The development of memory in childhood

The development of memory in childhood

Nelson Cowan, Editor *University of Missouri*
Charles Hulme, Series Editor *University of York*

Psychology Press
a member of the Taylor & Francis group

Psychology Press, Publishers
Taylor and Francis
27 Church Road
Hove East Sussex, BN3 2FA
UK

British Library Cataloguing in Publication Data
A catalogue record for this book is available from the British Library.

Library of Congress Cataloging-in-Publication Data are available

ISBNs: 0-86377-495-4 HB
       0-86377-496-2 PB

Printed and bound in the United Kingdom by Biddles Ltd, Guildford and King's Lyn

Contents

Contributors

Patricia J. Bauer, *Institute of Child Development, University of Minnesota, 51 East River Road, Minneapolis, MN 55455-0345, USA*

David F. Bjorklund, *Department of Psychology, Florida Atlantic University, Boca Raton, FL 33432, USA*

Nelson Cowan, *Department of Psychology, University of Missouri, 210 McAlester Hall, Columbia, MO 65211, USA*

Rhonda N. Douglas, *Department of Psychology, Florida Atlantic University, Boca Raton, FL 33432, USA*

Robyn Fivush, *Department of Psychology, Emory University, Atlanta, GA 30322, USA*

Peter Gerhardstein, *Department of Psychology, Rutgers University, Busch Campus, New Brunswick, NJ 08903, USA*

Gail S. Goodman, *Department of Psychology, University of California, Davis, CA 95616-8686, USA*

Robert Guttentag, *Department of Psychology, University of North Carolina, Greensboro, NC 27412, USA*

Mary Holland Joyner, *Department of Psychology, University of North Carolina, Davie Hall, CB #3270, Chapel Hill, NC 27599-3270, USA*

Beth Kurtz-Costes, *Department of Psychology, University of North Carolina, Davie Hall, CB #3270, Chapel Hill, NC 27599-3270, USA*

CONTRIBUTORS

Jayanthi Mistry, *Department of Child Studies, Eliot-Pearson Hall, Tufts University, Medford, MA 02155, USA*

Charles A. Nelson, *Institute of Child Development, University of Minnesota, 51 East River Road, Minneapolis, MN 55455-0345, USA*

Alan J. Parkin, *Laboratory of Experimental Psychology, University of Sussex, Falmer, Brighton BN1 9QG, UK*

Jianjian Qin, *Department of Psychology, University of California, Davis, CA 95616-8686, USA*

Jodi A. Quas, *Department of Psychology, University of California, Davis, CA 95616-8686, USA*

Allison D. Redlich, *Department of Psychology, University of California, Davis, CA 95616-8686, USA*

Carolyn Rovee-Collier, *Department of Psychology, Rutgers University, Busch Campus, New Brunswick, NJ 08903, USA*

CHAPTER 1

Introduction

Nelson Cowan

Memory is the food of mental growth. What 3-year-old Vera remembers about a row boat trip may be used by her in many ways that are worth contemplating. As soon as the trip ends, she might compare the recent memory of rocking in the waves with the feeling of standing on solid earth, and that can help her intuitive understanding of nature and physics. Her vocabulary may be developing as she mentally replays some words her father said during the trip: "Don't stand up while we're in motion, sweetie . . . squat down if you want to move around in the boat." In motion . . . squat down.

The next day one might find her playing out a scenario for boat trips with some small action figures and a friend. The figurines drive to the lake, the mom and dad go into the little shack and talk to the man at the desk, they get the boat, get the paddles, and hold the boat steady while stepping in. Vera may all the while build up more general social rules from instances such as this, perhaps subconsciously: "My parents care about me; they like me to have fun. But they want me to be safe; they want to control everything. I like to control it myself when I feel safe." The same for natural facts: "It's colder over the water; the water makes it windy; the birds seem excited when the sun comes out."

Later on in life the whole episode may fade. The boat trip may become confused with several other trips that had the same feeling to them or had many features in common. Instead of remaining specific instances, they may blend into a general memory such as, "those times when the folks used to take us out to that lake we lived near." The memory may be buried by newer understandings that Vera takes on as her mind grows, making the boat trip irrelevant or obscure; or the memory might be rethought and forever altered. Yet, peculiar incidents might stand out, even if they are of no obvious significance, such as the name of the park, or "that time that the fish jumped pretty high out of the water."

Vera might become a good rower or athletically keen in general, without remembering the experiences that served as good practice. There is memory "in the muscles," and other memory in the mind and – so it seems – in the heart.

This vignette is a contemplation of how important memory can be to a developing person, in so many different ways, both conscious and unconscious. This kind of contemplation can take us only so far, of course. It tells us what may be true. There is a lot that we know but also much that is unknown, and to get closer to the truth one must consider extensive evidence and decide what to believe, what not to believe, and when to suspend judgment for the time being. The more that one wants to know the truth, the more interested one becomes in methods that can help in finding that truth.

Thus, this is a scientific book about memory development in childhood. It would be difficult to understand all of this topic from one point of view, and therefore we have put together eleven points of view in the next eleven chapters. Together, I think you will find that they paint a broad mural. In order to know their topic better, researchers of memory development typically specialize in a subtopic or point of view that they find most interesting, and this book includes chapters on a number of different but interlocking aspects of memory development by specialists in those aspects.

Chapter 2 is on the development of memory in infancy. Infants cannot tell you what they remember, so this field depends on creating new methods for learning what infants know or think. It is startling how much progress has been made in this area and how much the infants' responses tell us that they have learned! The limits in learning are also interesting and important, though; infants clearly do not learn in exactly the same way as adults and it is fascinating to get in their minds a bit.

Chapter 3 is on neurological factors in memory development. Here again, the progress is striking. The new neuroimaging devices have begun to show us how we actually can link brain areas to particular aspects of memory, if we keep in mind that there may be different ways to interpret some of the brain images.

Chapter 4 is on the development of memory in early childhood. It has been known since the days of Jean Piaget that young children's thought processes are very different from those of older children. They are more magical in nature, not as constrained by the laws of nature; and young children often have difficulty seeing things from another's point of view. Yet, they are accomplishing the important work of building a mental structure and a language. They absorb an enormous amount of knowledge. All of this makes their memory very distinctive and interesting.

Chapter 5 is on the development of declarative and procedural memory. Declarative memory is the memory that one can deliberately bring up or "declare," whether it be a fact or an episode (such as Vera's built up knowledge about boating trips in general or memory of this one in specific); whereas procedural memory is the knowledge of how to do something, which need not be accompanied by knowledge of how, when, or where the procedure was learned in the first place (such as Vera's acquired ability to row). Because declarative memory is more consistently dependent on the mental framework in which the event was encoded, one finds very different developmental courses for declarative versus procedural memory.

2

Chapter 6 is on the development of event memory, which is a detailed view of a particular, important sort of declarative memory. The question is, as one charts the course of development, how the changing brain structure affects the way in which the memories of specific events in one's personal life are stored.

Chapter 7 is on the development of working memory, which refers to the information that must be held in mind while one is solving a problem or completing some mental task. It can be the words in a sentence that are held in mind until it can be comprehended, or the items that one wants to buy at the store.

The information held in mind can include recent events as well as facts learned long ago, which must be brought back to mind in order to interpret the problem or find a solution. The ability to hold the necessary information in mind changes dramatically with age and accounts for many developmental improvements in thinking. (Vera used working memory to compare motion in water and on land, and she used it to reflect upon the meanings of new words her father said to her.)

Chapter 8 is on the development of mnemonic strategies. One of the ways in which either working memory or long-term memory is made to succeed is through the use of mental tricks or acquired methods that make the stimulus array seem more orderly, or that help keep information in mind. This chapter charts the child's progress in improving the use of such strategies. (Vera might have repeated to herself, "don't stand up in the boat," which would be an example of one simple form of covert verbal rehearsal, a strategy used in working memory. She would have been unlikely to have used other mnemonic strategies at that age; but an older child, say a 10-year-old, might try not to leave a toy in the boat by thinking, "When we return and I see this picnic table I'll think of the toy.")

Chapter 9 is on the development of processing resources used for memory. Processing resources refer to limited mental capacities, so that if you use certain resources on one task they are temporarily unavailable for other tasks. These resources certainly include attentiveness, the general notion being that events that are more closely attended are better remembered. Resources may also include mental processes that are more closely related to specific tasks. It seems clear that Vera's use of processing resources will improve as she matures, but we would like to know more about how they will mature and what effects that will have on her memory.

Chapter 10 is on the development of metamemory. One reason that Vera would not have a strategy to try and remember a toy is that, at her young age, she is not yet aware that there is a danger of forgetting the toy. Knowledge of how one's memory operates (or fails to operate), termed "metamemory," changes with age in interesting ways that will be examined. Metamemory is an important quality that allows better strategies to be used as children mature; you cannot easily fix a memory problem if you do not yet know about it.

Chapter 11 is on children's autobiographical memory and eyewitness testimony. Suppose Vera is unlucky enough to witness an armed robbery in the lake office. Can we rely on her account of what happened, in court? What aspects of her testimony are valid, and under what conditions of questioning? If Vera has emotional instabilities or problems later on in her life, how much stock should her therapist place in her description of what happened early in her life? These practical questions are closely related to the theoretical ones we have asked earlier in the book, and they have a theoretical, philosophical side all their own.

Oh yes. I have forgotten to tell you where Vera lives. Canada? Spain? Anyway, does it matter? That is an empirical question. Chapter 12 is on cross-cultural aspects of memory development. It will discuss ways in which the characteristics of a culture can influence how and what children remember.

In reading these chapters, there are certain questions that you might keep in mind. I put these questions to the contributing authors, and each of them has dealt with the questions insofar as these seemed relevant to the topic. Keeping these questions in mind as a checklist may help you to gain more from the chapters.

1. What is the definition of the chapter's topic?
2. What are a few intuitively clear examples of it?
3. Why is it potentially important on theoretical or practical grounds, and what do we want to know about it?
4. How can it be measured objectively?
5. What are the most important developmental principles or issues regarding that topic?
6. Are there studies with adults or animals that help to explain the topic or its principles?
7. What are the relevant developmental findings, and how can they be interpreted? (This takes up the most space in each chapter.)
8. How is our understanding of the general principles affected by our knowledge of this research?
9. Are there related findings in adult aging that make an interesting comparison to the childhood development of this topic? What general principles may hold across the entire developmental lifespan?
10. What are some of the most important remaining unknowns, and how might they be explored further? How are they being explored?
11. Are there any important concluding observations that one could make?

Armed with these questions and any others of your own choosing, you are ready to proceed. The world of childhood memory awaits!

CHAPTER 2

The development of infant memory

Carolyn Rovee-Collier and Peter Gerhardstein

Infant memory: A classic paradox

Since the time of Freud, who advocated that adult behavior could be traced to our infantile experiences, the long-term effects of infants' early experiences have invoked a great deal of theoretical interest. Most developmental psychologists have traditionally assumed that infants' early experiences lay the groundwork for their later behavioral and cognitive development. That is, they have thought that the effects of early experiences progressively accumulate, producing an organism who is increasingly complex. Implicit in this assumption is the capacity for long-term memory in infancy: If infants' early experiences are to affect their later behavior, then they must possess some relatively enduring record of those experiences – some means of preserving the effects of those experiences until they draw on them in the future. Paradoxically, however, most psychologists also believe that prelinguistic infants are incapable of remembering their past experiences over the long term. Ironically, this belief also originated with Freud (1935), who proposed that early traumatic memories were forced into an unconscious state (i.e., repressed), where they continued to motivate behavior but could not be recalled. Freud's proposal found support in the phenomenon of infantile amnesia – the phenomenon that most adults cannot recall memories from their childhood prior to the age of 3 or 4 (e.g. Allport 1937; Loftus 1993; Pillemer & White 1989; Schachtel 1947).

More recently, infantile amnesia has been attributed to maturational deficiencies in the ability of young infants to encode and store memories over the long term (Kagan & Hamburg 1981; Pillemer & White 1989; Schacter & Moscovitch 1984). Behavioral evidence that infants' novelty preferences persist for only seconds or minutes at most following initial familiarization (for reviews, see Olson & Strauss 1984; Werner & Perlmutter 1979) and neuropsychological evidence that the brain mechanisms presumed to mediate long-term memory are compromised by damage in lesioned animals and aging amnesics have led many researchers to infer that these same mechanisms are relatively late to mature (e.g. Bachvalier & Mishkin 1984; McKee & Squire 1993; Nadel, Willner & Kurz 1985; Nadel & Zola-Morgan 1984; Schacter & Moscovitch 1984) . This maturational-deficiency view has been challenged, however, by evidence from a number of laboratories that prelinguistic infants can remember some events, particularly those in which they actively participated, for periods ranging from weeks to years (see Rovee-Collier & Hayne 1987 for review; Hayne 1990; Myers et al. 1987, 1994; Perris et al. 1990). This has left open the question of why so few early memories are remembered.

Procedures used to study memory with young infants

Novelty preference procedures

Most of what was originally known about infants' memorial abilities came from studies of infant looking patterns using either the paired-comparison or habituation paradigm. These procedures exploit the fact that infants older than 8–10 weeks of age tend to look longer at a novel stimulus than at a familiar (or pre-exposed) one (for review, see Fagan 1984). The continued extent of the infant's novelty preference after a delay is thought to index the extent of the infant's visual recognition memory. In general, measures of visual recognition memory, irrespective of paradigm or infant age, indicate that forgetting is complete after only a few seconds or minutes during the first year of life (Rose 1981; for review, see Werner & Perlmutter 1979). Because these measures are usually obtained within a single, brief session, they can be considered to index the infant's short-term memory. Short-term memory in adults, as in most species, is age-invariant and lasts for only a few seconds to minutes (for review, see Rovee-Collier & Hayne 1987).

Bruner (1964) argued that what is important about memory is not that an organism possesses it but that it can be retrieved and used to guide behavior (see also Nelson 1984). In fact, the central assumption of novelty-preference paradigms – that what the infant recognizes can be inferred from the extent to which he or she subsequently *ignores* a pre-exposed stimulus – is inconsistent with this function. Indeed, most authorities on memory agree that only those aspects of a prior event that are represented in the memory of that event can cue its retrieval (for review, see Tulving 1983). By definition, then, novel stimuli cannot serve as retrieval cues for the memory of an event. Moreover, to the extent that novel stimuli compete with effective retrieval cues for attention, they actually impede memory processing: Unless the pre-exposed stimulus is attended at the time of testing, the requisite retrieval cues cannot be sampled, and retrieval cannot be initiated. Thus, novelty preference paradigms make use of a somewhat obtuse dependent measure, in which the extent to which a subject indicates recognition is assessed by the extent to which the pre-exposed stimulus is *not* a cue for retrieval.

Paired-comparison paradigm Fantz (1958) made the original observation that infants' distribution of looking between members of a pair of visual patterns was nonrandom, with some patterns being fixated reliably longer than others. His paired-comparison paradigm was subsequently modified to study the effect of briefly pre-exposing infants to a particular stimulus then testing the infant with a pair of stimuli – the pre-exposed stimulus and a completely novel one – presented concurrently. The duration of an infant's looking at a novel stimulus is expressed as a proportion of the infant's total duration of time spent looking at the novel stimulus (A) and at the pre-exposed one (B) during the paired-comparison test (A/A+B). The mean proportion of looking at the novel stimulus is then statistically tested against a proportion of 0.50, that is, random looking at the two simultaneously presented cues.

Fagan (1970) was the first to introduce a delay between infants' pre-exposure to the sample and the paired-comparison test with the pre-exposed and the novel stimuli and sought the longest delay after which infants still showed a novelty preference. This delay defined the upper limit of the infant's visual recognition memory. That is, the fact that infants look randomly at the two test stimuli is taken as evidence that they have forgotten the pre-exposed target and again perceive the two test stimuli as equally novel. Using this paradigm, Rose (1981) found that 6-month-olds exhibited a significant novelty preference only when tested immediately after the pre-exposure procedure, whereas 9-month-olds exhibited a significant novelty preferences after 90–160 seconds.

The habituation paradigm This procedure was inspired by Sokolov's neuronal model of the habituation of the orienting reflex (Sokolov 1963). Sokolov's model assumes that the individual constructs an internal representation of each attended stimulus, or an engram. Attention to a given stimulus on each subsequent occasion is determined by the magnitude of the discrepancy between the physical stimulus and its internal representation. When the engram matches the physical stimulus (zero discrepancy), the individual no longer attends to it. The decline in attention to a previously encountered stimulus, therefore, reflects the reduction of the effective stimulus, which is the discrepancy or the degree of novelty. As time passes, however, the internal representation decays, and the discrepancy between the template and the physical stimulus correspondingly increases. When there is no longer any trace of the template, the discrepancy is again at a maximum. By this account, when the habituated stimulus is again attended as fully as a completely novel stimulus, forgetting is assumed to be complete.

In habituation studies of infant visual recognition memory, successive trials with one stimulus are presented until a criterion of response decrement is reached (typically, 50 per cent of the mean response magnitude during the first two or three trials), at which point different groups of infants are tested for retention after different delays with either the habituation stimulus (a no-shift group) or a novel stimulus. When testing immediately follows the final habituation trial, responding to the habituation stimulus is low, and habituation generalizes to the novel test stimulus as a function of its similarity to the habituation stimulus. When a delay is introduced between the habituation trials and the posthabituation test trial, spontaneous recovery to the original habituation stimulus increases with the length of the delay interval, and infants will ultimately fixate the test stimulus for as long as they did during their original encounter with it. When this occurs, forgetting of the original stimulus is assumed to be complete, and this delay is taken as an index of the limit of infants' visual recognition memory (for review, see Olson & Sherman 1983).

Stinson (1971, in Werner & Perlmutter 1979) obtained a classic forgetting function using a variation of the habituation procedure in which 4-month-olds learned to produce high-amplitude sucks that were reinforced by the brief presentation of a visual reinforcer (e.g. the mother's face and voice on a screen). As the effectiveness of the reinforcer waned over repeated presentations, high-amplitude responding gradually decreased from its peak rate. When the response decrement reached a criterion level, a delay was imposed between the final reinforcer presentation on the current trial and its subsequent presentation on the next trial. Responding remained low when 0 and 15 seconds intervened between training and testing. When the delay exceeded 30 seconds, however, high-amplitude responding returned to its original level, indicating that forgetting was complete by this delay.

Conditioning paradigms

In a 1976 review of what was known about the development of memory in infants and children, Campbell and Coulter concluded:

> Child development psychologists have not yet studied memory over long time intervals. Our best estimates come from retrospective studies of early childhood memories. . . . We cannot overemphasize the differences between these indices of long-term memory in man and those used to study memory in the developing rat. The human is asked to recall events of early childhood in the absence of any stimuli associated with that era. The rat, on the other hand, is returned to a highly distinctive setting and asked to reproduce a specific response. If these same procedures were used with man, it seems quite likely that evidence for long-term memory would appear much earlier (Campbell & Coulter 1976: 144–145).

Both classical and operant conditioning paradigms provide direct measures of long-term retention (Bolles 1976) and, not surprisingly, have yielded quite different estimates of the limits of infant long-term retention than those obtained by researchers using novelty-preference paradigms.

Classical conditioning A few sporadic classical conditioning studies using longitudinal procedures with older infants in the early 1930s provided some evidence of retention for periods of several months (Jones 1930, 1931; Marinesco & Kreindler 1933), but the enterprise was thereafter neglected for almost a half-century.

The work of Little et al. (1984) stands as the only systematic study of the retention of classically conditioned responses in the newborn. Infants received

50 presentations of a conditioned stimulus (CS-tone) that overlapped and terminated with an air puff-US (unconditioned stimulus) that caused infants to blink. The interval between the CS and US (the interstimulus interval, or ISI) was either 500 or 1500 milliseconds. In addition, infants received 20 randomly interspersed CS-alone test trials. Previously, Little (1970) had found that infants exhibited classical conditioning only at the longer of these ISIs, despite the fact that adults typically exhibit it only at the shorter ISI. Infants were trained at either 10, 20, or 30 days of age and received a retention session 10 days later. Thus, for example, infants who were trained for the first time at 20 days served as maturational controls for infants who had been trained at 10 days and tested at 20 days (see Figure 2.1). The difference between the number of responses

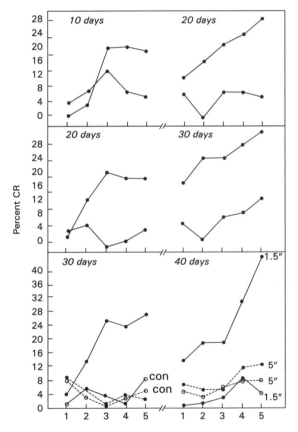

Figure 2.1 Percentage of conditioned responses on CS-US trials by infants initially trained at 10, 20, or 30 days of age (left panels) and retrained in a second session 10 days later (right panels). Infants received either a 500-msec or 1500-msec ISI. Performance of a random control group (dashed lines) is shown in the bottom panel. Reprinted with permission from Little, A. H., L. P. Lipsitt, & C. Rovee-Collier 1984. Classical conditioning and retention of the infant's eyelid response: Effects of age and interstimulus interval. *Journal of Experimental Child Psychology* **37**, 512–24. Copyright © 1984, Academic Press, Inc.

during the retention test and during initial training (i.e., savings) was the measure of retention. Significant savings was displayed by all except infants initially trained at 10 days of age, and infants trained at 20 days responded significantly more during their retention test than infants being trained for the first time at 30 days of age.

Operant conditioning A series of operant conditioning studies using the mobile conjugate reinforcement paradigm has systematically documented long-term retention on the part of infants between 2 and 7 months of age. This series was launched by a report (Rovee & Fagen 1976) that 3-month-olds remembered a learning contingency between footkicking and mobile movement for 24 hours. Moreover, infants' rate of responding during a brief nonreinforcement phase at the outset of each succeeding daily session vertically reflected their rate of responding during an identical nonreinforcement phase at the end of the preceding session. Because reinforcement had not yet been introduced at the time when the long-term retention test was conducted, the response carry-over from the preceding session 24 hours earlier could reflect only what infants brought into the session with them and not new learning or savings at the time of testing.

In the *mobile conjugate reinforcement paradigm*, the intensity of reinforcement (mobile movement) is proportional to the rate and vigor of the infant's kicking, so that each infant controls the value of its own reinforcement. This aspect of the procedure eliminates the necessity of equating reinforcers across ages when this paradigm was subsequently used with older infants. In the mobile paradigm, infants show a rapid increase in kick rate during the first 3–6 minutes of acquisition that is not merely a result of behavioral arousal, elicited by the moving mobile (Rovee & Rovee 1969; Rovee-Collier et al. 1978).

Sullivan et al. (1979) subsequently standardized the retention procedure so that 2- and 3-month-olds, all trained and tested at home, now receive a 15-minute session on 2 successive days and a procedurally identical test session after a specified delay. For 3 minutes at the outset of the session (baseline), a soft ribbon is connected without slack from one of the infant's ankles to an "empty" suspension stand that is clamped to one crib rail (see Figure 2.2a) while the mobile is suspended from a stand affixed to the opposite rail. In this arrangement, the infant can view the mobile, but kicks cannot move it. Next, the experimenter hooks the ribbon to the same stand as the mobile for 9 minutes (acquisition) (see Figure 2.2b). In this arrangement, each kick conjugately activates the mobile. Finally, each session ends with another 3-minute nonreinforcement period (immediate retention test) when the mobile is again visible but kicks will not move it. All retention tests, regardless of delay, were conducted in this manner. Because 5 minutes is typically required to extinguish responding at this age (Rovee & Rovee 1969), the mean response rate during the final 3-minute nonreinforcement phase usually reflects the mean response rate during the final 3 minutes of acquisition and thus indexes the infant's final level of conditioning. Occasionally, an infant detects the with-

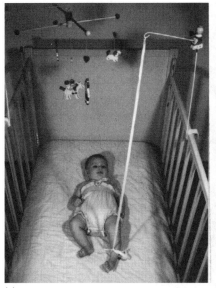 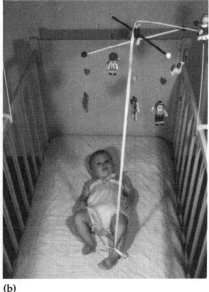

(a)   (b)

Figure 2.2 The experimental arrangement used with 3-month-olds during (a) baseline, when the mobile and the ribbon are suspended from different stands and kicking cannot move the mobile, and (b) acquisition, when kicking moves the mobile via an ankle ribbon. Reprinted with permission from Rovee-Collier, C., M. W. Sullivan, M. K. Enright, D. Lucas, J. W. Fagen 1980. Reactivation of infant memory. *Science* **208**, 1159–61. Copyright © 1980, American Association for the Advancement of Science.

drawal of reinforcement or becomes bored at the end of training; in this case, the actual final level of conditioning serves as the index of learning for that infant instead.

Hill et al. (1988) adapted the mobile paradigm for use with 6-month-olds, hanging the mobile from a floor microphone stand, placing them in a sling-seat inside a playpen (see Figure 2.3), and using sessions that were one-third shorter in each phase. The 6-month-olds learn the task more rapidly than the 3-month-olds, within the first 1–3 minutes of acquisition.

The response measures that are obtained during nonreinforcement periods at the outset and at the end of training (baseline and immediate retention test, respectively) serve as reference points for the individual's memory performance during an identical nonreinforcement period that is administered at the outset of a temporally distant session (the delayed recognition test). If an infant's kick rate during the long-term retention test is equal to or greater than it was during the immediate retention test, then retention is "perfect" (retention ratio = 1.00), that is, the infant has shown no forgetting. Even if infants exhibit a significant degree of forgetting during the long-term test, their forgetting is not considered to be "complete" until their test rate has returned to the original baseline level (baseline ratio = 1.00).

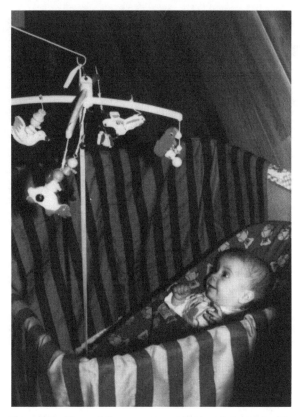

Figure 2.3   The mobile arrangement used with 6-month-olds.

The logic of using the mobile paradigm to study infant memory is straight-forward: Because prelinguistic infants lack a verbal response to tell us if they recognize a particular test stimulus, they are taught a motoric one that they can use for this purpose – an operant footkick that activates a crib mobile that displays the critical visual information. (In addition to being displayed directly on the mobile components, the critical information can be displayed on a cloth liner that is draped around the sides of the crib or playpen where learning takes place.) After a delay, infants are merely shown either the original mobile or one on which the original visual information has been altered. They then say whether or not they recognize the test cue by whether or not they produce the learned response. If they do recognize it, then they kick at a rate greater than their baseline; that is, they say "yes." If they do not recognize it, then their kick rate is not above baseline; that is, they say "no." Using this procedure, Vander Linde et al. (1985) found that forgetting occurred within 3 days of training at 2 months of age, Sullivan et al. (1979) obtained forgetting within 6–8 days of training at 3 months of age, and Hill et al. (1988) observed gradual forgetting over the first 2 weeks after training at 6 months of age (see Figure 2.4).

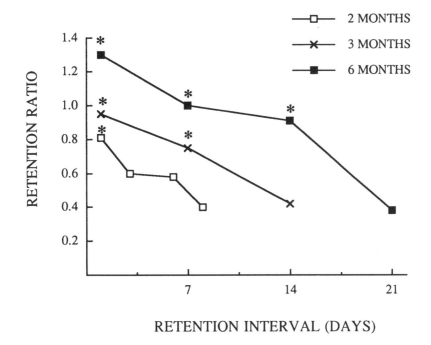

Figure 2.4 Performance of independent groups of 2-, 3-, and 6-month-old infants on a delayed recognition test with the original training mobile. Asterisks indicate that retention is significant. Reprinted with permission from Hill, W. H., D. Borovsky, & C. Rovee-Collier 1988. Continuities in infant memory development over the first half-year. *Developmental Psychobiology* **21**, 43–62. Copyright © 1988, John Wiley & Sons, Inc.

Auditory localization paradigm

Myers et al. (1987) exploited the fact that five children who had participated on multiple occasions in a study of auditory localization until they were 40 weeks old were still available for retention testing 2 years later. As in the original study, the children were brought to a laboratory room, and their reaching to objects in the light and in the dark was recorded. All contextual and other cues that had been present during the original study were again present during the test. Five other children who had not participated in the original study formed an age-matched control group that experienced the same test procedures. The researchers found that the children remembered many aspects of their earlier experience, particularly some of the original action sequences. Compared to the controls, they exhibited more reaching and play behavior overall. However, the infants' reaching and play behavior did not differ for objects that had been used in the original study and those that had not. Rather, they appeared to remember more general aspects of their original experience.

13

Subsequently, Perris et al. (1990) retested 1½- and 2½-year-olds who had participated on a single occasion in an auditory localization study involving reaching in the dark when they were 6½ months old. As before, children who had participated in the study as infants reached out more often and with greater success than children who had not. In addition, the previous participants were less emotional in the darkened test room, as if they found it somewhat familiar. Most important, these data demonstrate that children with language were capable of remembering something from the period before they had language, even if what they remembered was a feeling of familiarity and some general features of the test situation.

Procedures used with older infants and toddlers

Conditioning paradigms

To study the learning and memory of infants between 9 and 18 months of age, we have developed a paradigm as similar as possible to the mobile conjugate reinforcement paradigm except that infants press a lever to move a miniature train around a circular track (Campos-de-Carvalho et al. 1993; Figure 2.5).

Figure 2.5 The experimental arrangement used in the train task with 6- through 18-month-olds, shown here with a 6-month-old. Each lever press moves the train around the track for 2 seconds.

Recently, the procedure has also been used with 6-month-olds, whose retention in the train task is identical to that of 6-month-olds studied in the mobile paradigm (Hartshorn 1995).

In the train task, the stimulus array is highly complex and completely visible to the infant during the initial nonreinforcement period; when reinforcement is subsequently introduced, lever-pressing moves the train, just as kicking moved the previously visible mobile in the mobile paradigm, but the conjugate aspect has been eliminated: Each lever press while the train is moving is computer-tallied but has no effect on reinforcement, and the lever must be released after each response in order to deliver the next reinforcer. As in the mobile procedure, noncontingent reinforcement does not increase responding during acquisition phases, and the learning curves of all ages are indistinguishable as they are also indistinguishable from infants trained in the mobile paradigm. Finally, lever presses do not move the train during the long-term retention test, although infants attempt to do so by pressing if they recognize the test stimulus.

Infants are trained in their own homes in two sessions 24 hours apart and are tested at a later time in a procedurally identical session, but sessions are shorter at 9 and 18 months than at 6 months. Infants sit on their mother's lap or in a Sassy Seat® in front of a large viewing box; pressing a wide Plexiglas lever affixed to the front of the box moves a miniature train inside the box around a circular track, turns on flashing lights, and activates a toy car containing Sesame Street characters for 1–2 seconds. Infants tested in this paradigm remember progressively longer between 6 and 18 months of age (see Figure 2.6, p. 18).

Deferred imitation paradigm

In this paradigm, infants are shown a series of target actions on novel objects that are modeled by an adult. In the most stringent deferred-imitation procedure (e.g. Hanna & Meltzoff 1993; Meltzoff 1995), infants are not allowed to either touch or handle the novel test objects. After a prescribed delay, the infants are presented with the objects with no explicit reminding other than the objects and the test situation *per se* (i.e., a cued-recall procedure), and the number of target acts they produce is recorded. Age-matched controls are used to assess the degree to which infants of the test age spontaneously produce the target acts in the absence of having seen the actions being modeled.

In a less stringent version (e.g. Bauer & Hertsgaard 1993; McDonough & Mandler 1994; Meltzoff 1985, 1988), infants are allowed to imitate the modeled actions immediately after they are demonstrated and are tested again after a delay. Meltzoff (1995) has argued that immediate imitation allows infants to engage in motor practice of the target actions, which may influence the amount of subsequent recall. As a result, one cannot safely conclude whether, during the long-term test, infants remembered their motoric response or the actions they saw the model perform.

Meltzoff (1995) has reported that infants who were either 14 or 16 months of age and who saw the modeled actions without an immediate opportunity to model them (the most stringent procedure) could reproduce some of those actions as long as 4 months later (at 18 and 20 months of age, respectively), thus demonstrating that infants evidence retention of the stimulus in the absence of any opportunity to imitate (motorically) the modeled actions. Meltzoff noted that because these two sets of results spanned the age (18 months) at which infants presumably undergo a verbal "explosion," they argue against the existence of a newly emergent mechanism that prevents access to memories encoded prior to this age. A similar argument against such a mechanism arises from the findings of Myers et al. (1987), discussed earlier. Researchers using the less stringent criterion have found that toddlers could remember event sequences after periods ranging from 1 to 6 weeks (Bauer & Hertsgaard 1993; Bauer & Mandler 1989; Bauer & Shore 1987).

Multiple-activities paradigm

A third approach that has been used to study retention in toddlers is the multiple-activities paradigm. In this paradigm, children are usually brought to a laboratory where they engage in a series of structured activities. Later, they are returned to the laboratory and asked to re-enact the activities. If they do not do so spontaneously, they are provided with a series of progressive prompts. Retention is indexed in terms of the number of original activities the children reproduce at the time of testing without verbal prompting. Fivush and Hamond (1989), for example, engaged 24- and 28-month-old children in a series of play events involving four different toy animals (zebra, duck, monkey, giraffe) and tested all children for their retention of the events 14 weeks later. Children in a repeated experience condition, however, returned to the playroom and re-enacted the events 2 weeks after session 1, while children in a single experience condition did not. During the long-term test, children in the repeated experience condition recalled significantly more items than children in the single experience condition, revealing the benefit of an additional practice session on retention. Most striking, however, was the fact that children in the repeated experience condition exhibited no forgetting over the period between their 2-week and their 14-week visits.

In a similar study, Hudson (1994) brought 18-month-old children to the laboratory where they engaged in a series of eight structured activities, each at a different station in a large room. At one station, for example, the activity involved opening a particular cabinet door, getting out fish food, feeding the fish in a tank, and putting the food back; at another, the activity involved opening a particular drawer, removing crayons, scribbling on a sheet of paper, and so forth. The children received a re-enactment session on the same day, 2 weeks later, or 8 weeks later, and retention was measured 8 weeks after the second session. Age-matched controls were trained for only a single session prior to their 8-week retention test at either 20 or 22 months of age, or they

16

were familiarized with the experimental setting only 8 weeks prior to their "retention" test (a baseline control group). The timing of the second session in relation to the first had a significant impact on toddlers' retention. The control groups spontaneously exhibited only 1–2 activities during the long-term test. Likewise, toddlers whose training and re-enactment occurred within a single session performed relatively poorly during the long-term test. The re-enactment session improved retention significantly only when it occurred 8 weeks later, near the end of the time window (Rovee-Collier 1995) – that is, only when it occurred near the time that toddlers normally forget the activities altogether. Not only did this group spontaneously recall significantly more activities than any other group despite being tested 4 months after its initial session, but also the prompted retention of this group significantly exceeded that of all others when toddlers were returned to the laboratory for a third visit 6 months later (Hudson 1994).

Developmental changes in infant retention

As we noted at the outset of this chapter, it is commonly thought that memories of older infants are mediated by a fundamentally different system than memories of younger infants (e.g. Bachvalier 1990; Bachvalier & Mishkin 1984; Kagan & Hamburg 1981; Mandler 1990; McKee & Squire 1993; Nadel et al. 1985; Schacter & Moscovitch 1984). Infants as young as 20 days who had learned to blink to avoid a puff of air to their cornea when signaled by a tone remembered this contingency for as long as 10 days when *savings* was the measure of retention (Little et al. 1984). Using a more stringent *cued-recall* measure that required that infants produce a previously learned response in the absence of any opportunity for new learning, we found that infants from 2 through 18 months of age remembered progressively longer with age, even when infants of all ages had attained the same final level of learning and had exhibited the same level of retention 24 hours after training (Hartshorn et al. 1995). Thus, 2-month-olds remembered the mobile task for 1 day but not for 3 days; 3-month-olds exhibited perfect retention for 3–4 days but forgot within 6–8 days; 6-month-olds remembered the task for 2 weeks but not for 3; 9-month-olds remembered it for 6 weeks but not for 7; 12-month-olds remembered it for 8 weeks but not for 9; 15-month-olds remembered it for 10 weeks but not for 11; and 18-month-olds remembered it for 12 weeks but not for 13 (Hartshorn et al. 1995).

The age function for retention in Figure 2.6 offers no evidence that long-term memory abruptly improves during the third quarter of the first year of life, as has been conjectured by those who argue that a qualitatively different "late-maturing" memory system (declarative or explicit memory) emerges at about that time in development (Bachvalier 1990; Kagan & Hamburg 1981; Mandler 1990; McKee & Squire 1993; Schacter & Moscovitch 1984). Moreover,

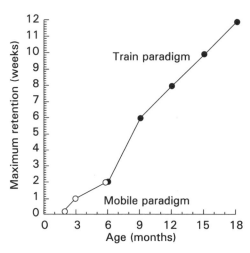

Figure 2.6 The maximum duration of retention of infants between 2 and 18 months of age who were tested in either the mobile paradigm (2–6 months) or on the train task (6–18 months) until they finally displayed complete forgetting (i.e., test performance at baseline). Retention is the same at 6 months irrespective of task. From Hartshorn, Aaron, Livolsi, Hille, & Rovee-Collier 1995.

it cannot be argued that the progressive increase in retention with age that is shown in Figure 2.6 is unique to the particular type of memory that is measured in conditioning paradigms: Although the retention estimates in Figure 2.6 were obtained with the same, standardized memory paradigm, they are remarkably similar to the duration of long-term retention that has been reported for same-aged infants who were tested in vastly different memory paradigms with quite different training parameters (Fivush & Hamond 1989; Hudson 1994; Meltzoff 1995; Sheffield & Hudson 1994).

The rate at which a forgotten memory is recovered by a reminder also increases over the first half-year of life and, undoubtedly, thereafter. At 3 months, evidence that the forgotten memory has been recovered does not emerge until 8 hours after exposure to the reminder, and its recovery does not peak until 3 days later (Fagen & Rovee-Collier 1983). During the reactivation process, the memory attributes that were forgotten first (i.e., those representing the details of the training mobile) are recovered after the memory attributes that were forgotten last (i.e., those representing its general features) (Hayne & Rovee-Collier 1995). At 6 months, however, evidence of the recovered memory appears after only 1 hour, and recovery peaks after 4 hours (Boller et al. 1990).

The specificity of infants' memories has been assessed by testing with a cue (e.g. the mobile, the crib or playpen liner in the immediate visual surround, the room) that differs in some way from the cue that was present at the time of original encoding. If the unaltered stimulus can cue retrieval after 24 hours but the altered mobile or liner cannot, then it can be concluded that the information was represented in the original memory and that changing it disrupted retention. If both the original and the altered stimulus can cue retrieval after a long retention interval, however, then it can be concluded that the infant has forgotten the details of the original stimulus and responded on the basis of the more general, still-remembered features that it shares with the altered cue.

The specificity of the cues needed for successful memory retrieval decreases as infants grow older. At both 2 and 3 months, infants detect even the most minute changes in the test mobile and fail to recognize it just 1 day after training if more than a single object has been substituted into the one they were trained with. Likewise, if the original mobile contains more than a single new object, it is completely ineffective as a reminder (for review, see Rovee-Collier & Hayne 1987). In contrast, 3-month-olds' retention is not impaired if their immediate visual surround is completely changed during the 1-day test. After 3 days, however, they do not recognize the training mobile if the cloth liner is changed but remember it perfectly if the liner is unchanged. Memory reactivation is also significantly impaired if the original mobile is presented as a reminder in the presence of a different cloth liner (Butler & Rovee-Collier 1989; Rovee-Collier et al. 1985), but memory reactivation is completely precluded if the reminder is presented in a different room even if the cloth liner is the same (Hayne et al. 1991). At 6 months, infants can discriminate a novel mobile from their training mobile after delays of 2 weeks while 3-month-olds can do so for only 3 days. Yet, older infants fail to recognize the training mobile after only 1 day in a novel context (Borovsky & Rovee-Collier 1990). Although their memory for the details of the training context appears to fade within a week, once the memory is forgotten it cannot be reactivated if the reminder is exposed in either an immediate visual surround (Borovsky & Rovee-Collier 1990) or room (Hartshorn 1995) that differs from the one where the memory was originally encoded.

The specificity of the cues required for memory retrieval at young ages can be reduced or eliminated, however, by training infants with a variety of cues (Greco et al. 1990; Hayne et al. 1987; Rovee-Collier et al. 1993b) or in a variety of contexts (Amabile & Rovee-Collier 1991; Rovee-Collier & DuFault 1991). Thus, both 3- and 6-month-olds who are trained with just two discriminably different mobiles will subsequently respond if the test or reminder mobile is different; likewise, infants who are trained in just two discriminably different contexts will subsequently recognize the mobile in yet another different one. Even so, there is no "cross-generalization" between cue and context. Infants trained with two different mobiles in a single context will not respond to a novel mobile if either the test or the reminding context is also changed (Shields & Rovee-Collier 1992).

As infants age, their retention continues to be impaired by a change in the focal cue, but only after a very short delay. Also, at both 9 and 12 months, a change in the room where a reminder is presented has no effect on retention in a delayed recognition paradigm except after the longest delays at which the infants still remember the task, when a room change impairs retention (Aaron et al. 1995). Similarly, Hanna and Meltzoff (1993) have reported that 14-month-olds can display deferred imitation of specific actions after a retention interval of 2 days despite a major change in the context within which they had originally viewed the actions being modeled (i.e., from the day-care center or laboratory to the home).

To summarize, although infants remember longer as they get older, the fundamental mechanisms that mediate their memory processing change only quantitatively – and not qualitatively–over the first year and a half. At all ages, infants have memories that are forgotten gradually, can be recovered by exposure to a reminder, and are modified by exposure to postevent information. While the memories of young infants are highly specific, the specificity of the focal cue and the contextual cues required for memory retrieval diminishes with age – possibly as infants increasingly experience a greater number of similar cues and contexts with age.

Reminder paradigms

Memory reinstatement

This phenomenon was discovered in 1966 by Campbell and Jaynes, who proposed that reinstatement was a means by which memories might be sustained over major developmental periods. The principle underlying reinstatement is simple: As a memory wanes, a brief exposure to the original event keeps the memory going – like throwing a new log on a fire that is dying out.

In Campbell and Jaynes' (1966) original study of reinstatement, they established conditioned fear by presenting two groups of 23-day-old rat pups with a series of 9 trials on which a shock (the US, or unconditional stimulus) was administered in either the black or white (the CS, conditional stimulus) compartment of a cage, followed by placement in the "safe" compartment for an equal period of time. A third group was not originally trained. Subsequently, one of the original conditioned-fear groups and the group that had received no prior fear conditioning received three CS–US trials every week for the next 3 weeks. When all groups were tested 4 weeks after the end of original training (or 1 week after the last CS–US pairing), only pups who had received both the early fear conditioning plus the intervening shocks showed a high degree of conditioned fear; the other groups showed none (see Figure 2.7). This demonstrated that both intermittent CS–US pairings in the absence of original training and fear conditioning in the absence of intermittent exposures were insufficient to account for the conditioned fear that the experimental group displayed after the 4-week delay. They used the term *reinstatement* to refer to the empirical fact that part of the original conditions were reinstated during presentation of the periodic reminders.

Subsequently, the reinstatement procedure has been used with young

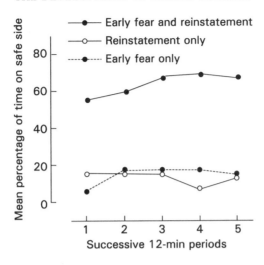

Figure 2.7 Retention of conditioned fear in young rats 28 days after their original fear conditioning as a function of their intervening experience. The reinstatement group was originally trained and also received intermittent shocks during the retention interval. (From Campbell & Jaynes 1966.)

preschoolers trained to criterion on object-location paired-associates (Howe et al. 1993) and school-aged children trained on picture pairs (Hoving & Choi 1972; Hoving et al. 1972). The general finding at all ages is that reinstatement procedures improve long-term retention after delays ranging from 4 to 8 weeks.

Memory reactivation

The memory reactivation paradigm grew out of the reinstatement paradigm when Spear (1973; Spear & Parsons 1976) subsequently discovered that rat pups also could remember their early fear conditioning a month later if they were exposed only once, the day before their long-term retention was tested, to some fragment of the original event – for example, the shock or the tone. This fragment of the original event, also called a *reminder*, presumably primed or *reactivated* the latent or dormant memory, thereby increasing its accessibility. As a result, the otherwise forgotten memory was again expressed during the subsequent retention test. The finding that a forgotten memory could be reactivated revealed more generally that memories that appear to be forgotten may actually not be permanently lost but potentially may be recovered by a reminder.

It is important to distinguish between reinstatement and reactivation, both of which are reminder procedures. In the reinstatement procedure, the memory is maintained over a period of time by intermittent exposures during the retention interval to some of the original conditions of training, for example, the contingency. In the reactivation procedure, described below, the forgotten memory is recovered by a single exposure at the end of the retention interval to some of the original conditions of training. Thus, reinstatement forestalls forgetting, while reactivation alleviates it.

In the late 1970s, we modified the classical fear-conditioning reactivation paradigm so that its critical components were maintained in an operant, appetitive (mobile) paradigm and demonstrated that a reactivation treatment could also alleviate forgetting with human infants (Rovee-Collier et al. 1980; for review, see Rovee-Collier & Hayne 1987). Since then, the procedure has also been used with toddlers (Sheffield & Hudson 1994) and preschool children. In our work, a reactivation treatment is administered after forgetting is

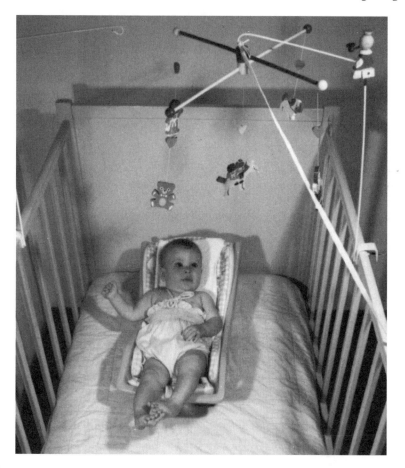

Figure 2.8 The experimental arrangement during a reactivation treatment at 3 months. The experimenter, hidden from the infant's view, pulls the ribbon attached to the mobile hook, activating it non-contingently for 3 minutes at the same rate that the infant had kicked during the final 3 minutes of acquisition 2–4 weeks earlier. Reprinted with permission from Rovee-Collier, C., M. W. Sullivan, M. K. Enright, D. Lucas, & J. W. Fagen 1980. Reactivation of infant memory. *Science* **208**, 1159–61. Copyright © 1980, American Association for the Advancement of Science.

complete, and whether or not the memory was recovered is confirmed later, during a delayed recognition test. Controls are either trained but receive no reactivation treatment prior to testing or receive the reactivation treatment without having initially been trained. In the mobile studies, a reactivation treatment involves briefly (2–3 minutes) and passively exposing the infant to either the moving mobile, the cloth liner, or both in advance of the long-term test. During the reactivation treatment, the ankle ribbon is not connected to the mobile, and infants are seated in a sling-seat to minimize their spontaneous activity (see Figure 2.8). In the train studies, infants view the moving train for 2 minutes while the lever is inoperative (Hartshorn 1995).

Twenty-four hours after a successful reactivation treatment, retention is typically perfect. At 3 months, excellent retention is seen either 2, 3, or 4 weeks after training. If a single reactivation treatment is administered 5 weeks after training, it is effective for many individuals but does not provide evidence of memory recovery for a group. At 3 months of age, once a memory has been re-activated, it is reforgotten at the same rate that it was forgotten originally (see Figure 2.9). Reactivated memories, therefore, are not transient but can continue to influence behavior weeks after the event originally occurred. Finally, a memory that has been reactivated more than once is even longer lasting. After a single reminder at 3 months, for example, the reactivated memory is forgotten within a week of reminding. Hayne (1990), however, found no evidence of for-getting 2 weeks after reminding – 6 weeks after original training – when 3-month-olds received two reminders, on days 20 and 27 after training. Repeated reactivations could theoretically eventuate in memories that are

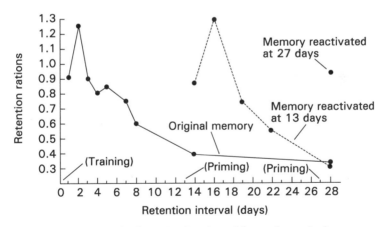

Figure 2.9 The forgetting and reforgetting functions of the newly acquired memory and the reactivated memory as a function of the number of days since either training or reminding when retention testing occurred. A reminder was presented only once, on day 13, 27, or 34 after the end of training. Subjects were independent groups of 3-month-olds tested only once. Reprinted with permission from Rovee-Collier, C., Sullivan, M. W., Enright, M. K., Lucas, D., & Fagen, J. W. (1980). Reactivation of infant memory. *Science* **208**, 1159–61. Copyright © 1980 by the American Association for the Advancement of Science.

almost continuously accessible, achieving the status of "semantic" or "generic" memory.

In summary, a reactivation paradigm differs from a standard delayed recognition paradigm in that the researcher reminds or primes with either the original or an altered stimulus considerably in advance of the long-term test in the reactivation paradigm, while the experimenter simply tests with one of these with no prior cuing in the delayed recognition paradigm. The reactivation treatment restores a memory to the same level as that attained shortly after training, and multiple reminders can protract retention.

Comparisons between newly acquired and reactivated memories

Newly acquired and reactivated memories share many characteristics, but they are not identical. First, although memory performance during a delayed recognition test declines gradually over time, memory performance after a reactivation treatment is all-or-none, unaffected by the interval between training and reminding. As noted above, 3-month-olds exhibit perfect retention 24 hours after a reminder whether it was exposed 2, 3, or 4 weeks after training. (Ultimately a point is reached after which a single reminder is not effective.) Second, newly acquired memories are readily modified, but reactivated memories are not (see below). Third, the magnitude of a newly acquired memory is affected by the amount of training (number of trials, session time), but the magnitude of a reactivated memory is not. And fourth, delayed recognition performance depends heavily on goals and expectations; reactivation, which is a purely perceptual identification process, devoid of an active memory component, does not.

Finally, while newly acquired memories are readily modified or updated (see pp. 30–2), we have found that a reactivated memory of the original context is very difficult to modify. Because the original memory cannot be reactivated at all if the reminder mobile or context is novel, it is first necessary to remind infants with the original mobile in the original context in order to initiate the memory reactivation process. Once the reactivation process has begun, we then attempt to modify the reactivated memory by passively exposing infants to either a novel mobile or context. Although the newly acquired memory can be modified by exposure to a new context in the complete absence of the training mobile, the reactivated memory cannot be modified even if the training mobile is present when the new context is exposed (Boller & Rovee-Collier 1994).

We subsequently discovered that the reactivated memory could be modified only if infants' kicks were explicitly reinforced for 2 minutes in the novel context – an adaptation of the original reinstatement phenomenon (Campbell & Jaynes 1966). When a brief contingency experience was introduced immediately after reminding, infants did recognize the mobile in the novel exposure context during the delayed recognition test. A no-training control group also received the reactivation treatment in one context and the

2-minute reinforcement experience in another, but this group received no training prior to reactivation. This control group exhibited no retention when tested in the novel exposure context either 1 day later or even 2 hours later. Because the 2-minute reinforcement period after reminding did not support retention unless infants had previously been trained, we conclude that the effect of the brief reinforcement phase in the novel context must have "piggy-backed" onto the original training memory even though the recovery of that memory was not yet complete when the 2-minute reinforcement experience took place (Boller & Rovee-Collier 1994).

These data suggest that infants' memories that are reactivated after long delays are unlikely to be expressed in a context different from the original encoding context unless the infants are provided with information that the current context, like the old one, is predictive.

Factors affecting retention

Event timing

How information from two separate, temporally discrete events becomes integrated or linked is a central problem in cognition. For the infant, whose knowledge base is still relatively meager, the integration of new information with old (i.e., information in memory) is particularly critical. As it turns out, there is a limited period, or *time window*, during which such integration can take place (Rovee-Collier 1995). Thus, new information that is encountered before the time window has shut will be integrated into or accumulated with what came before, and information that is encountered after the time window has shut will not. Understanding whether an infant's prior experiences will affect his or her future behavior depends on knowing whether the memory can still be retrieved at that future time, that is, on the width of the time window.

As an example of the operation of a time window, 3-month-olds successfully classified a novel exemplar of a category as a category member if they viewed it within 4 days of category training but not if they viewed it 6 days afterwards. Thus, the time window for their recognizing a new category member closed after 4 days (Rovee-Collier et al. 1993b). This conclusion was verified by testing them in a reactivation paradigm: For infants who had viewed the novel exemplar 4 days after training, the novel exemplar was an effective reminder 3 weeks later for the memory of category training; for infants who had first viewed the novel exemplar 6 days after training (after the time window had presumably shut), however, the novel exemplar was not an effective reminder. Thus, the novel exemplar was classified as a category member and included in the memory of category training only when it was encountered before the time window shut. As such, it could be a reminder for that memory; otherwise it could not.

25

In addition, the width of the time window for a given memory (i.e., the duration of its retention) expands each time the memory is retrieved (*number of retrievals*). Furthermore, it expands more when the delay prior to retrieval is longer (*difficulty of retrieval*). This is as true for adults (Anderson et al. 1994; Bjork 1975) and other species (Hendersen 1985) as it is for infants. We have already described how retention is protracted for an additional week at 3 months by a second reminder (Hayne 1990). The retention advantage of retrieving a memory later in the time window, however, is illustrated by the fact that when 3-month-olds viewed the novel exemplar immediately after category training, when the time-window first opened, they recognized it for 4 days; but when they viewed it at the end of the time window (4 days after training), then they recognized it for an additional 10 days, that is, for 2 weeks after training (Rovee-Collier et al. 1993b).

We also asked if there were a time window within which the effects of two widely separate distant training sessions could be integrated and outside of which they could not (Rovee-Collier et al. 1995). In an initial experiment, the retention of different groups of 3-month-olds was tested 8 days after the first of two training sessions. The groups differed from one another only in terms of when their second training session occurred in relation to their first. When session 2 followed session 1 after delays of 1–3 days, infants exhibited excellent retention during the long-term test. When session 2 followed session 1 by 4 days, however, they exhibited none; their retention was no better than that of a control group who received no second session at all. Apparently, when the second session occurred after the time window had shut, the effects of the two training sessions did not accumulate, and infants treated the second session as if it were unique (i.e., as another "first" session).

In addition, when the second session occurred near the end of the time window, long-term retention was significantly better than when the second session more closely followed the first session, when the time window opened. These data demonstrate that the *timing* of a succeeding event determines whether it will be integrated with what came before or will be treated as unique – a result that has obvious implications for the development of the knowledge base and for the future retention of that event.

Amount of training

One of the few laws of memory is that retention is better with more training (Cohen 1985). When more training is defined in terms of "more sessions," the improved retention can be attributed to the fact that the memory has been retrieved more often (see above discussion). When more training is defined in terms of "more training time," however, more retrievals cannot explain the improved memory performance.

In two experiments with 3-month-olds, we varied either the number of operant training sessions or the duration of a single training session, measuring retention either 1, 7, 14, or 21 days later (Ohr et al. 1989). In the first experiment, infants were trained for one, two, or three sessions lasting 9 minutes each on separate days. After one training session, infants remembered for 1 day but not for 7 days; after two sessions, infants remembered for 7 days but not for 14; and after three sessions, they remembered for 14 days but not for 21. Thus, each additional 24-hour session protracted retention by 1 week, even though all groups had learned the contingency at the same rate in a single session and had attained the same final level of acquisition. In the second experiment, we trained all infants for a single session that lasted 6, 9, 12, or 18 minutes and tested retention 7, 14, or 21 days later. Neither the 6- nor the 9-minute training groups remembered the task 7 days later. Infants who were trained for 12 minutes remembered for 7 but not for 14 days, and infants who were trained for 18 minutes remembered for 14 days but not for 21. Thus, each 6-minute increment in the duration of training increased retention by 1 week. These data confirm that increasing the amount of training protracts retention in infants as in adults, whether amount of training is defined in terms of the number of sessions or training time.

Distribution of training

A factor that is closely related to the amount of training is how a given amount of total training time is programmed or distributed. In both animals and human adults, distributed training leads to better retention than massed training (Bryan 1980; Glenberg 1979). Cornell (1980), using a novelty-preference paradigm, pre-exposed infants for a total of 20 seconds with either 3 or 60 seconds between trials. Although both conditions produced a novelty preference after a 5-second delay, the 60-second intertrial interval yielded superior retention after delays as long as 60 minutes.

In studies using the mobile conjugate reinforcement paradigm, 2-month-olds remembered better (for 2 weeks) when their training was distributed over three 6-minute sessions than when it occurred in a single 18-minute session (Vander Linde et al. 1985). As was the case above, the number of retrievals could have accounted for this result. Alternatively, the benefits of distributed training could have stemmed from exposing subjects to different learning contexts over time, thereby increasing the number and variety of their potential retrieval cues. The longer the delay between successive retrievals, the more variable the context is likely to be when the next retrieval does occur. This account is known as the *encoding-variability hypothesis* (Glenberg 1979).

At 3 months of age, identically trained infants remembered after 2 weeks in both conditions (Enright et al. 1983), performing like infants in the Ohr et al. (1989) study who had received three 9-minute training sessions. (Whether infants would have remembered as long had their sessions been shorter is unknown.) Recall, however, that when a succeeding trial occurs later in the time window (see pp. 25–6, above), retention is more protracted until, at some point, the succeeding trial falls outside of the time window and offers no retention advantage at all (Rovee-Collier et al. 1995).

Affect

Emotions are viewed as internal contextual cues that, like external contextual cues, are encoded as part of the memory of an event. Because memory retrieval depends on how closely the cues present during a retention test match those that were present during original encoding, differences in the affective context between encoding and retrieval can impair retention.

Fagen and his colleagues reported that 3-month-olds who cry during training in the mobile conjugate reinforcement paradigm forget more rapidly than infants who do not (for review, see Fagen & Prigot 1993). In their initial study, infants were trained with a 10-object mobile for two sessions and, shortly into the third session, were shifted to a 2-object mobile (a nonpreferred mobile) for the remainder of that session. Following the shift, approximately 50 per cent of the infants cried at some point during the remainder of the session. When tested with either the 10- or the 2-object mobile 1 day later, both noncriers and criers displayed excellent retention; 7 days later, however, noncriers still displayed excellent retention, but criers displayed none (Fagen et al. 1985).

In a subsequent study, they found that the degree of retention displayed by criers during the 7-day test depended on the interval between the end of training with the 10-object mobile and the point at which infants were shifted to the 2-object one. As the shift interval was increased from 0 (immediately) to 2, 5, 15, or 30 minutes, retention progressively improved. With a 30-minute shift interval, the retention of the noncriers and criers did not differ 7 days later (Fagen et al. 1989). This result is reminiscent of the phenomenon of retrograde amnesia, in which memory progressively improves as a function of the amount of time that has elapsed since the occurrence of a traumatic event.

Memory networks

By at least 6 months of age, prelinguistic infants have already begun to develop networks of associations or mnemonic links between memories that were independently established but share a common feature. This characteristic, also known as associative memory, was previously thought to characterize only the memory of children and adults with language. Historically, it has been thought that the presentation of a retrieval cue activates a memory at a given node in the memory network, with this activation then spreading to other nodes linked to the original one. As a result, the memories associated with those nodes also are activated such that they become accessible for retrieval when an appropriate retrieval cue is detected.

In the first study demonstrating this phenomenon with infants, Timmons (1994) on separate days taught 6-month-old infants to move a mobile by kicking and to turn on a music box by arm-pulling – two different paired associates – in a highly distinctive context. In a delayed recognition test 3 days later, infants produced only the particular response that had originally been associated with a given test cue, regardless of which response they had learned last. This result confirmed that infants' memories of each paired associate had been stored independently and that their retrieval was highly specific to the cue that was presented at the time of testing.

In a second experiment, Timmons trained the infants as before, but this time she waited until both of the memories had been forgotten (i.e., for 3 weeks), at which time she exposed half of them to the mobile and half of them to the music box as a memory prime in a reactivation paradigm. The next day, all infants received a long-term retention test with the mobile as the retrieval cue. As expected, infants who were both primed and tested with the mobile exhibited the mobile-appropriate response to the mobile retrieval cue – the typical finding in memory reactivation studies. Surprisingly, however, infants who were primed with the music box but tested with the mobile also exhibited the mobile-appropriate response – and no other – to the mobile test cue (see Figure 2.10). Because these infants' memories had never been primed with the mobile and because they also had forgotten the mobile memory at the time when the music-box memory was primed, it is clear that activation of the memory node corresponding to the music box paired-associate subsequently activated the memory node corresponding to the mobile paired-associate by virtue of a link between the two memory nodes in a common network. That is, the two memories were mnemonically linked, such that priming with the music box brought

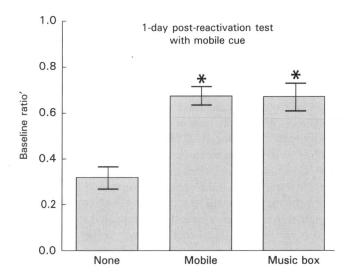

Figure 2.10 Recovery of a forgotten cue-response association by 6-month-olds who were trained 3 weeks earlier to move a mobile and operate a music box by arm-pulling or foot-kicking. Infants in the two experimental groups were exposed for 2 minutes to the music box as a reminder and were tested with the mobile 1 day later. An asterisk indicates that infants exhibited significant retention during the long-term test. Controls who were tested without having been reminded exhibited no retention. (From Timmons 1994.)

to mind the memory of the mobile task, which had been acquired in the same context.

A similar result was found by Sheffield and Hudson (1994) in a study with 14- to 18-month-old toddlers. Using the multiple-activities paradigm, they allowed toddlers to engage in six different structured activities at different stations in the laboratory. After toddlers' memory of their visit had been forgotten, they were returned to the laboratory, and half of the activities were modeled by the experimenter while the children merely watched. Twenty-four hours later, children were asked to produce the three activities they had not seen modeled and the three that they had. As expected, children of this age who had not been originally trained but who had viewed the modeling exhibited deferred imitation of the three actions they had seen modeled the day before, and children who were not exposed to the reactivation treatment (the modeling) remembered none. However, children who had originally been trained and had also seen three activities modeled were able to re-enact the remaining three activities, despite not having engaged in them for 10 weeks. Thus, as in the Timmons (1994) study, directly reactivating some activities led to the indirect reactivation of others in a common network – again probably mediated by the common context in which the activities were initially performed.

These results have major implications for day-to-day memory processing. If memories in an associative network need not be directly reactivated in order to be recovered, then in the normal course of interacting with their environment, infants and older individuals are likely to encounter retrieval cues that indirectly prime other memories in the mnemonic network in addition to directly priming those in which the cues are represented. Although indirect priming increases the possibility that individuals will have a ready response for related situations that they are likely to encounter, it also increases the possibility that the indirectly reactivated memories are accessible for modification by new circumstances either at the time of retrieval or afterwards, depending upon how rapidly they are reforgotten. This, in turn, jeopardizes the likelihood of their retrieval in the future and may contribute, in part, to infantile amnesia. On the other hand, if memories are strengthened each time they are retrieved, then their retrieval via indirect reactivation could increase the probability that these same memories will be retrieved in the future, although some details of the original memory may be lost over repeated retrievals, whether the retrieval is direct or indirect (Hitchcock & Rovee-Collier 1996).

Updating memories

Despite the considerable specificity of infants' memories for both the focal cue (the mobile) and the context within which it is encountered, infants' memories are readily modified or updated by information they encounter subsequent to training (Rovee-Collier & Boller 1995). If either 3- or 6-month-olds are trained for 2 days and then briefly and merely passively observe a novel object that is physically different but functionally similar to the prior training mobile, for example, then they will integrate a representation of that object with their prior memory representation. In the future, that object is capable of cueing the training memory during either during a delayed recognition test or a reactivation treatment (Boller et al. 1995; Greco et al. 1990; Rovee-Collier et al. 1993a). Infants' memory of the training context can be modified in the same way. If 6-month-olds are exposed to a novel context for only 2 minutes immediately following the conclusion of training in session 2, then they subsequently are able to recognize the training mobile in that novel exposure context as well as in a context that they have never seen prior to the delayed recognition test. This is important because infants of this age otherwise completely fail to recognize their training mobile in a novel test context. At both 3 and 6 months, infants who have been merely exposed, passively and only once, to a novel mobile or a novel context, behave in the same fashion as infants who were explicitly trained with a different mobile or in a different context for an entire session.

The modification of infants' training memory by subsequently encountered information is not a recency effect: When infants are exposed to the new information after session 1 instead of after session 2, the same result is obtained. If the exposure occurs immediately before session 1, however, then infants do not respond to the pre-exposed information (either the mobile or the liner) during the delayed recognition test, even though the exposures before and after session 1 are equally contiguous with training in that session. These results suggest that infants' memories are encoded in terms of meaningful events. Before infants have learned that they can move a mobile in the presence of a particular cloth liner, mobiles and cloth liners have no particular significance for them; they are not proactively associated with the training memory. Once the training memory has been established, however, then infants have a meaningful event to which the subsequently encountered mobiles and liners can be "glued" (Boller et al. 1995; Boller & Rovee-Collier 1992).

In view of its specificity, the relative ease with which a newly acquired memory can be modified by virtue of mere observation is surprising. At 6 months, for example, infants' memory for a context that was present during an entire training session can be recoded merely by exposing the infants for only 2 minutes to a different context after the session is over. The mobile need not even be present during the exposure for the memory to be altered (Boller & Rovee-Collier 1992).

Our research using the passive exposure procedure to modify infants' memories is analogous to the retroactive interference procedure that has been used to study the effects of misleading postevent information on adults' eyewitness testimony (e.g. Belli 1989; Loftus 1979; Loftus & Hoffman 1989; McCloskey & Zaragoza 1985). In both the infant and the adult studies, novel information that is introduced after an initial event is over modifies subjects' performance on a later ensuing retention test. This modification typically takes two forms: (1) retention of the original event is impaired, and (2) the novel postevent information is treated as if it were represented in the original memory. Also, the longer the interval between the original event and exposure to the postevent information, the more likely is the postevent information to affect subsequent retention in both adults (Loftus et al. 1978) and infants (Boller et al. 1996; Rovee-Collier et al. 1994). Presumably, as the original memory trace becomes weaker, it is easier to modify.

In recent years, considerable controversy has arisen concerning the fate of the original memory trace. We have found evidence, however, that the original memory has not been overwritten, at least after short exposure delays when its details are still highly accessible. Although both 3- and 6-month-olds fail to recognize their original training mobile after having been passively exposed to a novel mobile 1 day after training (Rovee-Collier et al. 1994; Muzzio & Rovee-Collier 1996, respectively), they can still be reminded by the original mobile 2–3 weeks later, indicating that their memory of the first session is still intact. Their poor retention of the original memory, therefore, is temporary and may result either from a temporary state of inhibition or a conflict between competing memories. After long exposure delays, however, only the exposure mobile can reactivate the forgotten memory; the original one no longer can (Muzzio & Rovee-Collier 1996; Rovee-Collier et al. 1994).

Whatever the fate of the original memory might be after long exposure delays, our data clearly reveal that memory recoding does occur for what transpires within a single session. Apparently, young infants treat each daily session as a new event and form a new memory representation for each. Their memory of a given session is recoded in terms of the novel information (e.g. a mobile or context) that they encounter after that session is over, when the training memory was still highly active, but their memories of prior sessions remain intact. These results suggest that when cues in a subsequent session retrieve the memory of one or more prior sessions of which those cues or attributes are a part, the retrieved representation is only a copy of the original, which remains undisturbed. The retrieved memory, in turn, becomes a part of a newly created memory of the current session, that is, a new memory token of the event.

Infantile amnesia revisited

Returning to the issue of infantile amnesia, we can conclude with certainty that it does not result either from a maturational deficiency in the brain mechanisms that encode and maintain long-term memories in infants or from other memorial deficits on the part of the very young (Rovee-Collier 1990). As this chapter has documented, infants' memories of events in which they participate are highly enduring and become even more so after repeated encounters with reminders. In addition, their memories are highly specific; by 3 months, they include information about the incidental context or place where the event took place, and by 6 months, they include some information of the temporal order of stimuli that were encountered within a session (Gulya 1996). These facts are inconsistent with views that early memories are short-lived, highly generalized and diffuse, and devoid of place information for most of the first year of life (e.g. Mandler 1990; Nadel & Zola-Morgan 1984; Nelson 1984; Olson & Strauss 1984; Schacter & Moscovitch 1984).

The discovery that inactive or forgotten memories can be reactivated, both directly and indirectly, and substantially prolonged by exposure to reminders, along with new evidence about how the characteristics of repeatedly reactivated memories change, offers new prospects for understanding how infants' early experiences can accumulate and affect their later behavior. Finally, the finding that infants' prior memories are readily updated or modified to reflect the demands and circumstances of their current social and physical world suggests that many of our earliest memories may have been progressively modified or retrieved so often that their original forms can no longer be recognized. Given the rapidity with which the infant's social position and physical and cognitive skills change over the first 3 years of life in particular, we find this account of infantile amnesia highly plausible. From a functional perspective, this may not be such a bad thing. Insofar as so much of what we needed to know when we were young is not useful when we are older, it would seem to be highly adaptive for these early memories to be forgotten.

References

Aaron, F., K. Hartshorn, P. Klein, M. Ghumman, & C. Rovee-Collier 1995. *Effects of cue and context changes on infant memory retrieval.* Paper presented at the meeting of the Eastern Psychological Association, Boston, MA.

Allport, G. W. 1937. *Personality: A psychological interpretation.* New York: Holt.

Amabile, T. A. & C. Rovee-Collier 1991. Contextual variation and memory retrieval at six months. *Child Development* **62**, 1155–66.

Anderson, M. C., R. A. Bjork, & E. L. Bjork 1994. Remembering can cause forgetting: Retrieval dynamics in long-term memory. *Journal of Experimental Psychology: Learning, Memory, and Cognition* **20**, 1063–87.

Bachvalier, J. 1990. Ontogenetic development of habit and memory formation in primates. In *The development and neural bases of higher cognitive functions.* A. Diamond (ed.). *Annals of the New York Academy of Sciences* **608**, 457–77.

Bachvalier, J. & M. M. Mishkin 1984. An early and a late developing system for learning and retention in infant monkeys. *Behavioral Neuroscience* **98**, 770–8.

Bauer, P. J. & L. A. Hertsgaard 1993. Increasing steps in recall of events: Factors facilitating immediate and long-term memory in 13.5- and 16.5-month-old children. *Child Development* **64**, 1204–23.

Bauer, P. J. & J. M. Mandler 1989. One thing follows another: Effects of temporal structure on 1- to 2-year-olds' recall of events. *Developmental Psychology* **25**, 197–206.

Bauer, P. J. & Shore, C. M. 1987. Making a memorable event: Effects of familiarity and organization on young children's recall of action sequences. *Cognitive Development* **2**, 327–38.

Belli, R. F. 1989. Influences of misleading postevent information: Misinformation interference and acceptance. *Journal of Experimental Psychology: General* **118**, 72–85.

Bjork, R. A. 1975. Retrieval as a memory modifier. In *Information processing and cognition: The Loyola Symposium*, R. L. Solso (ed.), 123–44. Hillsdale, NJ: Erlbaum.

Boller, K., M. C. Grabelle, & C. Rovee-Collier 1995. Effects of postevent information on infants' memory for a central target. *Journal of Experimental Child Psychology* **59**, 372–96.

Boller, K. & C. Rovee-Collier 1992. Contextual coding and recoding of infant memory. *Journal of Experimental Child Psychology* **52**, 1–23.

Boller, K. & C. Rovee-Collier 1994. Contextual updating of reactivated memories. *Developmental Psychobiology* **27**, 241–56.

Boller, K., C. Rovee-Collier, D. Borovsky, J. O'Connor, & G. Shyi 1990. Developmental changes in the time-dependent nature of memory retrieval. *Developmental Psychology* **26**, 770–9.

Boller, K., C. Rovee-Collier, M. Gulya, & K. Prete 1996. Infants' memory for context: Timing effects of postevent information. *Journal of Experimental Child Psychology* **63**, 583–602.

Bolles, R. C. 1976. Some relationships between learning and memory. In *Processes of animal memory*. D. L. Medin, W. A. Roberts, R. T. Davis (eds.), 21–48. Hillsdale, NJ: Erlbaum.

Borovsky, D. & C. Rovee-Collier 1990. Contextual constraints on memory retrieval at 6 months. *Child Development* **61**, 1569–83.

Bruner, J. 1964. The course of cognitive growth. *American Psychologist* **19**, 1–15.

Bryan, R. M. 1980. *Retention of odor-shock conditioning in neonatal rats: Effects of distribution of practice*. Unpublished doctoral dissertation, Rutgers University, New Brunswick, NJ.

Butler, J. & C. Rovee-Collier 1989. Contextual gating of memory retrieval. *Developmental Psychobiology* **22**, 533–52.

Campbell, B. A. & X. Coulter 1976. Neural and psychological processes underlying the development of learning and memory. In *Habituation*, T. J. Tighe & R. N. Leaton (eds.), 129–57. Hillsdale, NJ: Erlbaum.

Campbell, B. A. & J. Jaynes 1966. Reinstatement. *Psychological Review* **73**, 478–80.

Campos-de-Carvalho, M., R. Bhatt, T. Wondoloski, P. Klein, & C. Rovee-Collier 1993. *Learning and memory at nine months*. Paper presented at the meeting of the International Society for the Study of Behavioral Development, Recife, Brazil.

Cohen, R. L. 1985. On the generality of the laws of memory. In *Perspectives on learning and memory*, L. G. Nilsson & T. Archer (eds.), 247–77. Hillsdale, NJ: Erlbaum.

Cornell, E. H. 1980. Distributed study facilitates infants' delayed recognition memory. *Memory and Cognition* **8**, 539–42.

Enright, M. K., C. Rovee-Collier, J. W. Fagen, & K. Caniglia 1983. The effects of distributed training on retention of operant conditioning in human infants. *Journal of Experimental Child Psychology* **36**, 209–25.

Fagan, J. F., III 1970. Memory in the infant. *Journal of Experimental Child Psychology* **9**, 217–26.

Fagan, J. F., III 1984. Infant memory: History, current trends, relations to cognitive psychology. In *Advances in the study of communication and affect, Vol. IX, Infant memory*, M. Moscovitch (ed.), 1–27. New York: Plenum.

Fagen, J. W., P. S. Ohr, L. K. Fleckenstein, & D. R. Ribner 1985. The effect of crying on long-term memory in infancy. *Child Development* **56**, 1584–92.

Fagen, J. W., P. S. Ohr, J. M. Singer, & S. J. Klein 1989. Crying and retrograde amnesia in young infants. *Infant Behavior and Development* **12**, 13–24.

Fagen, J. W. & J. A. Prigot 1993. Negative affect and infant memory. In *Advances in infancy research, Vol. VIII*, C. Rovee-Collier & L. P. Lipsitt (eds.), 169–216. Norwood, NJ: Ablex.

Fagen, J. W. & C. Rovee-Collier 1983. Memory retrieval: A time-locked process in infancy. *Science* **222**, 1349–51.

Fantz, R . L. 1958. Pattern vision in young infants. *Psychological Record* **8**, 43–7.

Fivush, R. & N. R. Hamond 1989. Time and again: Effects of repetition and retention interval on 2 year olds' event recall. *Journal of Experimental Child Psychology* **47**, 259–73.

Freud, S. 1935. *A general introduction to psychoanalysis*. New York: Clarion.

Glenberg, A. M. 1979. Component-levels theory of the effects of spacing of repetitions on recall and recognition. *Memory and Cognition* **7**, 95–112.

Greco, C., H. Hayne, & C. Rovee-Collier 1990. The roles of function, reminding, and variability in categorization by 3-month-old infants. *Journal of Experimental Psychology: Learning, Memory, and Cognition* **16**, 617–33.

Gulya, M. 1996. *Memory for serial order at 6 months of age*. Unpublished master's thesis, Rutgers University, New Brunswick, NJ.

Hanna, E. & A. N. Meltzoff 1993. Peer imitation by toddlers in laboratory, home, and day-care contexts: Implications for social learning and memory. *Developmental Psychology* **29**, 702–10.

Hartshorn, K. 1995. *Delayed recognition, reactivation, and memory specificity at 6 months in an operant paradigm*. Unpublished master's thesis, Rutgers University, New Brunswick, NJ.

Hartshorn, K., F. Aaron, D. Livolsi, S. Hille, & C. Rovee-Collier 1995. *Infant learning and memory between 9 and 12 months*. Paper presented at the meeting of the Eastern Psychological Association, Boston, MA.

Hayne, H. 1990. The effect of multiple reminders on long-term retention in human infants. *Developmental Psychobiology* **23**, 453–77.

Hayne, H., & C. Rovee-Collier 1995. The organization of reactivated memory in infancy. *Child Development* **66**, 893–906.

Hayne, H., C. Rovee-Collier, & M. A. Borza 1991. Information for place information. *Memory and Cognition* **19**, 378–86.

Hayne, H., C. Rovee-Collier, & E. E. Perris 1987. Categorization and memory retrieval by three-month-olds. *Child Development* **58**, 750–60.

Hendersen, R. 1985. Fearful memories: The motivational significance of forgetting. In *Affect, conditioning, and cognition: Essays in the determinants of behavior*, F. R. Brush & J. B. Overmeier (eds.), 43–53. Hillsdale, NJ: Erlbaum.

Hill, W. H., D. Borovsky, & C. Rovee-Collier 1988. Continuities in infant memory development over the first half-year. *Developmental Psychobiology* **21**, 43–62.

Hitchcock, D. F. A. & C. Rovee-Collier 1996. The effect of repeated reactivations on memory specificity in infants. *Journal of Experimental Child Psychology* **62**, 378–400.

Hoving, K. L. & K. Choi 1972. Some necessary conditions for producing reinstatement effects in children. *Developmental Psychology* **6**, 214–17.

Hoving, K. L., L. Coates, M. Bertucci, & D. C. Riccio 1972. Reinstatement effects in children. *Developmental Psychology*, **6**, 426–9.

Howe, M. L., M. L. Courage, & L. Bryant-Brown 1993. Reinstating preschoolers' memories. *Developmental Psychology* **29**, 854–69.

Hudson, J. A. 1994. *Reinstatement of toddlers' event memory: A matter of timing.* Paper presented at the Practical Aspects of Memory Conference, College Park, MD.

Jones, H. E. 1930. The retention of conditioned emotional reactions in infancy. *Journal of Genetic Psychology* **37**, 485–98.

Jones, H. E. 1931. The conditioning of overt emotional response. *Journal of Educational Psychology* **22**, 127–30.

Kagan, J. & M. Hamburg 1981. The enhancement of memory in the first year. *Journal of Genetic Psychology* **138**, 3–14.

Little, A. H. 1970. *Eyelid conditioning in the human infant as a function of the interstimulus interval.* Unpublished master's thesis, Brown University, Providence, RI.

Little, A. H., L. P. Lipsitt, & C. Rovee-Collier 1984. Classical conditioning and retention of the infant's eyelid response: Effects of age and interstimulus interval. *Journal of Experimental Child Psychology* **37**, 512–24.

Loftus, E. F. 1979. *Eyewitness testimony.* Cambridge, MA: Harvard University Press.

Loftus, E. F. 1993. Desperately seeking memories of the first few years of childhood: The reality of early memories. *Journal of Experimental Psychology: General* **122**, 274–7.

Loftus, E. F. & H. G. Hoffman 1989. Misinformation and memory: The creation of new memories. *Journal of Experimental Psychology: General* **118**, 100–4.

Loftus, E. F., D. G. Miller, & H. J. Burns 1978. Semantic integration of verbal information into a visual memory. *Journal of Experimental Psychology: Human Learning and Memory* **4**, 19–31.

Mandler, J. M. 1990. Recall of events by preverbal children. In *The development and neural bases of higher cognitive functions*, A. Diamond (ed.), *Annals of the New York Academy of Sciences* **608**, 485–503.

Marinesco, G. & A. Kreindler 1933. Des réflexes conditionnels: L'organization des réflexes conditionnels chez l'enfant. *Journal de Psychologie* **30**, 855–86.

McCloskey, M. & M. Zaragoza 1985. Misleading postevent information and memory for events: Arguments and evidence against memory impairment hypotheses. *Journal of Experimental Psychology: General* **114**, 381–7.

McDonough, L. & J. M. Mandler 1994. Very long-term recall in infants: Infantile amnesia reconsidered. *Memory* **2**, 339–52.

McKee, R. D. & L. R. Squire 1993. On the development of declarative memory. *Journal of Experimental Psychology: Learning, Memory, and Cognition* **19**, 397–404.

Meltzoff, A. N. 1985. Immediate and deferred imitation in fourteen- and twenty-four-month-old infants. *Child Development* **56**, 62–72.

Meltzoff, A. N. 1988. Infant imitation and memory: Nine-month-olds in immediate and deferred tests. *Child Development* **59**, 217–25.

Meltzoff, A. N. 1995. What infant memory tells us about infantile amnesia: Long-term recall and deferred imitation. *Journal of Experimental Child Psychology* **59**, 497–515.

Muzzio, I. A. & C. Rovee-Collier 1996. Timing effects of postevent information on infant memory. *Journal of Experimental Child Psychology* **63**, 212–38.

Myers, N. A., R. K. Clifton, & M. G. Clarkson 1987. When they were very young: Almost-threes remember two years ago. *Infant Behavior and Development* **10**, 123–32.

Myers, N. A., E. E. Perris, & C. Speaker 1994. Fifty months of memory: Longitudinal study in early childhood. *Memory* **2**, 385–415.

Nadel, L., J. Willner, & E. M. Kurz 1985. Cognitive maps and environmental context. In *Context and learning*, P. D. Balsam & A. Tomie (eds.), 385–406. Hillsdale, NJ: Erlbaum.

Nadel, L. & S. Zola-Morgan 1984. Infantile amnesia: A neurobiological perspective. In *Advances in the study of communication and affect. Vol. IX, Infant memory*, M. Moscovitch (ed.), 145–72. New York: Plenum.

Nelson, K. 1984. The transition from infant to child memory. In *Advances in the study of communication and affect, Vol. XI, Infant memory*, M. Moscovitch (ed.), 103–30. New York: Plenum.

Ohr, P., J. Fagen, C. Rovee-Collier, H. Hayne, & E. Vander Linde 1989. Amount of training and retention by infants. *Developmental Psychobiology* **22**, 69–80.

Olson, G. M. & T. Sherman 1983. Attention, learning, and memory in infants. In *Handbook of child psychology, Vol. II, Infancy and developmental psychology*, M. M. Haith & J. J. Campos (eds.), 1001–80. New York: Wiley.

Olson, G. M. & M. S. Strauss 1984. The development of infant memory. In *Advances in the study of communication and affect, Vol. XI, Infant memory*, M. Moscovitch (ed.), 29–48. New York: Plenum.

Perris, E. E., N. A. Myers, & R. K. Clifton 1990. Long-term memory for a single infancy experience. *Child Development* **61**, 1796–807.

Pillemer, D. B. & S. H. White 1989. Childhood events recalled by children and adults. In *Advances in child development and behavior, Vol. XXI*, H. W. Reese (ed.), 297–340. San Diego, CA: Academic.

Rose, S. A. 1981. Developmental changes in infants' retention of visual stimuli. *Child Development* **52**, 227–33.

Rovee, C. & J. W. Fagen 1976. Extended conditioning and 24-hour retention in infants. *Journal of Experimental Child Psychology* **21**, 1–11.

Rovee, C. & D. T. Rovee 1969. Conjugate reinforcement of infant exploratory behavior. *Journal of Experimental Child Psychology* **8**, 33–9.

Rovee-Collier, C. 1990. The "memory system" of prelinguistic infants. In *The development and neural bases of higher cognitive functions*, A. Diamond (ed.), *Annals of the New York Academy of Sciences* **608**, 517–36.

Rovee-Collier, C. 1995. Time windows in cognitive development. *Developmental Psychology* **51**, 1–23.

Rovee-Collier, C., S. A. Adler, & M. A. Borza 1994. Substituting new details for old? Effects of delaying postevent information on infant memory. *Memory and Cognition* **22**, 644–56.

Rovee-Collier, C. & K. Boller 1995. Interference or facilitation in infant memory? In *Interference and inhibition in cognition*, C. J. Brainerd & F. N. Dempster (eds.), 61–104. San Diego, CA: Academic.

Rovee-Collier, C., M. A. Borza, S. A. Adler, & K. Boller 1993a. Infants' eyewitness testimony: Effects of postevent information on a prior memory representation. *Memory and Cognition* **21**, 267–79.

Rovee-Collier, C. & D. DuFault 1991. Multiple contexts and memory retrieval at 3 months. *Developmental Psychobiology* **24**, 39–49.

Rovee-Collier, C., M. K. Enright, D. Lucas, J. W. Fagen, & M .J. Gekoski 1981. The forgetting of newly acquired and reactivated memories of 3-month-old infants. *Infant Behavior and Development* **4**, 317–31.

Rovee-Collier, C., S. Evancio, & L. A. Earley 1995. The time window hypothesis: Spacing effects. *Infant Behavior and Development* **18**, 69–78.

Rovee-Collier, C., C. Greco-Vigorito, & H. Hayne 1993b. The time window hypothesis: Implications for categorization and memory modification. *Infant Behavior and Development* **16**, 149–76.

Rovee-Collier, C., P. C. Griesler, & L. A. Earley 1985. Contextual determinants of infant retention. *Learning and Motivation* **16**, 139–57.

Rovee-Collier, C. & H. Hayne 1987. Reactivation of infant memory: Implications for cognitive development. In *Advances in child development and behavior, Vol. XX*, H. W. Reese (ed.), 185–238. New York: Academic.

Rovee-Collier, C., B. A. Morrongiello, M. Aron, & J. Kupersmidt 1978. Topographical response differentiation in three-month-old infants. *Infant Behavior and Development* **1**, 323–33.

Rovee-Collier, C., M. W. Sullivan, M. K. Enright, D. Lucas, & J. W. Fagen 1980. Reactivation of infant memory. *Science*, **208**, 1159–61.

Schachtel, E. G. 1947. On memory and childhood amnesia. *Psychiatry*, **10**, 1–26.

Schacter, D. L. & M. Moscovitch 1984. Infants, amnesics, and dissociable memory systems. In *Advances in the study of communication and affect, Vol. IX*, M. Moscovitch (ed.), 173–216. New York: Plenum.

Sheffield, E. & J. Hudson 1994. Reactivation of toddlers' event memory. *Memory* **2**, 447–65.

Shields, P. J. & C. Rovee-Collier 1992. Long-term memory for context-specific category information at 6 months. *Child Development*, **63**, 175–214.

Sokolov, E. N. 1963. *Perception and the conditioned reflex*. New York: Macmillan.

Spear, N. E. 1973. Retrieval of memories in animals. *Psychological Review* **80**, 163–94.

Spear, N. E. & P. J. Parsons 1976. Analysis of a reactivation treatment: Ontogenetic determinants of alleviated forgetting. In *Processes of animal memory*, D. L. Medin, W. A. Roberts, & R. T. Davis (eds.), 135–65. Hillsdale, NJ: Erlbaum.

Stinson, F. S. 1971. *Visual short-term memory in 4-month infants*. Unpublished doctoral dissertation, Brown University, Providence, RI.

Sullivan, M. W., C. Rovee-Collier, D. M. Tynes 1979. A conditioning analysis of infant long-term memory, *Child Development* **50**, 152–62.

Timmons, C. R. 1994. Associative links between discrete memories in infancy. *Infant Behavior and Development* **17**, 431–45.

Tulving, E. 1983. *Elements of episodic memory*. New York: Oxford University Press.

Vander Linde, E., B. A. Morrongiello, & C. Rovee-Collier 1985. Determinants of retention in 8-week-old infants. *Developmental Psychology* **21**, 601–13.

Werner, J. S. & M. Perlmutter 1979. Development of visual memory in infants. In *Advances in child development and behavior, Vol. XIV*, H. W. Reese & L. P. Lipsitt (eds.), 1–56. New York: Academic.

Acknowledgements

Preparation of this chapter was supported by a Research Scientist Award (K05-MH00902) and Grant R37-MH32307 from the National Institute of Mental Health to the first author.

CHAPTER 3

The neurobiological basis of early memory development

Charles A. Nelson

The formal study of memory has a long and distinguished history, dating back (at least) to the mid-nineteenth century (e.g. Dunn 1845; Ebbinghaus 1885 a,b; for brief reviews on the history of research on memory, see Schacter 1987; Roediger 1990). Three themes common to research conducted from the mid-1800s through to the latter half of the twentieth century (e.g. 1970s) were concerns with the limits of memory, the contents of memory, and increasingly, the cognitive architecture of memory. However, relatively ignored until the late twentieth century was a concern with the ontogeny of memory, and interest in the biological bases of memory. As will be evident in this volume, there is now a plethora of research on memory development, due in large measure to the development of methods amenable to the study of the infant and child. In addition, the biological bases of memory has also received considerable study of late (e.g. Mishkin & Appenzeller 1987; Squire 1986, 1987). However, as will become apparent in this chapter, the juxtaposition of these themes – the biological bases of early memory development – has received relatively little attention. It is the goal of this chapter to review what is currently known about this topic, and to put forth a number of theoretical proposals on the relation between brain and memory development.

This chapter will begin with a brief exposition as to why the study of brain and memory in the context of development is so important, and why so little attention has been paid to this topic. I will then briefly describe current views of mature memory function, including its neurobiological basis. Here I will argue that there are multiple types of memory, each of which is subserved by somewhat independent neural systems. I will next turn my attention to the literature on infant memory. Here I will focus on describing the various ways that early memory has been studied, and relate what is known about the infant's behavior to what is known about corresponding changes in the brain. Based on this discussion, I will conclude that different "types" of adult memory have their origin in the infancy period. In the final section of this chapter I will offer suggestions as to how the study of the relation between brain and memory development can be improved.

It should be noted why I have elected to focus on *early* memory. Since my overarching goal is to explore the neurobiological bases of memory development, it is necessary to superimpose the time course of behavior onto that of brain. Unfortunately, because relatively little is known about brain development beyond the first few years of life, it is necessary to restrict our discussion of brain–memory relations to this time period. In addition, because memory beyond the preschool period changes little *relative* to changes observed over the first 1–2 years of life, it seemed most efficacious to document these early changes, as they likely provide the foundation for these latter changes. (For an elaboration on this point, and many of the ideas expressed in this chapter, see Nelson 1995.)

Brain, memory and development: History of the problem

The failure to consider the biological bases of memory development is unfortunate, not only because the study of development is important in its own right, but also because the implications that such study has for understanding mature function. For example, the argument has been made that studying memory impairment in the human adult and inducing memory deficits in the monkey may provide methods of converging operations on the study of "normal" memory. In both cases it is assumed that insight into a particular part of the brain can be gained by observing the changes in function that occur when some particular structure has been altered by disease (as in the case of the human) or surgical lesion (as in the case of the animal). These methodological approaches are not without their shortcomings, however, including the difficulty of generalizing from a clinical to a normal population, and the issue of what is a suitable species for developing an animal model. A developmental approach, on the other hand, provides for the ability to study how the components of a memory system are assembled at the outset. Such a prospective view has at least two advantages. First, it is unnecessary to assume that the manipulation of a given structure has not influenced any other structure (e.g. it is a lesion of the hippocampus proper that results in a particular deficit in behavior, and not a lesion of the rhinal cortex that contains the inputs and outputs to/ from the hippocampus; for discussion, see Webster et al. 1995). Second, the identification of the various neural and behavioral components that comprise a memory system may be more reliable if the assembly of such a system is studied as it unfolds (a developmental approach), than if one attempts to *infer* such components from the breakdown of mature function (a cognitive neuropsychological approach).

It is not difficult to account for why the study of brain and memory development has lagged behind similar study of mature function. First, the scientific domain to which the study of early memory has historically fallen – developmental psychology – has focused much of its efforts on developing methods for studying *behavior*, a not insignificant problem given the nonverbal and motorically immature nature of our species' young. As a result, relatively little attention has been paid to the rapid theoretical and methodological advances being enjoyed by its complement discipline of developmental neuroscience. Second, many of the current methods for imaging brain function and brain structure in the human adult are invasive (e.g. Positron Emission Tomograph – PET), and thus cannot be used with normal, healthy infants and children, (for examples of uses of PET with neurologically compromised infants, see Chugani 1994; Chugani & Phelps 1986; de Schonen et al. 1993). Finally, many of these procedures, even when not invasive (e.g. functional Magnetic Resonance Imaging – fMRI), impose demands on attention and motor resources that are unrealistic for use with infants and young children (e.g. the ability to remain motionless and/or to sustain attention for long periods of time).

The field of developmental cognitive neuroscience has begun to overcome some of these obstacles. It has done so by studying infant non-human primates using the methods used with adults of these same species (e.g. lesion method; 2-deoxyglucose; see Bachevalier 1990, 1992), and by studying human infants using the same tools as used to study human adults (e.g. event-related potentials, or ERPs; Nelson 1994). When these advances are combined with knowledge accrued through the study of overt behavior, it becomes possible to provide a fuller and more complete description of memory development and its associated brain bases than is otherwise possible. It is to outline such an account that is the primary goal of this chapter.

Models of mature memory function

Contemporary views of adult memory suggest that memory is not a unitary trait. A number of investigators have argued, for example, that there may be two types of memory, referred to by different authors as declarative vs. procedural, declarative vs. nondeclarative, explicit vs. implicit, memory vs. habit, etc. (for discussion, see Sherry & Schacter 1987). Although the terms differ, declarative or explicit memory is usually taken to refer to memory that can be stated explicitly or *declared*, that can be brought to mind as an image or proposition in the absence of ongoing perceptual support, and/or of which one is consciously aware. Procedural or implicit memory, on the other hand, is often taken to reflect memory that is embedded in skilled activity or procedures; in addition, it is memory of which one is generally *not* consciously aware (Squire 1986, 1987). [1] The distinctions between these types of memory were originally based on psychological dissociations (e.g. Tulving 1985), whereby performance might be found to vary depending on the particular task used to evaluate memory (e.g. implicit memory is revealed when exposure to a stimulus affects performance on a task that does not require the subject to explicitly remember that stimulus; e.g. Graf & Schacter 1985). Increasingly, however, these subdivisions have been further reinforced by work with human adults using the methods of cognitive neuropsychology, and lesion studies conducted with non-human primates (for a good lay discussion of both methods, see Puri & Mishkin 1994). These methods are briefly described below.

Cognitive neuropsychology

Interest in relating brain function to brain structure has existed for many years. However, it is arguably the case of patient H. M. that brought this cognitive neuropsychological approach into widespread use. In brief, H. M. suffered from a seizure disorder originating in the temporal lobes that could not be treated pharmacologically. As is currently the case, if such seizures are left unchecked, they result initially in cognitive and emotional impairments (particularly impairments in memory), but can ultimately result in death (i.e., by way of depriving the brain of oxygen). To relieve such seizures, H. M.'s surgeon bilaterally resected (i.e., removed) the anterior two-thirds of *both* temporal lobes, including the hippocampus and amygdala. Although H. M.'s seizures were brought under control, he suffered from a profound memory impairment afterwards (for details of this early work, see Milner et al. 1968; Scoville & Milner 1957). Most notable was the observation that, although H. M. was able to recall with great accuracy the events from early in his life, he seemed entirely unable to form new memories; indeed, it has been commented that H. M. lives entirely in the present (for a lay description of the history of research with H. M., see Hilts 1995). What was even more remarkable, however, was that H. M.'s memory impairment was limited to the types of memory we now think of as explicit or declarative memory; that is, he appeared to have no conscious recall or recognition of previously learned (i.e., learned subsequent to surgery) material. However, memory for information acquired through skilled motor activity, such as copying a figure whose image appears in a mirror (mirror tracing), appeared intact, as did priming (see note 1). The explanation for this apparent discrepancy in performance is that memory for material for which conscious awareness is not required, and/or that was acquired through skilled motor activity depends on different neural circuitry than conscious forms of memory, such as recall and recognition. Presumably the latter types of memory depend on structures that lie in the temporal lobes (the very areas that were resected), particularly the hippocampus.

Lesion method

Work with H. M. and patients like H. M. (e.g. WC1606, reported by Bechara et al. 1995, and R. B., reported by Zola-Morgan et al. 1986) laid the foundation for examining the relation between brain and memory in our own species. However, the study of clinical populations can be a tricky venture for a variety of reasons. For example, one must entertain the possibility that the observed deficits might also be due to lesions that exist in the brain that lie *outside* of the identified area but that cannot be easily imaged. A second concern is whether the data from a given patient can be generalized to other patients, let alone groups of normal individuals. Because of these concerns, it became necessary to con-

44

duct studies with animals, in which precise and confirmable lesions could be induced. By adopting this approach one could examine memory function before and after inducing a lesion. In addition, one could eventually verify the precise location of the lesion (using various histological methods) after the animal had been sacrificed. An additional advantage of the animal model was that the work with the human could guide which exact regions of the brain should be lesioned in the animal, thereby tightening the linkage between brain and behavior.

Excellent reviews of this literature exist, and the reader is referred to these papers for details (e.g. see Winocur 1992; Zola-Morgan & Squire 1992). Suffice to say, a similar dissociation between types of memory (e.g. explicit vs. implicit) and the neural substrate underlying these types of memory (e.g. medial temporal lobe vs. striatum) has been found, at least in general terms. For example, lesions of the hippocampus and surrounding region result in impairments on a variety of tasks thought to reflect explicit memory (e.g. Delayed Non-Match to Sample), leaving performance on nonexplicit memory tasks unaffected (e.g. habit; cf. Bachevalier & Mishkin 1984).

Before proceeding, it should be stressed that the use of animal models also presents difficulties, including first, to what extent one can generalize from animals to humans, secondly, the relatively small number of animals that are typically evaluated (often fewer than five; cf. Miller & Desimone 1994, in which two animals were used, and Pellizzer et al. 1995, in which only one animal was used), and thirdly, the subtle and often ignored fact that different species of animal can vary enormously, and thus the question of which species makes the best model becomes critical.

Summary   Collectively, the work from cognitive neuropsychology and lesion studies with non-human primates has suggested that different types of memory are subserved by different neural systems. Thus, the explicit memory system appears to be subserved by structures that lay in the medial temporal lobe (e.g. hippocampus, rhinal cortex; for example, see Petri & Mishkin 1994; Squire & Zola-Morgan 1991; Zola-Morgan & Squire 1992). Less is known about the implicit memory system, although this system likely does *not* involve medial temporal lobe structures (e.g. Knopman & Nissen 1987), the cerebellum (e.g. Daum et al. 1993b), or the frontal lobes, but most likely *does* involve the structures that comprise the striatum (e.g. caudate; for example, Saint-Cyr et al. 1988; see Petri & Mishkin 1994; Salmon & Butters 1995). Additional explanation of these brain areas is provided in subsequent sections of this chapter.

Background to the problem of ontogeny

Research on the ontogeny of memory is less theoretically developed than the work on adult memory. This can be accounted for by four observations. First, with the exception of a handful of investigators working in developmental cognitive neuroscience (for examples, see Bachevalier 1990, 1992; Diamond 1990; Janowsky 1993; Nelson 1994, 1995; Overman et al. 1992; Webster et al.

Table 3.1 Tasks used to study memory development in the human and the monkey (infancy period).

Tasks	Human	Monkey
Visual expectations	x	
Conditioning	x	
Delayed non-matching sample (DNMS)	x	x
Visual paired comparison	x	x
Habitation	x	
Cross-modal recognition memory	x	x
Sequencing/deferred imitation	x	

1995), few students of memory development have been concerned with the brain. Secondly, unlike the adult, infants do not typically suffer discrete brain lesions, making neuropsychological dissociations among different types of memory impossible (e.g. infants only rarely suffer from strokes that selectively target the temporal lobes, but rather suffer more global infarcts). Thirdly, cognitive and linguistic limitations on the part of infants greatly limit the methods by which one can study early memory. Thus, unlike the study of the adult, cognitive dissociations among memory tasks cannot easily be performed with infants. Finally, a seemingly insurmountable issue (common to both the animal literature and the human infant literature) concerns the assertion that explicit memory requires conscious awareness. If our index of conscious awareness is that subjects respond verbally, neither monkeys nor the preverbal human would ever satisfy this criterion. However, if we modify the standards so that purposeful behavior (e.g. reaching to obtain a reward or stimulus; crying at the departure of the caretaker; discovering rules in a problem set) or the ability to ascertain the interrelationship among items or events by the use of stored information (e.g. the ability to recognize a particular facial expression despite its being portrayed by several different models, all of whom vary in the intensity in which the expression is depicted) meets our criterion of "awareness," then it may be possible to agree that a particular task reflects explicit memory. However, it may be helpful to relax the psychological criterion of conscious awareness and replace it instead with a more parsimonious view that if different neural systems are involved in different memory tasks, then these tasks may reflect different "types" of memory (see pp. 69–70 for an elaboration on this point). Collectively, however, it is these reasons that likely account for the paucity of brain-based theories regarding the ontogeny of memory.

How, then, might one approach the question of when in development different memory systems emerge, and what neurobiological events correlate with their emergence? As a starting point I will begin by examining what is required of the infant when tested in different memory paradigms. Different task demands *may* suggest that different types of memory are involved in performing in the various tasks (although admittedly one cannot rule out the possibility that different *processes* are involved, not different types of memory qua

Table 3.2 Neural structures thought to underlie different memory tasks and maturational time table (in postnatal months) for the emergence of behaviour and anatomy (human).

Tasks	Structures	Maturational Time Frame (months)
Visual expectancies	striatum	1–3/3–?
Conditioning (for acquisition)	cerebellum	3/3–?
	brainstem	3?/–?
Conditioning (for retention)	hippocamps	1–12/
DNMS	hippocampus/ rhinal cortex	1–12/ 18–45
DNMS	cortical area TE	12–36/12–36
VPC	hippocampus	2–3/1–12
Habituation	hippocampus?/rhinal cortex	0–12
Sequencing/deferred imitation	hippocampus+?	9–12+?
Cross-modal recognition memory	amygdala/hippocampus	6–12

memory). However, as stated earlier, dissociation among different tasks is more difficult in the infant than in the adult, as first, one cannot rely on verbal performance, second, the kinds of motor performance one can evaluate in infants is very limited, and third, general cognitive immaturity on the part of the infant precludes the investigator from adopting many of the tasks used with adults (unlike their use with, for example, preschoolers or even toddlers). As a result, a formal task analysis will be impossible, although it will hopefully provide a first approximation to the question of isolating different types of memory.

As I describe the various tasks used to study memory in the human, I will also note whether these same (or similar) tasks have been applied to the study of neurologically impaired adult humans or infant monkeys (see Table 3.1). The rationale for including this literature is that some insight may be gained by relating the manipulation of brain structures to the manipulation of task performance. It must be noted, however, that relatively few of the procedures used with adults or animals have been performed with human infants (although some notable exceptions will be described). By drawing such a parallel it should become possible to *correlate* the task performance of human infants with that of human adults and infant monkeys, although drawing direct comparisons will not be possible.

The next step in this process of describing the ontogeny of memory will be to superimpose the time course for the emergence of function against that for the emergence of structure. Thus, what do we know about the development of those areas/regions/circuits of the brain that might be involved in performance in the various tasks that have been described? Such a superimposition may allow us to derive *neural* dissociations among memory types. I shall use this information as a form of converging evidence for the behavioral data that will have already been reviewed. As a result, it should become possible to provide a first approximation as to what "types" of memory might realistically develop at different ages, and how the emergence of function is made possible by the emergence of structure (see Table 3.2 for an illustration).

The study of early memory and its relation to brain development

Tasks that might reflect forms of implicit memory

Visual expectancies Marshall Haith and colleagues have utilized corneal photography to examine the infant's ability to form expectations about future events (for review, see Haith et al. 1993). Eye movements are recorded as infants fixate a series of lights which, when lit in succession, create a certain pattern. Of particular interest is whether infants correctly anticipate the next light in the sequence, and whether their reaction times decline when the sequence changes. These authors have demonstrated that infants as young as 3.5 months will rapidly "learn" the sequence of lights as reflected by anticipating the next light in the sequence. In addition, when the learned pattern is interrupted, reaction time increases, suggesting that the infant recognized the change in sequence (Haith et al. 1988; Wentworth & Haith 1992).

Unfortunately, this exact paradigm has not yet been performed in a neuropsychological or cognitive neuroscience context. As a result, one must attempt to identify a task that has been used in this context in the adult human or monkey that approximates that used by Haith and colleagues with human infants. One such task includes a procedure used by Knopman and Nissen to examine a form of procedural learning, and that has been thought to depend on the striatum (a constellation of structures, including the caudate and putamen, that lie deep within the cortex). One example should suffice (see Knopman 1991; Knopman & Nissen 1987). Subjects were presented with a series of lights. There were four lights in a row, and ten rows altogether. One light in each row came on, and the subject was required to push a key corresponding to each light. The sequence of ten lights made a pattern, and after the tenth light came on the sequence began anew. Elderly adults with Alzheimer's disease (AD) and healthy elderly controls served as subjects. Both groups of subjects showed decreased reaction times as the ten-light sequence emerged, and both groups showed increased reaction times when the sequence of lights was unexpectedly changed. These results suggest that both groups learned the sequence. Only the control subjects, however, professed *awareness* (as indexed verbally) that a sequence of lights had been presented.

The observation that the AD patients were selectively impaired on the explicit memory aspects of the task (i.e., awareness of the pattern), but unimpaired on the procedural memory aspects (i.e., learning as inferred from reaction times) is intriguing. Given that the AD patients were tested in the early stages of the disease, when neuropathology was (presumably, as this was not confirmed) restricted to the medial temporal lobes, it seemed reasonable to conclude that this region of the brain was *not* involved in task performance. Determining which precise region(s) was involved is a bit more difficult, although a reasonable hypothesis is that in this task, as in other procedural memory tasks, an intact striatum is required (see Salmon & Butters 1995 for discussion). Given that the AD patients suffered no known pathology of these structures, it was assumed that the normative procedural learning that was observed was due to intact striatal structures. Collectively, then, it seems reasonable to assume that an intact striatum made possible the procedural learning that was evidenced by comparable task performance in both groups, but medial temporal lobe impairment in the AD group prevented these subjects from possessing explicit knowledge of the lights' sequence.

Although infants in the visual expectancy paradigm were not required to push buttons, the latency with which they move their eyes indicated that they had learned the sequence of moving lights. Whether they were "aware" of the emerging pattern will never be determined. However, the similarity between the infant paradigm and that employed with adults by Knopman and Nissen (1987) suggests that the performance in the former task did not depend on temporal lobe structures but may well have depended on striatal structures. The question that logically follows is whether such an assertion is biologically plausible.

The neural bases of procedural memory   Relatively little is known about the development of the human striatum. It is known that the structures that comprise the striatum (caudate and putamen; see Figures 3.1–3.2) are the first of the telencephalic (forebrain) structures to begin myelinating, and that the structures that comprise the basal ganglia (caudate, putamen, globus pallidus, subthalamic nucleus, and substantia nigra) are differentiated at birth. Within the basal ganglia, the inner segment of the globus pallidus is well myelinated by the eighth postnatal month, although the outer segment does not reach adult levels of myelin until beyond the first postnatal year (for discussion, see Sidman & Rakic 1982). These findings are in agreement with metabolic studies. For example, Chugani and colleagues (Chugani 1994; Chugani & Phelps 1986; Chugani et al. 1987) have reported that the basal ganglia display increases in metabolic activity earlier than most regions of the cortex.

Based on these data, it seems reasonable to propose that the striatum may support performance in the visual expectancy paradigm and as such, may reflect a form of procedural memory akin to that in the adult.

Conditioning   Although the study of learning continues to occupy the research agendas of many neuroscientists and clearly occupied the agenda of many psychologists interested in adult functioning for much of the twentieth century, considerably less work has been done in the context of early development. In addition, although attention was paid to the question of whether infants were even capable of learning and/or of being conditioned (see Lipsitt 1990), much of what remains today is in the narrow field of instrumental conditioning. Unfortunately, the two procedures most widely used with the human infant have never been used with the primate. Similarly, the neural bases underlying task performance have not been established, as these procedures have not been utilized in either a basic or cognitive neuroscience framework. As a result, the relation between brain and learning in the context of human development remains largely a black hole. To remedy this situation, the model

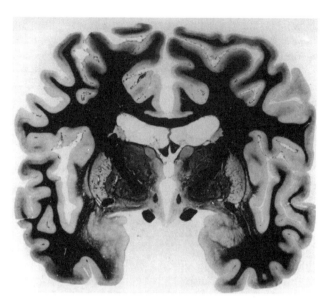

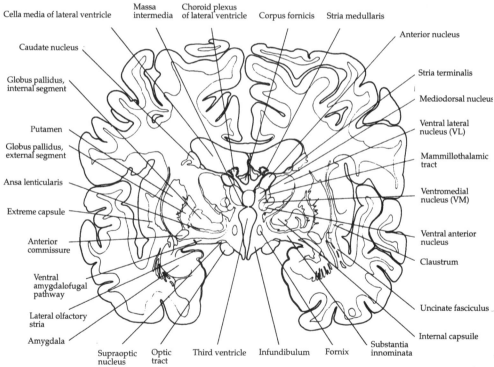

Cella media of lateral ventricle

Massa intermedia

Choroid plexus of lateral ventricle

Corpus fornicis

Stria medullaris

Anterior nucleus

Caudate nucleus

Globus pallidus, internal segment

Putamen

Globus pallidus, external segment

Ansa lenticularis

Extreme capsule

Anterior commissure

Ventral amygdalofugal pathway

Lateral olfactory stria

Amygdala

Supraoptic nucleus

Optic tract

Third ventricle

Infundibulum

Fornix

Substantia innominata

Stria terminalis

Mediodorsal nucleus

Ventral lateral nucleus (VL)

Mammillothalamic tract

Ventromedial nucleus (VM)

Ventral anterior nucleus

Claustrum

Uncinate fasciculus

Internal capsuile

Figure 3.1 Some of the structures that comprise the striatum, including the putamen and caudate (left side, top and bottom portions of figure), thought to be involved in procedural memory. (From *Fundamental neuroanatomy*, by W. J. H. Nauta & M. Feritag 1986, and reprinted with permission.)

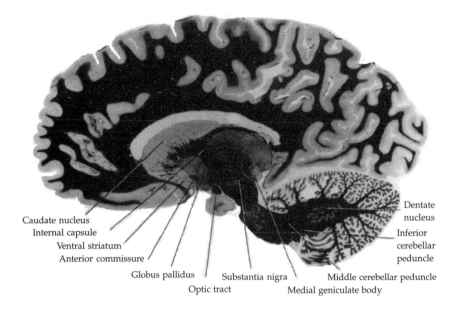

Caudate nucleus
Internal capsule
Ventral striatum
Anterior commissure

Globus pallidus   Substantia nigra
Optic tract   Medial geniculate body

Dentate
nucleus
Inferior
cerebellar
peduncle
Middle cerebellar peduncle

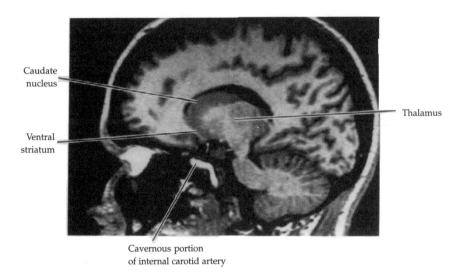

Caudate
nucleus

Ventral
striatum

Thalamus

Cavernous portion
of internal carotid artery

Figure 3.2 Upper figure represents myelin-stained region of the brain, revealing (in saggital view) two striatal structures, the caudate nucleus and globus pallidus, thought to be involved in procedural memory; lower figure represents Magnetic Resonance Image (MRI) of a comparable brain region. (From *The human brain and spinal cord*, 2nd edn, by L. Heimer. Copyright 1995 by Springer-Verlag, and reprinted with permission.)

of brain–behavior relations I will propose will depend to a great extent on peripheral work with non-primate species, and to a very limited extent, on work with the human adult. This approach is less than satisfactory, but is necessary in order to establish some linkages between brain and conditioned behavior.

There have been two primary methods by which memory has been studied using conditioning. One involves instrumental conditioning, and the other the conditioned eye-blink response.

Instrumental conditioning

Sucking behavior   DeCasper and colleagues have used non-nutritive sucking to examine newborn infants' recognition of their mother's voice. Infants are allowed to suck on a non-nutritive nipple until a baseline suck rate is established. Different auditory stimuli are then presented each time the infant sucks. Some of these stimuli are presumed to be familiar to the infant, whereas others are not. If the infant's sucking behavior can be modified by the presentation of a particular stimulus, then memory for this stimulus is inferred.

This work has demonstrated that infants, within a day or two of being born, can not only recognize their mother's voice (e.g. DeCasper & Fifer 1980), but can distinguish between a story the mother had read out loud during the last weeks of pregnancy (i.e., a familiar story) and a novel story (e.g. DeCasper & Spence 1986; for elaboration, see DeCasper & Spence 1991). For example, these authors have reported that listening to the mother's voice, or the voice of their mother reading a familiar nursery rhyme, modifies sucking, whereas listening to the voice of a stranger or the voice of the mother reading an unfamiliar nursery rhyme does not. It is assumed that this pattern of results must be due to the prenatal experience of hearing the mother's voice.

Leg kick conditioning   The other method by which memory is inferred from instrumental behavior concerns conditioned leg kicking. This procedure has been extensively developed by Rovee-Collier and colleagues (for review, see Rovee-Collier 1990). Because this work is reviewed in the current volume, only a cursory description will be provided.

In brief, infants are positioned on their backs in a crib, with a mobile suspended above them. After obtaining some baseline level of kicking, a ribbon is attached to the mobile at one end and to the infant's leg at the other. Infants as young as 3 months readily draw the association between their leg movement and the movement of the mobile, and the highly reinforcing properties of the mobile's movement generally results in a substantial increase of leg kicking relative to baseline. After some retention interval the infant is again placed in the crib, and a test period is administered. Here the infant might be presented with the same or different mobile in the same or different context (e.g. the crib bumper might change).

Although there are many variants of this procedure (e.g. introducing a reinstatement period between initial conditioning and the recognition test), the results in nearly all cases are robust; infants as young as 3 months show evidence of savings after intervals as long as 2–4 weeks, so long as reinstatement is provided (e.g. Rovee-Collier & Hayne 1987).

Neural bases of instrumental conditioning Unfortunately, the two procedures described in this section have never been used in a neuroscience context, with primates or any other species (in the case of the sucking response, the questions addressed by DeCasper may be unique to the human, although it would be interesting to determine if newborn monkeys recognize their mother's vocalizations). It is therefore extraordinarily difficult to ascertain the neural bases of these forms of memory. A *possible* analogy to Rovee-Collier's work might be the instrumentally conditioned limb flexion response. Here animals (often cats) are first conditioned to associate a tone (CS) with a shock (UCS) applied to the leg. The animal must then learn to flex the leg during the time the CS is presented before the CS terminates in the UCS. In a representative example of this procedure, Voneida and colleagues (e.g. Voneida et al. 1990) demonstrated that lesions in the olivary-cerebellar complex result in severe loss of the response. The lesions resulting in the greatest loss involved damage to the rostral parts of the dorsal and medial accessory olivary nuclei (which receives inputs from the forelimb spinal cord and cerebral cortical areas). In contrast, rostralmedial olivary lesions had little effect on behavior.

Comparing the instrumental conditioned response to the limb flexion response bears some risks. However, it may be possible to speculate that in the former procedure, portions of the olivary-cerebellar complex are involved, at least in terms of learning the task. The critical components of this complex likely include cerebellar Purkinje cells, which receive input from the contralateral inferior olivary complex via the climbing fibers, and from the mossy fibers, which transmit a wide range of sensory input. The underlying neuroanatomy therefore includes the cerebellum and certain deep nuclei of the brainstem (see Figures 3.3–3.4). Consistent with the latter argument is the observation that lesions of certain cerebellar nuclei can block acquisition of some forms of motor learning, such as the eye-blink conditioned response (e.g. Steinmetz et al. 1992), and aversive signaled bar-press learning (e.g. Steinmetz et al. 1993). However, we might also speculate that the ability to recognize the mobile itself is mediated by the hippocampus. (This point will be elaborated below.)

Classical conditioning Although studies of classical conditioning are widespread in the behavioral neuroscience literature, little work has been done in this context with human infants. However, there is evidence that infants (including newborns) can be conditioned in general (e.g. Marquis 1931; Wickens & Wickens 1940). Of particular relevance to the goals of the current chapter is the small literature on the conditioned eye-blink response. Subjects are initially presented with a tone (CS). Shortly thereafter (coincident with the tone) a puff of air is presented to the eye (UCS). This combination results in a blink (UCR). After a certain number of trials, the CS alone results in a blink (CR). Although this paradigm has been used little since the mid-1970s, a brief syn-

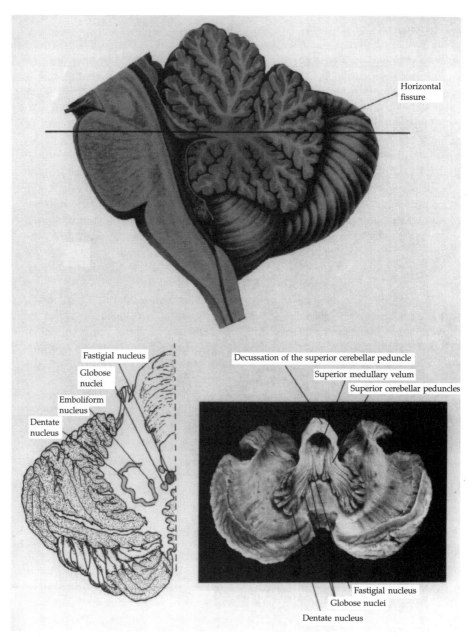

Horizontal
fissure

Fastigial nucleus

Globose
nuclei

Emboliform
nucleus

Dentate
nucleus

Decussation of the superior cerebellar peduncle

Superior medullary velum

Superior cerebellar peduncles

Fastigial nucleus
Globose nuclei
Dentate nucleus

Figure 3.3 A near-horizontal section of a cerebellar preparation (upper figure); lower figure is a gross anatomic preparation revealing some of the intracerebellar nuclei thought to be involved in conditioning. (From *The human brain and spinal cord*, 2nd edn., by L. Heimer. Copyright 1995 by Springer-Verlag, and reprinted with permission.)

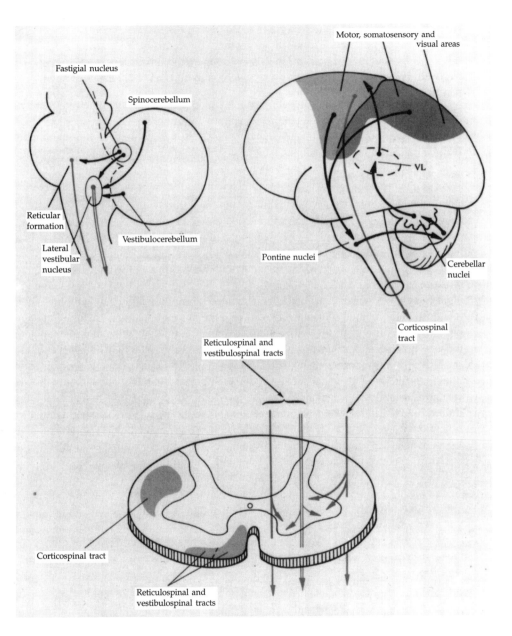

Figure 3.4 Schematic drawing of the cerebellum and motor system, thought to be involved in conditioning. (From *The human brain and spinal cord*, 2nd edn., by L. Heimer. Copyright 1995 by Springer-Verlag, and reprinted with permission.)

opsis of this literature would suggest that the conditioned eye-blink response appears to develop between 10 and 30 days in the human (see Lipsitt 1990).

Neural bases of classical conditioning Unfortunately, studies of classical conditioning in the primate in a basic or cognitive neuroscience context have not yet been conducted. Thus, it is necessary to look to other literatures for assistance in this regard. Although this is not an optimal solution, it will have to suffice if I am to be successful in *speculating* about the neural bases of such conditioning.

Animal studies In general, the neural circuitry involved in eye-blink conditioning in the mature rabbit has been well worked out by Thompson and colleagues (for review, see Woodruff-Pak et al. 1990; Woodruff-Pak & Thompson 1988). Here it has been demonstrated that the cerebellum and its associated brainstem circuitry are responsible for acquisition. The general hypothesis proposed by Thompson, Woodruff-Pak and colleagues has been that the CS activates mossy fibers of the cerebellum, while the US activates climbing fibers. Cerebellar Purkinje cells are the most likely candidates. Finally, although the cerebellum is responsible for acquisition of the eye-blink response, the hippocampus may be involved in the storage process. For example, activity in the CA1 region increases within trials early in the acquisition phase, but only when learning is occurring.[2]

Human data A number of studies examining the conditioned eye-blink response in the human have been conducted. For example, Daum et al. (1993b) has reported that patients with cerebellar pathology (e.g. due to ischemic lesions) or who had undergone surgical resection of the cerebellum demonstrated a severe impairment in acquiring the conditioned eye-blink response. Interestingly, these patients were aware of the reinforcement contingencies. Similarly, Woodruff-Pak (1993) has reported that patient H. M., who had undergone a bilateral resection of the temporal lobes (see p. 44), can acquire the conditioned eye-blink response, although he is not aware of having done so.[3] Collectively, the human literature is in agreement with the animal literature: Specifically, acquiring the conditioned eye-blink response requires the cerebellum, and does not require medial temporal lobe structures.

Thus far I have argued that instrumental conditioning involves the cerebellum and certain deep nuclei of the brainstem, and that the conditioned eye-blink response requires the cerebellum (at least for its acquisition). In this context it is important to ask whether there are data to support the assertion that these structures/nuclei are sufficiently mature early in life to support such conditioning.

Relatively little is known about the development of either the cerebellum or deep nuclei. During prenatal development the cerebellum lags behind the cortex by several weeks (see Kandel et al. 1991). Nevertheless, PET studies have revealed that glucose activity (perhaps a corollary of synapse formation) in the cerebellum during the first postnatal year of life more closely approximates adult values than virtually any other region of the brain (Chugani 1994;

Chugani & Phelps 1986). Portions of the superior and inferior cerebellar peduncles and the decussation of the superior cerebellum peduncles (see Figure 3.5) are developed at birth. In addition, myelination patterns of the entire cerebellum appear adult-like by 3 postnatal months (Barkovich et al. 1988). Thus, although the development of the cerebellum initially (i.e., prenatally) lags behind that of the cortex, rapid development appears to occur towards the end of the last part of gestation and the first part of postnatal life. These general findings may possibly account for the high motor learning potential and conditionability of the young infant.

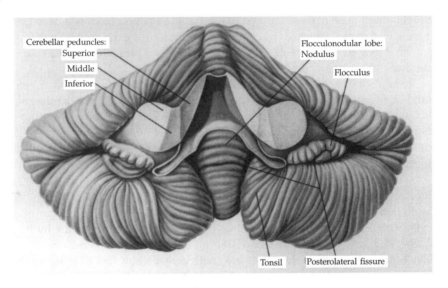

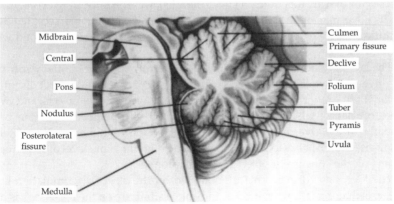

Figure 3.5 Upper portion of the figure represents a ventral view of the cerebellum (thought to be involved in conditioning) when detached from the brainstem; lower portion represents a midsagittal section through the brainstem and cerebellum. (From *Principles of neural science*, 3rd edn, by E. R. Kandel, J. H. Schwartz, & T. M. Jessell. Copyright 1991 by Springer-Verlag, and reprinted with permission.)

Tasks that might reflect forms of explicit memory

Delayed non-match to sample (DNMS) The DNMS has long been used extensively to study memory in the non-human primate (Mishkin & Delacour 1975), and has recently been extended to the human infant and child. In the version of the task relevant to the present discussion, monkeys are presented with a sample object. When this object is removed, a food reward is revealed. The monkey is then presented with the sample object and a novel object. Reaching for the novel object is rewarded with food. In this manner the animal must acquire a general rule that the novel object is the correct object. On each trial, new stimuli serve as sample and comparison (i.e., trial-unique procedure). Once the animal has learned to reach for the novel object as indexed by a high level of performance (e.g. 90 per cent criterion), the demand on memory can be increased by imposing greater delays between presentation of the sample and test objects.

It should be noted that what makes this task "explicit" is that the animal (and presumably the human – see pp. 45–7) must be "aware" of what the rule is in order to carry it forward to new instances (recall that each trial contains new stimuli). In addition, the fact that the rule is remembered even after a delay has ensued is consistent with what is required in other tasks of explicit memory (e.g. recall).

A number of studies have demonstrated that it is not until 4 months that monkey infants even begin to learn the DNMS task, and it is not until 1 year that adult performance is approached (Bachevalier & Mishkin 1984). Overman and colleagues have recently extended this procedure to the study of the human infant, and have reported that 12–15-month-old human infants require extensive training to perform the DNMS task, with considerably less training necessary by the time infants are between 18 and 32 months old. However, even the oldest children in this study (45–81 months) were significantly worse than adults (Overman et al. 1992). When one imposes the commonly accepted 3 or 4:1 ratio of monkey years to human years, these human data correspond well with the monkey data.

The late development of adult-like DNMS performance was initially surprising, given how well infant monkeys do on a task of concurrent object discrimination. In this latter task, animals are presented with pairs of objects, and over repeated, daily trials, they are required to select one member of the pair consistently. In the Overman et al. (1992) report, 3-month-old animals that took 720 trials to learn DNMS took only 16 trials to attain the same level of 90 per cent correct on the concurrent object discrimination task.

The high level of performance obtained on the object discrimination task suggests that the failure of animals to behave similarly on the DNMS task is not due to problems in perception, reaching, motivation, or associating a stimulus with a response. Thus, it was initially concluded (e.g. Bachevalier & Mishkin 1984) that delayed maturation on the DNMS task reflected the (relatively) late development of visual recognition memory.

This explanation no longer seems tenable. A study conducted by Diamond (1992, 1995; also see preliminary report in Diamond 1990) indicated that if infants are required only to *look* at the novel object and not reach for it, adult-like performance on the DNMS task is obtained by 6–12 months.[4] This report has been replicated by Overman et al. (1993), who administered the standard DNMS task to four groups of infants (10–15 months, 18–20 months, 22–38 months, and 45–107 months) and to adults. A video camera recorded visual fixations on each DNMS trial. The authors reported that in *all* age groups longer looking was obtained to the novel vs. familiar stimulus. Based on these results (and those of Diamond), it seems reasonable to conclude that adult performance on the DNMS task must require more than visual recognition memory, as even the youngest infants in this study discriminated the novel from familiar stimulus. It is unclear what other ability is being tapped. One possibility may be that the strong tendency to prefer novelty overrides (until the second or third year of life) reinforcement contingencies. (This proclivity to prefer novelty is discussed on pp. 60–5.) A second possibility (discussed by Diamond 1995) is the infant's ability to resist interference (e.g. providing a reward for displacing the sample stimulus during the familiarization phase may distract infants from shifting their attention from the sample to the novel stimulus during the test phase).

The neural bases of DNMS performance   These more recent behavioral observations regarding DNMS performance conform to the results of recent studies examining the neural bases of DNMS performance. Mishkin, Bachevalier, and colleagues had initially demonstrated that lesions of the medial temporal lobe (hippocampus, amygdala, and surrounding tissue, such as the entorhinal cortex; see Figures 3.6–3.7) impaired performance on the DNMS task (Mishkin et el. 1984). A similar pattern of results has also been reported in the human (Owen et al. 1995). In addition, Colombo and Gross (1994) have reported single unit activity in both the hippocampus and inferior temporal lobe (IT) in monkeys performing in the Delayed Match-To-Sample task (a variant of the DNMS task that requires the animal to choose the familiar stimulus instead of the novel stimulus). Because of the late onset of adult-like DNMS performance, it had therefore been assumed that these structures mature late. However, more recent observations call this assumption into question. First, and perhaps most importantly, Bachevalier and colleagues have demonstrated that the DNMS task may also depend critically on the inferior temporal regions TE and TEO (see Figure 3.8), not just the hippocampus. These authors have reported that neonatal (early) lesions or adult (late) lesions of the hippocampus, amygdala, and surrounding tissue (i.e., H+A+ lesion) both significantly reduce adult performance. However, only late lesions of area TE impaired performance on the DNMS task, whereas early lesions had no effect (Bachevalier 1990, 1992; Bachevalier et al. 1991; Bachevalier & Mishkin 1992; Webster et al. 1995). Accordingly, the DNMS task (at least the conventional reaching version) may well depend additionally (and critically) on cortical area TE, as well as on subcortical limbic areas such as the hippocampus (this point will be elaborated below).

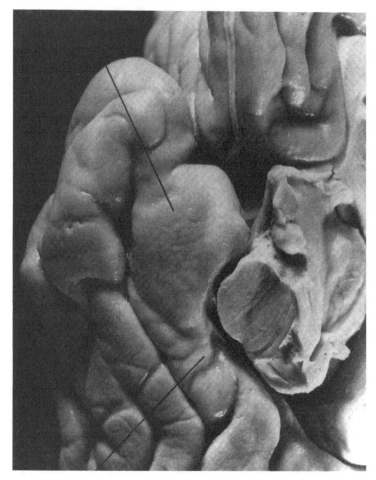

Figure 3.6 The entorhinal area (indicated by line at top of figure), a region thought to be involved in explicit memory, and the parahippocampal gyrus (indicated by line at bottom of figure). (From *The human brain and spinal cord*, by L. Heimer. Copyright 1995 by Springer-Verlag, and reprinted with permission.)

The development of medial temporal lobe structures In contrast to the rat, there is increasing evidence that in the primate (human and non-human), the hippocampus matures relatively early in postnatal life. For example, the pyramidal neurons of the CA3 region of the monkey brain are adult-like at birth (Seress & Ribak 1995a), as is the distribution of muscarinic receptors (receptors for acetylcholine) in the monkey limbic cortex (in contrast to those in the cortex, which mature later; O'Neil et al. 1986). Second, the volume of human limbic cortex and the size of surrounding limbic structures (e.g. hippocampus) rapidly become adult-like in the second half of the first year of life (Kretschmann et al. 1986), although most of the structures that comprise

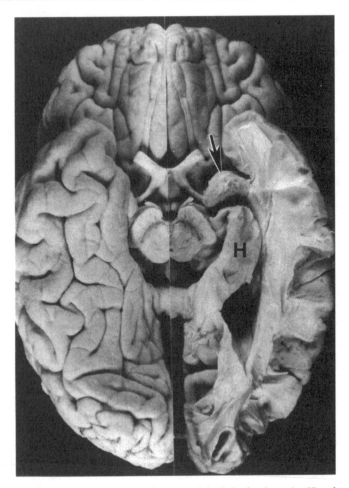

Figure 3.7 Blunt dissection of the the amygdaloid body (arrow); **H** refers to the hippocampal formation, an area thought to be involved in pre-explicit memory. (From *The human brain and spinal Cord*, 2nd edn, by L. Heimer. Copyright 1995 by Springer-Verlag, and reprinted with permission.)

the hippocampal formation are cytoarchitecturally mature – except for the dentate – *prenatally* (Janas 1994). Third, the subiculum (which links the entorhinal cortex with the hippocampus) and the hippocampus proper mature relatively early in human postnatal development (Humphrey 1966). Fourth, the entorhinal cortex (which links the hippocampus with the cortex) has already begun to form synapses and express neurotransmitters by mid-gestation in the monkey, and may already have begun to form extrinsic connections (Berger & Alvarez 1994; Berger et al. 1993); it is also the area that shows the most advanced areal differentiation in the cortex in the human – an event that occurs by the tenth prenatal week (Kostovic et al. 1990). Fifth,

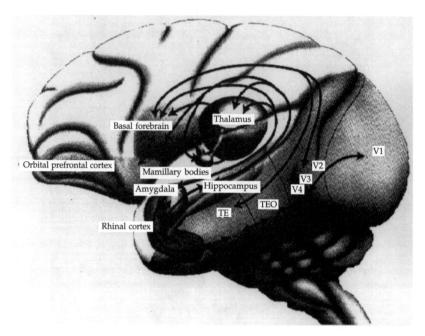

Figure 3.8 A schematic view of the structures thought to be involved in explicit memory, including the hippocampus, rhinal cortex, and area TE. (Adapted from Bachevalier, J., O. Pascalis, & W. Overman 1995 with permission).

dendrite development in the hippocampus precedes that in the visual cortex (Paldino & Purpura 1979), a structure known to be quite functional by the second half of the first year of life (see Aslin 1989 for review of behavioral data; see Bourgeois & Rakic 1993 for discussion of physiological data). Sixth, metabolic activity in the temporal lobes increases substantially by 3 postnatal months, and precedes that of prefrontal cortex by several months (Chugani 1994; Chugani & Phelps 1986). The only area within the hippocampal formation that appears to have somewhat protracted postnatal development is in the area of the dentate gyrus, where adult levels of synapses are not attained until 10 months in the monkey (or 3–4 years in the human; see Eckenhoff & Rakic 1991: Note, though, that most dentate cells originate prenatally in the monkey; see Seress & Ribak 1995b).

Collectively, the data cited above support the conclusion that the human and non-human primate hippocampus and surrounding structures (excluding the dentate) mature early in life, and thus the late development of DNMS performance is unlikely to be due to delayed hippocampal development.

If one accepts the argument that the hippocampus develops early, one can then ask whether there are other infant memory tasks that are also dependent on this structure. As reviewed below, the answer to this question appears to be "yes".

Visual paired-comparison task (VPC) This procedure was developed by Robert Fantz as a method of examining early perceptual function, although it was rapidly adopted by those studying early memory. What Fantz discovered was that infants had a proclivity to respond to novel stimuli (Fantz 1956). Specifically, when given a choice between a familiar stimulus and a novel stimulus, infants older than 2–3 months would "prefer" (i.e., look longer at) the latter (for discussion, see Fagan 1990). What determined whether a stimulus was novel or familiar was accomplished by providing the infant with previous experience with one of them. Thus, infants would typically be shown a pair of identical stimuli for some period of study (e.g. 60 sec), followed by a test phase. During the test phase the familiar stimulus would appear on one side of the screen, and the novel stimulus (i.e., a stimulus not previously seen) would appear on the other side. Corneal reflections were recorded from the infants' eyes, thereby determining which of the stimuli the infant fixated more.

There are many variants of the visual paired comparison procedure, such as varying the length of the familiarization period, or imposing a delay between familiarization and test. In nearly all cases, however, the observation that infants "prefer" to look at a novel stimulus more than a familiar stimulus has been interpreted by most investigators as evidence of recognition memory. Such evidence has most reliably been obtained in infants older than 2–3 months (for discussion, see Fagan 1990). In terms of the impact of imposing a delay, the longest delay that human infants appear able to tolerate has been 48 hours for abstract patterns and 2 weeks for faces (Fagan 1970, 1973). And, although not exhaustively studied, infant pig-tailed macaques have been shown to tolerate a delay of 24 hours (Gunderson & Swartz 1985).

Habituation procedure This procedure is a variant of the visual paired comparison paradigm. Here infants are presented with a single stimulus repeatedly, until their looking declines to some predetermined value (e.g. a typical criterion of habituation would be that infants have two consecutive looks that are 50 per cent less long than their first one or two looks). After the infant has habituated, a novel stimulus is presented. If infants' looking recovers (i.e., dishabituates), it is assumed that they have identified this stimulus as novel, or more parsimoniously, have determined that this is not the familiar stimulus (for discussion, see Bornstein 1985).

Like the visual paired comparison procedure, there are many variants of the habituation procedure, including (a) using different criterial values, (b) imposing a delay between habituation and test, and (c) exposing infants to a *category* of stimuli (e.g. different male faces) and examining whether infants generalize their looking from a new exemplar of the old category (e.g. a previously unseen male face), and discriminate this category from a new category (e.g. female faces). In general, however, longer looking to the novel stimulus relative to the familiar stimulus has been interpreted as evidence of recognition memory. Such evidence has been obtained in infants as young as a few days old (e.g. Slater 1995), although generally results are more robust somewhat after the neonatal period. In terms of delays, infants are typically able to remember the familiar stimulus for periods of time ranging from 24 to 48 hours. However, it should be stressed that in the *auditory* modality, there are data suggesting that newborns (1–2 days old) are able to recognize a word after a delay of 24 hours (Swain et al. 1993).

Although there are a number of parallels between the visual paired comparison and habituation procedures, perhaps the most important is that in both procedures, memory for the familiar stimulus is inferred from longer looking at the novel stimulus.[5] One fundamental difference, however, is that in the former procedure, infants' recognition memory is (potentially) facilitated by providing perceptual support for the recognition decision; that is, both stimuli are presented simultaneously for comparison. In contrast, in the habituation procedure the stimuli are presented one at a time, and thus any such comparison must (presumably) be done on the basis of some perceptual or representational scratch pad. One would think that providing perceptual support for deciding which stimulus is familiar and which is novel would lower the demands on memory, in which case one should expect lower age estimates using this procedure vs. the habituation procedure. However, whatever advantage this facet of the procedure possesses may be offset by two potential disadvantages. The first is that for younger infants in whom head control has not yet matured, looking back and forth may prove problematic. A second is that presenting two stimuli simultaneously may cause interference and actually *increase* the demands on memory. Given the advantages and disadvantages of each procedure, it may not be surprising that the age estimates of when infants show evidence of memory is comparable.

Neural basis of novelty preferences   There are two sources of evidence to suggest that novelty preferences (at least as examined in the VPC procedure) are mediated by the hippocampus and surrounding structures. First, Bachevalier et al. (1993) presented 5-, 15-, and 30-day-old infant monkeys, and adult monkeys, with pairs of identical stimuli for 30 seconds. A 10 sec delay then ensued, followed by two 5 sec test trials. The authors reported that monkeys older than 15 days of age showed robust novelty preferences. However, if the amygdala, hippocampus, and surrounding cortex were removed bilaterally (H+A+ lesion), such preferences failed to obtain. Additionally, lesions of area TE in infancy have no effect on VPC performance, although lesioning this same area in the adult will effectively yield a severe impairment in task performance (Webster et al. 1995). From these results it may be concluded that the hippocampus and surrounding tissue probably support novelty preferences, at least in the infancy period. However, as may be the case for DNMS performance (see earlier discussion), area TE may contribute to novelty preferences in the juvenile or adult monkey. I shall return to this point in a later discussion.

Turning now to studies of the human, McKee and Squire (1993) tested elderly subjects using a procedure that was nearly identical to that employed by Bachevalier et al. (1993). Here pairs of identical stimuli were initially presented (familiarization phase), followed by 5 sec test trials containing pairs of familiar and novel stimuli. Duration of looking was monitored and recorded. The authors reported that neurologically normal adults showed novelty preferences after delays as long as several hours (a result similar to that obtained with adult monkeys). However, adults suffering from bilateral damage to the hippocampal formation or diencephalic regions only showed such preferences when the delay between familiarization and test was less than 1 sec; when such delays exceeded 2 min, no such preferences were evident.

Collectively, these studies demonstrate that intact temporal lobe structures are responsible for novelty preferences (at least as evaluated in the VPC procedure), and that such structures become operational in the monkey by approximately 15 days of life.

Does dependence on the hippocampus make a task "explicit"?

If the VPC task reflects explicit memory in the adult sense of the term, one must account for why infants do not demonstrate evidence of recognition or recall memory until the second half of the first year of life when tested in other, presumably "explicit-like" tasks. This point will be illustrated below.

Cross-modal recognition memory   A task that has proven to be more difficult for the infant than visual recognition memory is cross-modal recognition memory. Here infants are familiarized to a stimulus in one sense modality, without benefit of experience gained through other modalities. They are then presented with the familiar stimulus and a novel stimulus (singly, or in pairs) in a different modality. For example, an infant might be allowed to feel an object without being allowed to see it. The infant is then presented with a *picture* of the object initially seen, along with a picture of a novel object. Longer looking at the picture of the novel object is used to infer recognition of the familiar object. In order for infants to be successful on this task, they must encode the familiar stimulus in one modality, transfer the representation of this stimulus to a second modality, retain this representation in memory (for whatever delay ensues between familiarization and test), and then discriminate the familiar and novel objects. (Of course, an alternate possibility is for infants to retain information from the original modality during the delay period, and transfer this information to the new modality at the time of test.)

A general finding from this literature (for review, see Rose & Ruff 1989) has been that it is not until 6 to 8 months of age that infants become successful on this task; that is, not until then do they consistently prefer the novel stimulus. The fact that performance on this task develops later than on unimodal (e.g. visual) recognition memory tasks may suggest that (a) additional limbic structures may be required for forming cross-modal associations, and/or (b) tasks that require more than simple novelty preferences may not be within the infant's behavioral repertoire until after the first 6 months or so, when additional neural development has occurred.

In terms of the first assertion, a likely candidate for the involvement of limbic structures in addition to the hippocampus is the amygdala. For example, Murray and Mishkin (1985) have reported that bilateral lesions of the amygdala impair the ability to make cross-modal associations. In subsequent work, Murray and Gaffan (1994) demonstrated that the amygdala may play less of a role in cross-modal associations *per se* than in stimulus–stimulus associations. In either case, these findings suggest that when cross-modal recognition is required, involvement of both the amygdala and hippocampus is necessary; the latter structure for mediating novelty preferences, the former for drawing cross-modal (or stimulus–stimulus) associations (and possibly also memory).

Although it has been impossible to examine *directly* amygdala and hippocampal involvement in cross-modal recognition memory in the human infant, there are indirect data that support such an assertion. Using a task modeled after that used in behavioral studies, my colleagues and I (Nelson et al. 1993) allowed 8-month-old infants to feel an object for 60 sec, without benefit of seeing the object. Cortical event-related potentials (ERPs) were then recorded as the infants were presented with alternating pictures of the familiar object and a novel object. In previous studies by our group (for review, see Nelson 1994), a baseline response invoked by a familiar stimulus and a positive slow wave response invoked by a novel stimulus has been interpreted to reflect, respectively, the recognition of a familiar event and the updating of working memory for a partially encoded event. In the present study, this same pattern was observed; specifically, the picture of the object that infants had been familiarized to haptically invoked a baseline response, whereas the picture of the novel object invoked a positive slow wave response. Although it is difficult to ascertain with certainty the neural substrate responsible for generating the observed ERPs, we interpreted the data as suggesting the involvement of the limbic structures responsible for recognition memory and for cross-modal associations. In addition, although we did not report data on younger infants, pilot studies conducted since then have failed to observe this response in 6-month-old infants (Nelson, unpublished), nor in 8-month-old infants who were born prematurely (Richards et al. 1994).

Collectively, the human infant ERP data, coupled with the monkey data, suggest that cross-modal recognition memory depends on limbic structures in addition to the hippocampus, and requires more than simple novelty preferences. Thus, it seems reasonable to conclude that simple novelty preferences (presumably mediated by the hippocampus) may not reflect the end state of mature explicit memory.

Memory for event sequences/deferred imitation   Another task that might be thought of as reflecting a form of explicit memory is memory for event sequences. Here infants are shown a sequence of events (generally two to five steps long) involving real objects (e.g. a rattle, cup, etc.), and are "asked" to reproduce this event sequence either immediately or after some delay (e.g. a doll is undressed, put in a bathtub, washed, then dried, then re-clothed; note that completely arbitrary sequences are also used in addition to causal sequences). Work by Bauer (e.g. Bauer 1992; see also Ch. 4 in this volume), Mandler (e.g. Mandler 1990; Mandler & McDonough 1995), and Meltzoff (e.g. Meltzoff 1990, 1995) have demonstrated that by approximately 9 to 12 months infants are able to observe an event or sequence of events acted out by the investigator, and at some later date reproduce this sequence. The delay tolerated between initial observation of the sequence and subsequent reproduction of the sequence varies as a function of age. For example, Bauer et al. (1994) have demonstrated that 16–18-month-old infants are able to remember this sequence for as long as 8 months; 12-month-olds can also remember the sample sequence but the effects are less robust.

Although the neural bases for performance in this task could not be addressed in this work, more recent work with human adults has been. McDonough et al. (1995) tested neurologically normal controls and adults suffering from amnesia (with confirmed or suspected damage to the medial temporal lobe) using a paradigm virtually identical to that used with infants. Specifically, subjects were shown a series of eight different action sequences on one day, and on the next day tested under two conditions: either instructed to imitate the previously seen sequences or simply observed to see if they did so spontaneously. The authors reported that only the control subjects were able to reproduce the sequences, and did so under both instructed and uninstructed conditions. In contrast, the subjects with amnesia failed to reproduce the sequences in either condition. As was the case for the McKee and Squire (1993) study described earlier (in which adults with amnesia failed to prefer a novel stimulus after a 2 minute or more delay), the results of the present study suggests that the hippocampus and surrounding structures supports memory for event sequences (or deferred imitation).

Collectively, the data from the cross-modal recognition and event memory tasks point to a different time frame of development relative to tasks that require simple novelty preferences. Although all the tasks reviewed in this section require the hippocampus, it appears that the type of memory evaluated in the cross-modal and sequencing tasks differ slightly from that evaluated by the visual paired comparison and habituation procedures. This could be due to a number of factors, including the necessity for structures other than the hippocampus to be involved (e.g. the amygdala, for cross-modal or stimulus–stimulus associations), and for abilities other than simple novelty preferences to be involved.

In order to reconcile the apparent differences in age of onset between these tasks and those cited earlier, I would suggest that the form of "explicit" memory that is dependent on the hippocampus early in life differs qualitatively from that observed later in the first year. Indeed, it has recently been proposed (Nelson 1994; Nelson & Collins 1991; Webster et al. 1991a) that novelty preferences early in life may be reflexive or obligatory in nature, and thus this form of memory differs qualitatively from that observed in tasks like the DNMS task. Recent evidence from my laboratory (Nelson & Collins 1991, 1992) using cortical event-related potentials (ERPs) supports this assumption. We used ERPs to disentangle how often a stimulus was presented from whether that stimulus was novel or familiar. Infants were presented with *two* faces equally often, for ten trials each. The aim here was to familiarize infants to two events, not one. Infants were then presented with three classes of events. On 60 per cent of the trials one of the faces seen during familiarization was presented (*Frequent-Familiar* event). On a random 20 per cent of the trials the *other* familiarization face was presented (*Infrequent-Familiar* event). Finally, on *each* of the remaining 20 per cent of the trials (12 in all), a different face was presented (*Infrequent-Novel* events). If infants had fully encoded both events during familiarization, then we might expect them to respond equivalently to these same two faces presented during test, and distinguish these faces from the novel faces. What in fact was found, however, was that at 4 months infants failed to distinguish among the three classes of events. At 6 months they appeared to respond both to how often the stimuli were presented (i.e., they distinguished between familiar stimuli presented frequently vs. infrequently) and whether the stimuli had been seen before (they distinguished between the familiar stimuli and the novel stimuli). At 8 months infants' ERPs distinguished only between the novel and familiar events; event frequency was no longer a factor in their ERP response. The change in performance noted across these three age groups suggested that the so-called "novelty reaction" in infants younger than 6 months may in fact be an obligatory response to infrequently presented events. It is only by approximately 8 months that infants ignore event frequency and attend instead to whether a stimulus is novel or familiar.[6]

If this interpretation is correct, this would suggest that novelty preferences, at least until 6–8 months of life, may be "reflex-like" in nature (a similar argument has also been proposed by others; cf. Bachevalier et al. 1991). It would follow, then, that memory inferred from novelty preferences, despite being dependent on limbic structures, might differ qualitatively from memory as evaluated in, for example, the DNMS task, which is also supported (in part) by the limbic system.

One way to account for this difference would be to examine other developments that might occur in the brain that underlie performance in these tasks. For example, as mentioned earlier, the granule cell layer (dentate) may develop later than most other regions of the hippocampal formation. Axons in the entorhinal cortex perforate the subiculum to reach the dentate, and efferents from the dentate feed back to other hippocampal structures. As a result, the development of this structure would seem to play an important role in the general neural circuitry of the hippocampal formation. Second, it has recently been reported that in the monkey, adult levels of glucose utilization are not obtained in area TE until approximately 4 months of age, the age at which infants first begin to succeed on the DNMS task (Bachevalier et al. 1991). In contrast, and as reviewed earlier, the hippocampus appears to be functionally developed within the first month or so of life. This suggests that whatever role TE plays in novelty preferences does not emerge until 4 months in the monkey, and nearly a year in the human. Third, it has been reported (Webster et al. 1991b; Webster et al. 1995) that in unlesioned monkeys, a transient projection is observed from area TEO (see Figure 3.8) to the lateral basal nucleus of the amygdala; this projection is retracted later in development and is not present in the adult. However, when area TE is removed during the neonatal period, this normally transient projection *is* seen in the adult. In addition, projections from area TEO to the dorsal part of the lateral nucleus of the amygdala, which are normally transient and disappear in the adult, tend to expand into the zone normally occupied by terminals from area TE when TE is lesioned in infancy. It has been speculated that the sparing in DNMS performance that has been noted with early TE lesions may be due to the retention of these early transient projections (see Webster et al. 1995). Similarly, the presence of these transient projections early in life in the intact animal, followed by their regression, may account for some forms of limbic-dependent memory to precede other forms; for example, VPC vs. DNMS.

What I am proposing, then, is that there may be two forms of explicit memory in the infant. One is an early form that depends predominantly on the limbic system (hippocampus in particular), and that results in preferences for novelty that are reflexive in nature. This form accounts for performance on any task that involves a novelty preference but where task demands (e.g. familiarization and test stimuli presented in a single modality) or delays are minimal (e.g. seconds vs. minutes, hours, or weeks). Between 6 and 12 postnatal months this early form is supplanted and/or modified by a second form, which depends on cortical structures (e.g. area TE) as well as further elaboration of limbic structures (e.g. dentate). This latter form is likely to be responsible for the emergence of function in cross-modal recognition memory tasks, sequencing and/or deferred imitation tasks, and the DNMS task.

Summary

At the outset of this chapter I suggested that there are at least two major types of memory, and that each type (explicit, implicit) depends on different neural circuits.[7] I then described the various tasks that have been used to study memory in the infant. Based on the demands each of these tasks makes on memory, I then related each "type" of memory to what is known about the (assumed) neural circuitry associated with each task. Two broad categories of tasks that reflect forms of implicit memory were described. The visual expectancy paradigm was characterized as reflecting procedural memory. This adult classification was based on similarity to tasks used with adults, in whom striatal structures are thought to mediate task performance, and in whom the temporal lobe (cf. Knopman & Nissen 1987) and cerebellum are thought *not* to be involved (e.g. cerebellar lesions seem not to affect procedural learning in the adult human; see Daum et al. 1993b). In contrast, memory tasks that require conditioning (be it leg kick or eye-blink) seem to depend on the cerebellum and deep nuclei of the brainstem for acquisition, and possibly the hippocampus for retrieval and/or maintenance (particularly in the case of leg kick conditioning, where visual recognition memory is required).

In terms of tasks that reflect forms of explicit memory, it was concluded that tasks that rely solely on novelty preferences (e.g. simple visual paired comparison), when no or only very brief delays are required (e.g. <2 sec) depend disproportionately on the hippocampus. Because of this dependence, it was proposed that novelty preferences reflect an early-developing form of explicit memory – perhaps the term *pre-explicit* memory would be appropriate. However, explicit memory in the adult is known to depend more broadly on the hippocampus and rhinal cortex, and importantly, the inferior temporal cortex (e.g. TE). Infant tasks that also draw on these structures were thought to include tasks that (a) depend on recognition memory more generally (e.g. crossmodal), (b) require the infant to "recall" (although this could be too strong a word) a sequence of events seen previously, or (c) demand the coordination of recognition memory and action schemes (e.g. reaching for a novel object). Because these latter tasks more closely resemble what is required in adult tasks of explicit memory, and because the demands of these tasks draw more broadly on both medial and inferior temporal cortical regions, it was proposed that a more adult-like form of explicit memory supplants pre-explicit memory towards the end of the first year of life. The developmental trajectory of explicit memory probably continues through the next several years of life, as further developments in medial and inferior temporal lobe transpire.[8]

Given the nature of the task demands and the relative maturity of the associated neural circuitry underlying both conditioning studies and procedural memory tasks just outlined, it would seem reasonable to propose that less subsequent development would be evident here than in forms of explicit memory. In these former cases memory appears early in life, and at least in the case of conditioning, remains robust for at least the next several months. Unfortunately, since the dependent measures used in these tasks do not easily lend themselves to the study of older infants and children (although see Ch. 2 in this volume for discussion), it may be difficult to confirm this prediction (e.g. to the best of the author's knowledge, Rovee-Collier has not conducted leg kick conditioning studies in older infants).

One difficulty in laying out the framework of brain–memory relations proposed in this chapter has been the paucity of studies in which there has been a direct investigation of the ontogeny of memory from a developmental or cognitive neuroscience perspective. To this end it might be useful to suggest a few avenues for future research.

Suggestions for improving our understanding of the neurobiological bases of memory development

One line of investigation that has already shown great promise has been to conduct parallel studies with human infants/children and age-matched non-human primates. Several examples of this work already exist, such as the DNMS studies conducted by Overmann (e.g. Overmann et al. 1993). In addition to continuing this behavioral work, it might also be profitable to conduct "comparative" electrophysiological studies as well. For example, in some of the ERP work conducted by the author, it has been assumed that the positive slow wave response of the ERP invoked by certain events reflects a form of memory updating; it has been further assumed in some cases that this response may originate in structures that mediate explicit or pre-explicit memory (e.g. hippocampus, amygdala; see Nelson 1995; Nelson et al. 1993). One way to confirm this latter claim might be to conduct studies with infant primates with and without lesions of the relevant structures.

A second recommendation would be to test memory function in human adults, both neurologically normal and impaired, using the procedures used to test infants. Work currently coming from Squire's lab, using the VPC and sequencing tasks (e.g. McDonough et al. 1995; McKee & Squire 1993) nicely reflects such an endeavor. The advantage of this approach is that one can also conduct standard adult tasks in conjunction with the infant tasks, and in so doing provide a measure of converging operations.

A related recommendation is to begin to develop tasks with human infants that are based on tasks already being used with human adults. Perhaps the best example might include priming studies. Several of the tasks used with the adult that are thought to reflect implicit memory do not require a verbal response, and the motor requirements might easily be modified for use with infants. In so doing headway might be made in evaluating the development of implicit memory over the first year or two of life.

My final suggestion is for developmental cognitive neuroscientists and psychologists to begin to consider developing some of the more powerful neuroimaging techniques for use with infants and young children. One such example would be the use of functional Magnetic Resonance Imaging (fMRI). Unlike conventional MRI, fMRI permits one to sample data quickly (e.g. every 20 msec), and to do so periodically. In so doing one can record data on an intermittent basis, mitigating the need for the subject to remain motionless. Equally important, however, is the ability to image the brain while the subject is engaged in some task. Although it may be some time before this procedure is modified and deemed safe for human infants, its use in young children is already on the horizon (Casey et al. 1995).

Conclusions

The theoretical perspective offered in this chapter has primarily comprised piecing together various perspectives on memory – notably those from developmental psychology, basic and cognitive neuroscience, and cognitive neuropsychology. It has been proposed that memory is likely to be dependent on the striatum (procedural memory), on the cerebellar/olivary complex and possibly the hippocampus (conditioning), and on portions of the limbic system (pre-explicit memory) develop within the first few months of life. Between 6 and 12 months pre-explicit memory may be supplanted by a more adult-like form of temporal lobe memory (explicit memory).

As students of memory well know, memory continues to improve through early adolescence, at which point adult-like performance is typically obtained. Although these developments likely use as a scaffold the neurological changes detailed in this chapter, accounting for these changes is a challenge to which developmental cognitive neuroscientists must also rise.

Notes

1. Recent work on a number of fronts has further parsed implicit memory into at least two types. As described in the text, one form of implicit memory is reflected in procedures, such as learning acquired through motor activity. A second form of implicit memory may be priming, which some think may itself take two forms: perceptual and conceptual (for discussion, see Tulving & Schacter 1990). For example, *perceptual priming* tests might involve presenting stimuli in a study phase that reappear briefly or in degraded form during a test phase. A subject's faster or more accurate identification of the test items relative to similar but unstudied items is taken as evidence of such priming. In contrast, an example of *conceptual priming* might be when subjects exhibit an increased likelihood of generating a target word after previous exposure to a semantically related word (e.g. the word *donkey* primes for later recognition of *animal*). As a rule, both implicit memory (broadly defined) and priming (if we think of priming as reflecting a form of implicit memory) are typically preserved in amnesia.
2. I am not arguing that all forms of classical conditioning involve this circuitry; rather, I am simply suggesting that this is the circuitry that underlies the conditioned eye-blink response.
3. I had earlier pointed out that the hippocampus may be required for *retaining* the conditioned eye-blink response. Although H. M. has no hippocampus, and appears to retain this response after a period of weeks, his may not be the best case to evaluate this proposal. Specifically, in animals the resection of the hippocampus typically immediately precedes or follows training and testing. In H. M.'s case, his hippocampus was removed 38 years earlier. Thus, one cannot rule out some recovery of function over this period of time
4. It must be acknowledged that requiring the infant to look instead of reach may change the fundamental nature of this task so that it may be inappropriate to

consider this a looking time "equivalent" of the standard DNMS task, but rather a substantial modification. Indeed, the looking time version of the DNMS task reported by Diamond (1995) bears great similarity to the traditional visual paired comparison task (discussed on pp. 62–3). For this reason, the Overman et al. (1993) method of recording looking while simultaneously recording reaching has a certain theoretical appeal.

5. It should be stressed that evidence of *discrimination* has been inferred from longer looking at the *familiar* stimulus as well. For example, Meltzoff and Moore (1977) familiarized newborn infants to a pacifier of a certain shape, and then presented them with a picture of the pacifier they had experienced by sucking on it, and a picture of a novel pacifier. Infants looked longer at the picture of the familiar pacifier, which was taken as evidence of discrimination. Similarly, Pascalis et al. (1995) have shown that under some conditions newborn infants will prefer to look at the mother's face vs. a stranger's face. It strikes the author as problematic to accept preferences for either the familiar *or* novel stimulus as equivalent. Perhaps a more parsimonious explanation is that preferences for familiar stimuli might best be considered as evidence of recognition, whereas preferences for novel stimuli be considered as evidence of both discrimination and recognition.

6. It should be noted that attention is easily drawn to an infrequently presented stimulus well beyond the infancy period, even when it is not novel or relevant to attend to (for task purposes). For example, we (Nelson & Nugent 1990) have found that although 4- to 6-year-old children will evince a P300 response to a 20 per cent target event, they will also show the same response to a 20 per cent *non-target* event. This suggests that the compelling nature of responding to infrequently presented stimuli, even when instructed to ignore them, is maintained well beyond the infancy period.

7. Not fitting neatly into the broad categories of explicit and implicit memory is *working memory*. Working memory is typically thought of as the ability to hold information in mind until some action can be initiated (e.g. reach for an object previously hidden for a few seconds). Because tests of working memory typically involve tasks that require the subject/animal to coordinate a number of abilities and skills (e.g. inhibition, coordination of action schemes, sensitivity to reward), it has been difficult to isolate the neurobiological bases of the memory features of a given task (e.g. the A not B task). For these reasons, coupled with space limitations, I have elected not to discuss the development of the neurobiology of working memory. For recent discussions of this literature in the context of development, see Diamond 1990; Gilmore & Johnson 1995; Nelson 1995).

8. As other chapters in this volume make clear, improvements in memory exist well beyond the infancy period. Unfortunately, and as stated at the outset of this chapter, little is known about brain development in the primate (human and non-human) beyond the first few years of life. Thus, it would be premature to speculate about the brain bases of memory development in the childhood years. However, it does seem reasonable to suggest that if the use of strategies contributes to improvements in memory, then the involvement of the prefrontal cortex would not be surprising.

References

Aslin, R. 1989. Visual and auditory development in infancy. In *Handbook of Infant Development*, J. D. Osofsky (ed.), 2nd edn., 5–97. New York: Wiley.

Bachevalier, J. 1990. Ontogenetic development of habit and memory formation in primates. In *Development and neural bases of higher cognitive functions*, A. Diamond (ed.), 457–84. New York: New York Academy of Sciences Press.

Bachevalier, J. 1992. Cortical versus limbic immaturity: Relationship to infantile amnesia. In *Minnesota Symposia on Child Psychology: Developmental neuroscience*, *Vol. XXIV*, M. R. Gunnar & C. A. Nelson (eds.), 129–53. New York: Erlbaum.

Bachevalier, J., M. Brickson, & C. Hagger 1993. Limbic-dependent recognition memory in monkeys develops early in infancy. *NeuroReport* **4**, 77–80.

Bachevalier, J., C. Hagger, & M. Mishkin 1991. Functional maturation of the occipitotemporal pathway in infant rhesus monkeys. In *Brain work and mental activity*, N. A. Lassen, D. H. Ingvar, M. E. Raichle, & L. Friberg (eds.), 231–40. Copenhagen: Munksgaard.

Bachevalier, J. & M. Mishkin 1984. An early and a late developing system for learning and retention in infant monkeys. *Behavioral Neuroscience* **98**, 770–8.

Bachevalier, J. & M. Mishkin 1992. *Dissociation of the effects of neonatal inferior temporal cortical versus limbic lesions on visual recognition in 10-month-old rhesus monkeys.* Unpublished paper.

Bachevalier, J., O. Pascalis, & W. Overman 1995. *The development and neural basis of visual recognition memory in primates.* Unpublished paper.

Baddeley, A. D. 1986. *Working memory.* Oxford: Oxford University Press.

Baddeley, A. D. 1992. Working memory. *Science* **255**, 556–9.

Baillargeon, R. 1993. The object concept revisited: New directions in the investigation of infants' physical knowledge. In *Visual perception and cognition in infancy*, *Carnegie-Mellon Symposia on Cognition, Vol. XXIII*. C. E. Granrud (ed.), 265–315. Hillsdale, NJ: Erlbaum.

Baillargeon, R., J. DeVos, & M. Graber 1989. Location memory in 8-month-old infants in a non-search AB task: Further evidence. *Cognitive Development* **4**, 345–67.

Baillargeon, R. & M. Graber 1988. Evidence of location memory in 8-month-old infants in a nonsearch AB task. *Developmental Psychology* **24**, 502–11.

Barkovich, A. J., B. O. Kjos, D. E. Jackson, & D. Norman 1988. Normal maturation of the neonatal and infant brain: MR imaging at 1.5 T. *Neuroradiology* **166**, 173–80.

Bauer, P. J. 1992. Holding it all together: How enabling relations facilitate young children's event recall. *Cognitive Development* **7**, 1–28.

Bauer, P. J., L. A. Hertsgaard, & G. A. Dow 1994. After 8 months have passed: Long-term recall of events by 1- and 2-year-old children. *Memory* **2**, 353–83.

Bechara, A., D. Tranel, H. Damasio, R. Adolphs, C. Rockland, & A. R. Damasio 1995. Double dissociation of conditioning and declarative knowledge relative to the amygdala and hippocampus in humans. *Science* **269**, 1115–18.

Bell, M. A. & N. A. Fox 1992. The relations between frontal brain electrical activity and cognitive development during infancy. *Child Development* **63**, 1142–63.

Berger, B. & C. Alvarez 1994. Neurochemical development of the hippocampal region in the fetal rhesus monkey. II. Immunocytochemistry of peptides, calcium-binding proteins, DARPP–32, and monoamine innervation in the entorhinal cortex by the end of gestation. *Hippocampus* **4**, 85–114.

Berger, B., C. Alvarez, & P. S. Goldman-Rakic 1993. Neurochemical development of the hippocampal region in the fetal rhesus monkey. I. Early appearance of peptides, calcium-binding proteins, DARPP–32, and monoamine innervation in the entorhinal cortex during the first half of gestation (E47 to E90). *Hippocampus* **3**, 279–305.

Biederman, I. & E. E. Cooper 1992. Size invariance in visual object priming. *Journal of Experimental Psychology: Human Perception and Performance*, **18**, 121–33.

Bornstein, M. H. 1985. Habituation as a measure of visual information processing in human infants: Summary, systematization, and synthesis. In *The measurement of audition and vision in the first year of postnatal life: A methodological overview*, G. Gottlieb & N. A. Krasnegor (eds.), 253–300. Norwood, NJ: Ablex.

Bourgeois, J.-P. & P. Rakic 1993. Changes in synaptic density in the primary visual cortex of the Macaque monkey from fetal to adult stage. *Journal of Neuroscience* **13**, 2801-20.

Butler, J. 1986. *A contextual hierarchy in infant memory.* Unpublished master's thesis. Rutgers University, New Brunswick, NJ.

Butler, J. & C. Rovee-Collier 1989. Contextual gating of memory retrieval. *Developmental Psychobiology* **22**, 533–52.

Casey, B. J., J. D. Cohen, P. Jezzard, R. Turner, D. C. Noll, R. J. Trainor, J. Giedd, D. Kaysen, L. Hertz-Pannier, & J. L. Rapport 1995. Activation of prefrontal cortex in children during a non-spatial working memory task with functional MRI. *Neuroimaging* **2**, 221–9.

Chugani, H. T. 1994. Development of regional brain glucose metabolism in relation to behavior and plasticity. In *Human behavior and the developing brain*, G. Dawson & K. Fischer (eds.), 153–75. New York: Guilford.

Chugani, H. T. & M. E. Phelps 1986. Maturational changes in cerebral function in infants determined by [18]FDG positron emission tomography. *Science* **231**, 840–3.

Chugani, H. T., M. E. Phelps, & J. C. Mazziotta 1987. Positron emission tomography study of human brain functional development. *Annals of Neurology* **22**, 487–97.

Colombo, M. & C. G. Gross 1994. Responses of inferior temporal cortex and hippocampal neurons during delayed matching-to-sample in monkeys (*Macaca fascicularis*). *Behavioral Neuroscience* **108**, 443–55.

Daum, I., H. Ackermann, M. M. Schugens, C. Reimold, J. Dichgans & N. Birbaumer 1993a. The cerebellum and cognitive functions in humans. *Behavioral Neuroscience* **107**, 411–19.

Daum, I., M. M. Schugens, H. Ackermann, W. Lutzenberger, J. Dichgans, & N. Birbaumer 1993b. Classical conditioning after cerebellar lesions in humans. *Behavioral Neuroscience* **107**, 748–56.

DeCasper, A. J. & W. P. Fifer 1980. Of human bonding: Newborns prefer their mother's voices. *Science* **208**, 1174–76.

DeCasper, A. J. & M. J. Spence 1986. Prenatal maternal speech influences newborns' perception of speech sounds. *Infant Behavior and Development* **9**, 133–50.

DeCasper, A. J. & M. J. Spence 1991. Auditory mediated behavior during the perinatal period: A cognitive view. In *Newborn attention: Biological constraints and the influence of experience*, M. J. S. Weiss & P. R. Zelazo (eds.), 142–76. Norwood, NJ: Ablex.

de Schonen, S., C. Deruelle, J .Mancini, & O. Pascalis 1993. Hemispheric differences in face processing and brain maturation. In *Developmental neurocognition: Speech and face processing in the first year of life*, B. de Boysson-Bardie, S. de Schonen, P. Juscyzk, P. McNeilage, & J. Morton (eds.), 149–63. Dordrecht: Kluwer.

Diamond, A. 1985. Development of the ability to use recall to guide action, as indicated by infants' performance on AB. *Child Development* **56**, 868–83.

Diamond, A. 1990. The development and neural bases of memory functions as indexed by the AB and delayed response tasks in human infants and infant monkeys. In *Development and neural bases of higher cognitive functions*, A. Diamond (ed.), 267–317. New York: New York Academy of Sciences Press.

Diamond, A. 1992. Recognition memory assessed by looking vs. reaching: Infants' performance on the visual paired comparison and delayed non-matching to sample tasks. *Institute for Research in Cognitive Science Report* 92–11.

Diamond, A. 1995. Evidence of robust recognition memory early in life even when assessed by reaching behavior. *Journal of Experimental Child Psychology* **59**, 419–74.

Diamond, A. & B. Doar 1989. The performance of human infants on a measure of frontal cortex function, the delayed response task. *Developmental Psychobiology* **22**, 271–94.

Diamond, A. & P. S. Goldman-Rakic 1989. Comparison of human infants and rhesus monkeys on Piaget's AB task: Evidence for dependence on dorsolateral prefrontal cortex. *Experimental Brain Research* **74**, 24–40.

Diamond, A., S. Zola-Morgan, & L. R. Squire 1989. Successful performance by monkeys with lesions of the hippocampal formation on AB and object retrieval, two tasks that mark developmental changes in human infants. *Behavioral Neuroscience* **103**, 526–37.

Dunn, R. 1845. Case of suspension of the mental faculties. *Lancet* **2**, 588–90.

Ebbinghaus, H. 1885a. *Uber das Gedachtnis* [Memory]. Leipzig: Duncker & Humblot.

Ebbinghaus, H. 1885b. *Memory: A contribution to experimental psychology*. New York: Dover.

Eckenhoff, M. F. & P. Rakic 1991. A quantitative analysis of synaptogenesis in the molecular layer of the dentate gyrus in the rhesus monkey. *Developmental Brain Research* **64**, 129–35.

Ellis, A. E., A. Matthews, & C. A. Nelson 1994. Pre-term and full-term infants' performance on the AB task: Implications for brain development. Unpublished paper.

Fagan, J. F. III 1970. Memory in the infant. *Journal of Experimental Child Psychology* **9**, 217–26.

Fagan, J. F. III 1973. Infants' delayed recognition memory and forgetting. *Journal of Experimental Child Psychology* **16**, 424–50.

Fagan, J. F. III 1990. The paired-comparison paradigm and infant intelligence. In *Development and neural bases of higher cognitive functions*, A. Diamond (ed.), 337–64. New York: New York Academy of Sciences Press.

Fagen, J. W., C. K. Rovee-Collier, & M .G. Kaplan 1976. Psychophysical scaling of stimulus similarity in 3-month-old infants and adults. *Journal of Experimental Child Psychology* **22**, 272–81.

Fantz, R. L. 1956. A method for studying early visual development. *Perceptual and Motor Skills* **6**, 13–15.

Gilmore, R. O. & M. H. Johnson 1995. Working memory in infancy: Six-month-olds' performance on two versions of the oculomotor delayed response task. *Journal of*

Experimental Child Psychology **59**, 397–418.

Goldman, P. S. 1971. Functional development of the prefrontal cortex in early life and the problem of neuronal plasticity. *Experimental Neurology* **32**, 366–87.

Goldman, P. S. & H. E. Rosvold 1972. The effects of selective caudate lesions in infant and juvenile rhesus monkeys. *Brain Research* **43**, 53–66.

Goldman-Rakic, P. S. 1985. Toward a neurobiology of cognitive development. In *Neonate Cognition*, J. Mahler (ed.), 285–306. Hillsdale, NJ: Erlbaum.

Goldman-Rakic, P. S. 1987. Circuitry of the prefrontal cortex and the regulation of behavior by representational knowledge. In *Handbook of Physiology: Section I: The nervous system. Vol. V. Higher functions of the brain*, F. Plum & V. Mountcastle (eds.), 373–417. Bethesda, MD: American Physiological Society.

Graf, P. & D. L. Schacter 1985. Implicit and explicit memory for new associations in normal and amnesic subjects. *Journal of Experimental Psychology: Learning, Memory, and Cognition* **11**, 501–18.

Gunderson, V. M. & K. B. Swartz 1985. Visual recognition in infant pigtailed macaques after a 24-hour delay. *American Journal of Primatology* **8**, 259–64.

Haith, M. M., C. Hazan, & G. S. Goodman 1988. Expectation and anticipation of dynamic visual events by 3.5-month-old infants. *Child Development* **59**, 467 (1989).

Haith, M. M., N. Wentworth, & R. Canfield 1993. The formation of expectations in early infancy. In *Advances in infancy research*, C. K. Rovee-Collier & L. P. Lipsitt (eds.), Norwood, NJ: Ablex.

Heimer, L. 1995. *The human brain and spinal cord*, 2nd edn. New York: Springer-Verlag.

Hilts, P. J. 1995. *The strange tale of Mr. M. and the nature of memory*. New York: Simon & Schuster.

Humphrey, T. 1966. The development of the human hippocampal formation correlated with some aspects of its phylogenetic history. In *Evolution of the forebrain*, S. Hassler (ed.), 104–16. Stuttgart: Thieme.

Huttenlocher, P. R. 1979. Synaptic density in human frontal cortex: Developmental changes and effects of aging. *Brain Research* **163**, 195–205.

Huttenlocher, P. R. 1990. Morphometric study of human cerebral cortex development. *Neuropsychologia* **28**, 517–27.

Huttenlocher, P. R. 1994. Synaptogenesis, synapse elimination, and neural plasticity in human cerebral cortex. In *Threats to optimal development: Integrating biological, psychological, and social risk factors, Minnesota Symposium on Child Psychology, Vol. XXVII*, C. A. Nelson (ed.), 35–54. Hillsdale, NJ: Erlbaum.

Jacobson, C. F. 1936. Studies of cerebral function in primates. *Comparative Psychology Monographs* **13**, 1–68.

Janas, M. S. 1994. *The developing human foetal brain: A qualitative and quantitative study of the hippocampal formation in the normal, the abnormal, and the potentially abnormal human foetus*. Unpublished doctoral dissertation, Faculty of Health Sciences, University of Copenhagen.

Janowsky, J. 1993. The development of memory systems. In *Brain development and cognition: A reader*, M. H. Johnson (ed.). Cambridge, MA: Blackwell.

Jernigan, T. L., D. A. Trauner, J. R. Hesselink, & P. A. Tallal 1991. Maturation of human cerebrum observed in vivo during adolescence. *Brain* **114**, 2037–49.

Kail, R. 1990. *The development of memory in children*, 3rd edn. New York: Freeman.

Kandel, E. R., J. H. Schwartz, & T. M. Jessell 1991. *Principles of neural science*, 3rd edn.

New York: Elsevier.

Knopman, D. S. 1991. Long-term retention of implicitly acquired learning in patients with Alzheimer's disease. *Journal of Clinical and Experimental Neuropsychology* **13**, 880–94.

Knopman, D. S. & M. J. Nissen 1987. Implicit learning in patients with probable Alzheimer's disease. *Neurology* **37**, 784–8.

Korsakoff, S. S. 1889. Etude medico-psycholoque sur une forme des maladies de la mémoire [Medical-psychological study of a form of diseases of memory]. *Revue Philosophique* **28**, 501–30.

Kostovic, I., Z. Pentanjek, & M. Judas 1990. The earliest areal differentiation of the human cerebral cortex: Entorhinal area. *Society for Neuroscience Abstract* **16**, 846.

Kretschmann, J.-J., G. Kammradt, I. Krauthausen, B. Sauer, & F. Wingert 1986. Growth of the hippocampal formation in man. *Bibthca anatomy* **28**, 27–52.

Lipsitt, L. P. 1990. Learning processes in the human newborn: Sensitization, habituation, and classical conditioning. In *Development and neural bases of higher cognitive functions*, A. Diamond (ed.), 113–27. New York: New York Academy of Sciences Press.

Ludemann, P. & C. A. Nelson 1988. The categorical representation of facial expressions by 7-month-old infants. *Developmental Psychology* **24**, 492–501.

Mandler, J. M. 1990. Recall of events by preverbal children. In *Development and neural bases of higher cognitive functions*, A. Diamond (ed.), 485–516. New York: New York Academy of Sciences Press.

Mandler, J. M. & L. McDonough 1995. Long-term recall of event sequences in infancy. *Journal of Experimental Child Psychology* **59**, 457–74.

Marquis, D. 1931. Can conditioned responses be established in the newborn infant? *Journal of Genetic Psychology* **39**, 479–90.

McDonough, L., J. M. Mandler, R. D. McKee, & L. R. Squire 1995. The deferred imitation task as a nonverbal measure of declarative memory. *Proceedings of the National Academy of Sciences* **8**, 7580–4.

McKee, R. D. & L. R. Squire 1993. On the development of declarative memory. *Journal of Experimental Psychology: Learning, Memory, and Cognition* **19**, 397–404.

Meltzoff, A. 1990. Towards a developmental cognitive science: The implications of cross-modal matching and imitation for the development of representation and memory in infancy. In *Development and neural bases of higher cognitive functions*, A. Diamond (ed.), 1–37. New York: New York Academy of Sciences Press.

Meltzoff, A. N. 1995. What infant memory tells us about amnesia: Long-term recall and deferred imitation. *Journal of Experimental Child Psychology* **59**, 497–515.

Meltzoff, A. N. & M. K. Moore 1977. Imitation of facial and manual gestures by human neonates. *Science* **198**, 75–8.

Miller, E. K. & R. Desimone 1994. Parallel neuronal mechanisms for short-term memory. *Science* **263**, 520–2.

Milner, B., S. Corkin & H.-L. Teuber 1968. Further analysis of the hippocampal amnesic syndrome: A 14 year follow-up study of H. M. *Neuropsychologia* **6**, 215–34.

Mishkin, M. & T. Appenzeller 1987. The anatomy of memory. *Scientific American* **256**, 2–11.

Mishkin, M. & J. Delacour 1975. An analysis of short-term visual memory in the monkey. *Journal of Experimental Psychology: Animal Behavior Processes* **1**, 326–34.

Mishkin, M., B. Malamut, & J. Bachevalier 1984. Memories and habits: Two neural systems. In *Neurobiology of learning and memory*, G. Lynch, J. L. McGaugh, & N. M. Weinberger (eds.), 65–77. New York: Guilford.

Moscovitch, M. 1992. Memory and working-with-memory: A component process model based on modules and central systems. *Journal of Cognitive Neuroscience* 4, 257–67.

Mumby, D. G. & J. P. J. Pinel 1994. Rhinal cortex lesions and object recognition in rats. *Behavioral Neuroscience* 108, 11–18.

Murray, E. A. & D. Gaffan 1994. Removal of the amygdala plus subjacent cortex disrupts the retention of both intramodal and cross-modal associative memories in monkeys. *Behavioral Neuroscience* 108, 494–500.

Murray, E. A. & M. Mishkin 1985. Amygdalectomy impairs cross-modal association in monkeys. *Science* 228, 604–6.

Nauta, W. J. H. & M. Feritag 1986. *Fundamental neuroanatomy*. New York: Freeman.

Nelson, C. A. 1994. Neural correlates of recognition memory in the first postnatal year of life. In *Human development and the developing brain*, G. Dawson & K. Fischer (eds.), 269–313. New York: Guilford.

Nelson, C. A. 1995. The ontogeny of human memory: A cognitive neuroscience perspective. *Developmental Psychology* 31, 723–35.

Nelson, C. A. & P. F. Collins 1991. Event-related potential and looking time analysis of infants' responses to familiar and novel events: Implications for visual recognition memory. *Developmental Psychology* 27, 50–8.

Nelson, C. A. & P. F. Collins 1992. Neural and behavioral correlates of recognition memory in 4- and 8-month-old infants. *Brain and Cognition* 19, 105–21.

Nelson, C. A., M. Henschel, & P. F. Collins 1993. Neural correlates of cross-modal recognition memory in 8-month-old infants. *Developmental Psychology* 29, 411–20.

Nelson, C. A. & K. Nugent 1990. Recognition memory and resource allocation as revealed by children's event-related potential responses to happy and angry faces. *Developmental Psychology* 26, 171–9.

O'Neil, J. B., D. P. Friedman, J. Bachevalier, & L. G. Ungerleider 1986. Distribution of muscarinic receptors in the brain of a newborn rhesus monkey. *Society for Neuroscience Abstracts* 12, 809.

Overman, W. H., J. Bachevalier, F. Sewell, & J. Drew 1993. A comparison of children's performance on two recognition memory tasks: Delayed nonmatch-to-sample vs. visual paired-comparison. *Developmental Psychobiology* 26, 345–57.

Overman, W., J. Bachevalier, M. Turner, & A. Peuster 1992. Object recognition versus object discrimination: Comparison between human infants and infant monkeys. *Behavioral Neuroscience* 106, 15–29.

Owen, A. M., B. J. Sahakian, J. Semple, C. E. Polkey, & T. W. Robbins 1995. Visuospatial short-term recognition memory and learning after temporal lobe excisions, frontal lobe excisions, or amygdalo-hippocampectomy in man. *Neuropsychologia* 33, 1–24.

Paldino, A. M. & D. P. Purpura 1979. Branching patterns of hippocampal neurons of human fetus during dendritic differentiation. *Experimental Neurology* 64, 620–31.

Paller, K A. 1990. Recall and stem-completion priming have different electrophysiological correlates and are modified differentially by directed forgetting. *Journal of Experimental Psychology: Learning, Memory, and Cognition* 16,

1021–32.

Paller, K. A. & M. Kutas 1992. Brain potentials during memory retrieval provide neurophysiological support for the distinction between conscious recollection and priming. *Journal of Cognitive Neuroscience* **4**, 375–91.

Pascalis, O. & S. de Schonen 1994. Recognition memory in 3–4 day old human neonates. *NeuroReport* **5**, 1721–4.

Pascalis, O., S. de Schonen, J. Morton, C. Deruelle, & M. Fabre-Grenet 1995. Mothers' face recognition by neonates: A replication and an extension. *Infant Behavior and Development* **18**, 79–85.

Pearson, R. C. A., M. M. Esiri, R. W. Hiorns, G. K. Wilcock, & T. P. S. Powell 1985. Anatomical correlates of the distribution of the pathological changes in the neocortex of Alzheimer's disease. *Proceedings of the National Academy of Sciences USA* **82**, 4531–4.

Pellizzer, G., P. Sargent, & A. P. Georgopoulos 1995. Motor cortical activity in a context-recall task. *Science* **269**, 702–5.

Petersen, S. E., P. T. Fox, M. I. Posner, M. Mintun, & M. E. Raichle 1990. Positron emission tomographic studies of the processing of single words. *Journal of Cognitive Neuroscience* **1**, 153–70.

Petri, H. L. & M. Mishkin 1994. Behaviorism, cognition, and the neuropsychology of memory. *American Scientist* **82**, 30–7.

Piaget, J. 1952. *The origins of intelligence in children*. New York: International Universities Press.

Proctor, A. W., S. L. Lowe, A. M. Palmer, P. Franceis, M. M. Esiri, G. C. Stratmann, A. Najlerahim, A. J. Patel, A. Hunt, & D. M. Bowen 1988. Topographic distribution of neurochemical changes in Alzheimer's disease. *Journal of the Neurological Sciences* **84**, 125–40.

Richards, M. L. M., K. Thomas, M. K. Georgieff, & C. A. Nelson 1994. *Evoked potential responses of recognition memory in premature infants*. Paper presented at the Western Society for Pediatric Research, Carmel, CA.

Roediger, H. L. III 1984. Does current evidence from dissociation experiments favor the episodic/semantic distinction? *Behavioral and Brain Sciences* **7**, 252–4.

Roediger, H. L. III 1990. Implicit memory: Retention without remembering. *American Psychologist* **45**, 1043–56.

Roediger, H. L. III, S. Rajaram, & K. Srinivas 1990. Specifying criteria for postulating memory systems. In *The development and neural bases of higher cognitive functions*, A. Diamond (ed.). New York: New York Academy of Sciences.

Rose, S. A. & H. A. Ruff 1989. Cross-modal abilities in human infants. In *Handbook of infant development*, J. D. Osofsky (ed.), 318–362. New York: Wiley.

Rosenblith, J. F. 1992. *In the beginning*. 2nd edn. Newbury Park, CA: Sage.

Rovee-Collier, C. 1990. The "memory system" of prelinguistic infants. In *Development and neural bases of higher cognitive functions*, A. Diamond (ed.), 517–42. New York: New York Academy of Sciences Press.

Rovee-Collier, C. K. & J. W. Fagen 1981. The retrieval of memory in early infancy. In *Advances in infancy research, Vol. I*, L. P. Lipsitt & C. K. Rovee-Collier (eds.), 225–54. Norwood, NJ: Ablex Press.

Rovee-Collier, C. & H. Hayne 1987. Reactivation of infant memory: Implications for cognitive development. In *Advances in child development and behavior, Vol. XX*, H. W. Reese (ed.), 185–238. New York: Academic.

Saint-Cyr, J. A., A. E. Taylor, & A. E. Lang 1988. Procedural learning and neostriatal dysfunction in man. *Brain* **111**, 941–59.

Salmon, D. P. & N. Butters 1995. Neurobiology of skill and habit learning. *Current Opinion in Neurobiology* **5**, 184–90.

Schacter, D. L. 1987. Implicit memory: History and current status. *Journal of Experimental Psychology: Learning, Memory, and Cognition* **13**, 501–18.

Schacter, D. L. & E. Tulving 1994. What are the memory systems of 1994? In *Memory systems of 1994*, D. L. Schacter & E. Tulving (eds.), 1–38. Cambridge, MA: MIT Press.

Scoville, W. B. & B. Milner 1957. Loss of recent memory after bilateral hippocampal lesions. *Journal of Neurology, Neurosurgery, and Psychiatry* **20**, 11–21.

Seress, L. & C. E. Ribak 1995a. Postnatal development of CA3 pyramidal neurons and their afferents in the Ammon's horn of Rhesus monkeys. *Hippocampus* **5**, 217–31.

Seress, L. & C. E. Ribak 1995b. Postnatal development and synaptic connections of hilar mossy cells in the hippocampal dentate gyrus of rhesus monkeys. *Journal of Comparative Neurology* **355**, 93–110.

Sherry, F. & D. L. Schacter 1987. The evolution of multiple memory systems. *Psychological Review* **94**, 439–54.

Sidman, R. L. & P. Rakic 1982. Development of the human central nervous system. In *Histology and histopathology of the nervous system*, W. Haymaker & R. D. Adams (eds.), 3–145. Springfield IL: C. C. Thomas.

Slater, A. 1995. Visual perception and memory at birth. *Advances in Infancy Research* **9**, 107–62.

Squire, L. R. 1986. Mechanisms of memory. *Science* **232**, 1612–19.

Squire, L. R. 1987. *Memory and brain.* New York: Oxford Press.

Squire, L. R. 1992. Declarative and nondeclarative memory: Multiple brain systems supporting learning and memory. *Journal of Cognitive Neuroscience* **4**, 232–43.

Squire, L. R. 1994. Declarative and nondeclarative memory: Multiple brain systems supporting learning and memory. In *Memory systems 1994*, D. L. Schacter & E. Tulving (eds.), 203–31. Cambridge, MA: MIT Press.

Squire, L. R., J. G. Ojemann, F. M. Miezin, S. E. Petersen, T. O. Videen, & M. E. Raichle 1992. Activation of the hippocampus in normal humans: A functional anatomical study of memory. *Proceedings of the National Academy of Sciences, USA* **89**, 1837–41.

Squire, L. R. & S. Zola-Morgan 1991. The medial temporal lobe memory system. *Science* **253**, 1380–6.

Steinmetz, J. E., D. G. Lavond, D. Ikovich, C. G. Logan, & R. F. Thompson 1992. Disruption of classical eyelid conditioning after cerebellar lesions: Damage to a memory trace system or a simple performance deficit? *Journal of Neuroscience* **12**, 4403–26.

Steinmetz, J. E., S. F. Logue, & D. P. Miller 1993. Using signaled barpressing tasks to study the neural substrates of appetitive and aversive learning in rats: Behavioral manipulations and cerebellar lesions. *Behavioral Neuroscience* **107**, 941–54.

Swain, I. U., P. R. Zelazo, & R. K. Clifton 1993. Newborn infants' memory for speech sounds retained over 24 hours. *Developmental Psychology* **29**, 312–23.

Thompson, R. F. 1986. The neurobiology of learning and memory. *Science* **233**, 941–7.

Thompson, R. F. 1991. Neural mechanisms of classical conditioning in mammals. In *Behavioral and neural aspects of learning and memory*, J. R. Krebs & G. Horn (eds.), 63–72. Oxford: Clarendon.

Tulving, E. 1985. How many memory systems are there? *American Psychologist* **40**, 385–98.

Tulving, E. & D. L. Schacter 1990. Priming and human memory systems. *Science* **247**, 301–306.

Voneida, T. J., D. Christie, R. Bogdanski, & B. Chopko 1990. Changes in instrumentally and classically conditioned limb-flexion responses following inferior olivary lesions and olivocerebellar tractotomy in the cat. *Journal of Neuroscience* **10**, 3583–93.

Webster, M. J., J. Bachevalier, & L. G. Ungerleider 1995. Development and plasticity of visual memory circuits. In *Maturational windows and adult cortical plasticity*, B. Julesz & I. Kovacs (eds.). New York: Addison-Wesley.

Webster, M. J., L. G. Ungerleider, & J. Bachevalier 1991a. Lesions of inferior temporal area TE in infant monkeys alter cortico-amygdalar projections. *Developmental Neuroscience* **2**, 769–72.

Webster, M. J., L. G. Ungerleider, & J. Bachevalier 1991b. Connections of inferior temporal areas TE and TEO with medial temporal-lobe structures in infant and adult monkeys. *Journal of Neuroscience* **11**, 1095–116.

Wentworth, N. & M. M. Haith 1992. Event-specific expectations of 2- and 3-month-old infants. *Developmental Psychology* **28**, 842–50.

Wickens, D. D. & C. Wickens 1940. A study of conditioning in the neonate. *Journal of Experimental Psychology* **25**, 94–102.

Wilson, F. A. W., S. P. O. Scalaidhe, & P. S. Goldman-Rakic 1993. Dissociation of object and spatial processing domains in primate prefrontal cortex. *Science* **260**, 1955–8.

Winocur, G. 1992. The hippocampus and prefrontal cortex in learning and memory: An animal model approach. In *Neuropsychology of memory*, 2nd edn., L. R. Squire & N. Butters (eds.), 429–39. New York: Guilford.

Woodruff-Pak, D. S. 1993. Eyeblink classical conditioning in H. M.: Delay and trace paradigms. *Behavioral Neuroscience* **107**, 911–25.

Woodruff-Pak, D. S., C. G. Logan, & R. F. Thompson 1990. Neurobiological substrates of classical conditioning across the life span. In *Development and neural bases of higher cognitive functions*, A. Diamond (ed.), 150–78. New York: New York Academy of Sciences Press.

Woodruff-Pak, D. S. & R. F. Thompson 1988. Cerebellar correlates of classical conditioning across the life span. In *Life-span development and behavior, Vol. IX*, P. B. Baltes, R. M. Lerner, & D. M. Featherman (eds.), 1–37. Hillsdale, NJ Erlbaum.

Yakovlev, P. I. & A.-R. LeCours 1967. The myelogenetic cycles of regional maturation of the brain. In *Regional development of the brain in early life*, A. Minkowski (ed.), 3–70. Oxford: Blackwell Scientific.

Zola-Morgan, S. & L. R. Squire 1992. The components of the medial temporal lobe memory system. In *Neuropsychology of memory*, 2nd edn., L. R. Squire & N. Butters (eds.), 325–35. New York: Guilford.

Zola-Morgan, S., L. R. Squire, & D. G. Amaral 1986. Human amnesia and the medial temporal region: Enduring memory impairment following a bilateral lesion limited to field CA1 of the hippocampus. *Journal of Neuroscience* **6**, 2950–67.

CHAPTER 4

Development of memory in early childhood

Patricia J. Bauer

As the previous chapters have demonstrated, from very early in life, infants are capable of some amazing mnemonic feats. At only a few days old they demonstrate recognition memory (e.g. Slater 1995). For some stimuli (e.g. faces), recognition takes place after delays of as long as 2 weeks (see Fagan 1990 for discussion). Rovee-Collier and her colleagues have shown that by 2 months of age infants are able to retain conditioned responses for up to 3 days (Greco et al. 1986); by 6 months, the retention interval increases to 14 days (Hill et al. 1988), and can be extended to 28 days by a brief reinstating experience (i.e., exposure to some component of the original test event) (Rovee-Collier & Fagen 1981; see Ch. 2 in this volume, for a review). Recent research indicates that some experiences may have even longer lasting effects: Myers et al. (1994) provided evidence that experiences in the first year of life still may influence behavior at the age of 5 years. Thus, virtually from birth, infants are affected by experiences, the influences of which may be revealed even after a long time has elapsed. In fact, DeCasper and Spence (1986) suggest that even *prenatal* experiences may later manifest themselves in changes in behavior toward stimuli!

By the second half of the first year of life infants not only evidence the influence of prior experiences through behaviors such as looking longer or kicking harder, but also demonstrate the capacity to recall specific past events or episodes, in some cases, long after they occurred. The development of this ability is the primary focus of this chapter. In particular, the focus is on developments in recall that occur late in the first and throughout the third year of life, the period during which the human organism develops from a preverbal infant to a verbal young child. As will become evident, for both conceptual and methodological reasons, the development of recall ability during this period is a relatively new area of research attention. Nevertheless, it is already abundantly clear that by late in the first year of life children evidence the ability to recall specific events. What is more, in spite of some obvious areas of further and later developments in recall, it now is clear that, contrary to traditional conceptualizations, there are many continuities in this critical mnemonic process.

Traditional conceptualizations of young children's ability to recall the past

Until quite recently, it was widely assumed that infants and very young children were unable to form memories of specific events that would be available for recall later in time. The assumption was apparent both in general theories of cognitive development and in theories of memory phenomena. The perspectives converged in provision of accounts of the source of infantile or childhood amnesia – the inability of most adults to recall events that happened before their third or fourth birthday (e.g. Rubin 1982; Sheingold & Tenney 1982; Winograd & Killinger 1983; although see Usher & Neisser 1993 for adults' reports of events from the age of 2 years). Freud referred to the absence among adults of recollections of unique events experienced in the first years of life as the "remarkable amnesia of childhood. . .the forgetting which veils our earliest youth from us and makes us strangers to it" (1916/1966: 326). A variety of explanations for the amnesia have been advanced. Virtually all share the perspective that over the course of development, recall processes change qualitatively. For example, in addition to his more widely known explanation of infantile amnesia, namely, that memories of early childhood exist, but are repressed (Freud 1916/1966), Freud also proposed that the memories created by very young children are qualitatively different from those formed later in life. Early in development, children were thought to retain traces, fragments, or images of events, but not to retain coherent representations of past experiences (Freud 1905/1953). Freud suggested that childhood amnesia exists because adults failed to reconstruct or "translate" these fragments into a coherent narrative (see Pillemer & White 1989 for further discussion of this and related proposals).

Predictions of qualitative change in what information is encoded, in how it is encoded, or both, also serve as the centerpiece of more contemporary social (e.g. Neisser 1967, 1988; Schachtel 1947) and cognitive (e.g. Wetzler & Sweeney 1986; White & Pillemer 1979) accounts of the absence of memories from infancy and early childhood. Although these accounts differ widely in their attributions, they have in common the notion that cognitive structures change qualitatively over time. After the change, children are thought capable of forming memories of specific events or episodes that they later are able to recall. Before the qualitative change, they either cannot form such memories (e.g. Piaget 1952), or early memories become inaccessible over the course of development (e.g. Bower 1981; Neisser 1962, 1988).

It is important to note that by suggesting that infants were unable to recall specific events, investigators were not ignoring the fact that they learn and otherwise benefit from past experience. As examples in the opening paragraph of this chapter illustrate, there is ample evidence of facilitated processing of previously encountered information, even by very young infants. However, because these demonstrations are not necessarily indicative of *recall*, they do not represent a challenge to the traditional assumption of the period of infancy as one devoid of the capacity to construct and maintain accessible event memories. Recall entails retrieving a cognitive structure, established on the basis of past experience, in the absence of ongoing perceptual support for that experience (Mandler 1986). Recall is, by definition, a conscious product. When an adult provides a verbal report of a past experience there is ample evidence that the remembered material has been made accessible to the conscious mind. Because the subjects of research on memory for experiences early in life are preverbal or barely verbal, we are unable to query them to ensure their awareness that their behaviors result from some previous experience. There is ambiguity then as to whether the basis on which we infer memory, namely, a change in nonverbal behavior, results from conscious recollection or unconscious influence.

Multiple forms of memory and development

The distinction between a mnemonic behavior based on conscious recollection versus one resulting from an unconscious influence is fundamental. Memory researchers have proposed a variety of classification schemes to capture the phenomena reflective of these different processes, including, but not limited to, distinctions between explicit and implicit (Schacter 1987), declarative and procedural (Cohen & Squire 1980; Mandler 1984), and declarative and non-declarative (Zola-Morgan & Squire 1990) memory. The precise distinctions captured by these classifications are not identical. Nevertheless, they overlap to a large extent, and as reviewed in C. A. Nelson (Ch. 3 in this volume) and discussed in more depth in Parkin (Ch. 5 in this volume), they have in common a view that memory is best conceived not as a unitary trait, but as comprised of different systems, which serve distinct functions and are characterized by fundamentally different rules of operation (Sherry & Schacter 1987; Squire 1992; Tulving 1985).

Explicit or declarative memory captures most of what we think of when we refer to "memory" or "remembering" (Zola-Morgan & Squire 1993). It involves the capacity for conscious recollection of names, places, dates, events, and so on. In contrast, implicit, procedural, or nondeclarative memory represents a variety of nonconscious abilities, including the capacity for learning habits and skills, priming, and some forms of classical conditioning. A defining feature of nondeclarative memory is that the impact of experience is made evident through a change in behavior or performance, but that the experience leading to the change in not consciously accessible (Zola-Morgan & Squire 1993). Declarative memory is characterized as fast (e.g. supporting one-trial learning), fallible (e.g. memory traces degrade, retrieval failures occur), and flexible (i.e., not tied to a specific modality or context). Nondeclarative memory is characterized as slow (i.e., with the exception of priming, it results from

85

gradual or incremental learning), reliable, and inflexible (Sherry & Schacter 1987; Squire et al. 1993). What tasks tapping declarative memory have in common is that they require recollection of a specific episode. In contrast, what tasks tapping nondeclarative memory have in common is that recollection of a specific episode is not required, and in most cases (priming being an exception), learning proceeds gradually, as a result of repeated practice.

Implications for developmental research

When applied to the developmental literature, the distinction between declarative and nondeclarative memory helps to explain why the assumption of infants' inability to recall the past has been held so tenaciously. Methodologically, it has been very difficult to elicit from infants the behaviors that clearly can be identified as indicative of the function of declarative as opposed to nondeclarative processes. Many of the behaviors that infants can perform, such as looking for a longer period of time, or kicking more vigorously, cannot with confidence be attributed to the function of declarative memory. However, the past decade made it increasingly clear that 1- to 2-year-olds *must* be capable of recalling the past. First, K. Nelson (1986) and her colleagues showed that children as young as 3 years of age already have well-organized representations of familiar events, such as going to McDonald's (e.g. Hudson 1986; K. Nelson & Gruendel 1981, 1986; Slackman et al. 1986). This indicates that the capacity to form stable event representations must have developed prior to the age of 3. Secondly, preschoolers are able to provide verbal reports of events that occurred during their second year of life. In some cases the events occurred when the children were as young as 24 months, and were recalled 6 months to 2 years later (Fivush et al. 1987; Fivush & Hamond 1989, 1990; Hamond & Fivush 1991; see Fivush, Ch. 6 in this volume, for a review). Thus, although the majority of *adults* do not seem able to remember events that occurred before their third birthday, children apparently can.

Verbal report may provide the clearest indication of recall of a specific past event. However, because they are largely pre- or early-verbal, children younger than 3 cannot adequately be tested using this methodology. Even from preschoolers, verbal reports are elicited only with a great deal of prompting and directed questioning by adults (Fivush et al. 1987; Fivush & Hamond 1990). In Hamond and Fivush (1991), for example, 78 per cent of the information provided by 3- to 5-year-olds in a structured interview was elicited by prompts and directed questions from the adult interviewer. Moreover, as compared with nonverbal measures of recall memory (described below), verbal measures underestimate the mnemonic competence of children as old as 6 years of age (Fivush et al. 1992; Price & Goodman 1990; Smith et al. 1987). For example, in Goodman et al. (1990), 5-year-olds recalled twice as much information when they were asked to act out an event than when asked to provide a verbal report of it.

In order to investigate recall memory in children younger than 3, researchers have turned to the use of nonverbal methods. Diary studies have yielded some evidence of recall by children in the first year of life (e.g. Ashmead & Perlmutter 1980; K. Nelson & Ross 1980; Todd & Perlmutter 1980). Unfortunately, parental diaries capture only spontaneous indications of memory, which in very young children are not frequent (e.g. Ratner 1980; although see K. Nelson 1988 for a suggestion that the extent to which young children spontaneously talk about the past may be underestimated). In addition, diary studies do not afford experimental control. What really is needed is a nonverbal analogue to verbal recall: The mnemonic behavior must be derived from a task that engages the same cognitive processes as those involved in verbal recall, yet not require of subjects a verbal response.

Establishing the criteria for nonverbal measures of recall

Identifying nonverbal measures that clearly indicate recall is not an easy task. The major reason is that there is no agreed-upon set of necessary and sufficient criteria (i.e., no "defining" features) for determining whether a nonverbal behavior is indicative of recall of a specific event or episode. There are, however, "characteristic" features. Two nonverbal tasks possess these characteristic features and, as a result, have been used to test the development of recall memory: (a) object hiding and retrieval, and (b) elicited imitation (Mandler 1997). Object hiding and retrieval tasks are just what their name implies: The infant or child watches as an object is hidden; after a delay the child is permitted to retrieve the object (e.g. DeLoache 1984; Diamond 1990; Piaget 1954). In elicited-imitation tasks props are used to demonstrate (or "model") a specific action or action sequence. Either immediately after demonstration, or after some delay, the child is allowed to imitate the actions that the model produced. Because elicited imitation of actions or action sequences not only possesses the features that characterize recall, but also can be used to examine memory for events similar to those tested in older children, it has become the paradigm of choice for studying recall of events by children in the period of transition from infancy to early childhood.

With elicited imitation, aspects of original learning and later testing of memory contraindicate suggestions that the infant's or child's behavior is mediated by a mechanism other than recall. First, it is unlikely that elicited imitation evidences acquisition of a nondeclarative procedural or sensorimotor memory. Gradual or incremental learning is characteristic of procedural or sensorimotor acquisition (Bachevalier 1992; Mandler 1988, 1990; Schacter & Moscovitch 1984). In contrast, in the elicited-imitation paradigm, acquisition of to-be-remembered material is based on brief exposure to modeled and, in many cases, novel events. The opportunity for reproduction of the events occurs only after they have been demonstrated; there is no opportunity for practice during exposure to the events. Further, the opportunity to reproduce the test events prior to imposition of a delay is not necessary for later reproduction (e.g. Bauer et al. 1995; Mandler & McDonough 1995; Meltzoff 1988a,b,

1995). These conditions are not conducive to procedural or sensorimotor acquisition (Mandler 1990; Meltzoff 1990; Schacter & Moscovitch 1984).

It also is unlikely that the infant's or child's behavior in elicited imitation evidences unconscious priming or reactivation, processes by which previously experienced information becomes activated in memory without awareness that it has been encountered before, and without deliberate search (e.g. Graf et al. 1984). It has been demonstrated that these processes are highly dependent upon specific features of the stimuli: Changes across, as well as within, modality diminish the influence of prior experience (thus, one source of the characterization of nondeclarative memory as "inflexible") (Schacter 1990). In adults, for example, word fragment priming effects decrease when target words are presented in the visual modality, but are tested auditorally (Jackson & Morton 1984). Even within the visual modality, priming effects decrease when, for example, target words are presented in script, but at test are presented in typed form (Roediger & Blaxton 1987). Similar levels of specificity are required to reactivate previously conditioned responses in infants. For example, in the conjugate reinforcement paradigm, unless they are trained on a variety of exemplars, if even a single feature of the design on the liner of the crib in which 6-month-old infants are trained is changed (e.g. the shape of the figures is changed from a square to a circle), they respond as if they have had no previous training (Rovee-Collier & Shyi 1992).

In contrast, performance on the elicited-imitation task, like that on commonly used tests of declarative memory, is less affected by changes across or within modality. In fact, as Meltzoff (1990) has pointed out, the elicited-imitation task is a cross-modal one: The model is observed visually and later matched with the child's own actions. Imitation occurs even when the target action has been demonstrated by a televised model. For example, in Meltzoff (1988c), 14-month-olds visually perceived a two-dimensional model and later matched the behavior with their own actions using three-dimensional props. Moreover, within a modality, manipulations of the specific features of the stimuli have little effect on imitative performance. In Bauer and Dow (1994), 16- and 20-month-olds were tested for reproduction of target sequences immediately and after a 1-week interval. At delayed testing the props for some of the sequences were changed. The new props could be used to produce events that were structurally identical to the originals (e.g. both versions of the event might involve pretending to put a character to bed), but with different surface instantiations (i.e., in one version, a large bear might be put into a large wooden bed, whereas in another version, a small dog might be put into a plastic crib). Comparison of performance on sequences with and without changes to the props revealed virtually no decrease in performance associated with the manipulation. In sum, the circumstances of the elicited-imitation task contraindicate the possibility that performance on it could be supported by some form of nondeclarative memory. Consistent with this argument is the recent finding that adult human amnesics (in whom declarative memory processes are disrupted) are unable to perform an age-appropriate version of the task (McDonough et al. 1995).

Finally, not only is performance on the elicited-imitation task indicative of declarative memory, but also it can be differentiated from other demonstrations of declarative memory, such as are evidenced in some recognition tasks. The available props do provide perceptual support or cues to recall. However, this is not a critical distinction because all recall is cued, either by an external prompt (e.g. "Tell me what you remember about X"), or by an internal association (Spear 1978). Moreover, in the case of recall of the multi-step sequences that are used in elicited imitation, critical information about the *order* in which the event should unfold is not even perceptually cued: Once the model is gone, so are cues to temporal order. To reproduce previously modeled actions and action sequences then, information about what is to be performed, and in what order, must be encoded during demonstration and later retrieved from a representation of the event, in the absence of ongoing perceptual support. The circumstances of elicited imitation thus closely mimic those of standard verbal recall paradigms (Mandler 1990), and the behaviors derived from it meet the definition of recall (see Bauer 1995b; Bauer & Mandler 1992; Bauer et al. 1994; Mandler 1990; Meltzoff 1990 for further discussion).

Nonverbal evidence of recall of events in infancy and early childhood

Using the nonverbal measure of elicited imitation, researchers have asked a variety of questions about recall memory in older infants and young children. What all of the studies have in common is the basic technique: Props are used to produce a specific action or sequence of actions that the infant or child later is allowed to imitate. Depending upon the age group, the target event may be a single action or a sequence of several actions. Procedurally, depending upon the issue under consideration, researchers modify the basic technique in a number of ways. Variations include (a) inclusion of a pre-modeling baseline period during which spontaneous production of the target actions or sequences is assessed (to insure that the actions or sequences would not be performed without the benefit of their demonstration), (b) modeling the action or event sequence as many as three times in succession (to insure that the infants or young children, whose attention may "wander" during demonstration, actually have had a chance to encode the activity), (c) using narration to accompany demonstration of the action or sequence (either as an attention maintaining technique, or to assess the influence of language on memory), and (d) allowing immediate imitation of an action or sequence, delayed recall of which is to be tested later (thereby allowing for a direct assessment of the amount of forgetting that occurred over the delay interval). Notably, with few exceptions, these procedural variations have little to no effect on performance.

Regardless of procedure, what is clear is that children encode and retain information about the actions and sequences that they see performed, and that under a variety of circumstances, they are able to retrieve the information, even after long delays.

Immediate recall

Meltzoff (1988b) and McDonough (1991) tested the ability of infants 9 and 11 months of age, respectively, to reproduce single object-specific actions. In the case of the 9-month-olds, the modeled events were novel (e.g. depressing a recessed button in a box, causing it to "beep"); in the case of the 11-month-olds, some of the events were novel (e.g. pulling two pieces of pipe apart to reveal a hidden toy), whereas others would be considered to be more familiar (e.g. "feeding" a stuffed bear using a schematic bottle). Even 9-month-old infants are able to imitate actions such as these immediately after seeing them modeled. For example, in Meltzoff (1988b), of the three actions demonstrated, half of the infants produced none or one of them, and half produced two or all three of them.

By combining two or more actions into a sequence, researchers are able to test young children's recall of events that begin to approximate more closely those tested in older children. Thus far, the youngest infants to be tested for immediate recall of event sequences have been 11 months of age; they have been tested for recall of sequences depicting familiar events and events that are novel. An example of a "familiar" event is *Putting teddy-bear to bed*, modeled as putting a stuffed bear in a doll bed, and covering it with a blanket. An example of a novel event is using a transparent box and a large button to *Make a rattle*: push the button through a flexible diaphragm at the top of the box, and shake the box to make it rattle. By accurately imitating event sequences such as these, children as young as 11 months of age demonstrate immediate recall of both familiar and novel events (Bauer & Mandler 1992; Mandler & McDonough 1995). It is particularly important that young children are able to recall novel events, because it is only for these that there is certainty that the basis for recall was the specific sequence to which the children were exposed. On sequences depicting familiar events, the basis for reproduction conceivably could be prior knowledge of a common routine. For this reason, researchers primarily have focused on children's recall of novel actions and sequences.

Over the 1- to 2-year age period there is a steady increase in the length of the sequence that can be recalled accurately. By the time children reach 20 months, they approach ceiling in terms of reproduction of three-act events (Bauer & Dow 1994; Bauer & Hertsgaard 1993; Bauer & Thal 1990). By 24 months, children reliably reproduce events that are five steps in length (Bauer & Travis 1993). By age 30 months, they reliably reproduce events such as "building a house," which may involve as many as eight steps: (1) sand the house, (2) put a nail into a predrilled hole, (3) hammer the nail, (4) saw the house, (5) load a dump truck with bricks, (6) dump the bricks, (7) put a chimney on the roof of the house, and (8) paint the house (Bauer & Fivush 1992). These data make it clear that children of a young age are able to remember specific events over the very short term.

Recall after days or weeks

In addition to testing infants' immediate imitation, Meltzoff (1988b) and McDonough (1991) also included tests of 9- and 11-month-olds' (respectively) recall of single object-specific actions after a delay of 24 hours. Notably, even though they never had been allowed to imitate the actions prior to imposition of the delay (i.e., different infants were tested for immediate and 24-hour de- layed recall), 50 per cent of 9-month-olds recalled at least two of the three novel actions, and fully 20 per cent of them remembered all three of the novel actions that they had seen modeled 24 hours earlier (Meltzoff 1988b). Thus, not only are 9-month-old infants able to recall single object-specific actions imme- diately after seeing them modeled, but also they are able to retain information about the modeled activities over delays of at least 24 hours. By 14 months children can reproduce novel actions after a delay of at least one week (Meltzoff 1988a). Over the same delay, children aged 13 months also are able to maintain information about the temporal order of actions in multi-step event sequences (Bauer & Hertsgaard 1993). That is, after 1 week's delay, children produce a greater number of target actions, and a greater number of correctly ordered actions, relative to baseline. Their performance after a 1-week delay typically is lower than at immediate testing (i.e., children evidence some for- getting). Nevertheless, they remember the events. By 20 months of age, on short event sequences, children evidence little to no decrement in performance over delays of 2 to 6 weeks: Delayed recall performance is equivalent to that at immediate testing (Bauer & Mandler 1989; Bauer & Shore 1987).

That such young children are able to recall specific novel events and sequences over delays of 24 hours to several weeks is impressive indeed. It cer- tainly challenges one of the fundamental assumptions of traditional perspec- tives on memory in infancy and early childhood. That is, it renders untenable the suggestion that prior to the advent of qualitative change in how experience is encoded, young children simply are unable to form accessible event memo- ries (e.g. Piaget 1952). However, unless children are shown to remember over longer retention intervals, it remains a distinct possibility that these early memories, although accessible for some period after initial experience, become inaccessible over the course of development (e.g. Bower 1981; Neisser 1962, 1988). There are many factors that may contribute to failures in storage or retrieval of memory for an individual episode. In contrast, there generally are considered two categories of explanation for why once-accessible memories from an entire period of life might later become inaccessible: immaturity of the neural substrate necessary for retention over the long term, and lack of a means by which early memories later can be made available for verbal expression. The first of these possibilities is consistent with a neurobiological explanation for the absence of memories from early in life. A brief review of current understanding of the neural substrate subserving recall will serve to make the point (see C. A. Nelson, Ch. 3 in this volume, for a detailed review; see also C. A. Nelson 1995). The second explanation is discussed later in the chapter (see pp. 99–102).

The neural substrate of long-term recall

Since the mid-1980s work with adults suffering from anterograde amnesia (i.e., the inability to form new declarative memories), as well as with animal models of the syndrome, has resulted in significant progress in identifying the specific neural substrate underlying the formation of memories that are enduring and accessible over time. Data from a variety of sources suggest that a cortico-limbic-diencephalic circuit, involving the hippocampal formation and surrounding cortices, is the substrate subserving long-term recall (Mishkin & Appenzeller 1987; Squire & Zola-Morgan 1991). Specifically, the hippocampal formation is necessary for the consolidation of new memories for specific episodes, and appears necessary for the retrieval of recently established memories (i.e., those established within days or weeks) (e.g. Squire 1992; Zola-Morgan & Squire 1990). Its role in maintenance of memory for a specific episode is, however, time limited: Retrieval of memories for events that happened long ago is not dependent upon the integrity of the hippocampal formation. Rather, recall of events from the remote past is thought dependent upon neocortical association areas, implying that they serve as the storage sites for long-term memories (Squire 1992; Zola-Morgan & Squire 1993). Thus, the establishment and maintenance of specific event memories over long delays requires the functioning of both the hippocampal formation and the neocortical association areas, as well as the reciprocal connections between them (Bachevalier & Mishkin 1994).

Although there is not unanimous agreement as to when the components of the hippocampal formation become fully mature, behavioral data indicate that they may be functional at an early age (see C. A. Nelson, Ch. 3 in this volume, for discussion). In contrast, the neocortical components and the reciprocal connections between the hippocampus and the neocortex appear to develop more slowly (Bachevalier 1990; Bachevalier et al. 1993; Bachevalier & Mishkin 1994). This presents the possibility that delayed maturation of the neocortical association areas, their connections, or both, may limit the persistence of declarative memory early in life (Bachevalier & Mishkin 1994; Squire et al. 1993). In other words, early in development the functional hippocampal system may be able to support recall over a matter of days or even weeks, but the immaturity of neocortical association areas might preclude recall over the longer term. Necessary to address this possibility are data on young children's recall after delays of weeks to months. Without such data it is impossible to know whether 1-year-olds are able to retain accessible memories over periods of days or weeks, but are unable to consolidate and stabilize information for re-call after a long time period.

Long-term recall of specific events

Because of the relative "youth" of research on long-term recall in infancy and early childhood, there are only a few studies in which retention over delays of weeks and months has been tested. Nevertheless, based on these studies it is clear that even young children are able to recall specific events over long delays. Thus far the longest retention interval over which young children have been tested for recall of specific novel multi-step event sequences is 8 months. Bauer et al. (1994) tested children 21, 24, and 29 months of age for their recall of events that they experienced 8 months previously, as 13-, 16-, and 20-month-olds. To evaluate memory after the long delay, performance of the experienced children was compared to that of age- and gender-matched control children who never before had seen the test events (naive controls). Although the naive children spontaneously produced some of the target actions and sequences, in all three age groups, performance by the experienced children was signifi-cantly greater than that by the naive controls (Bauer et al. 1994). Thus, even the youngest children maintained organized representations of the novel events over the long delay.

Although representing the longest interval over which recall of multi-step events has been tested, Bauer et al. (1994) do not stand alone in suggesting very long-term recall by children in the 1- to 2-year age range. Meltzoff (1995) observed recall by 18- and 20-month-olds of single, novel object-specific actions that they had experienced 4 months previously, as 14- and 16-month-olds. Hudson and Sheffield (1995) observed recall after 6 months of events that children originally had experienced at 18 months of age. Finally, McDonough and Mandler (1994) reported that 63 per cent of 23-month-olds reproduced one of four single object-specific actions (i.e., "feeding" a schematic bottle to a stuffed bear) that they had experienced 12 months previously, when they were only 11 months of age. Together these data indicate that by late in the first year of life, children have the capacity to recall specific events after long periods of time. They thus contraindicate suggestions that insufficient development of the neural substrate necessary to consolidate and stabilize event representa-tions would result in the inaccessibility of memories after a long delay.

The argument that the neural substrate necessary for long-term recall is "in place" in the 1-year-old does not imply that it is fully mature, only that it is sufficiently functionally mature to support recall over long time periods. Nor does this suggestion imply that were we to happen upon the correct retrieval cue, we would be able to uncover declarative memories from earliest infancy. On the contrary, as discussed above and in more detail in C. A. Nelson (Ch. 3 in this volume), significant neural development must take place in order to support long-term recall. Data from a variety of sources indicate that these developments do not occur until the second half of the first year of life. Thus, it is only as infants approach the end of the first year that we anticipate emergence of the ability to recall information after a long delay. Consistent with this expectation, a preliminary report of a study yet in progress suggests that 9 months may represent an important watershed in the development of long-term recall ability. Even after multiple exposures to two-act events, approximately half of 9-month-olds are unable to recall them after 1 month (Carver 1995). On the flip side, what this means is that 50 per cent of infants *are* able to recall at least some events, even over such a long delay. Because in the elicited-imitation paradigm pronounced individual differences seem to be the exception, rather than the rule, this pattern is particularly suggestive of a period of transition, the timing of which often is marked by unevenness in development within the population.

Summary of evidence of recall of events in infancy and early childhood
In summary, the data reviewed thus far demonstrate accurate recall of specific events by children who were as young as 9 months at the time of experience of them. Children remember over the short term, as well as over delays of several months, thus demonstrating that they are able to construct and maintain memories of specific events that endure and are accessible over time. Notably, although age may place a lower bound on the capacity for long-term recall of specific events, once the capacity is in place, age does not seem to be the primary determinant of the length of the retention interval that children can tolerate. In contrast to steady increases with age in the amount of information that children can recall accurately (from two-step events at 11 months to eight-step events at 30 months: Bauer & Mandler 1992 and Bauer & Fivush 1992 respectively), there does not seem to be a "growth chart" type function that determines for how long children will retain event-related information. Rather, as suggested by Meltzoff, although younger infants may take longer to encode certain stimuli than older infants, once an event is encoded, the "retention interval per se is not a narrowly delimiting factor in early infancy" (Meltzoff 1988b: 224). If age is not the primary determinant of whether or for how long an event will be remembered, what does determine recall?

Determinants of long-term recall during the transition from infancy to early childhood

A review of the literature reveals two major determinants of recall of events by children during the transition from infancy to early childhood: The organization of event representations and the availability of cues or reminders of to-be-remembered events profoundly affect long-term memory in this age period. As will become evident, there is considerable continuity in the effects of these factors on very young children as compared with older children and adults.

Organization of event representations

The first determinant of event memory is how well the mental representation of the event is organized. The organization of an event representation is influenced by at least two factors: (a) the nature of the temporal relations among the components of the event, and (b) familiarity, or repeated experience of the event (Mandler 1986).

Effects of temporal structure Younger children, as well as older children and adults, show superior ordered recall of events characterized by enabling relations, compared with events that are arbitrarily ordered. Enabling relations are said to exist when, for a given end-state or goal, one action in a sequence is both temporally prior to and necessary for a second action in the same sequence. For example, in making a milkshake, physical law dictates that the ingredients be put into the blender before the lid is put on. Likewise, to avoid losing the ingredients to the counters or walls of the kitchen, the lid must be put on the blender before the motor is turned on. In contrast, actions in an event are said to be arbitrarily ordered when there are no inherent constraints on their temporal position in a sequence. To continue the example, in making a milkshake, whether the ice cream or the chocolate sauce is put in first is a matter of personal preference alone: It has no consequences for the outcome of the event.

That enabling relations facilitate recall in older children is readily apparent in the literature (e.g. Hudson & Nelson 1986; Price & Goodman 1990; Slackman et al. 1986). Preschool-age and older children show a consistent pattern of superior ordered recall of events characterized by enabling relations, compared with events that lack such relations, and thus, are arbitrarily ordered (e.g. Hudson & Nelson 1986; Price & Goodman 1990; Ratner et al. 1986; Slackman & Nelson 1984; Slackman et al. 1986). It also is apparent that enabling relations facilitate recall in very young children. In several studies researchers have contrasted recall of novel events containing enabling relations (such as making a rattle of two nesting cups and a rubber ball: put the ball into one cup, cover it with the other cup, shake the cups to make a rattle) with that of novel arbitrarily ordered events (such as making a party hat: put a pom-pom on the top of a cone-shaped base, attach a sticker to the front of the cone, attach a colored band around the base of the cone) (e.g. Bauer & Dow 1994; Bauer & Hertsgaard 1993; Bauer & Travis 1993; Mandler & McDonough 1995). The findings from these studies are remarkably consistent.

First, children produce an equivalent number of individual actions on novel-enabling and novel-arbitrary events. This suggests that they find the two event types equally interesting. Moreover, it precludes the possibility that differences in ordered recall are an artifact of a larger number of opportunities to produce ordered pairs (i.e., production of individual actions and production of pairs of actions are not independent). Second, although children produce an equivalent number of individual actions, they do not produce an equivalent number of ordered pairs of actions: Children's ordered recall of novel-enabling events is consistently greater than that of arbitrarily ordered ones. The advantage is apparent both at immediate testing (e.g. Bauer 1992; Bauer & Thal 1990; Bauer & Travis 1993) and at delayed testing (e.g. Bauer & Dow 1994; Bauer & Hertsgaard 1993; Bauer & Mandler 1989; Bauer et al. 1995; Mandler & McDonough 1995). It also is apparent even after several experiences of arbitrarily ordered events in an invariant temporal order (Bauer & Travis 1993) (see Bauer 1995b, for a review; see Bauer 1992, 1995b; Bauer & Travis 1993 for discussion of the means by which enabling relations in events may influence ordered recall). Finally, the results of control conditions make clear that the robust facilitating effect of enabling relations in events cannot be attributed to the problem-solving abilities of young children: Children who have not seen the target events modeled do not "figure out" how to produce them (e.g. Bauer 1992; Bauer et al. 1995).

Effects of familiarity or repeated experience   Familiarity, or repeated experience of an event, also influences organization and, thereby, recall for young as well as older children. Although repeated experience is not necessary for accurate recall (e.g. Hudson 1986; Smith et al. 1987), it aids memory both in terms of (a) the amount of information that is remembered (e.g. Fivush 1984; Hudson 1986, 1990), and (b) the length of time over which events can be recalled (Fivush & Hamond 1989). For example, Fivush and Hamond (1989) found that when asked to re-enact test events after a 3-month delay, 24- and 29-month-old children who had experienced the events twice recalled more about them than children who had experienced them only once. Moreover, children with repeated experience recalled as much after the 3-month retention interval as they had after only 2 weeks.

Similar facilitating effects of repeated experience have been observed in children in the second year of life. For children aged 13 and 15 months, repeated experience is not necessary for recall of events over the short term: After 1 week, children of this age recall both the individual target actions and the temporal order of actions of novel events experienced only once (Bauer & Hertsgaard 1993; Bauer et al. 1995). Nevertheless, particularly over the longer term, repeated experience clearly facilitates recall. For events experienced only once, relative to performance after a 1-week delay, performance after 1 month falls off precipitously. In contrast, events experienced three times before imposition of a 1-month delay are well recalled. Notably, recall after 1 month of events experienced three times is comparable to that after 1 week of events experienced only once (Bauer et al. 1995). The effects of repeated experience are not due to an increased likelihood of children spontaneously generating the target sequences as a result of greater comfort with the testing situation or familiarity with the props: Children who are given repeated experience with the setting, the experimenter, and the props, but who are not exposed to the modeled events, produce no more target actions and sequences at their second testing than they do at their first (Bauer & Dow 1994). Thus, the facilitating effects of repeated experience accrue only with exposure to the target events.

Research by Hudson and Sheffield (1995) indicates that the timing of subsequent exposures to events affects the efficacy of repeated experience. They provided different groups of children with either one or two experiences of a number of activities; the multiple experiences were separated by intervals of either 15 minutes, 2 weeks, or 8 weeks. Echoing Fivush and Hamond (1989) and Bauer et al. (1995), after 2.5 months, children who had received two experiences of the activities recalled more about them, relative to children who had experienced them only once. Notably, as the time between experiences increased, so did the facilitating effects of repeated exposure. The effects of timing were particularly pronounced when the children were tested again, this time 6 months after their last exposure to the events: Children who had received the experiences spaced 8 weeks apart recalled as much as they had fully 6 months earlier; the remaining groups recalled proportionally less. These results suggest that subsequent experience of an event is especially facilitative of recall if it occurs after a significant delay, and thus, nearer the time the event presumably otherwise would be forgotten (Hudson & Sheffield 1995).

Availability of cues or reminders of events

Just as well-organized representations of events result in an advantage in recall, cues or reminders of previously experienced events (a) support retention of information about them, and (b) facilitate retrieval after a delay.

Effects of reminding on storage   When one subsequently is re-exposed to a previously experienced event it is appropriate to regard the re-exposure as a "repeated experience" of the original event. However, except in the laboratory, it rarely is the case that an event is re-experienced precisely as it was experienced originally (even in the laboratory there inevitably are minor variations across experiences). More likely, something that resembles the original event to a greater or lesser extent will be encountered and serve as a reminder of the original event.

Hudson and Sheffield have demonstrated that a variety of experiences serve to remind young children of previously experienced events, thereby prolonging the interval over which information about them is retained. For example, Sheffield and Hudson (1994) exposed 14- and 18-month-old children to six novel activities (e.g. pulling a string to make a Mickey Mouse toy "talk"). At a subsequent session half of the children were passively re-exposed to a subset of three of the activities: They watched as the experimenter demonstrated the target actions, but they did not themselves produce them. Twenty-four hours after re-exposure the children were tested for recall of all six activities; the children who experienced the activities only once also were tested for recall. In an effect that parallels those of repeated experience (described above), children who had been passively re-exposed to the events recalled more than children who had not been re-exposed. This demonstrates that children need not perform the actions themselves in order to benefit from re-exposure (see also

Bauer et al. 1995). More importantly for present purposes, the children who had been passively re-exposed to a subset of the activities recalled more of *all* of the activities, including those that they had not seen remodeled. Sheffield and Hudson interpret this effect as evidence that the reminder of a subset of activities may "spread" to others associated with them, effectively reinstating the entire experience in memory.

Hudson and Sheffield (1995) demonstrated that exposure to some types of representations of previously experienced events also may serve to remind children of them. However, their effects may not be as strong or as long lasting. Specifically, exposure to a videotape of another child performing activities that the subjects previously had themselves performed was effective in reminding 18-month-olds when they were tested after a delay interval of 24 hours; it was not effective after a delay of 8 weeks. The use of still photographs of the activities (accompanied by appropriate verbal narration) was effective in reminding 24-month-olds, but not 18-month-olds (Hudson & Sheffield 1995). Finally, verbal narration alone has been shown to be effective in preserving memories in 3-year-old children (Hudson 1993); it has little effect on 2-year-olds (Hudson 1991, 1993). [1] Together, these studies demonstrate that even young children may be reminded of events during a retention interval and that, as a result of reminding, recall is facilitated. They also suggest that with development, children become sensitive to a wider range of reminding experiences.

Effects of reminding on retrieval   In addition to affecting the storage of information, reminders also affect information retrieval. Preschool-age children report more information when, at test, they are provided with specific cues or otherwise reminded of to-be-remembered events (e.g. Fivush 1984; Fivush et al. 1984; Fivush & Hamond 1990; Hudson 1990; Hudson & Fivush 1991). Although verbal rehearsal alone may not be effective in preserving young children's memory for events (Hudson 1993), verbal reminders provided at the time of retrieval facilitate recall even in very young children. For example, in Bauer et al. (1995), in addition to the props used to produce the event (which always are present when recall is tested, and thus serve as one type of reminder), at delayed testing the experimenter also provided a verbal reminder of the event in the form of a label for it. For example, on *Make a rattle*, the experimenter presented the props and said "You can use this stuff to make a rattle. Show me how you make a rattle." Following provision of the verbal information, the children were given the opportunity to produce the events.

After a short delay (i.e., 1 week), verbal reminding had a small yet significant facilitating effect on 15-month-olds' performance: Children reminded of the events showed no significant decrement in performance over the delay; children not reminded exhibited a significant decrease in ordered recall. Over a longer delay of 1 month, the effects of reminding were more pronounced. Children remembered events of which they were not reminded; they recalled significantly more of events of which they were reminded (Bauer et al. 1995). In fact, with reminding, performance after 1 month was roughly equivalent to that after 1 week. At least for 20-month-old children, verbal reminding still is effective in aiding retrieval even after delay intervals of as many as 14 months (Bauer & Wewerka 1997). Critically, the effects of reminding cannot be attributed to "suggestion" of plausible event sequences: Children who are exposed to verbal reminders, but who are not exposed to the modeled events, do not generate the target actions and sequences (Bauer & Hertsgaard 1993; Bauer et al. 1995). It is only when children have seen sequences produced that they exhibit performance indicative of recall of the specific events to which they have been exposed.

Summary of determinants of recall

In summary, factors known to influence recall of events by older children and adults also influence recall in very young children. Specifically, organization of the event representation has a pronounced effect on recall. Events constrained by enabling relations are well recalled, even over substantial delays. In addition, events with which children are familiar, or have had repeated experience, are well recalled, also over long delays. Reminding children of previously experienced events effectively serves to preserve event memories over longer periods of time than they otherwise would be remembered. A variety of experiences, including re-exposure to a subset of target activities, exposure to videotaped presentations, and for older children, still photographs, serve to remind children of past events. Finally, events of which children are verbally reminded at the time of retrieval also are well recalled, even by quite young children, after long delays.

The transition to verbal expression of event memory

By virtue of the fact that the focus of this chapter has been on recall of events by pre- and early-verbal children, the demonstrations of mnemonic competence that have been reviewed have been nonverbal. In contrast, for older children and adults, evidence of memory for past events is provided through verbal recollection. This difference may sound trivial. Of course older children are able to provide verbal reports of their past experiences: They have command of the verbal medium. However, the difference between younger and older children in the mode of expression of memory remains as one of the most notable exceptions to the catalogue of continuities in recall processes across a wide developmental span. Moreover, this difference may have profound implications for conclusions drawn about the continued accessibility of very early memories. Following K. Nelson and Ross (1980), Pillemer and White (1989: 321) argue that, if young children are able to recall specific past events over long periods of time, then their "memories should not only be expressible through behavior, they also should become verbally expressible when the child has the ability to reconstrue preverbal events in narrative form".

Although there is no evidence that early memories later become verbalizable, there remains the possibility that the transition to language changes the way that memories are encoded and stored. The resulting incompatibility of representational formats may render inaccessible memories of events from early in life (see Pillemer & White 1989 for discussion).

What evidence bears on the issue of children's ability to express their early memories verbally? It is clear that children can provide verbal reports of events experienced in the distant past (e.g. Fivush et al. 1987; Hamond & Fivush 1991; see Fivush, Ch. 6 in this volume, for review). Indeed, it was in part this fact that provided the original impetus for research on pre- and early-verbal children's event memory. However, a striking characteristic of these early reports is the amount of work that an interviewer must do to obtain them. For children younger than 24 months, it is the adult partner who provides both the structure and the content of the verbal report: The adult tells "what happened" in the event and the child confirms, denies, or repeats the information (e.g. Eisenberg 1985; Fivush 1991; Peterson & McCabe 1992; Sachs 1983). Between 2 and 2.5 years parents begin to substitute "yes" or "no" questions with memory questions, thus requiring that children provide at least some mnemonic content. Nevertheless, the structure of the report is provided by the adult who both cues memory and directs the memory search. It is not until after the age of 3 that children begin to initiate conversations about the past and to provide coherent narratives about them (e.g. Fivush et al. 1987).

Young children's difficulty in talking about the past stands in sharp contrast to their rapidly developing ability to talk about the "here and now." This led Bauer (1995a) to suggest that it is the decontextualized nature of the circumstances under which verbal reports of the past typically are elicited that renders young children particularly dependent upon the scaffolding provided by the adult. Consider that in the typical study of verbal expression of memory, at the time of the report, the child is not only temporally, but also spatially, separated from the to-be-recalled material. In this situation, children may be especially dependent upon the support provided by the discourse partner (Eisenberg 1985; Sachs 1983). If it is the decontextualized nature of the activity that limits young children's ability to talk about the past, then "contextualizing" the task, by allowing children to return to the physical location of a previous experience, providing the props involved in the original event, or both, should alleviate the heavy dependence upon an adult partner.

Although relevant data are not plentiful, there does exist in the literature evidence that with the aid of contextual support, children are able to talk about events from the distant past, and even about events that they experienced only as preverbal infants. A striking and well-documented example comes from Myers et al. (1987). In this study children participating in an auditory localization experiment were, as infants, exposed to a screen decorated with a picture of a whale. When at 32 months the children were tested for their memory of aspects of the original testing situation, the picture initially was hidden from

100

view. In response to the experimenter's request to "guess what picture is under here," one child responded "whale" (Myers et al. 1987: 128). Thus, there is some evidence that children are able to express verbally material that in all likelihood was encoded nonverbally (see K. Nelson & Ross 1980; Todd & Perlmutter 1980 for additional examples derived from parental diary reports of early mnemonic behavior).

Additional evidence on later verbal accessibility of early memories comes from Bauer and Wewerka (1995). In this study, using elicited imitation, children who were 13, 16, and 20 months of age at the time of experience of events were tested for recall of them at delay intervals of either 1, 3, 6, 9, or 12 months (thus, the children were 14 to 32 months at the time of testing). Although the researchers did not elicit them, the children spontaneously produced verbalizations in the course of the session. Whereas approximately half of the verbalizations that the children produced were devoted to labeling the available props and making general requests and comments (e.g. "Can I have some more toys?"), the other half were devoted to expression of memory for the target events. For example, the children asked how to produce or they verbally described the outcome of particular events, verbally performed target actions, and requested as yet unseen props and events. Thus, although they were not asked to do so, the children verbally demonstrated that they remembered the events to which they had been exposed (Bauer & Wewerka 1995). This study thus provides evidence of verbal memory for specific events by 1- to 2-year-old children. Critically, because the verbal reports were spontaneous, neither their content nor their structure was provided by the adult partner.

The data from Bauer and Wewerka (1995) also allow some insight into what determines whether memory will be expressed verbally. As measured by parental report on the MacArthur Communicative Development Inventory (an externally validated, stable, and reliable measure of early language competence: Fenson et al. 1994), productive vocabulary at the time of exposure to the events was moderately correlated with but not predictive of nonverbal expression of memory (i.e., through imitation). In contrast, productive vocabulary at the time of exposure to the events was correlated with verbal expression of memory, and as revealed by regression analyses, accounted for a significant portion of the variance in predicting verbal memory, even after removal of the variance associated with other relevant predictor variables (Bauer & Wewerka 1995). What these data indicate is that the availability of a verbal means of encoding an event does not *determine* whether that event will be recalled: Even children with very low levels of language development at the time of exposure were able to express their memory for the events nonverbally. However, the availability of a verbal means of encoding is related to later *verbal* expression of memory. In turn, verbal expression may be what determines whether a memory will survive the transition from infancy to early childhood (see, e.g. K. Nelson 1993 for discussion). Relevant to this suggestion are data from a follow-up study with a subset of the children from Bauer and Wewerka (1995).

When, once again in supportive context, the children were tested at 36 to 40 months, the only variable to predict verbal expression of memory was previous verbal expression of memory (Bauer & Wewerka 1997). The tentative conclusion to be drawn from this work is that greater language capacity at the time of experience of an event supports early verbal expression of event memory; in turn, early verbal expression uniquely predicts verbal accessibility of memory at age 3.

Conclusions and implications

Until relatively recently, a widely held assumption was that children younger than 2 to 3 years of age simply were not capable of remembering specific events from the past. Advances in our understanding of the recall abilities of children only slightly older have forced revision of this assumption. When asked, preschool-age children provide well-organized accounts of everyday events and personally meaningful experiences that in some cases occurred when they were as young as 24 months. This indicated that children younger than 2 years would be the subjects of inquiry into the onset of the ability to recall the past. Even adopting conservative criteria for what is considered evidence of recall, it has become apparent that 24 months is not the earliest age at which children are able to remember the past. By late in the first year of life children accurately recall specific events after delays of weeks and even months. In doing so they demonstrate that they are capable of forming memories of unique events that endure and are accessible over time.

Factors known to influence recall of events by older children and adults also influence recall in very young children, thus demonstrating considerable continuity in mnemonic processes. Specifically, organization of the event representation has a pronounced effect on recall. Events constrained by enabling relations, and events with which children are familiar, or have had repeated experience, are well recalled, even over substantial delays. As it does for older children, reminding young children of previously experienced events effectively serves to preserve event memories over longer periods of time than they otherwise would be remembered. Events of which children are verbally reminded at the time of retrieval are also well recalled, even by quite young children, after long delays. Results from a number of different control groups demonstrate that the effects of these determinants should not be attributed to the problem-solving abilities of young children, to the effects of increased familiarity with the experimenter, experimental setting, or the props themselves, or to suggestions of plausible event sequences. Rather, they are due to children remembering previously experienced events.

Because they are largely pre- and early-verbal, the subjects of research in the period of transition from infancy to early childhood primarily have been tested for recall of events using nonverbal measures. However, young children also are able to demonstrate event memory verbally. When they are presented with the props that they previously used to produce specific target events, they spontaneously talk not only about the perceptually available props, but also about the non-obvious target actions and sequences that they previously performed with them. Children's early "memory talk" is related to their reported level of productive language at the time of experience of the events; later memory talk is related to early memory talk.

In light of the mnemonic "feats" that even quite young children are able to perform, it seems appropriate to inquire as to what is yet to develop in memory development. The titles to subsequent chapters in this volume provide strong clues as to the numerous aspects of memory that undergo significant change in early childhood and beyond. Conspicuous by its omission until later chapters is discussion of the form of episodic memory known as autobiographical memory. Autobiographical memories, or personal memories (Brewer 1986), involve recollection of specific episodes, accompanied by a sense of personal involvement. In other words, they are memories of specific past events in which the subject was an involved participant; they constitute one's life story or personal past. It is the absence of this type of memory from early in life that characterizes the phenomenon of infantile amnesia. The question now to be asked is whether early memories, such as those described herein, are strictly episodic or might also be autobiographical.

It is likely that until young children can be made to speak in complete sentences and verbally describe their experiences in narrative form, an answer to the question of whether early memory is at all autobiographical will continue to elude us. This is because, for adults, recollections of a unique episode from one's past usually include the same categories as are included in a full narrative, namely, the *who, what, where, when, why*, and *how* of an event (K. Nelson 1993). This has led to the suggestion that, developmentally, the emergence of autobiographical memory is linked with the acquisition of narrative form to use as a frame for structuring and remembering experience (see, e.g. K. Nelson 1993; Pillemer & White 1989). Into the narrative frame one inserts informa-tion about the actors, actions, intentions, and affective experiences of those involved in the event. Thus, it is the advent of narrative organization that allows one to begin to construct the personal history that is the hallmark of autobiographical memory. Conversely, the absence of narrative form is what differentiates early memories of specific episodes from later, more adult-like, autobiographical memories. A number of authors describe the development of narrative form, and thus of autobiographical memory, as a product of social construction, established in the context of talking about and sharing past experiences (see, e.g. Fivush 1988; K. Nelson 1993; Pillemer & White 1989 for further discussion).[2]

To regard the development of autobiographical memory as a distinct form of episodic memory has certain advantages. Prominent among them is that it resolves the issue of the apparent lack of correlation between the onset of episodic memory and the onset of personal memory (Bauer 1993). Unfortunately, however, the resolution may come at the expense of new issues. One issue is that such a distinction necessitates identification of clear criteria for differentiation of the different forms of memory. At present, what seems to differentiate "run-of-the-mill" episodic memories from personal or autobiographical ones is that the latter are structured in a narrative form that also conveys a sense of personal involvement in the recounted experience. Episodic memories from the second year of life generally lack these qualities (K. Nelson 1993). Assignment of significance to these differences should, however, be made with caution. Traditionally, a child's inability to provide a verbal report of an experience was equated with an inability to remember the experience. In essence, early memory was defined out of existence. Equating the onset of a specific type of episodic memory with the development of the narrative form, with verbal expression of personal relevance, or both, carries with it the same potential. There is no doubt that use of conventional narrative form to report on past experience makes it easier to detect the presence of accessible, personally relevant memories from early in life. However, its unavailability should not be taken as evidence of the absence of such memories (see Bauer 1993 for further discussion). Determination of whether accomplishment of the narrative form is indicative of a new type of memory, or whether it signals the development of a convention for reporting memories, awaits establishment of clear criteria for differentiating episodic memory, which is evident by late in the first year of life, from autobiographical or personal memory.

Notes

1. Given the results reported in the next section, it seems likely that this failure has more to do with young children's lack of comprehension of the function of reminiscence/than with the efficacy of verbal information as an aid to memory.
2. A number of other explanations for the offset of infantile amnesia and the onset of autobiographical memory recently have been advanced. Discussion of these alternative perspectives is beyond the scope of this chapter. The interested reader is referred to Howe and Courage (1993) for an account emphasizing the importance of self development, and to Perner and Ruffman (1995) for an account emphasizing the importance of autonoetic consciousness, or the awareness of having experienced remembered events.

References

Ashmead, D. & M. Perlmutter 1980. Infant memory in everyday life. In *New directions for child development: Children's memory*, M. Perlmutter (ed.), 1–16. San Francisco, CA: Jossey-Bass.

Bachevalier, J. 1990. Ontogenetic development of habit and memory formation in primates. In *The development and neural bases of higher cognitive functions*, A. Diamond (ed.), 457–77. New York: New York Academy of Science.

Bachevalier, J. 1992. Cortical versus limbic immaturity: Relationship to infantile amnesia. In *Developmental behavioral neuroscience; The Minnesota Symposia on Child Psychology, Vol. XVIV*, M. R. Gunnar & C. A. Nelson, 129–53. Hillsdale, NJ: Erlbaum.

Bachevalier, J., M. Brickson, & C. Hagger 1993. Limbic-dependent recognition memory in monkeys develops early in infancy. *Neuroreport* **4**, 77–80.

Bachevalier, J. & M. Mishkin 1994. Effects of selective neonatal temporal lobe lesions on visual recognition memory in rhesus monkeys. *Journal of Neuroscience* **14**, 2128–39.

Bauer, P. J. 1992. Holding it all together: How enabling relations facilitate young children's event recall. *Cognitive Development* **7**, 1–28.

Bauer, P. J. 1993. Identifying subsystems of autobiographical memory: Commentary on Nelson. In *Memory and affect in development; Minnesota Symposia on Child Psychology, Vol. XXVI*, C. A. Nelson (ed.), 25–37. Hillsdale, NJ: Erlbaum.

Bauer, P. J. 1995a. *From the mouths of babes: The transition from nonverbal to verbal expression of memory*. Paper presented to the American Psychological Society, New York.

Bauer, P. J. 1995b. Recalling past events: From infancy to early childhood. *Annals of Child Development*, **11**, 25–71.

Bauer, P. J. & G. A. A. Dow 1994. Episodic memory in 16- and 20-month-old children: Specifics are generalized, but not forgotten. *Developmental Psychology* **30**, 403–17.

Bauer, P. J. & R. Fivush 1992. Constructing event representations: Building on a foundation of variation and enabling relations. *Cognitive Development* **7**, 381–401.

Bauer, P. J. & L. A. Hertsgaard 1993. Increasing steps in recall of events: Factors facilitating immediate and long-term memory in 13.5- and 16.5-month-old children. *Child Development* **64**, 1204–23.

Bauer, P. J., L. A. Hertsgaard, & G. A. Dow 1994. After 8 months have passed: Long-term recall of events by 1- to 2-year-old children. *Memory* **2**, 353–82.

Bauer, P. J., L. A. Hertsgaard, & S. S. Wewerka 1995. Effects of experience and reminding on long-term recall in infancy: Remembering not to forget. *Journal of Experimental Child Psychology* **59**, 260–98.

Bauer, P. J. & J. M. Mandler 1989. One thing follows another: Effects of temporal structure on 1- to 2-year-olds' recall of events. *Developmental Psychology* **25**, 197–206.

Bauer, P. J. & J. M. Mandler 1992. Putting the horse before the cart: The use of temporal order in recall of events by one-year-old children. *Developmental Psychology* **28**, 441–52.

Bauer, P. J. & C. M. Shore 1987. Making a memorable event: Effects of familiarity and organization on young children's recall of action sequences. *Cognitive Development* **2**, 327–38.

Bauer, P. J. & D. J. Thal 1990. Scripts or scraps: Reconsidering the development of sequential understanding. *Journal of Experimental Child Psychology* **50**, 287–304.

Bauer, P. J. & L. L. Travis 1993. The fabric of an event: Different sources of temporal invariance differentially affect 24-month-olds' recall. *Cognitive Development* **8**, 319–41.

Bauer, P. J. & S. S. Wewerka 1995. One- to two-year-olds' recall of events: The more expressed, the more impressed. *Journal of Experimental Child Psychology* **59**, 475–96.

Bauer, P. J. & S. S. Wewerka 1997. Saying is revealing: Verbal expression of event memory in the transition from infancy to early childhood. In *Developmental spans in event comprehension and representation: Bridging fictional and actual events*, P. van den Broek, P. J. Bauer, & T. Bourg (eds.). Hillsdale, NJ: Erlbaum.

Bower, G. H. 1981. Mood and memory. *American Psychologist* **36**, 129–48.

Brewer, W. F. 1986. What is autobiographical memory? In *Autobiographical memory*, D. C. Rubin (ed.), 25–49. New York: Cambridge University Press.

Carver, L. J. 1995. *A mosaic of nine-month-olds' memories: Looking time, ERP, and elicited imitation measures.* Poster presented to the Society for Research in Child Development, Indianapolis, IN.

Cohen, N. J. & L. R. Squire 1980. Preserved learning and retention of pattern analyzing skill in amnesia: Dissociation of knowing how and knowing that. *Science* **210**, 207–9.

DeCasper, A. J. & M. J. Spence 1986. Prenatal maternal speech influences newborns' perceptions of speech sounds. *Infant Behavior and Development* **9**, 133–50.

DeLoache, J. S. 1984. Oh where, oh where: Memory-based searching by very young children. In *Origins of cognitive skills*, C. Sophian (ed.), 57–80. Hillsdale, NJ: Erlbaum.

Diamond, A. 1990. Rate of maturation of hippocampus and the development of progression of children's performance on the delayed non-matching to sample and visual paired comparison tasks. In *The development and neural bases of higher cognitive functions*, A. Diamond (ed.), 394–426. New York: New York Academy of Science.

Eisenberg, A. R. 1985. Learning to describe past experiences in conversation. *Discourse Processes* **8**, 177–204.

Fagan, J. F. 1990. The paired-comparison paradigm and infant intelligence. In *The development and neural bases of higher cognitive functions*, A. Diamond (ed.), 337–64. New York: New York Academy of Science.

Fenson, L., P. S. Dale, J. S. Reznick, E. Bates, D. J. Thal, & S. J. Pethick 1994. Variability in early communicative development. *Monographs of the Society for Research in Child Development*, **59**(5).

Fivush, R. 1984. Learning about school: The development of kindergartners' school scripts. *Child Development* **55**, 1697–709.

Fivush, R. 1988. The functions of event memory. In *Remembering reconsidered: Ecological and traditional approaches to the study of memory*, U. Neisser & E. Winograd (eds.), 277–82. New York: Cambridge University Press.

Fivush, R. 1991. The social construction of personal narratives. *Merrill-Palmer Quarterly* **37**, 59–81.

Fivush, R., J. T. Gray, & F. A. Fromhoff 1987. Two-year-olds talk about the past. *Cognitive Development* **2**, 393–410.

Fivush, R. & N. R. Hamond 1989. Time and again: Effects of repetition and retention interval on 2-year-olds' event recall. *Journal of Experimental Child Psychology* **47**, 259–73.

Fivush, R. & N. R. Hamond 1990. Autobiographical memory across the preschool years: Toward reconceptualizing childhood amnesia. In *Knowing and remembering in young children*, R. Fivush & J. A. Hudson (eds.), 223–48. New York: Cambridge University Press.

Fivush, R., J. A. Hudson, & K. Nelson 1984. Children's long-term memory for a novel event: An exploratory study. *Merrill-Palmer Quarterly* **30**, 303–16.

Fivush, R., J. Kuebli, & P. A. Clubb 1992. The structure of events and event representations: A developmental analysis. *Child Development* **63**, 188–201.

Freud, S. 1905/1953. Three essays on the theory of sexuality. In *The standard edition of the complete psychological works of Sigmund Freud, Vol. VII*, J. Strachey (ed.), 135–243. London: Hogarth.

Freud, S. 1916/1966. *Introductory lectures on psychoanalysis*. Translated and edited by J. Strachey. New York: Norton.

Goodman, G. S., L. Rudy, B. L. Bottoms, & C. Aman 1990. Children's concerns and memory: Issues of ecological validity in the study of children's eyewitness testimony. In *Knowing and remembering in young children*, R. Fivush & J. A. Hudson (eds.), 249–84. New York: Cambridge University Press.

Graf, P., L. R. Squire, & G. Mandler 1984. The information that amnesic patients do not forget. *Journal of Experimental Psychology: Learning, Memory, and Cognition* **10**, 164–78.

Greco, C., C. Rovee-Collier, H. Hayne, P. Griesler, & L. Earley 1986. Ontogeny of early event memory: I. Forgetting and retrieval by 2- and 3-month-olds. *Infant Behavior and Development* **9**, 441–60.

Hamond, N. R. & R. Fivush 1991. Memories of Mickey Mouse: Young children recount their trip to Disneyworld. *Cognitive Development* **6**, 433–48.

Hill, W. L., D. Borovsky, & C. Rovee-Collier 1988. Continuities in infant memory development. *Developmental Psychobiology* **21**, 43–62.

Howe, M. A. & M. L. Courage 1993. On resolving the enigma of infantile amnesia. *Psychological Bulletin* **113**, 305–26.

Hudson, J. A. 1986. Memories are made of this: General event knowledge and development of autobiographic memory. In *Event knowledge: Structure and function in development*, K. Nelson (ed.), 97–118. Hillsdale, NJ: Erlbaum.

Hudson, J. A. 1990. Constructive processing in children's event memory. *Developmental Psychology* **26**, 180–7.

Hudson, J. A. 1991. Learning to reminisce: A case study. *Journal of Narrative and Life History* **1**, 295–324.

Hudson, J. A. 1993. Reminiscing with mothers and others: Autobiographical memory in young two-year-olds. *Journal of Narrative and Life History* **3**, 1–32.

Hudson, J. A. & R. Fivush 1991. As time goes by: Sixth graders remember a kindergarten experience. *Applied Cognitive Psychology* **5**, 346–60.

Hudson, J. A. & K. Nelson 1986. Repeated encounters of a similar kind: Effects of familiarity on children's autobiographical memory. *Cognitive Development* **1**, 253–71.

Hudson, J. A. & E. Sheffield 1995. *Extending young children's event memory: Effects of reminders on 16- to 24-month-olds' long-term recall*. Paper presented to the American Psychological Society, New York.

Jackson, A. & J. Morton 1984. Facilitation of auditory word recognition. *Memory and Cognition* **12**, 568–74.

Mandler, J. M. 1984. Representation and recall in infancy. In *Infant memory: Its relation to normal and pathological memory in humans and other animals*, M. Moscovitch (ed.), 75–101. New York: Plenum.

Mandler, J. M. 1986. The development of event memory. In *Human memory and cognitive capabilities: Mechanisms and performance*, F. Klix & H. Hagendorf (eds.), 459–67. New York: Elsevier Science.

Mandler, J. M. 1988. How to build a baby: On the development of an accessible representational system. *Cognitive Development* **3**, 113–36.

Mandler, J. M. 1990. Recall of events by preverbal children. In *The development and neural bases of higher cognitive functions*, A. Diamond (ed.), 485–516. New York: New York Academy of Science.

Mandler, J. M. 1997. Representation. In *Cognition, perception, and language*, D. Kuhn & R. Siegler (eds.), *Vol. II* of the *Handbook of Child Psychology*, W. Damon (ed.).

Mandler, J. M. & L. McDonough 1995. Long-term recall of event sequences in infancy. *Journal of Experimental Child Psychology* **59**, 457–74.

McDonough, L. 1991. *Infant recall of familiar actions with de-contextualized objects.* Poster presented to the Society for Research in Child Development, Seattle, WA.

McDonough, L. & J. M. Mandler 1994. Very long-term recall in infants: Infantile amnesia reconsidered. *Memory* **2**, 339–52.

McDonough, L., J. M. Mandler, R. D. McKee, & L. R. Squire 1995. The deferred imitation task as a nonverbal measure of declarative memory. *Proceedings of the National Academy of Sciences* **92**, 7580–84.

Meltzoff, A. N. 1988a. Infant imitation after a 1-week delay: Long-term memory for novel acts and multiple stimuli. *Developmental Psychology* **24**, 470–6.

Meltzoff, A. N. 1988b. Infant imitation and memory: Nine-month-olds in immediate and deferred tests. *Child Development* **59**, 217–25.

Meltzoff, A. N. 1988c. Imitation of televised models by infants. *Child Development* **59**, 1221–9.

Meltzoff, A. N. 1990. The implications of cross-modal matching and imitation for the development of representation and memory in infants. In *The development and neural bases of higher cognitive functions*, A. Diamond (ed.), 1–37. New York: New York Academy of Science.

Meltzoff, A. N. 1995. What infant memory tells us about infantile amnesia: Long-term recall and deferred imitation. *Journal of Experimental Child Psychology* **59**, 497–515.

Mishkin, M. & T. Appenzeller 1987. The anatomy of memory. *Scientific American* **256**, 80–9.

Myers, N. A., R. K. Clifton, & M. G. Clarkson 1987. When they were very young: Almost-threes remember two years ago. *Infant Behavior and Development* **10**, 123–32.

Myers, N. A., E. E. Perris, & C. J. Speaker 1994. Fifty months of memory: A longitudinal study in early childhood. *Memory* **2**, 383–415.

Neisser, U. 1962. Cultural and cognitive discontinuity. In *Anthropology and human behavior*, T. E. Gladwin & W. Sturtevant (eds.), 54–71. Washington, DC: Anthropological Society of Washington.

Neisser, U. 1967. *Cognitive psychology.* Englewood Cliffs, NJ: Prentice-Hall.

Neisser, U. 1988. Five kinds of self-knowledge. *Philosophical Psychology* **1**, 35–59.

Nelson, C. A. 1995. The ontogeny of human memory: A cognitive neuroscience perspective. *Developmental Psychology* **31**, 723–38.

Nelson, K. 1986. *Event knowledge: Structure and function in development.* Hillsdale,

NJ: Erlbaum.

Nelson, K. 1988. The ontogeny of memory for real events. In *Remembering reconsidered: Ecological and traditional approaches to the study of memory*, U. Neisser & E. Winograd (eds.), 244–276. New York: Cambridge University Press.

Nelson, K. 1993. Events, narratives, memory: What develops? In *Memory and affect in development; Minnesota Symposia on Child Psychology, Vol. XXVI*, C. A. Nelson (ed.), 1–24. Hillsdale, NJ: Erlbaum.

Nelson, K. & J. Gruendel 1981. Generalized event representations: Basic building blocks of cognitive development. In *Advances in developmental psychology, Vol. I*, M. E. Lamb & A. L. Brown (eds.), 131–58. Hillsdale, NJ: Erlbaum.

Nelson, K. & J. Gruendel 1986. Children's scripts. In *Event knowledge: Structure and function in development*, K. Nelson (ed.), 21–46. Hillsdale, NJ: Erlbaum.

Nelson, K. & G. Ross 1980. The generalities and specifics of long-term memory in infants and young children. In *New directions for child development – children's memory*, M. Perlmutter (ed.), 87–101. San Francisco, CA: Jossey-Bass.

Perner, J. & T. Ruffman 1995. Episodic memory and autonoetic consciousness: Developmental evidence and a theory of childhood amnesia. *Journal of Experimental Child Psychology* **59**, 516–48.

Peterson, C. & A. McCabe 1992. Parental styles of narrative elicitation: Effect on children's narrative structure and content. *First Language* **12**, 299–321.

Piaget, J. 1952. *The origins of intelligence in children*. New York: International Universities Press.

Piaget, J. 1954. *The construction of reality in the child*. New York: Basic Books.

Pillemer, D. B. & S. H. White 1989. Childhood events recalled by children and adults. In *Advances in child development and behavior, Vol. XXI*, H. W. Reese (ed.), 297–340. San Diego, CA: Academic.

Price, D. W. W. & G. S. Goodman 1990. Visiting the wizard: Children's memory for a recurring event. *Child Development* **61**, 664–80.

Ratner, H. H. 1980. The role of social context in memory development. In *New directions for child development – children's memory*, M. Perlmutter (ed.), 49–67. San Francisco, CA: Jossey-Bass.

Ratner, H. H., B. S. Smith, & S. Dion 1986. Development of memory for events. *Journal of Experimental Child Psychology* **41**, 411–28.

Roediger, H. L. & T. A. Blaxton 1987. Effects of varying modality, surface features, and retention interval on priming in word-fragment completion. *Memory and Cognition* **15**, 379–88.

Rovee-Collier, C. K. & J. W. Fagen 1981. The retrieval of memory in early infancy. In *Advances in infancy research, Vol. I*, L. P. Lipsitt (ed.). Norwood, NJ: Ablex.

Rovee-Collier, C. K. & G. C. W. Shyi 1992. A functional and cognitive analysis of infant long-term retention. In *The development of long-term retention*, C. J. Brainerd, M. L. Howe, & V. F. Reyna (eds.), 3–55. New York: Springer-Verlag.

Rubin, D. C. 1982. On the retention function for autobiographical memory. *Journal of Verbal Learning and Verbal Behavior* **21**, 21–38.

Sachs, J. 1983. Talking about the there and then: The emergence of displaced reference in parent–child discourse. In *Children's language, Vol. IV*, K. Nelson (ed.), 1–27. New York: Gardner.

Schachtel, E. 1947. On memory and childhood amnesia. *Psychiatry* **10**, 1–26.

Schacter, D. L. 1987. Implicit memory: History and current status. *Journal of Experi-*

mental *Psychology: Learning, Memory, and Cognition* **13**, 501–18.

Schacter, D. L. 1990. Perceptual representation systems and implicit memory. In *The development and neural bases of higher cognitive functions*, A. Diamond (ed.), 543–67. New York: New York Academy of Science.

Schacter, D. L. & M. Moscovitch 1984. Infants, amnesics, and dissociable memory systems. In *Infant memory: Its relation to normal and pathological memory in humans and other animals*, M. Moscovitch (ed.), 173–216. New York: Plenum.

Sheffield, E. G. & J. A. Hudson 1994. Reactivation of toddlers' event memory. *Memory* **2**, 447–65.

Sheingold, K. & Y. J. Tenney 1982. Memory for a salient childhood event. In *Memory observed*, U. Neisser (ed.), 201–12. San Francisco, CA: Freeman.

Sherry, F. & D. L. Schacter 1987. The evolution of multiple memory systems. *Psychological Review* **94**, 439–54.

Slackman, E. A., J. A. Hudson, & R. Fivush 1986. Actions, actors, links, and goals: The structure of children's event representations. In *Event knowledge: Structure and function in development*, K. Nelson (ed.), 47–69. Hillsdale, NJ: Erlbaum.

Slackman, E. A. & K. Nelson 1984. Acquisition of an unfamiliar script in story form by young children. *Child Development* **55**, 329–40.

Slater, A. 1995. Visual perception and memory at birth. In *Advances in infancy research, Vol. IX*, C. Rovee-Collier & L. P. Lipsitt (eds.), 107–62. Norwood, NJ: Ablex.

Smith, B. S., H. H. Ratner, & C. J. Hobart 1987. The role of cueing and organization in children's memory for events. *Journal of Experimental Child Psychology* **4**, 1–24.

Spear, N. E. 1978. *The processing of memories: Forgetting and retention*. Hillsdale, NJ: Erlbaum.

Squire, L. R. 1992. Memory and the hippocampus: A synthesis from findings with rats, monkeys, and humans. *Psychological Review* **99**, 195–231.

Squire, L. R., B. Knowlton, & G. Musen 1993. The structure and organization of memory. *Annual Review of Psychology* **44**, 453–95.

Squire, L. R. & S. Zola-Morgan 1991. The medial temporal lobe memory system. *Science* **253**, 1380–6.

Todd, C. M. & M. Perlmutter 1980. Reality recalled by preschool children. In *New directions for child development: Children's memory*, M. Perlmutter (ed.), 69–85. San Francisco, CA: Jossey-Bass.

Tulving, E. 1985. How many memory systems are there? *American Psychologist* **40**, 385–98.

Usher, J. A. & U. Neisser 1993. Childhood amnesia and the beginnings of memory for four early life events. *Journal of Experimental Psychology: General* **122**, 155–65.

Wetzler, S. E. & J. A. Sweeney 1986. Childhood amnesia: A conceptualization in cognitive-psychological terms. *Journal of the American Psychoanalytic Association* **34**, 663–85.

White, S. H. & D. B. Pillemer 1979. Childhood amnesia and the development of a socially accessible memory system. In *Functional disorders of memory*, J. F. Kihlstrom & F. J. Evans (eds.), 29–73. Hillsdale, NJ: Erlbaum.

Winograd, E. & W. A. Killinger, Jr. 1983. Relating age at encoding in early childhood to adult recall: Development of flashbulb memories. *Journal of Experimental Psychology: General* **112**, 413–22.

Zola-Morgan, S. & L. R. Squire 1990. The primate hippocampal formation: Evidence for a time-limited role in memory storage. *Science* **250**, 288–90.

Zola-Morgan, S. & L. R. Squire 1993. Neuroanatomy of memory. *Annual Review of Neuroscience* **16**, 547–63.

Acknowledgements

Preparation of this chapter was supported by a NICHD First Independent Research Support and Transition (FIRST) award (HD28425). Address correspondence to Patricia J. Bauer, Institute of Child Development, 51 East River Road, University of Minnesota, Minneapolis, MN 55455–0345, or to pbauer@maroon.tc.umn.edu.

CHAPTER 5

The development of procedural and declarative memory

Alan J. Parkin

One of the problems that has plagued recent research on human memory is the parallel existence of different taxonomic systems for the classification of memory phenomena. This chapter is ostensibly about the development of declarative and procedural memory – memory systems that are respectively characterized as accessible or not accessible to consciousness. However, to restrict myself simply to studies using that terminology would avoid most of the relevant literature. Thus this chapter cannot get off the ground unless I first discuss what I take to mean by declarative and procedural memory and how my use of these terms relates to other overlapping systems of classification such as that of episodic and semantic memory.

Episodic, semantic, and procedural memory

Tulving has made a seminal distinction between episodic and semantic memory in which a division is drawn between memory for personal events and general knowledge about the world. Remembering what one did last night was a test of episodic memory whereas knowing that Lima was the capital of Peru addressed semantic memory. Later a third category, procedural memory, was added. This form of memory was contrasted with episodic and semantic memory in that its contents were not consciously accessible – a typical example being the knowledge we possess to carry out skills such as riding a bicycle or typing a letter. Later Tulving developed this tripartite approach to memory organization by associating each form of memory with a different state of conscious experience. Procedural memory was considered divorced from any conscious accompaniment and termed "anoetic," semantic memory described as "noetic" so as to reflect a basic feeling of assuredness, and episodic memory as "autonoetic" or self-knowing (e.g. Tulving 1985, 1995).

Although the distinction between episodic and semantic memory is most frequently explained as a distinction between event and fact memory, this fails to emphasize an important point about how events themselves might be remembered. An event in one's life can be remembered because the retrieval of that event is accompanied by a degree of recollective experience (most typically reported as associated imagery) which serves give memory for that event authenticity – i.e. an event is "recognized as something formerly experienced" (Tulving 1985: 3). It is this type of experience that Tulving views as genuine episodic or autonoetic remembering. In contrast, memory for an event can be achieved without any full-blown recollection and this type of memory is assumed to arise from part of semantic memory that contains knowledge about oneself – here individuals are aware that an event has happened to them but this is not, contemporaneously, associated with experiential awareness of the event itself.

Tulving (1985) suggested a paradigm within which noetic and autonoetic forms of remembering might be distinguished. Subjects were presented with individual words and then asked to remember them either under free recall instructions or in the presence of semantic cues. On recall, subjects had also to classify each item into either the "remember" (R) or "know" (K) category. These categories were co-extensive with Tulving's notions of autonoetic and noetic remembering. Thus an R response would accompany recognition associated with specific event recollection while K was used to describe items recognized on the basis of general item familiarity. Subjects were able to make this distinction effectively and it was found that virtually all items produced under free recall were classed as R whereas a good proportion of items produced under cued recall conditions were classed as K. This finding, which we will return to later, suggests that the greater an individual's free recall relative to their cued recall, the more episodic information they have available.

Declarative memory

So far the case for Tulving's three-way classification of memory phenomena would appear to have strong support. However, there have been objections made to the episodic–semantic distinction. Tulving evolved his organizational theory at a time when neuropsychological data were beginning to have their first major impact on cognitive psychology. The study of amnesic patients had already provided all the proof needed to accept the distinction between short-term and long-term store and initial observations also suggested that the characteristics of amnesia provided strong evidence for the existence of three separable forms of memory (Parkin 1996a, b). Thus amnesic patients were observed to have intact procedural learning evidenced by preserved abilities such as musical skills, and intact semantic memory as shown by their normal performance on tests of verbal and nonverbal intelligence. In contrast these patients had immense difficulties in recalling events from both the post-illness and, in varying degrees, from the pre-illness periods of their lives (usually termed anterograde and retrograde amnesia respectively).

Problems arose, however, when the amnesic evidence was scrutinized in more detail. As noted, amnesic patients invariably exhibit some retrograde amnesia and examination of this indicated that the loss reflected both episodic and semantic memories. Thus not only would patients exhibit poor performance on tests of autobiographical memory, but also they would, in parallel, perform badly on tests of general knowledge about the same time periods: accounts of their personal life would, in Tulving's terms, be bereft of both autonoetic and noetic types of recollection. Preserved language function as support for the selective preservation of semantic memory was seen as spurious and attributed to the fact that language tests assess early acquired knowledge. As it is well known that early memories are more resistant to brain insult, the sparing of language could merely reflect the same preservation that is also seen for early events (Parkin 1996b). Indeed, when studies have examined the ability of amnesic patients to define words introduced at later stages in life they showed a pronounced memory deficit (Verafaellie & Roth 1996).

These difficulties led to the view that the distinction between episodic and semantic memory is not such a clear-cut one. Rather these two forms of memory should be subsumed under the term declarative memory, in which the defining feature is a memory accessible to conscious inspection (Squire 1987). An important point here is that the episodic and semantic memory distinction is not abandoned but, instead, it is proposed that these forms of memory are two qualitatively different expressions of the same system. More specifically, episodic memory can be seen as some record of the particular pattern of semantic memory activation at any point in time – just as the "black-box" flight recorder contains a moment-by-moment account of the state of an aircraft's control system. In contrast, procedural memory represents a separable form of memory whose contents are not consciously addressable.

Explicit and implicit memory

Before moving to the main subject matter one further classification system must be considered. Only a psychological version of Rip Van Winkle could have overlooked the distinction between explicit and implicit memory. Briefly, disquiet over the systems approach led some to consider a task-based approach to memory in which paradigms were classified as either demanding recollection of a previous event (explicit) or not requiring this recollection (implicit) – in the latter case it is important to note that an implicit task merely lacks any demand on recollection; it does not exclude a potential role for explicit remembering (Schacter 1987).

Perhaps the only incontrovertible test of explicit memory is free recall, but implicit memory has many means of assessment. Most widely used are tests of perceptual learning such as picture completion and verbal priming. In the former subjects are, for example, exposed to a degraded picture which is systematically made more informative until identification occurs. The task is then repeated and subjects' ability to identify previously exposed pictures compared with novel pictures is measured. Any savings in rate of identification for the previously exposed pictures is considered an expression of implicit memory. In a verbal priming task subjects are exposed to target words (e.g. MATERIAL) and then given word puzzles to solve. These may take the form of a fragment completion test – what word can you make by filling in the blanks _AT_RI_L – or a stem completion task – what is the first word that "pops" into your mind beginning with MAT___? In both of these tasks production of the target word at a level above baseline is considered a measure of implicit memory.

Although task-based we must consider how this distinction maps on to our declarative–procedural dichotomy. Explicit memory falls neatly into the declarative category but the allocation of implicit memory phenomena is less clear cut. Some tests of procedural memory meet the criterion of implicit quite readily simply because conscious recollection cannot, by the very nature of the learning taking place, play anything but a peripheral role. Consider the widely used pursuit rotor task in which, across successive trials, an individual must learn to keep a light beam on a dot tracing an erratic circular path. Learning occurs on this task but what is being learned cannot be articulated in any way. It is for this reason that amnesic patients, in whom effective recollective experience is essentially zero, can learn this task as effectively as normal people.

A similar situation occurs in studies that contrast explicit recognition of stimuli with subjects' autonomic responses to those stimuli. Within the neuropsychological literature it is well established that patients with an impairment in recognizing familiar faces (prosopagnosia) will nonetheless indicate recognition of those faces when measures of skin conductance are taken. Thus for once-familiar faces there will be higher levels of skin conductance than for novel faces (Bauer 1984).

However, as we noted earlier, implicit memory tasks are classified as such because they do not demand rather than preclude conscious recollection of previous learning event. This allows the possibility that recollection *may* play a role in implicit task performance, thus making it difficult to define the form of memory being tested. Some skills, for example, may take time to become truly implicit because, during the early stages of acquisition, they are mediated by explicit recollections. As a young cricketer I remember being told that my bowling would always be better if my right arm brushed my ear on delivery. For a time I consciously recollected this advice as I came in to bowl. However, with practice this recollection was no longer needed. In fact is now clear that, once a skill is properly acquired, attempts to mediate it by previously beneficial explicit influences are detrimental.

Providing skills are strongly acquired there seems little difficulty in equating these procedural memories as examples of implicit remembering. But what of the other implicit measures more commonly used in experimental studies? In both perceptual learning and verbal priming one can make a plausible case that the information mediating the implicit memory response is not consciously accessible. This is most evident in perceptual learning of the type described earlier where the information underlying savings is not easily verbalized. Further, it is not difficult to extend this argument to the underlying knowledge that mediates simple priming effects – indeed recent theoretical accounts of priming, such as Schacter's Perceptual Representation System (Schacter & Tulving 1994) or Hayman and Tulving's (1989) Quasi-Memory System, propose low-level mechanisms which would preclude conscious access (see below).

The problem with implicit measures such as verbal priming and picture completion is that they can potentially be contaminated by explicit influences. In both cases a subject's recollection of the original learning event could facilitate performance by constraining response options – thus completion of a fragment might be aided by recollection of the solution from the learning phase. This issue has proved a major problem for memory investigators but it is not an insuperable one. In a study I carried out with Riccardo Russo using picture completion (Russo & Parkin 1993), we found an apparent deterioration in the implicit memory of elderly subjects. However, using parallel measures of explicit memory, we showed that this age effect was wholly due to elderly subjects making less use of their explicit memory of the learning episode. Thus the equation of implicit tasks such as perceptual learning and verbal priming with procedural memory can be made only if explicit influences on performance are ruled out.

Another point that must be stressed is that procedural memory cannot be thought of as a single entity.[1] Thus the memory systems responsible for performing tasks such as verbal priming and picture completion may have little or no overlap. Indeed studies that have attempted to examine relationships between different forms of procedural memory have shown no association (Witherspoon & Moscovitch 1989). Rather, procedural memory must be considered as an umbrella term encompassing different forms of memory all sharing the property of being inaccessible to consciousness but otherwise functionally distinct.

Finally how does the concept of semantic memory cut across the implicit–explicit distinction? Answering a question such as, "Is a banana yellow?" seems to meet the criterion of implicit, as I certainly do not need access to a specific event in order to answer. However, I feel uncomfortable in equating this form of remembering with other implicit measures because there is a more general attachment with the past – I am aware that my past experience is the basis of my answer even though I am not dependent on a specific event. This contrasts with the production of a genuine implicit response in, for example, a verbal priming experiment, in which the whole point is that performance is thought, subjectively, to be purely a current event unmediated by past experience. I am thus inclined to consider semantic memory as essentially explicit in that information retrieved as such has an inherent attachment to the past which imbues within it the certainty needed for effective utilization.

117

Components of declarative and procedural memory

The above discussion has proceeded to a point where I feel able to use the terms declarative and procedural memory reasonably unambiguously in relation to other taxonomies of the memory system. Doubtless there will be those who disagree with some of what I propose but the system I have outlined in Figure 5.1 does enable me to impose a single classification structure on a literature and to define how different classes of memory paradigm are organized within it.

Focus

In considering the focus of this chapter I was confronted with a potentially vast literature. Declarative memory, as defined, technically covers all consciously accessible knowledge. Procedural memory is also a sizeable topic embracing as it does the acquisition of motor skills and other areas that I have not touched on such as conditioned responding. Moreover, writers such as Karmiloff-Smith (1992) have made extensive reference to the concept of procedural memory in cognitive development, particularly with regards to the emergence of language. To provide a manageable focus I have restricted myself to studies in which there has been a direct comparison of procedural and declarative memory for the same material and those in which there has been an attempt to characterize qualitative changes in the nature of declarative memory. Within these high constraints I nonetheless hope to provide an account of an area of high potential interest within cognitive development.

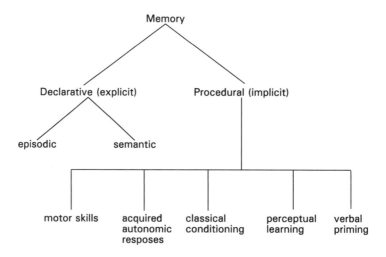

Figure 5.1 A proposed taxonomy of the memory system.

The development of procedural memory

In contrast to the vast literature on adults the amount of data concerning the development of procedural memory in early life is remarkably small. Carroll et al. (1985) are accredited with the first investigation in which they first asked children ranging from 5 to 10 years and adults to name a series of pictures. Subsequently the pictures were re-presented and both naming latency and recognition were measured. Predictably, recognition memory improved with age but the facilitation of naming was equal across all age groups, thus suggesting that this form of procedural memory was stable. However, as Naito and Komatsu (1993) have pointed out, there are a number of methodological reservations about this study which make the results somewhat inconclusive concerning the developmental course of procedural memory.

In a study I carried out with Sarah Streete (Parkin & Streete 1988) we first exposed 3-, 5- and 7-year-old children plus adults to the series of degraded pictures designed by Snodgrass et al. (1987): See Figure 5.2. Subjects were required to name each picture and, if they failed, successively more informative versions were presented until identification was achieved. Retention was tested by re-presenting the pictures and measuring the degree of savings in renaming the pictures successfully. Subjects were also given a test of their ability to recollect seeing the pictures. In our original paper we reported that the absolute amount of savings increased with age but, when savings was recalculated as a proportion of original learning, the amount of savings appeared age invariant.

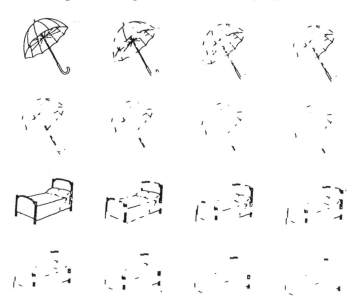

Figure 5.2 Examples of fragmented pictures used by Parkin and Streete (1988) and the subsequent study by Russo et al. (1995).

We treated this view with caution and I presented a subsequent reanalysis of these findings using the formula recommended by Snodgrass (1989) for calculating savings (Parkin 1993). In this analysis allowance is made for the different baseline performance levels of the age groups. Almost inevitably older children produce higher baseline performance and thus have less potential to show priming effects. The Snodgrass formula allows for this and calculations using it then indicated a clear developmental trend. However, we were unable to conclude that this reflected purely procedural memory because there was also an age-related improvement in recollection of the study phase. When savings were analyzed as a function of whether or not a picture could be recognized it was found that savings scores were much better for recognized pictures except in the youngest group, where recognition was at chance. Because the youngest group showed good levels of savings we can minimally conclude that procedural memory is effective before recollective memory for the same information is occurring. But the data are silent as to the developmental of procedural memory because the upward trend observed could reflect contamination arising from recollection of the study episode.

Two other earlier studies have appeared to show age invariance in procedural memory abilities. Greenbaum and Graf (1989) showed 3- and 5-year-old children sets of line drawings of objects usually seen in a particular location such as a zoo. The children were asked to name and then remember them. Immediately afterwards they heard a short story about going to one of the locations and were asked what they might typically find there. Priming effects were measured by comparing the probability of giving a response from the learning phase with a baseline condition. In addition, children's recall of the pictures was measured. As age increased so did the amount of words produced on the word production task. However, the extent of priming, measured in proportional terms, did not change significantly with age. This contrasted with the recall measure, which showed the expected age-related increase in performance. This study again suggests age invariance of procedural memory but the absence of an adult group precludes a firm conclusion on this point.

Naito (1990) required three groups of children (6, 8, and 11 years) plus adults to answer either a physical or elaborative question about a series of words. Either a word completion test or free recall test for the words followed. Regardless of age group there was a reliable priming effect and, even though the absolute amounts of word completion increased with age, the degree of priming, in proportional terms, remained the same. One must note, however, that what trends exist are upward. Recall did increase with age, with the effects being most apparent with elaborative encoding.

Russo et al. (1995) addressed the inconclusive results of Parkin and Streete (1988) by repeating the same type of study but incorporating additional design elements that enabled the contaminating effects of explicit memory to be partialled out of the priming measure (Russo & Parkin 1993). Using this procedure it was found that no age differences in priming between children of different ages and adults were found when analysis was restricted to those picture sequences which subjects could not recall from the original learning episode. Moreover it should be noted that Russo et al. used the scoring procedure recommended by Snodgrass rather than a simple proportional savings score.

Drummey and Newcombe (1995) have also recently examined a paradigm (testing procedure) similar to that used by Parkin and Streete. Pictures were exposed in a more naturalistic setting using a technique in which the target items were gradually deblurred. Priming was measured by examining the extent to which pictures could be recognized in a more blurred form on subsequent testing. Recognition of the items was tested by exposing fully focused versions of the pictures and requiring their discrimination from novel items. As expected, there was an age effect in recognition but the priming data were somewhat more complex to interpret. First, all groups showed a significant priming effect – this included a group of 3-year-olds tested after 3 months and whose recognition ability was not above chance. The priming data were analyzed using the Snodgrass correction and produced a strange outcome. Priming appeared to increase from 3 to 5 years and then decline in the adult group. On the basis of the authors' statistics the only reliable difference is a decline in priming between 5 years and adulthood. However, with an average increase in priming of 48 per cent between 3 and 5 years one cannot comfortably assume no developmental trend in childhood. In this connection it is unfortunate that the authors do not report the same type of analysis as Russo et al., in which priming effects for recognized and non-recognized items are reported separately.

Lorsbach and Morris (1991) examined the ability of second and sixth grade children on a task in which subjects were first asked to name pictures as quickly as possible. On the next day the test was repeated and, following naming, subjects indicated whether or not they had seen the picture before. Priming was assessed by comparing naming latency for the previously exposed pictures with that for new pictures. An age effect was found on recognition but there was no statistically reliable difference in the degree of naming facilitation as a function of age. However, this conclusion warrants comment. Examination of the authors' Figure 5.1 shows that there is an obvious tendency for the younger children to show a *greater* priming effect than the older children – a finding reflected in an interaction between aging and priming that just misses conventional significance.

A similar type of study involving faces is reported by Ellis et al. (1993). In the first experiment children from three age groups (5, 8, and 11 years) initially viewed pictures of classmates and made decisions about expression or gender. In the next phase they were shown a sequence of faces and asked to decide as quickly as possible whether they knew the person or not. Half of the known faces had also been presented in the earlier orientation phase and it was found that all three groups of children showed priming in that recognition of previously exposed faces was faster than that for non-exposed familiar faces. This finding was then replicated in a similar design comparing only 5-year-olds and adults. In both experiments there is a large effect of age on reaction times but no interaction between age and the extent of priming. As a result the authors conclude that the priming effect they observe is invariant with age.

Newcombe and Fox (1994) examined the abililty of 9- and 10-year-old children to recognize pictures of former classmates. Recognition levels, although not very good, were significantly above chance. Skin conductance data were also collected to assess the relation between autonomic responses and recognition. Increased skin conductance occurred to faces of previous classmates compared with controls. However, the extent of this autonomic responding was unrelated to whether children explicitly recognized the faces. These data thus indicate that the procedural memory system mediating autonomic responses to faces is independent of that governing explicit recognition (see also Newcombe & Lie 1995). A final study was recently reported by DiGuilio et al. (1994) using two measures of priming (identification of degraded words and a modification of Gollin's picture completion task) and measures of recall. Comparisons were made between children of 8 and 12 years of age and the typical pattern was found: No apparent age effect on the procedural measures despite reliable age-related improvements in recall.

Lorsbach and his colleagues have also contrasted procedural and declarative memory within a developmental framework. Their studies have explored both the performance of normal children and those with learning disabilities. Lorsbach and Worman (1989) compared third- and sixth-grade learning disabled (LD) children with similar age groups of normal (NLD) children on tests of picture recall and a picture completion task similar to that used by Parkin and Streete (1988). Predictably the NLD children were superior on recall measures but no group differences were found on the picture completion task. Lorsbach and Worman (1990) compared similar groups using a paired-associate learning paradigm and found an advantage for the NLD children on cued recall but no difference in a priming measure derived from the same procedure. In a further study Lorsbach et al. (1992) presented LD and NLD children with pictures or words and then measured memory in terms of picture recognition or speed of picture naming. LD children showed an advantage in recognition and were also better at remembering if a test item had originally been presented as a word or picture. But, contrary to their earlier studies, they found that the LD group showed greater evidence of priming compared to NLD children.

Organic amnesia in childhood

As noted earlier, studies of adult amnesics have indicated the selective preservation of procedural memory. It is therefore of interest to consider the development status of children who suffer from the same aetiologies that give rise to amnesia in adults. One of the most notable causes of human amnesia is herpes simplex encephalitis (HSE) and this illness is just as common in children as it is in adults. It is therefore surprising that so few instances of the associated memory disorder in children have been reported. Partly, this may reflect a different developmental course of the infection and the fact that the symptoms may be more widespread – "autism," for example, has been given as a diagnosis in a number of cases (see Parkin & Leng 1993). The only clear-cut case of amnesia in childhood following HSE is that of T. C. (Wood et al. 1989). T. C. contracted the illness at age 9 and as a result developed severe memory problems on tasks involving recall. Yet, as her education progressed, she managed to keep up with her peer group as assessed by WISC and graduated from high school. When reassessed at the age of 20, however, she could recall nothing of two complex figures she had just copied accurately and was unable to remember anything about a previously heard short story.

Ostergaard (1987) also reports a case of amnesia in childhood following cerebral oedema linked to near drowning. Patient C. C. showed severe deficits on tests of list and story recall, and memory for a complex picture. Impairments were also noted on tests of semantic memory including reading vocabulary, lexical decision, and verbal intelligence. However, on the Gollin (1960) pictures C. C. showed savings similar to controls for retention intervals of up to 8 days. C. C. was also asked to learn a computer game ("Thunderbirds") which involved the usual perceptual motor skills for these games (i.e., firing rockets, dodging bombs) and learning various rules about how different aliens would attack. Learning was again evaluated over an 8-day period and C. C. showed learning similar to controls.

Ostergaard's study thus shows the dissociation in memory performance typical of amnesic patients in a young patient with normal performance only found on tests of procedural memory. The case of Wood et al. (1989) is, however, problematic in that a child with an obviously severe anterograde amnesia nonetheless graduated from high school. This may not, however, be as puzzling as it seems. It is well established that the acquisition of English grammar is largely an implicit process and there is also evidence that the learning of arithmetic has a large and separable procedural component (Temple 1994). It is possible that success on these procedural elements, plus others that may have contributed to the assessment, enabled a reasonable level of success to be achieved. The latter point is one also stressed by Ostergaard and Squire (1990) in their critique of the Wood et al. case. In addition they also stress that T. C.'s anterograde learning ability was not total (e.g. she showed reasonable immediate recall on a standard clinical test) and that this residual ability may well have been sufficient to account for her scholastic achievements.

PARKIN

The developmental status of procedural memory

Although the number of studies is not great there is sufficient evidence to come to some conclusions about the developmental nature of procedural memory. What seems without doubt is that procedural memory is operative at an early point in development. Studies of picture completion in 3-year-olds have, for example, shown reliable priming of pictures at a point where recognition of those pictures is at chance. The functional independence of procedural memory is also indicated by studies showing that this memory ability can remain normal when declarative abilities fail to develop. An additional finding, supported by most of the published studies, is that procedural memory appears age invariant.

Perhaps the most important of the above conclusions is that procedural memory appears age invariant. If correct, this finding suggests that the form of memory underlying picture completion priming is somewhat primitive – perhaps comprising the priming of fundamental units of perceptual analysis (e.g. geons – Biederman & Gerhardstein 1993). This would be consistent with Schacter's recent PRS account of pictorial priming effects, which he explains in terms of a presemantic structural processing system that is insensitive to object identity – a concept he derives from recent conceptualizations of visual object agnosia (see Parkin 1996a for a recent review). A system like this, which might well be stabilized very early in development, thus predicts no developmental increment in picture completion priming even though the same developmental span might reflect sizeable increments in object knowledge.

It is also possible to conceive of verbal priming being mediated at a primitive and thus age invariant level. Hayman and Tulving (1989) presented a target word (e.g. CATERPILLAR) and priming was measured by examining subjects' fragment completion responses. Priming was measured twice for each target using different but equally hard fragments (e.g. _AT_R__LL__?; C__E_PI__AR ?). This manipulation examined whether priming of CATERPILLAR was mediated by activation of a word-specific representation. If correct, this would predict that the two different fragments, all other factors constant, should be equally effective in showing priming because the critical factor determining priming is the likelihood of the fragment making contact with the activated word representation.

Priming effects were observed but no correlation was found between the effectiveness of any two fragments addressing the same target word. It was therefore suggested that priming in fragment completion was not mediated by the activation of word-specific representations. Instead repetition priming was held to be mediated by a "traceless quasimemory" (QM) system where learning occurs not by the establishment of traces representing the original stimulus, but by changes that affect lower levels of the perceptual system such that, on representation, a word will be processed more efficiently than previously because a word comprising those elements has already been experi-

124

enced. Thus changes in the QM system do not record that a *particular* stimulus has been presented; rather they increase the probability or speed in responding to a type of stimulus when it reoccurs and it is this that facilitates priming. Since there is no reason to suppose that the two different fragments map equally on to the presumed alterations in the QM system, there is no basis for expecting them to be equally effective in the priming process.

The QM system is similar to the visual word form system proposed by Schacter (1994) to account for verbal priming effects. Derived from Warrington and Shallice (1980), this idea proposes that there is a system which represents information about the visual and orthographic form of words. It is held to be presemantic on the grounds that dissociations involving the ability to read words without being able to comprehend them can occur. Moreover, because of observations that priming of unfamiliar nonwords can occur it is argued that priming does not involve any word-specific representations.

So far the above theories are specifying the mediation of priming at a relatively low level, i.e. presemantic, and, as such, might seem nicely consistent with claims of age invariance. However, I would urge caution. The argument for age invariance, by its very nature, depends on accepting a null result as proof of a hypothesis. This is an uncomfortable way to argue and, in the case of the procedural memory data, we must be particularly careful. More specifically, the possibility that scoring artifacts underlie the lack of a developmental trend must be considered. This point is evident in the early study of Greenbaum and Graf (1989) in which the lack of an age effect in target production occurs in a performance range of between 1.3 and 1.8 (out of 6) in the youngest and oldest subjects respectively.

Earlier we considered the issue of scoring procedural memory using a correction which takes account of absolute differences in baseline performance, and hence the scope for different aged subjects to show priming. This correction was used by Drummey and Newcombe (1995) and, as noted above, their data appear to show an upward trend in perceptual memory. Naito's (1990) data also indicates a big increase in baseline performance, particularly when comparing children with adults, thus making it difficult to be sure that priming levels really are equivalent with age – acceptance of age invariance here would depend on a reanalysis along the lines suggested by Snodgrass. The study by Lorsbach and Morris (1991) indicates a pitfall of using latency data to assess procedural memory. You will recall that these authors reported greater priming in younger subjects, as measured by latency difference, but this is confounded by higher overall latencies in the younger group. Thus the appearance of a larger difference in the young subjects may simply reflect a scaling effect on reaction times and any conclusion about age invariance on the basis of these data is not possible. Similarly the age invariance found by Ellis et al. (1993) is confounded by large age effects on reaction time and here it is also possible that potentially greater priming effects in older subjects may have been masked by a ceiling on reaction time speeds. Finally, the study by DiGuilio et al. (1994) also confounds the lack of an age effect on priming with an overall age-based increase in performance – thus once again the lack of an age effect could simply reflect less opportunity for priming in the older children.

At present only the study by Russo et al. (1995) appears to give good evidence of age invariance in procedural memory. Theoretical positions based on the age invariance assumption would thus do well to await the outcome of future research.

The development of declarative memory

As noted earlier, the broad definition of declarative memory includes all that would be considered as consciously accessible knowledge. Thus to attempt a developmental review of this, *per se*, would be an enormous task. My aim is far smaller in that I will consider one specific area – the development of declarative memory from the perspective of noetic versus autonoetic modes of remembering which, as we saw earlier, can refer to qualitatively different forms of event memory.

Perner and Ruffman (1995) have provided data concerning the ontogeny of autonoetic memory. Briefly their hypothesis is that event memory in young children is initially based on a noetic form of remembering to which is added a subsequent stage of autonoetic remembering. Further they argue that the transition from noetic to autonoetic forms of remembering occurs around the same developmental time point as that delineating the period of infantile amnesia – this refers to the widespread observation that adults have great difficulty retrieving memories from before the age of around 4 years (Dudycha & Dudycha 1941). In addition they argue that the transition from noetic to autonoetic forms of remembering is not an isolated cognitive event but one that is more generally related to a child's emerging theory of mind. Thus autonoetic memory is co-extensive with a more advanced theory of mind.

Developing their idea Perner & Ruffman note:

> For instance, consider two ways in which one might retain the fact that the word "butter" was on a list. For merely *knowing* that there was a word "butter" on the list it is sufficient to represent the proposition there was the word butter on the list. In contrast, for an act of proper *remembering*, in the specific narrow sense, it is also necessary to represent the additional fact that *one has seen the word on the list and that, therefore, one knows that the word has appeared on the list*. (Perner & Ruffman 1995: 517)

The latter experience is considered autonoetic in that the representation confirms that one has experience of an event that is known.

Perner and Ruffman (1995) draw attention to the similarity between the

126

cognitive operations involved in autonoetic remembering and those required to perform the theory of mind task designed by Wimmer et al. (1988). In this task children either observed an item being put in a box, were told what object was in a box, or given no information at all. Both 3- and 4-year-olds were able to decide accurately whether they knew what was in the box but there was a marked age difference in their ability to explain how they knew. The 4-year-olds correctly stated that they knew because they had seen or been told about the object or did not see anything whereas 3-year-olds seemed unable to explain their knowledge. Perner and Ruffman argue that the ability to make a link between seeing and knowing in this task, is qualitatively the same as that required for autonoetic remembering.

On this basis it is then argued that children prior to the age of 4 do not experience genuine episodic, autonoetic remembering. To test this idea two groups of young children were given tests of free recall and cued recall and their performance on these tasks compared their performance on "see-know" tasks similar to that of Wimmer et al. (1988). Based on Tulving's (1995) initial observations (see pp. 113–14) the assumption of the experiment was that the greater a child's free recall ability, relative to their cued recall performance, the more able that child was to make use of episodic memory. The data showed very clearly that enhanced free recall in the children was strongly associated with better performance on the "see-know" tasks – thus suggesting that episodic recollection is related to their growing understanding about the origin of knowledge.

Subsequent experiments extended this finding and controlled for potential artifacts. In the second experiment, for example, performance on a see-know test that does not employ a memory load is shown to correlate as strongly with free recall – this rules out a possible interpretation of the first experiment in that the task designed by Wimmer et al. (1988) has a memory load and, as such, it may be this that correlated with free recall. In a third study the relationship between see-know tasks and free recall was examined in a stepwise regression which showed that the relationship remained when the correlations between free recall and verbal and general intelligence were removed from the data .[2]

On the basis of these results Perner and Ruffman (1995) feel confident that the appearance of autonoetic remembering reflects the same ability as that enabling the child to appreciate the relationship between experience and the possession of knowledge. They also note that the proposed onset of autonoetic ability, around 4 years, also marks the temporal boundary of the infantile amnesia period. Thus they extend their argument by proposing that infantile amnesia arises because memories before the age of 4 are not represented in an autonoetic form. As a result adults cannot remember this period as episodic experiences even though they might know something about these events if assessed in another way.

If Perner and Ruffman are correct then a number of issues have to be resolved. Most important, perhaps, are the characteristics of memory before the age of 4 years. There is now plenty of evidence that declarative memory exists well before the age of 4. McKee and Squire (1993) have claimed that infants become proficient on a task involving declarative memory at around 5 months. They refer to the novelty preference paradigm in which an infant will look longer at a novel stimulus than one that was presented before. The authors demonstrate that the same phenomenon can be demonstrated in adults but, most importantly, not in adult amnesic subjects. Given that amnesic subjects are markedly compromised on tests of declarative memory, the ability of infants to do the task is attributed to a rudimentary form of declarative memory.

More direct evidence for declarative memory before the age of 4 years has come from studies that have asked young children to give accounts of their experiences. Consider the following conversation described by Fivush and Hamond (1990: 223).

> Child: Once on Halloween the kids was over and I had a princess dress on me.
>
> Adult: You had a princess dress on? Did you get any candy? Did you go door to door? What happened?
>
> Child: We went treating.
>
> Adult: You went treating! and who took you?
>
> Child: Andrea's mother took us. And my mom. . . and we brought a pumpkin too.
>
> Adult: What did you do with the pumpkin?
>
> Child: We lighted it.
>
> Adult: What did it look like? Was it scary?
>
> Child: Uh-huh. Dad made cuts in it with a razor. He made a face too. That was funny.

These comments were made by a child of just under 3 years of age and suggest very good recall of events during the years for which infantile amnesia will subsequently develop. Experimental studies also confirm this. Hamond and Fivush (1991), for example, investigated children who visited DisneyWorld at around the age of 3 or 4. Half the subjects were interviewed 6 months after the trip and the remainder after 18 months. All the children recounted a great deal of information about their DisneyWorld experience and there were no effects of retention interval. However, it was noted that older children tended to recall more detail and produce their memories more spontaneously than younger children.

Noting data of these kinds Perner and Ruffmann acknowledge the explicit nature of these young children's memory but emphasize what they consider to be very important differences. Thus they stress the need for prompting in young children and that their recall is dominated by the content of adults' questions. The dependence of early memories on cues is aptly illustrated in a study by Hudson and Fivush (1991), who investigated the ability of sixth-grade children to remember a kindergarten experience. When measured by free recall the children remembered virtually nothing, but when cues were given considerable memory appeared.

Perner and Ruffman's (1997) thesis therefore is that the reliance on cueing in young children's explicit memory is suggestive of a noetic form of remembering. The essence of the argument is that because of the preponderance of noetic judgements about cued recalled items in adults (see earlier) it follows, *ipso facto*, that heavy reliance on cues by younger children is also indicative of noetic remembering. This is, of course, a fairly strong inference and one would feel happier with additional evidence concerning possible experiential changes in memory around the borders of the infantile amnesia period. Perner and Ruffman stress the need to confirm that the recall of 6-year-olds is autonoetic but I would argue that it is just as important to show that explicit recall by 2- and 3-year-olds meets the definition of noetic. Given the subtlety of this distinction it will be interesting to see if additional empirical evidence can bear on this issue. In the adult literature, for example, it has been suggested that autonoetic remembering is reflected in enhanced sensitivity to manipulations such as levels of processing whereas noetic remembering does not show this effect (e.g. Gardiner 1988). One prediction, therefore, might be that children below the age of about 4 would not show a levels of processing effect in their recall.

To explain infantile amnesia Perner and Ruffman argue that very young children lack the ability to represent events "as experienced." As a result these early memories are based solely on descriptions of events and become confused with later memories depicting similar events. However, those later events remain distinctive because they have associated episodic information available. In support of this point they note work by Usher and Neisser (1993), who investigated the boundaries of infantile amnesia in adults as a function of the type of event addressed. Briefly, it was shown that memories concerning the birth of a sibling or hospitalization were available from the age of 2 onwards whereas those concerned with the death of a family member or a move could be recalled from age 3. These data thus suggest that if an event is unique or unusual it will penetrate the infantile amnesia barrier and remain accessible in later life.

A problem with Perner and Ruffman's account is their assumption that the enhanced availability of later childhood events is due to the association of episodic information with those memories. We know, for example, that noetic forms of remembering can occur for events following the infantile amnesia period, i.e. individuals are able to address events in a purely noetic form as indicated by their ability to ascribe some of their memories to familiarity-based as opposed to recollective experience. If post-infantile memories can be retrieved without reference to episodic information, then why cannot memories formed in the infantile period also be similarly retrieved?

A possible answer to this relates to a point I made earlier about the status of semantic memory in relation to the episodic–semantic distinction. My argument was that a typical semantic memory task cannot be thought of as implicit because, inherent in the production of general knowledge is an acknowledgement that performance is based on past experience. On the assumption that noetic remembering of a personal event is also tapping semantic memory then a similar argument prevails – an event has authenticity because, in some sense, it is associated with the potential for episodic recollection. Episodic memory is not therefore retrieved but its potential availability adds a "confirmatory atmosphere" to the noetic form of remembering. If one then assumes that this confirmatory association is essential for recall then the poor recall of early memories is understandable because they lack this quality.

Other points of view have been put forward to account for declarative memory development. Howe and Courage (1993) have argued that the personalization of event memory (i.e., episodic memory) is dependent on the parallel emergence of a sense of self. They provide a review of studies which have examined the emergence of self in young children based on paradigms exploring an individual's response to his or her mirror image. They note that this ability, which is considered co-extensive with the emergence of self-awareness, develops at between 18 and 24 months and that "the fact that this period corresponds with the onset of autobiographical memory is, we believe, more than mere coincidence" (Howe & Courage 1993: 319). In relation to our present concerns, what appears true is that the emergence of self-awareness coincides with the onset of children's ability to talk about past events in their lives (e.g. Hamond & Fivush 1991) but, in the stricter terminology argued for by Perner and Ruffman, this type of early remembering may not be episodic. Moreover, the Howe and Courage (1993) theory suffers as an account of infantile amnesia because the emergence of a sense of self occurs considerably earlier than the accepted boundary of infantile amnesia.

An alternative approach to the development of declarative memory has been put forward by Nelson and her colleagues (e.g. Hudson 1990; Nelson 1993). This theory, which one might term the social interaction theory, proposes that the development of autobiographical memory depends crucially on the child's ability to develop a narrative form of memory which in turn enables the child to share memory of experiences with others. Thus, as Fivush and Hamond (1990) point out, young children tend to recall events in a way that is not particularly memorable for an adult. When asked to recall a camping holiday, for example, one young child said "First we eat dinner, then go to bed, and then wake up and eat breakfast" (Fivush & Hamond 1990: 231).

A considerable amount of research has been carried out to investigate how the narrative form of memory changes with age. In a recent longitudinal study

Fivush et al. (1995) interviewed children about three novel past events (e.g. trips to science museums or amusement parks) at four different age points. The structure of these interviews was then analyzed in detail to assess their narrative structure. The analysis was quite complex, involving three categories of narrative element: structural (e.g. orientation in time and place, and character identification); referential (e.g. simple and complex actions); cohesion (e.g. use of simple and complex temporal markers such as "before," "after," "in order to," "usually").

Somewhat surprisingly even the youngest children (40 months) were able to produce quite coherent narratives of past events. However, as the children got older their narratives became more complex, coherent, and detailed. The study also incorporated evaluation of repeatedly recalled events and this again indicated the development of more complex narratives, particularly between the ages of 4 and 5. Support for the role of social interaction in the development of narrative memory is provided by Tessler and Nelson (1994). Following an earlier unpublished study by Engel, Tessler noted that mothers interacting with children could be divided into two basic types. *Elaborative* mothers talked about events in narrative terms (e.g. when did something happen) whereas *pragmatic* mothers talked primarily in instrumental terms (e.g. where did you put your shoes). Tessler found that this distinction had implications for what children remembered about a visit to a museum in that children of elaborative mothers recalled more about the visit than the offspring of pragmatic mothers. This finding indicates that the way parents talk about memory may have implications for how memory develops .[3]

The social interaction theory thus proposes that memory evolves by the gradual creation of an autobiographical component to memory which is dependent for this development on an increasing use of the narrative form to describe memory. Furthermore there is evidence that the nature of mother–child interactions when talking about memory facilitates autobiographical memory. Infantile amnesia is accounted for by arguing that memories formed prior to the age of 4 may not have a good narrative structure and therefore not amenable to the narrative form of memory retrieval characteristic of the post infantile amnesia period – a finding supported by the upturn in narrative qualities between 4 and 5 years (Fivush et al. 1995).

While the social interaction theory is framed in a different way, it may not be in opposition to the theory of mind framework put forward by Perner and Ruffman. As these authors state, "mothers' elaborated talk about past episodes provides one source of useful data that further the child's theory of mind" (Perner & Ruffman 1995: 544). In addition they also note studies showing that family interaction also appears to have a beneficial effect on the development of theory of mind (Perner et al. 1994).

The development of declarative memory remains an open but intriguing topic for future research. Perner and Ruffman's approach is an interesting and challenging way of treating the development of memory as an integral part of cognitive development rather than seeing memory as an "add on" which can be evaluated in paradigms wholly divorced from other aspects of cognition. In addition it is not antagonistic to other ideas concerning the emergence of declarative memory such as those stressing social interaction; indeed it is quite possible to argue that the emergence of a more complex narrative form of memory is an expression of exactly those changes specified in Perner and Ruffman's account. However, as we have seen, there are important limitations to the theory of mind approach at present. In particular, more evidence about the subjective qualities of young children's recollection is urgently required.

Conclusions and future directions

The evidence I have reviewed shows that young children can be proficient on tests of procedural memory when their ability on declarative memory tests addressing the same material is very poor. This has been illustrated particularly well with respect to perceptual learning but there is also evidence of verbal priming being present at an early stage. The literature has suggested that these procedural memory abilities may be fully established at an early age and this is consistent with recent theoretical accounts of what underlies these forms of procedural memory. However, I have urged caution on this point until further unambiguous data are reported.

Irrespective of the age invariance issue, the most compelling question is to explain what procedural memory is for. Durkin (1989) drew sharp attention to the lack of studies attempting to relate studies of memory to other issues in cognitive development. In an attempt to deal with this issue he considered a number of possible roles for procedural memory in the process of language acquisition. From our restricted focus the most relevant is his discussion of the "fast mapping" phenomenon in young children (Carey 1978). Briefly, it is proposed that when young children encounter a novel word they can rapidly draw upon the linguistic and nonlinguistic context for a partial understanding of the word's meaning. Typically, fast mapping is achieved by briefly introducing a new term in a relatively casual setting and then testing the child's subsequent ability to comprehend and use the term correctly. A mechanism of this kind is thought to be crucial in order to explain the speed at which a developing child can acquire new vocabulary (i.e., about nine new words a day).

In support of this view Durkin cites a study by Dockrell and Campbell (1986) in which a typical fast mapping procedure was used to teach children the meaning of a novel word *gombe*. It was found that children could subsequently use the word appropriately despite an inability to define it explicitly. Consistent with this is a subsequent study by Chapman et al. (1990) indicating that fast mapping ability is equivalent in normal young children and older, mental-age-matched children with Down's Syndrome – even though the latter have greatly reduced expressive language.

The idea that mechanisms mediating verbal priming could, in part at least, underlie fast mapping phenomena is an interesting one but, as yet, there is little direct evidence. Indeed what little evidence exists for verbal priming in young children comes from the visual domain. A fruitful area of research therefore might be to explore the relationship between auditory-verbal priming phenomena and language acquisition more directly.

At present the most obvious potential role for procedural memory involves the development of recognition memory. There is now growing acceptance that recognition memory comprises two elements – an explicit or declarative component and an implicit procedural component. The former constitutes what we have referred to as conscious recollection. The procedural component of memory reflects the idea that representation of a previously encountered stimulus allows that item to be perceived more fluently and that this additional fluency serves as a cue to recognition memory – a response that is expressed in terms of a non-recollective "familiarity-based" response (Johnston et al. 1991).

Given the role of perceptual fluency in recognition it is a parsimonious step to suggest that the mechanisms responsible for perceptual learning and those that underwrite perceptual fluency effects are one and the same. Connected with this it is interesting to note an additional analysis carried out in Drummey and Newcombe (1995) of a picture completion task in which they examined the degree of priming associated with recognized and non-recognized pictures. The authors found that greater priming for recognized pictures occurred only in the adult group – this finding was linked to that of Moscovitch and Bentin (1993), who showed that repetition priming effects in adults disappear when recognition memory for the same items is at chance. Discussing this, Drummey and Newcombe (1995) suggest that adults may become more proficient at using the occurrence of the additional activation underlying priming to facilitate recognition. This is an interesting idea that warrants further investigation.

Turning to the development of declarative memory, the most interesting issue appears to be the nature of explicit recall in the years immediately before and after the boundaries of infantile amnesia. Thus it is clear that children of 2 to 3 years can produce explicit recall of events but the issue is why these early memories become lost in later life. Perner and Ruffman's (1995) hypothesis suggests that a change in memorial representation takes place that is directly linked to the child's emerging theory of mind. In contrast the social interaction theorists argue that poor recall of early explicit memories occurs because these are not constructed around an effective narrative form. It would seem that this is a particularly fruitful area for future research and it will be interesting to see whether these apparently different accounts of declarative memory development can be distinguished at the empirical level.

Notes

1. At this point the reader might question the wisdom of the term "procedural" to embrace the various memory tasks I have considered. An alternative, following the suggestion of Squire and Zola-Morgan 1991, would be to replace this term with "nondeclarative." However, given the widespread use of the declarative–procedural distinction I felt that this would complicate matters unduly.
2. It should be noted that K. Nelson (1992) has criticized this position on the grounds that she failed to obtain a relationship between performance on a theory of mind task and autobiographical memory. However, these data are not described and, subsequent to this, no study of this kind has yet appeared.
3. An additional finding of Fivush et al. (1995) was that girls tended to produce more complex, elaborate, and personally significant narratives than boys. Various explanations of this are considered (e.g. the possibility that the girls are more linguistically advanced) but these do not account for the difference. Instead the authors suggest that the more advanced performance of the girls may arise because parents tend to have more sophisticated conversations with daughters. Indeed the inexperienced traveller in this literature should be aware of the contradictory uses of the term "episodic memory" by social interaction theorists and those proposing a link between memory development and theory of mind.

References

Bauer, R. M. 1984. Autonomic recognition of names and faces in prosopagnosia: A neuropsychological application of the guilty knowledge test. *Neuropsychologia* **22**, 457–69.

Biederman, I. & P. C. Gerhardstein 1993. Recognizing depth-rotated objects: Evidence and conditions for three-dimensional viewpoint invariance. *Journal of Experimental Psychology: Human Perception and Performance* **19**, 1162–1182.

Carey, S. 1978. The child as a word learner. In *Linguistic theory and psychological reality*, M. Halle, G. Miller, & J. Bresnan (eds.), Cambridge, MA: MIT Press.

Carroll, M., B. Byrne, & K. Kirsner 1985. Autobiographical memory and perceptual learning: A developmental study using picture recognition, naming latency, and perceptual identification. *Memory and Cognition* **13**, 273–9.

Chapman, R. S., E. Kay-Raining Bird, & S. E. Schwartz 1990. Fast mapping of words in event contexts by children with Down's Syndrome. *Journal of Speech and Hearing Disorders* **55**, 761–70.

DiGuilio, D. V., M. Seidenberg, D. S. O'Leary, & N. Raz 1994. Procedural and declarative memory: A developmental study. *Brain and Cognition* **25**, 79–91.

Dockrell, J. & R. Campbell 1986. Lexical acquisition strategies in the preschool child. In *The development of word meaning*, S. S. Kuczaj & M. D. Barrett (eds.). New York: Springer-Verlag.

Drummey, A. B. & N. Newcombe 1995. Remembering versus knowing the past: Children's explicit and implicit memory. *Journal of Experimental Child Psychology* **59**, 549–65.

Dudycha, G. J. & M. M. Dudycha 1941. Childhood memories: A review of the literature. *Psychological Bulletin* **38**, 668–82.

Durkin, K. 1989. Implicit memory and language acquisition. In *Implicit memory: Theoretical issues*, S. Lewandowsky, J. C. Dunn, & K. Kirsner (eds.), 73–96. Hillsdale, NJ: Erlbaum.

Ellis, H. D., D. M. Ellis, & J. A. Hosie 1993. Priming effects in children's face recognition. *British Journal of Psychology* **84**, 101–10.

Fivush, R., C. Haden, & S. Adam 1995. Structure and coherence of preschooler's personal narratives over time: Implications for childhood amnesia. *Journal of Experimental Child Psychology* **60**, 32–56.

Fivush, R. & N. Hamond 1990. Autobiographical memory across the preschool years: Toward reconceptualizing childhood amnesia. In *Knowing and remembering in young children*, R. Fivush & J. A. Hudson (eds.), 249–48. Cambridge: Cambridge University Press.

Gardiner, J. M. 1988. Functional aspects of recollective experience. *Memory and Cognition* **16**, 309–13.

Gollin, E. S. 1960. Developmental studies of visual recognition of incomplete objects. *Perceptual and Motor Skills* **11**, 289–98.

Greenbaum, J. L. & P. Graf 1989. Preschool period development of implicit and explicit remembering. *Bulletin of Psychonomic Society* **27**, 417–20.

Hamond, N. R. & R. Fivush 1991. Memories of Mickey Mouse: Young children recount their trip to DisneyWorld. *Cognitive Development* **6**, 433–48.

Hayman, C. A. G. & E. Tulving 1989. Is priming in fragment completion based on a "traceless" memory system? *Journal of Experimental Psychology: Learning, Memory and Cognition* **15**, 941–56.

Howe, M. L. & M. L. Courage 1993. On resolving the enigma of infantile amnesia. *Psychological Bulletin* **113**, 305–26.

Hudson, J. A. 1990. The emergence of autobiographic memory in mother–child interactions. In *Knowing and remembering in young children*, R. Fivush & J. A. Hudson (eds.) 166–96. Cambridge: Cambridge University Press.

Hudson, J. A. & R. Fivush 1991. As time goes by: Sixth graders remember a kindergarten experience. *Applied Cognitive Psychology* **5**, 347–60.

Johnston, W. A., K. J. Hawley, & J. M. G. Elliot 1991. Contribution of perceptual fluency to recognition judgment. *Journal of Experimental Psychology: Learning, Memory and Cognition* **17**, 210–33.

Karmiloff-Smith, A. 1992. *Beyond modularity: A developmental perspective on cognitive science*. Cambridge, MA: MIT Press.

Lorsbach, T. C. & A. K. Morris 1991. Direct and indirect testing of picture memory in second and sixth grade children. *Contemporary Educational Psychology* **16**, 18–27.

Lorsbach, T. C., J. Sodoro, & J. S. Brown 1992. The dissociation of repetition priming and recognition memory in language/learning disabled children. *Journal of Experimental Child Psychology* **54**, 121–46.

Lorsbach, T. C. & L. J. Worman 1989. The development of explicit and implicit forms of memory in learning disabled and nondisabled children. *Contemporary Educational Psychology* **14**, 67–76.

Lorsbach, T. C. & L. J. Worman 1990. Episodic priming in children with learning disabilities. *Contemporary Educational Psychology* **15**, 93–102.

McKee, R. D. & L. R. Squire 1993. On the development of declarative memory. *Journal of Experimental Psychology: Learning, Memory, and Cognition* **19**, 397–404.

Moscovitch, M. & S. Bentin 1993. The fate of repetition effects when recognition approaches chance. *Journal of Experimental Psychology: Learning, Memory and Cognition* **19**, 148–58.

Naito, M. 1990. Repetition priming in children and adults: Age-related dissociation between implicit and explicit memory. *Journal of Experimental Child Psychology* **50**, 462–84.

Naito, M. & S. Komatsu 1993. Processes involved in the childhood development of implicit memory. In *Implicit memory: New directions in cognition, development, and neuropsychology*, P. Graf & M. Masson (eds.), 231–60. Hillsdale, NJ: Erlbaum.

Nelson, K. 1992. Emergence of autobiographical memory at age 4. *Human Development* **35**, 172–7.

Nelson, K. 1993. The psychological and social origins of autobiographical memory. *Psychological Science* **4**, 7–14.

Newcombe, N. & N. A. Fox 1994. Infantile amnesia: Through a glass darkly. *Child Development* **65**, 31–40.

Newcombe, N. & E. Lie 1995. Overt and covert recognition of faces in children and adults. *Psychological Science* **6**, 241–5.

Ostergaard, A. L. 1987. Episodic, semantic and procedural memory in a case of amnesia at an early age. *Neuropsychologia* **25**, 341–57.

Ostergaard, A. & L. R. Squire 1990. Childhood amnesia and distinctions between forms of memory: A comment on Wood, Brown and Felton. *Brain and Cognition* **14**, 127–33.

Parkin, A. J. 1993. Implicit memory across the lifespan. In *Implicit memory: New directions in cognition, development, and neuropsychology*, P. Graf & M. Masson (eds.), Hillsdale, NJ: Erlbaum.

Parkin, A. J. 1996a. *Explorations in cognitive neuropsychology*. Oxford: Basil Blackwell.

Parkin, A. J. 1996b. *Memory and amnesia: An introduction*. Oxford: Basil Blackwell.

Parkin, A. J. & N. R. C. Leng 1993. *Neuropsychology of the amnesic syndrome*. Hove, UK: Erlbaum.

Parkin, A. J. & S. Streete 1988. Implicit and explicit memory in young children and adults. *British Journal of Psychology* **79**, 361–9.

Perner, J. & T. Ruffman 1995. Episodic memory and autonoetic consciousness: Developmental evidence and a theory of infantile amnesia. *Journal of Experimental Child Psychology* **59**, 516–48.

Perner, J., T. Ruffmann, & S. R. Leekam 1994. Theory of mind is contagious: You catch it from your sibs. *Child Development* **65**, 1224–34.

Russo, R., P. Nichelli, M. Gibertoni, & C. Cornia 1995. Developmental trends in implicit and explicit memory: A picture completion study. *Journal of Experimental Child Psychology* **59**, 566–78.

Russo, R. & A. J. Parkin 1993. Age differences in implicit memory: More apparent than real. *Memory and Cognition* **21**, 73–80.

Schacter, D. L. 1987. Implicit memory: History and current status. *Experimental Psychology: Learning, Memory and Cognition* **13**, 501–18.

Schacter, D. L. 1994. Priming and multiple memory systems: Perceptual mechanisms of implicit memory. In *Memory systems 1994*, D. L. Schacter & E. Tulving (eds.). Cambridge, MA: MIT Press.

Schacter, D. L. & E. Tulving 1994. What are the memory systems of 1994. In *Memory systems 1994*, D. L. Schacter & E. Tulving (eds.). Cambridge, MA: MIT Press.

Snodgrass, J. G. 1989. Sources of learning in the picture fragment completion task. In *Implicit memory: Theoretical issues*, S. Lewandowsky, J. C. Dunn, & K. Kirsner (eds.), 259–82. Hillsdale, NJ: Erlbaum.

Snodgrass, J. G., B. Smith, K. Feenan, & J. Corwin 1987. Fragmenting pictures on the Apple Macintosh computer for experimental and clinical applications. *Behavioral Research Methods and Instrumentation* **19**, 270–4.

Squire, L. R. 1987. *Memory and brain*. New York: Oxford University Press.

Squire, L. R. & S. Zola-Morgan 1991. The medial temporal lobe memory system. *Science* **253**, 1380–6.

Temple, C. M. 1994. The cognitive neuropsychology of the developmental dyscalculias. *Current Psychology of Cognition* **13**, 351–70.

Tessler, M. & K. Nelson 1994. Making memories: The influence of joint encoding on later recall by young children. *Consciousness and Cognition* **3**, 307–26.

Tulving, E. 1985. Memory and consciousness. *Canadian Psychology* **26**, 1–12.

Tulving, E. 1995. Organization of memory. Quo vadis? In *The cognitive neurosciences*, M. Gazzaniga (ed.). Cambridge, MA: MIT Press.

Usher, J. A. & U. Neisser 1993. Childhood amnesia and the beginnings of memory for four early life events. *Journal of Experimental Psychology: General* **122**, 155–65.

Verfaellie, M. & H. L. Roth 1996. Knowledge of English vocabulary in amnesia: An examination of premorbidly acquired semantic memory. *Journal of the International Neuropsychology Society*.

Warrington, E. K. & T. Shallice 1980. Word form dyslexia. *Brain* **30**, 99–112.

Wimmer, H., G.-J. Hogrefe, & J. Perner 1988. Children's understanding of informational access as a source of knowledge. *Child Development* **59**, 386–96.

Witherspoon, D. & M. Moscovitch 1989. Stochastic independence between two implicit memory tasks. *Journal of Experimental Psychology: Learning, Memory and Cognition* **15**, 22–30.

Wood, F. B., I. S. Brown, & R. H. Felton 1989. Long-term follow-up of a childhood amnesic syndrome. *Brain and Cognition* **10**, 76–86.

Acknowledgement

I am grateful to Wendy Clements for her comments on a previous draft of this chapter and also to Martin Conway for some useful suggestions.

CHAPTER 6

Event memory in early childhood

Robyn Fivush

Event memory in early childhood

A mother once reported to me that as she and her 34-month-old daughter were driving past an empty field, her daughter called out, "pumpkins, pumpkins!" Indeed, this was the field where they had gotten their Halloween pumpkin 8 months previously, and they had not driven past there since. The mother was startled that her young daughter was able to recall the event after such a long delay. "Isn't it true that young children have poor memories?" she asked me. Although this is a widely held assumption, research conducted since the early 1980s has demonstrated just the opposite; even quite young children have remarkably good memories for personally experienced events.

In this chapter, I review research on young children's event memory, with several questions in mind. How do children represent and recall personally experienced events? How do event representations change as a function of age, and as a function of increasing experience with specific kinds of events? And what are the developmental relations between recall of specific, one-time occurrences and recurring experiences? My focus throughout is on deliberate memory, in the sense that children are actively recalling past events. Although it is clear that past experiences influence behaviors beginning in early infancy (e.g. DeCasper & Spence 1986; Rovee-Collier & Shyi 1992; see Rovee-Collier, Ch. 2 in this volume), my concern is with children's abilities to represent and recall these experiences explicitly (see both Bauer and Parkin, Chs. 4 and 5 in this volume, for full discussions of this distinction). Representations of previous experiences allow us to predict and anticipate future events (Nelson 1986), and provide a sense of continuity through time essential to the formation of a self-concept (Fivush 1988). Children's developing abilities to represent and recall the past are the necessary foundations for understanding both their world and themselves. Thus it may be somewhat surprising that event memory was sparsely studied until the 1980s. Part of this is attributable to historical conceptions of early memory. In the first section of this chapter, therefore, I present a brief overview of the historical framework for understanding memory development before turning to a detailed review of the research on the development of children's event memory.

Historical background

In the 1960s and 1970s the prevailing view within developmental psychology was that young children's memory abilities were quite poor. Two avenues of research on memory development supported this interpretation. First, Piaget (Piaget & Inhelder 1973) had described preschoolers' inability to recall stories in their presented sequential order, or to reproduce the sequence of a presented series of items. Moreover, when engaging in these kinds of tasks, preschoolers were quite likely to intrude information not presented, and to confuse antecedents and consequences of actions. Based on these findings, as well as the findings across a diverse set of developmental tasks, Piaget concluded that preschoolers' thought was unorganized, fragmentary and idiosyncratic.

In the 1970s, information-processing approaches to development challenged many of Piaget's conclusions. Still, memory development research conducted within the information-processing tradition focused on children's abilities to engage in strategic intervention. When presented with a list of words, or a series of pictures or objects to recall, children younger than about 6 or 7 years of age tend not to engage spontaneously in activities that would ensure their subsequent recall, such as rehearsing presented items or grouping items into meaningful categories. Perhaps not surprisingly then, children perform abysmally on these kinds of tasks (see Kail 1990; Kail & Bisanz 1982 for reviews). Thus the general picture of very young children was that they were mnemonically incompetent.

Beginning in the mid-1970s, this conceptualization of the early memory system began to be called into question. Critical to this changing view was the growing recognition within developmental theory that the tasks and situations in which we assess young children play an integral role in the kinds of performances elicited and conclusions drawn (Brown & DeLoache 1978; Donaldson 1978; Gelman 1978). Whereas there is no question that older children perform better than younger children on tasks that require abstract and decontextualized thinking, young children often perform as well as older children in situations in which they can rely on meaningful information presented in motivating ways. This "contextual" view of development argues that human cognition occurs in social situations with real human goals and motivations guiding behavior (Laboratory of Comparative Human Cognition 1983; Vygotsky 1978; Werstch 1985). In order to understand the development of any given behavior, one must understand how that behavior functions to achieve meaningful goals in ongoing social interaction in the real world (Rogoff 1990). Indeed, in situations in which children are clearly motivated to remember, they show increased evidence of using deliberate mnemonic strategies (e.g. DeLoache et al. 1985), although it must be noted that younger children still do not perform as well as older children on these kinds of memory tasks (see Bjorkland, Ch. 8 in this volume, for a full discussion of the development of mnemonic strategies). It was within this changing view of early mnemonic competency that research on children's event memory emerged.

Children's memories of recurring events

In 1981, Nelson and Greundel published a seminal paper which demonstrated for the first time that preschool children had well-organized memories of personally experienced events (see also Nelson 1986; Nelson et al. 1983 for overviews). This research was groundbreaking in several ways. First, as Nelson and Greundel argue, if we want to understand how preschoolers represent and remember events, then we must focus on events that are important and meaningful in preschooler's lives. Thus, in this research, Nelson and Greundel asked children to recount familiar everyday events, such as going grocery shopping and going to McDonald's. Secondly, in this paradigm, children are not given information and asked to recall it; rather they are asked to generate accounts of events they have experienced. In this way, we can examine how children are naturally organizing information for recall. Finally, by asking children of different ages and with differing amounts of experience with events to recall them, we can begin to examine how children's event memory changes as a function of general cognitive development as well as increasing familiarity with the material being recalled.

When asked to recount these kinds of events, children ranging in age from 3 to 8 years responded in unpredicted ways. For example, when asked "What happens when you bake cookies?" one 3-year-old child responded, "Well, you bake them and eat them." And a 4-year-old recounted, "My mommy puts chocolate chips inside the cookies. Than ya put 'em in the oven . . . then we take them out, put them on the table and eat them." (examples are from Nelson & Gruendel 1981). Although sparse, these recounts are surprising. First, and most important, when children recount familiar events, they virtually always report the component actions in their appropriate temporal sequence. Note that for some events, actions must occur in a particular temporal order. For example when going to McDonald's, one must order food before paying, one must get the food before eating it, and so on. Other events, however, do not follow a logical temporal order. For example when going grocery shopping one can choose produce and then canned goods or the reverse. Clearly most real-world events are complex combinations of logical and arbitrary temporal orders (e.g. at the grocery store you must select the food before paying). Even very young children are sensitive to these distinctions, and report logically ordered events in their correct order, but report arbitrarily ordered events in more flexible ways. (Indeed, as discussed by Bauer, Ch. 4 in this volume, temporal organization is a critical factor in how events are represented and recalled even extremely early in development.)

Moreover, children report events at a general level, in two senses. First, children do not report what happened during one instance of the event (e.g. yesterday at McDonald's I got Chicken McNuggets and I spilled my Coke). Rather, they report what happens each and every time the event occurs (e.g. You order your food and then you pay and then sit and eat it). Second, children report these events in the second person, you, and the timeless present tense. In this way, it is clear that children are not recounting what they themselves did, but are recounting what one does, the culturally appropriate frame of the event.

These findings indicate that children have generalized, well-organized representations of familiar events, and these representations conform to a "script." A script is a type of schematically organized memory first described by Schank and Abelson (1977). Scripts are spatially-temporally organized sequences of actions that specify the actions, actors, and props that are most likely to be present during any given instantiation of an event. Research with adults demonstrates that scripts are a basic form of representation that allow us to navigate our world (Bower et al. 1979; Mandler 1983). Because we have well-organized scripts for recurring events, we can predict what is going to happen in the future and we can infer what must have happened in the past. In this way, scripts are dynamic and reconstructive (Bobrow & Norman 1975), and they provide the culturally shared background information necessary for understanding our world. Intriguingly, Nelson and Greundel's findings indicate that scripts are a developmentally early form of representation. Children as young as 3 years of age report familiar events in ways qualitatively similar to older children and adults, suggesting that even very young children are actively engaged in understanding and representing their everyday world.

Developmental differences

Although there are surprising developmental continuities in script reports, there are also developmental differences. Whereas children at all ages report component actions of events in their appropriate temporal order, older children's event reports appear more elaborate and complex than younger children's reports. Older children almost always report more of the component actions of events than do younger children. Older children also report more alternatives (e.g. you can order a hamburger *or* a cheeseburger), more conditional activities (e.g. *if* you go through the drive-through, then you order from your car), and more optional activities (e.g. you *might* get dessert) than younger children. The most obvious explanation of these differences rests on developmental differences in verbal recall; older children's script reports are more complex because their language is more complex than that of younger children.

The role of language in script reports In thinking about children's event memories, we need to make a distinction between the verbal report of the event and the underlying representation of the event (Nelson 1986). Information that is verbally recalled is clearly part of the representation, but not every-

142

thing that is represented will necessarily be recalled. This may be due to multiple reasons, including why one is reporting the event and to whom. But it ~~however~~ may also be due to developmental differences in language abilities. Younger children's underlying event representations may be just as complex as older children's representations, but they may have difficulty expressing this complexity in language. If this were the case, then we would expect younger and older children to be comparable on nonverbal measures of event knowledge. The findings are somewhat equivocal. When asked to select and sequence pictures of familiar events (Caarni & French 1984; Fivush & Mandler 1985), or to re-enact events behaviorally (Fivush et al. 1992; Nelson & Greundel 1981; Price & Goodman 1990; Ratner et al. 1986), younger children show more elaborated event knowledge than when asked to recall events verbally. However, although the developmental differences are attenuated, older children still recall more than younger children even when assessed nonverbally.

Whereas verbal measures seem to underestimate the elaborativeness of younger children's representations, they do not seem to underestimate the complexity of their representations. For example, although 4-year-old children can generate and reproduce picture sequences of familiar events almost as well as 5- and 6-year-olds, they cannot generate or reproduce these sequences backwards, as can older children (Fivush & Mandler 1985). These findings suggest that younger children's event knowledge is not as flexibly organized as is older children's (see also Fivush & Slackman 1986). Related to this, when asked to sort pictures of a clay-making event into categories, 5-year-old children put together pictures that share objects (e.g. all the actions performed with the bowl), whereas adults put together the pictures that share activities (e.g. mixing ingredients together) (Ratner et al. 1986). Thus younger children's event representations are not organized around goals to the same extent as are older children's and adults.

Overall, then, developmental differences in complexity of representations do not appear to be due to increasing linguistic sophistication. This is not to argue that language and memory are unrelated. The developing relations between language and event memory are quite complex and will be discussed in more detail below. Rather, the argument here is that the fact that older children verbally report more elaborate and complex event memories is not due solely to increasing language skills. Further support for this conclusion comes from studies on the role of experience on the development of event representations, discussed in the next section, and from studies examining how actions and objects which change across specific experiences are represented, discussed later in the chapter.

The role of experience on script reports In the early research, children were asked about events that are culturally familiar, such as going to McDonald's, going grocery shopping, and going to birthday parties. Although even the youngest children interviewed had experienced these events, clearly older children had experienced these events more often, and this may be one of the reasons why older children's script reports are more elaborate and complex. There are two ways to address this possible confound. One is to examine children of the same age who have had differing amounts of experience with a specific event, and the other is to examine children of different ages with the same amount of experience with an event.

In a study utilizing the first approach, Nelson and Greundel (1981) asked preschool children about having lunch at their day-care center. All of the children were 3 to 4 years of age at the time of the interview, but some of the children were new to the center and some had been there for several months. Those children with more experience reported more elaborated scripts than children who had just arrived. In a similar vein, Fivush (1984) asked kindergarten children to recount the school day routine on the second day of school, and again during the second week, the third week, and the tenth week of school. Although all the children had some preschool experience, the kindergarten routine contained several novel aspects, including a full day at school with lunch, individual lockers for each student, and many new activities. Even on the second day of school, children reported this event in a generalized, temporally organized fashion, suggesting that an organized event representation is formed on the very first encounter with an event. (I will return to this issue later.) More to the point, as experience with the kindergarten routine grew, children reported more component activities and more complex relations among activities. In particular, children's scripts became more conditional and more hierarchically organized over time. For example, on the second day of school, one child reported (examples are from Fivush & Slackman 1986):

> I just go to school. Then we do stuff. And then we have lunch or snack and then we go home. (The interviewer asks if anything happens.) We play a little and then we go to the gym sometimes, or else we can go to the playground. And then we have snack, and then in an hour, we have lunch. And then we can draw a picture or read and then we go home.

While this report is impressive in its elaboration and complexity, the following example of a report from the tenth week of school illustrates how much more detailed and conditional children's understanding of the school day routine becomes:

> I turn over my name. I do my handwriting. If I have time, I do my art project. Then we have meeting time. Then we have math time. Then we have another meeting with snack. Then sharing if it's Friday. If not, story with snack. And sharing if it's Friday. After snack and story, minigym. Go to the bathroom, have lunch, then you have a little play time. And then we have Ron's (science class) or nap.

Clearly, we are seeing many of the same kinds of changes in children's scripts with increasing event experience that we see with increasing age. This pattern suggests that children's event representations are becoming more complex as a function of increasing experience with an event. Yet children of different ages with the same amount of experience with an event still report it differently. Price and Goodman (1990) had 2.5- to 5-year-old children experience a wizard event three times. Whether assessed through verbal report or re-enactment, the older children recalled more of the component actions of the event than the younger children did. Most interesting, the older children recalled a causal connection between an action that occurred early in the sequence and one that occurred late in the sequence, whereas the younger children did not.

Similarly, Fivush et al. (1992) asked 3- and 5-year-old children to recall a play event they experienced once or four times. Older children recalled more verbally than did younger children, but younger children recalled as much as the older children during re-enactment. However, this was true only for action sequences that were invariant across experience. When the action sequence incorporated new objects or actions, 3-year-olds had much more difficulty recalling the event both verbally and behaviorally than did 5-year-olds. The 5-year-olds were easily able to incorporate alternative actions into their developing scripts, but 3-year-olds were not. Even with equal amounts of experience with an event, younger children have more difficulty representing causal connections and alternative actions within events than do older children, whether assessed verbally or behaviorally.

Overall, children's event representations become more complex with both age and experience with specific events. Increasing complexity of script reports with age cannot be attributed solely to increasing linguistic skills, but also seems to reflect an increasing developmental ability to represent events in more complex ways. However, the research also suggests that the structure of the event plays an important role in how it will be represented.

The structure of events

Not all events in the world have the same underlying structure. Some events are quite temporally constrained, whereas others are quite arbitrary in their temporal order. Furthermore, some events are very much the same upon each occurrence, whereas other events are quite variable across different experiences. How might the structure of an event influence the ways in which children come to represent that event? And how might this change developmentally?

Temporal structure One of the most robust findings in this body of research is that children report the component actions of events in their experienced temporal order. Yet, as noted above, some events in the world are more temporally constrained than others, and children seem to be sensitive to these differences. Events which follow a logical order, such that actions must occur in a specified sequence, are virtually always reported in that sequence, whereas events which follow a more flexible order are reported in a more variable sequence (Slackman & Nelson 1984). Intriguingly, children report events in their correct temporal order even after the very first experience with the event (Fivush 1984; Hudson & Nelson 1986; Ratner et al. 1986).

Moreover, children will "correct" temporal sequences in their recall. Hudson and Nelson (1983) presented 4- and 6-year-old children with stories about two familiar events, baking cookies and going to a birthday party. In each story some of the component actions were presented in an incorrect temporal order. For example, giving presents to the birthday child occurred as the guest was leaving the party. When asked to recall these stories, the younger children simply omitted the incorrectly sequenced actions from their recall. But the older children actually transformed these actions so that they made sense in the sequence. Giving birthday presents became getting party favours to take home. Omissions and transformations of incorrectly sequenced actions indicate that children's event representations are tightly temporally organized, and deviations from expected temporal sequence are not easily recalled.

The question is whether children understand the logical connections among actions or are simply reporting actions in their experienced order. That is, do children understand *why* particular actions occur in a particular order, or do they simply know *that* these actions occur in this order? In order to explore this issue, Fivush et al. (1992) asked children to recall two types of events, a logically ordered event (making fundough), in which each action was a prerequisite for the next action to occur, and an arbitrarily ordered event (sand play), in which the component actions were independent of each other. Even though the actions of the arbitrary event did not follow any logical order, they were always experienced in exactly the same order. Children aged 3 and 5 were asked to recall these events both verbally and behaviorally after one experience and after four experiences. Both verbal and behavioral recall showed similar patterns at both ages: Children recalled the component actions in their experienced order when recalling the logical event, but not when recalling the arbitrary event, and this pattern held after one experience and after four experiences. Even very young children are sensitive to the logical connections among actions in an event sequence; logically connected sequences are represented and recalled in their presented temporal order whereas arbitrary sequences do not seem to be, even when that arbitrary sequence is repeated across experiences. Young children are picking up on the logical structure of events in the world and are using this structure to help organize their event representations. Indeed, as discussed by Bauer (Ch. 4 in this volume), sensitivity to the logical structure of events in the world seems to be a basic component in the development of event representations even in infancy.

Event variability Although component actions of some events may always occur in the same temporal order, it is unlikely that every single experience with an event will contain exactly the same set of actions. When going to

McDonald's one may always get a "happy meal," but the toy included changes every time. Similarly, at school reading may always occur after recess, but the material read changes from day to day. How do children come to represent this kind of event variability? In the study by Fivush et al. (1992) discussed above, a third event that the children experienced contained just this kind of variability. At each experience, children made a "shape collage" but the actual shape, as well as some of the other materials used, changed at each experience. The 5-year-olds had no difficulty representing this change. When asked to re-enact the event with a new set of variations, they were easily able to do so, whether they had one previous experience or four. The 3-year-olds, in contrast, had more difficulty. After they had one experience (e.g. making a duck shape collage with feathers) and were asked to re-enact the event with a new set of items (e.g. a tree shape with leaves), they were completely befuddled. They simply looked at the new items and did not know what to do. However, after having four experiences, each one different, they had no problems when asked to re-enact the event with a fifth set of items.

Similar results were obtained by Bauer and Fivush (1992), when 36-month-old children were shown a series of complex event sequences with sets of toys and asked to re-enact them. Two of the sequences were exactly the same at each of four presentations over a 1-week period, but in two of the sequences, some of the objects varied from one presentation to the next. At the second session, when presented with a set of objects where some of the objects were now different from the original set, children were confused; they had more difficulty re-enacting these sequences than sequences in which none of the objects changed. However, by the third session, when presented with yet different objects, children were quite able to extend their developing event representations to include the varying objects. It seems that younger children may have more difficulty than older children in understanding that some aspects of events may change. They need more experience with how events can vary from time to time in order to build this variability into their representation of the event.

Kuebli and Fivush (1994) expanded on this finding in a study of 4- and 7-year-old children's representations of alternative actions within a recurring event. Children experienced two arts and crafts projects (making a puppet and making a bird) four times. Within each of these activities, one action changed with every experience and one action changed only at the third experience; the other three experiences were identical. Children's knowledge of these alternatives was assessed through spontaneous recall and probed questioning. Again, younger children had more difficulty representing the alternative actions within these events than did older children. When items changed at every experience, children at both ages reported these alternatives, but when items changed on only one occasion, 4-year-olds showed little awareness of this change. Even under very directed probing, young children often claimed no change had occurred. Younger children seem to need more experience with how an event can change across occurrences in order to represent this variability than do older children.

Summary

Quite clearly, even very young children have well-organized representations of familiar events. Children as young as 3 years of age report events in similar ways to older children and adults, and they are sensitive to the temporal structure of events in the world. With increasing experience with events, children report more of the component actions and they report more conditional actions, although older children still report more actions and more complex actions than younger children even with equal amounts of experience. Perhaps the most intriguing developmental difference is that younger children have more difficulty than older children representing variability within events, especially after just one or two experiences with how an event can change. If young children have difficulty representing minor variations within an event, how do they come to represent more overarching variations? In particular, how do they differentiate and represent single occurrences of recurring events? And how is this related to children's memories for novel events?

Children's memories for single instances of recurring events

Scripts represent what usually happens during any given occurrence of an event, allowing us to predict and anticipate our world. By focusing on what usually happens, however, we may lose information about specific instances of an event. For example, although we all have a script for eating lunch, it is very difficult to recall what you had for lunch a week ago Tuesday, unless you eat the same thing every day, or something out of the ordinary happened, such as a special lunch with a friend. The intuition that specific occurrences, or instantiations, of a recurring event are difficult to recall is borne out in research with adults. Although the results are somewhat complicated, the basic finding is that specific instantiations of an event that are not unusual in any way are extremely difficult to recall (Bobrow & Norman 1975; Graesser 1980; Smith & Graesser 1981). However, if something unusual happens during a specific instantiation, it becomes easier to recall. Different explanations of this finding have been advanced, but they all share in common the idea that specific episodes of an event are "tagged" in memory by their distinctive features (Graesser et al. 1979). Essentially, we recall the script and then the script representation "points" to the distinctive episode in memory.

Research with young children indicates that they, too, have great difficulty recalling specific episodes of recurring events if these episodes were not unusual in any way. Hudson and Nelson (1986) asked 3- and 5-year-old children about dinner at home and snack at daycamp. Children were asked both "what happens" and "what happened yesterday." At both ages, children were able to provide more information to the general question than the specific question. In a replication and extension of this finding, Pillemer et al. (1994) also asked 3- to 5-year-old children about last night's dinner at home. Again they found that children recalled little specific information, but with the provision of additional cues, children were able to recount specific details. Similarly, when Fivush (1984) asked kindergarten children about what happened yesterday at school, children provided very little information, although they were able to give general accounts of the school day routine. But again, when provided with specific cues, children were able to recall specific details about the day before.

Thus it seems that children retain memories of specific episodes of recurring events but these are difficult to recall without specific cues that help to differentiate this one occurrence from all other occurrences. This further suggests that children should be able to recall episodes that deviate in some significant way from the recurring event. In fact, there is some evidence that this is the case. Kindergarten children were asked what happens at museums in general, and also what happened at a special class trip to a museum of archeology (Fivush et al. 1984). The archeology museum was unusual in that children dug for artifacts in a large sandbox and made clay models of what they had found. Both immediately after the class trip and six weeks later, children were able to give both a general account of museum trips and specific details about the museum of archeology.

In more experimental analogues to the real-world research, similar findings emerge. The basic paradigm involves asking children to recall script-based stories in which atypical actions are embedded. As do adults, children tend to recall atypical actions quite well on immediate recall. In delayed recall, however, both adults and children intrude script information not included in the original presented story and have difficulty recalling the atypical actions (Adams & Worden 1986; Graesser et al. 1979, 1980; Smith & Graesser 1981). Over time, memories of specific episodes fade and scripted information becomes more prominent. In this way, memories of specific episodes become "normalized" to the script. However, Hudson (1988) has argued that distinctions must be made among the types of atypical actions that are presented and recalled. Actions which disrupt the goal of the event (e.g. you cannot order food in a restaurant because you were not given a menu) may be tagged differently in memory than actions which are mere distractions (e.g. the waiter spills some water on you). Children recall atypical actions which disrupt events better than atypical actions which are mere distractions, both immediately and at delayed recall (Davidson & Hoe 1993; Hudson 1988).

The overall pattern of results supports two conclusions. First, children, like adults, have difficulty recalling specific instances of events which do not deviate in any significant way from the script. However, when provided with specific cues, children can recall details about particular instances. Additionally, when the specific instance does deviate from the script, especially in ways that disrupt the goal of the event, children can recall the specific instance even after a few weeks. Note that these conclusions assume that there is already an established script from which the instance can deviate. How do children represent events after the first occurrence, and how does this representation develop with the first few experiences with an event?

Script formation

Perhaps the most likely explanation of how scripts form is that children form a specific event memory upon the first occurrence of an event (e.g. on the first trip to McDonald's the child remembers that she ordered a happy meal and the box had a puzzle on it and she ate all the french fries but only half the hamburger, and so on). After the second occurrence of the event, the child now has two episodic memories which share some similarities and some differences. After three experiences, there might be three episodic memories and so forth. At some point, the child would begin to compare the memories and note the similarities across occurrences leading to a generalized representation of what usually occurs.

Although this may seem the most logical possibility about how scripts are formed, the data do not support it. In fact, children seem to form scripts on the very first encounter with a new event. That is, even after one experience with a new event, children recount that event in a generalized, temporally ordered framework. This is quite clear from the example given above of one child's response when asked "what happens when you go to kindergarten?" on the morning of the second day of kindergarten. This recount conforms to the basic definition of a script. It is reported in the generalized "we do x" and the child does not include any idiosyncratic information about what happened to her on the first day. In contrast, when asked "what happened yesterday?" children gave specific details of their experience. For example, one child recounted having to come to school in a taxi because she missed the bus, and another child reported having special cookies in her lunch box.[1]

What these examples illustrate is that scripts and episodic memories are not on a continuum in the memory system, but rather seem to reflect different ways of representing events which can be present simultaneously. After one experience, children can report the specific details of what occurred, but they also seem to form a general framework such that they expect future occurrences of the event to conform to the first experience in important ways. Clearly, this script will change with increasing experience, as discussed above. But the basic framework of the event representation is established after just one experience (Fivush & Slackman 1986; Hudson & Nelson 1986; Ratner et al. 1986).

We know that once a script is firmly established, specific episodes are difficult to recall, but what about in the first few experiences of an event? After the first experience, children seem to have a skeletal script for the event, but they also seem to have a detailed memory of the first episode. How do children represent specific episodes during the first few experiences with an event?

Farrar and Goodman (1990) explored this question in a study of 4- and 7-year-old children's event memories. Children experienced a visit to the playroom either once, twice or four times. Obviously, in the one-time-only condition, children experienced only one event. In the two-experience condition, children experienced one event on the first experience and a somewhat different event on the second experience. In the four-experience condition, children experienced the same event three times on three successive occasions, and then experienced a somewhat different event on a fourth occasion. All children were then interviewed about their experiences. Children having only one experience were able to recall that experience quite well. But children experiencing two somewhat different experiences had more difficulty recalling either experience in detail, suggesting some confusion and interference in their memories. Older children who had multiple identical experiences before experiencing the different event were better able to recall the two events than children in the two-experience condition, but younger children still had difficulty in this condition, indicating that younger children were still confusing the two different experiences. Essentially, in the early phases of script development, younger children are somewhat disrupted by experiences which deviate from the typical, but older children are better able to represent these deviations.

Hudson (1990a) also examined this issue in a study of 3- and 5-year-old children's memories for a creative movement workshop. Children experienced either one workshop or four workshops. In the repeated experience condition, some of the activities were identical across experiences and some varied from time to time. Children were asked to recall the first workshop (whether it was the only one they experienced or the first in the series) immediately and after a delay. All children recalled the workshop quite well on immediate recall. Interestingly, after delay, children in the repeated experience group recalled more about the first workshop than children having only that experience, but they also intruded a great deal of information from the subsequent workshops into their memory of the first workshop. Again, it seems that children have some difficulty keeping specific instantiations of similar events separate in memory.

Summary

As in the findings on general script reports, children's reports of specific episodes of recurring events show a great deal of continuity across development. Younger children, like older children and adults, have difficulty recalling a specific instance of an event that does not deviate substantially from the script, but given specific cues, episodes can be recalled, often in great detail. Episodes which are quite different from the script, on the other hand, seem to be recalled quite well, even without specific cues. Further, atypical actions not central to the goal are well recalled immediately, but seem to fade over time as the episode is reconstructed to conform to the script. Also, somewhat surprisingly, children seem to form a generalized event representation upon the first occurrence with an event. The major developmental difference seems to be that younger children have more difficulty than older children in representing individual instantiations of an event during the early phases of script development. This is similar to the findings reported above about young children's difficulties in representing minor variations in the objects used during an event (Bauer & Fivush 1992; Fivush et al. 1992; Kuebli & Fivush 1994). All of these studies indicate that in the initial phases of forming and consolidating a script, young children are debilitated by variations among instantiations of the event to a greater extent than are older children (see Hudson et al. 1992, for a more detailed discussion of the developing relations between memories of single instances and recurring events).

Children's memories of novel events

The relation between children's generalized event representations and their memories of single, novel experiences is an intriguing one, partly because it is related to the phenomenon of "childhood amnesia." Although the explanation of childhood amnesia is still controversial, the empirical findings are quite clear; adults have difficulty recalling events that occurred before the age of about 3.5 to 4 (see Pillemer & White 1989, for a review; but see Usher & Neisser 1993 for a somewhat different interpretation). Both Hudson (1986) and Nelson (1988) initially theorized that this might be because young children do not form memories of specific experiences this early in development. Because children form a generalized event representation on the first experience of an event, Hudson and Nelson posited that scripts were a necessary precursor to specific event memories. It was not until children had a well-developed generalized memory system that they could begin to represent specific experiences in terms of how they differed from the script. Indeed, their early research found that 3- to 7- year-old children were better able to recount the general event than specific experiences (Hudson & Nelson 1986). However, in this study, they also found that children were sometimes able to give long, detailed recounts about special novel events, such as a visit to DisneyWorld or a first trip on an airplane. Thus, the initial formulation had to be modified (see Nelson 1988 for a full review).

What has become abundantly clear since the mid-1980s is that even quite young children are able to recall specific, novel experiences in some detail, and they can retain these memories over remarkably long periods of time (see Fivush 1993 for a review). For example, Fivush et al. (1987) asked 2.5- to 3-year-old children to recall events they had experienced either in the recent past (up to 3 months ago) or in the distant past (more than 3 months ago). All ten children interviewed were able to give accurate details about their past experiences, and were able to recall as much information about distantly experienced events as about more recently experienced events. In fact, all ten children were able to recall verbally at least one event that had occurred more than 6 months in the past. Similarly, Todd and Perlmutter (1980) found that 3- and 4-year-old children were able to recall accurate details of experienced events, although 4-year-olds recalled more information than 3-year-olds.

Some limitations of these first studies were that all the children were asked about different events, that had occurred at different times, and little information was available about how frequently these events had been discussed since their occurrence. In order to address these concerns, Hamond and Fivush (1990) asked 4- to 6-year-old children to recount a family trip to DisneyWorld. Not only were all the children asked about the same event, but they were all asked the same set of structured questions. Further, parents were asked to estimate how often the event had been discussed, either with or without photos, and when these discussions took place. Half of the children interviewed had been to DisneyWorld 6 months in the past and half had been there 18 months in the past. All children recalled quite a lot of accurate information about their experience. Most surprisingly, younger children recalled as much as older children and children who had been to DisneyWorld 18 months ago recalled as much as children who had been there 6 months ago. Children are able to remember a special event in great detail, and quite accurately, even over a very long period of time. Interestingly, the number of times the events had been discussed was not related to children's recall at 6 months, but after 18 months, those families that talked about the event more frequently had children who recalled more information than families that did not talk about the event as frequently. Verbal rehearsal may become increasingly important in keeping a memory alive as time since the experience increases.

It may not be just verbal rehearsal that facilitates memory. In an innovative series of studies, Hudson (1991; Sheffield & Hudson 1994) has been exploring the role of reactivation on retention of specific memories. Toddlers are brought to a playroom and experience an unusual series of activities. Some children return to the playroom to re-experience the event, either in part or in its entirety and then all the children return again at a later point and are asked to re-enact the event. Children who had the "reinstatement" remember substantially more at the final recall than children who did not, indicating that a behavioral rehearsal of even a part of the event can buffer against forgetting the entire event over relatively long delays. Thus even very young children are able to retain memories of specific experiences over long delays, but there may be developmental differences in how much and what kind of rehearsal is necessary to keep these memories alive. In particular, Hudson demonstrates that as children get older, the reinstatement of the memory can occur over longer delays; for very young children, the event may need to be reinstated quite soon after its occurrence in order to maintain the memory.

Summary

Recent research demonstrates that young children are able to recall specific, novel events over long periods of time. However, the type and frequency of rehearsal may play a critical role in the maintenance of memories, and may show developmental differences. In fact, this may be part of the explanation of childhood amnesia. Although young children can obviously encode and remember specific events from this early period of their life, these memories may become more and more inaccessible over time if they are not rehearsed.[2] Moreover the type and timing of the rehearsal may be developmentally sensitive.

The social-cultural context of event memories

Much of the research on developing event memories focuses on children's individual recounts of events. But clearly events in the real world occur in a social and cultural context. The ways in which events are talked about and how they are valued must surely play a role in children's developing event memory. For example, school is a highly valued activity in Western culture; children's participation in this activity must be influenced by the value placed upon it, which in turn will influence children's developing understanding and representation of the school day event. One way in which these values are expressed is in terms of how the event is talked about. Flannagan et al. (1995) examined mother–child conversations about the school day routine in middle- and working-class Anglo and Hispanic populations. Intriguingly, mothers with sons talked more about learning interactions at school, whereas mothers of daughters talked more about social interactions. These differences were somewhat more pronounced in the Hispanic than in the Anglo dyads, suggesting that gender and culture are important determinants of the kinds of interactions that mothers stress in discussing school with their young children. Why this is important is because it is likely that by focusing on particular aspects of events over others, mothers may be implicitly teaching their children what is important and valuable about their experiences.

These results highlight the fact that the ways in which events are talked about with children is a critical component of how children come to understand and represent events. As argued previously, age differences in children's event reports are not due solely to increasing language skills, but this does not mean that language plays no role in the development of event memory. Quite the contrary, there is a complex interaction between language and event memory (see Fivush & Haden 1996; Fivush et al. 1995 for discussions). The ways in which experiences are talked about before, during, and after the event all play a role in how children remember the event.

For example, Tessler and Nelson (1994) compared what mothers and 4-year-old children talked about during an event and children's subsequent

154

memory for the event. In two studies, one examining memories for a museum visit and one examining memories for a neighbourhood picture-taking excursion, they found that children recalled information that was mutually discussed by the mother and the child more than information talked about by only the mother or only the child. In an experimental analogue to this finding, Pipe et al. (1996) asked 5-year-old children to recall a "visit with the pirate" event, in which children dress up as pirates and hunt for buried treasure. Children experienced this event with an adult who either provided a full narrative of what was happening, or simply used "empty" language, such as "now, we'll do this." Children experiencing the event without narration recalled substantially less information and made many more errors in recall than children experiencing the event with narration. Clearly, the way in which events are talked about as they are occurring plays a critical role in children's memory for the event. Very likely, this is because the way in which the adult talks about the event helps the child to construct an organized representation.

Pipe et al. (in preparation) also found, however, that if children read a story about the event before the experience, it did not matter if the event was narrated during the experience for subsequent memory. If children already have an organized set of expectations about the event before it occurs, then they may not need the adult to help them organize the event as it is occurring. However, it is not quite clear what information children may be able to use to construct an organized representation before actually experiencing an event. Baker-Ward (1994) had children watch a video about visiting the dentist before their first visit; these children recalled no more information than children who had not seen the video. We simply have very little information at this point about how children can construct expectations for events that they have never directly experienced. In the only study of its kind, Murachver et al. (1994) asked 5-year-old children to recall a pirate event after directly experiencing the event, observing another child experience the event, or reading a story about the event. Children with direct experience recalled more information, and more organized information than children in the other groups after one exposure. Even after hearing the story several times, children in this condition did not recall the event as well as children with direct experience.

Overall, direct experience with an event accompanied by an adult providing an ongoing narrative about what is happening appears to lead to the most complete, accurate, and organized memory for young children. Children can form event memories through experience alone, without accompanying narration, and through narration alone without accompanying experience, but these memories do not seem to be as complete, or as accurate. Moreover, once children have experienced an event, the way in which it is discussed with others can still influence the subsequent memory. As we have already seen, children may need to "re-experience" the event, either through action or language to keep the event memory alive. But even beyond the simple effect of

155

rehearsal on the maintenance of memory, the particular ways in which events are reminisced about with others seems to be important.

Several studies have documented individual differences in the ways in which parents talk with their young children about past events (Fivush & Fromhoff 1988; Hudson 1990b; McCabe & Peterson 1991; Reese & Fivush 1993; Reese et al. 1993). Although different studies have used somewhat different measures, there is consensus that some parents are more elaborative than others. Elaborative parents give lots of rich, embellished information about the event during reminiscing, whereas less elaborative parents tend to ask the same questions repeatedly and to switch topics more frequently. Interestingly, children of more highly elaborative parents recall more information about the past. This is true both concurrently and longitudinally; parents who are highly elaborative early in development have children who recall more information about their past experiences later in development (McCabe & Peterson 1991; Reese et al. 1993). Children seem to be learning the narrative and linguistic skills for recounting their past through participating in highly elaborated conversations with their parents.

Developing relations between talking about events and remembering events is certainly complex, but the research conducted thus far indicates that this is a crucial aspect of children's developing event memory. The events of our lives are fundamentally social. Just as the temporal and variable structure of events influences children's developing events representations, the social structure of events is critical as well. Moreover, it is not just the way in which events are talked about as they are occurring that is important; the way in which events are talked about before and after they occur must be considered as well.

Scripts, episodes and novel events: What develops?

As this review indicates, conceptions of early memory have changed fundamentally since the early 1980s. We now know that even very young children recall a great deal of accurate, organized knowledge about events they have experienced in their everyday world. Children represent and recall familiar, recurring events, they recall specific episodes of recurring events under certain conditions, and they recall novel events in great detail. Moreover, there is substantial continuity in the form of these memories over a wide developmental span. Although older children and adults recall more information verbally than do younger children, the temporal structure of the recall is the same across development, as are the relations between generalized event memories and memories of specific instances. Further, many of the changes we see in event memory with increasing age are similar to the changes we see with increasing experience, indicating that some of these age differences are a function of expanding experience rather than developing cognitive abilities.

156

The major developmental difference in children's event memories seems to revolve around the representation of variability within recurring events, particularly during the early phases of script formation. Several studies have documented that 3- and 4-year-old children are confused by even minor variations across occurrences of an event during the first few experiences. Exactly why this is so and how this changes developmentally is still in question. Farrar and Goodman (1990) have proposed that in the initial stages of forming a representation, the "script-confirmation" phase, children (and adults) pay attention to what is the same in order to construct a general representation. Once the representation is stable, children (and adults) enter the "script-deployment" phase, in which they begin to pay attention to what is different and unique about this particular occurrence. It may be that younger children remain in the script-confirmation phase for longer than older children and adults.

In addition to considering the cognitive underpinnings of event memory, we must also consider the social situations in which memories are formed and recalled. Children encounter and recall new events as part of their ongoing social interactions in the world, and the ways in which these experiences are structured through language is critical.

Investigating children's event memory began with the premise that children's memory should be examined in more meaningful and familiar contexts. What we have learned from this approach is that memory is not something children have, but something that children use, in their everyday world, to anticipate and predict their environment and to share their experiences with others. It is this functional approach to understanding memory development that has led to new discoveries about how young children understand and represent their world.

Notes

1. Interestingly, although children responding to the "what happened yesterday?" question gave specific details, only about half of the children queried responded at all. That is, even on the morning of the second day of kindergarten, many children were unable to recall any specific details of the day before. As discussed in Fivush (1984) this is most likely due to children's difficulty in using "yesterday" as a retrieval cue. When given more specific information about occurrences of the day before, almost all the children could recall additional information. This is consistent with the discussion of children's memories for specific instantiations of recurring events.

2. Childhood amnesia appears to be quite a complex phenomenon and rehearsal may be only one contributing factor. Other factors that seem to play a role include the development of narrative skills (Fivush et al. 1995), the development of socially shareable memories (Nelson 1993; Pillemer & White 1989) and the development of an autobiographical self (Fivush 1988).

References

Adams, L. T. & P. E. Worden 1986. Script development and memory organization in preschool and elementary school children. *Discourse Processes* **9**, 149–66.

Bauer, P. J. & R. Fivush 1992. Constructing event representations: Building on a foundation of variations and enabling relations. *Cognitive Development* **7**, 381–401.

Bobrow, D. G. & D. Norman 1975. Some principles of memory schemata. In *Representation and understanding*, D. G. Bobrow & A. Collins (eds.). New York: Academic.

Bower, F. H., J. B. Black, & T. J. Turner 1979. Scripts in memory for texts. *Cognitive Psychology* **11**, 177–220.

Brown, A. L. & J. DeLoache 1978. Skills, plans and self-regulation. In *Children's thinking: What develops?*, R. S. Siegler (ed.), 3–36. Hillsdale, NJ: Erlbaum.

Caarni, E. & L. A. French 1984. The acquisition of "before" and "after" reconsidered: What develops? *Journal of Experimental Child Psychology* **37**, 394–403.

Davidson, D. & S. Hoe 1993. Children's recall and recognition memory for typical and atypical actions in script-based stories. *Journal of Experimental Child Psychology* **55**, 104–26.

DeCasper, A. J. & M. J. Spence 1986. Prenatal maternal speech influences newborns' perceptions of speech sounds. *Infant Behavior and Development* **9**, 133–50.

DeLoache, J., J. Cassidy, & A. L. Brown 1985. Precursors of mnemonic strategies in very young children. *Child Development* **56**, 125–37.

Donaldson, M. 1978. *Children's minds*. London: Norton.

Farrar, M. J. & G. S. Goodman 1990. Developmental differences in the relation between scripts and episodic memory: Do they exist? In *Knowing and remembering in young children*, R. Fivush & J. Hudson (eds.), 30–64. Cambridge: Cambridge University Press.

Fivush, R. 1984. Learning about school: The development of kindergartners' school scripts. *Child Development* **55**, 1697–709.

Fivush, R. 1988. The functions of event memory: Some comments on Nelson and Barsalou. In *Remembering reconsidered: Ecological and traditional approaches to memory*, U. Neisser & E. Winograd (eds.), 277–82. New York: Cambridge University Press.

Fivush, R. 1993. Developmental perspectives on autobiographical recall. In *Child victims, child witnesses: Understanding and improving testimony*, G. S. Goodman & B. L. Bottoms (eds.), 1–24. New York: Guilford.

Fivush, R. & F. A. Fromhoff 1988. Style and structure in mother–child conversations about the past. *Discourse Processes* **11**, 337–55.

Fivush, R., J. T. Gray, & F. A. Fromhoff 1987. Two year olds' talk about the past. *Cognitive Development* **2**, 393–409.

Fivush, R. & C. Haden 1996. Narrating and representing experience: Preschoolers developing autobiographical recounts. In *Event comprehension and representation*, P. van der Broek, P. J. Bauer, & T. Bourg (eds.), Hillsdale, NJ: Erlbaum.

Fivush, R., C. Haden, & S. Adam 1995. Structure and coherence of preschoolers' personal narratives over time: Implications for childhood amnesia. *Journal of Experimental Child Psychology* **60**, 32–50.

Fivush, R., C. A. Haden, & E. Reese 1996. Remembering, recounting and reminiscing: The development of autobiographical memory in social context. In *Recon-*

structing our past: An overview of autobiographical memory, D. C. Rubin (ed.). Cambridge: Cambridge University Press.

Fivush, R., J. Hudson & K. Nelson 1984. Children's long-term memory for a novel event: An exploratory study. *Merrill-Palmer Quarterly* **30**, 303–16.

Fivush, R., J. Kuebli, & P. A. Clubb 1992. The structure of events and event representations: Developmental analysis. *Child Development* **63**, 188–201.

Fivush, R. & J. Mandler 1985. Developmental changes in the understanding of temporal sequence. *Child Development* **56**, 1437–46.

Fivush, R. & E. Slackman 1986. The development of scripts. In *Event knowledge: Structure and function in development*, K. Nelson (ed.), 71–96. Hillsdale, NJ: Erlbaum.

Flannagan, D., L. Baker-Ward, & L. Graham 1995. Talk about preschool: Patterns of topic discussion and elaboration related to gender and ethnicity. *Sex Roles* **32**, 1–15.

Gelman, R. 1978. Cognitive development. *Annual Review of Psychology* **29**, 297–332.

Graesser, A. C., S. E. Gordon, & J. D. Sawyer 1979. Recognition memory for typical and atypical actions in scripted activities: Tests of a script pointer plus tag hypothesis. *Journal of Verbal Learning and Verbal Behavior* **18**, 319–32.

Graesser, A. C., S. B. Woll, D. J. Kowalski, & D. A. Smith 1980. Memory for typical and atypical actions in scripted activities. *Journal of Experimental Psychology: Human learning and Memory* **6**, 503–15.

Hamond, N. R. & R. Fivush 1990. Memories of Mickey Mouse: Young children recount their trip to DisneyWorld. *Cognitive Development* **6**, 433–48.

Hudson, J. A. 1986. Memories are made of this: General event knowledge an the developmental of autobiographic memory. In *Event knowledge: Structure and function in development*, K. Nelson (ed.), 97–118. Hillsdale, NJ: Erlbaum.

Hudson, J. A. 1988. Children's memory for atypical actions in script-based stories: Evidence for a disruption effect. *Journal of Experimental Child Psychology* **46**, 159–73.

Hudson, J. A. 1990a. Constructive processes in children's event memory. *Developmental Psychology* **2**, 180–7.

Hudson, J. A. 1990b. The emergence of autobiographic memory in mother–child conversation. In *Knowing and remembering in young children*, R. Fivush & J. A. Hudson (eds.), 166–96. New York: Cambridge University Press.

Hudson, J. A. 1991. *Effects of re-enactment on toddler's memory for a novel event.* Paper presented at the meetings of the Society for Research in Child Development, Seattle, WA.

Hudson, J. A., R. Fivush, & J. Kuebli 1992. Scripts and episodes: The development of event memory. *Applied Cognitive Psychology* **6**, 483–505.

Hudson, J. A. & K. Nelson 1983. Effects of script structure on children's story recall. *Developmental Psychology* **19**, 625–35.

Hudson, J. A. & K. Nelson 1986. Repeated encounters of a similar kind: Effects of familiarity on children's autobiographic memory. *Cognitive Development* **1**, 253–71.

Kail, R. 1990. *The development of memory in children.* New York: Freeman.

Kail, R. & J. Bisanz 1982. Information processing and cognitive development. In *Advances in child development and behavior, Vol. XVII*, H. W. Reese (ed.), 45–81. New York: Academic.

Kuebli, J. & R. Fivush 1994. Children's representation and recall of event alternatives. *Journal of Experimental Child Psychology* **58**, 25–45.

Laboratory of Comparative Human Cognition 1983. Culture and cognitive development. In *Cognitive development*, J. H. Flavell & E. M. Markman (eds.), *Vol. I* of the *Handbook of child psychology*, P. H. Mussen (ed.), 4th edn., 295–356. New York: Wiley.

Mandler, J. M. 1983. Representation. In *Cognitive development*, J. H. Flavell & E. M. Markman (eds.), *Vol. III* of the *Handbook of child psychology*, P. H. Mussen (ed.), 4th edn., 420–94. New York: Wiley.

McCabe, A. & C. Peterson 1991. Getting the story: A longitudinal study of parental styles in eliciting narratives and developing narrative skill. In *Developing narrative structure*, A. McCabe & C. Peterson (eds.), 217–53. Hillsdale, NJ: Erlbaum.

Murachver, T., M-E. Pipe, L. Owens, R. Gordon, & R. Fivush 1994. *Do, show, and tell: Children's event memories acquired through direct experience, observation and stories.* Unpublished paper.

Nelson, K. 1986. *Event knowledge: Structures and function in development.* Hillsdale, NJ: Erlbaum.

Nelson, K. 1988. The ontogeny of memory for real events. In *Remembering reconsidered: Ecological and traditional approaches to the study of memory*, U. Neisser & E. Winograd (eds.), 244–76. New York: Cambridge University Press

Nelson, K. 1993. The psychological and social origins of autobiographical memory. *Psychological Science* **1**, 1–8.

Nelson, K., R. Fivush, J. Hudson, & J. Lucariello 1983. Scripts and the development of memory. In *Contributions to human development*, M. T. H. Chi (ed.), *Vol. IX* of *Trends in memory development research*, 52–70. New York: Karger.

Nelson, K. & J. M. Gruendel 1981. Generalized event representations: Basic building blocks of cognitive development. In *Advances in development psychology, Vol. 1*, M. E. Lamb & A. L. Brown (eds.), 131–58. Hillsdale, NJ: Erlbaum.

Nelson, K. & J. Gruendel 1986. Children's scripts. In *Event knowledge: Structure and function in development*, K. Nelson (ed.), 21–46. Hillsdale, NJ: Erlbaum.

Piaget, J. & B. Inhelder 1973. *Memory and intelligence.* New York: Basic Books.

Pillemer, D. B., M. L. Picariello, & J. C. Pruett 1994. Very long term memories of a salient preschool event. *Journal of Applied Cognitive Psychology* **8**, 95–106.

Pillemer, D. B. & S. H. White 1989. Childhood events recalled by children and adults. *Advances in Child Development and Behavior* **21**, 297–340.

Pipe, M-E. J. Dean, J. Canning, & T. Murachver 1996. *Telling it like it was, is and will be: Effects of narration of children's event reports.* Paper presented at International Conference on Memory, Padova, Italy.

Price, D. W. W. & G. S. Goodman 1990. Visiting the wizard: Children's memory for a recurring event. *Child Development* **61**, 664–80.

Ratner, H. H., B. S. Smith, & S. A. Dion 1986. Development of memory for events. *Journal of Experimental Child Psychology* **41**, 411–28.

Reese, E. & R. Fivush, R. 1993. Parental styles for talking about the past. *Developmental Psychology* **29**, 596–606.

Reese, E., C. A. Haden, & R. Fivush 1993. Mother–child conversations about the past: Relationships of style and memory over time. *Cognitive Development* **8**, 403–30.

Rogoff, B. 1990. *Apprenticeship in thinking.* New York: Oxford University Press.

160

Rovee-Collier, C. & C. W. G. Shyi 1992. A functional and cognitive analysis of infant long-term memory retention. In *Development of long-term retention*, M. L. Howe, C. J. Brainerd, &V. F. Reyna (eds.). New York: Springer-Verlag.

Shank, R. & A. Abelson 1977. *Scripts plans goals and understanding*. Hillsdale, NJ: Erlbaum.

Sheffield, E. & J. A. Hudson 1994. Reactivation of toddlers' event memory. *Memory* **2**, 447–65.

Slackman, E. A., J. A. Hudson, & R. Fivush 1986. Actions, actors, links, and goals: The structure of children's event representations. In *Event knowledge: Structure and function in development*, K. Nelson (ed.), 47–69. Hillsdale, NJ: Erlbaum.

Slackman, E. A. & K. Nelson 1984. Acquisition of an unfamiliar script in story form by young children. *Child Development* **55**, 329–40.

Smith, D. A. & A. C. Graesser 1981. Memory for actions in scripted activities as a function of typicality, retention interval, and retrieval task. *Memory and Cognition* **9**, 550–9.

Tessler, M. & K. Nelson 1994. Making memories: The influence of joint encoding on later recall by young children. *Consciousness and Cognition* **3**, 307–26.

Todd, C. & M. Perlmutter 1980. Reality recalled by preschool children. In *New directions for child development: Children's memory*, M. Perlmutter (ed.), 69–86. San Francisco, CA: Jossey-Bass.

Usher, J. & U. Neisser 1993. Childhood amnesia and the beginnings of memory for four early life events. *Journal of Experimental Psychology: General* **122**, 155–65.

Vygotsky, L. S. 1978. *Mind in society: The development of higher psychological processes*. Cambridge, MA: Harvard University Press.

Wertsch, J. 1985. *Vygotsky and the social formation of mind*. Cambridge, MA: Harvard University Press.

CHAPTER 7

The development of working memory

Nelson Cowan

Working memory refers to ideas that are thought of, or made available to the mind, just when they are needed in order to carry out a mental task or solve a problem. A simple example is remembering a phone number so you don't have to keep your eye on the exact spot in the phone book while entering the number. As a slightly more complex example, suppose you need to add 39 and 46 without using paper or a calculator. To do so, you must keep in mind both of the numbers to be added while bringing to mind the procedure you will use to do this sort of addition. In the conventional procedure, after you add the numbers in the right-hand column, 9 and 6, you must remember to decompose the answer (15) into a 5 that goes in the right-hand column of the sum and must be remembered, and a 1 that is added to the left-hand column's numbers, making 1 + 3 + 4 = 8 in this second column. Then you must remember to adjoin the numbers in the two columns, forming the answer (85).

Two things may set these examples apart from memory as discussed in most places within this book: capacity limits and time limits. In contrast to the vast capacity of the human mind to learn information and retrieve it on occasion, the amount that one can bring to mind all at once, to perform a task or solve a problem, is quite limited. (To appreciate this, just ask a friend to get you seven unrelated items, as long as he or she is going into the kitchen anyway. You are more likely to get a confused or irritated reply than you are to get all seven items.) Moreover, this limited amount of information that is brought to mind at any one time can be kept in mind only briefly (say, less than about a minute) unless the person devotes intense effort to the task of retaining the information. (Remember the things you wanted to say to someone but forgot while that person was talking to you? How about the errand you forgot to run because something more interesting caught your attention first?)

Because this working memory is so important in daily life, it would be very helpful to know how it changes with development in childhood. If we knew that, we would know a lot about particular limitations on thinking and problem solving in children of various ages. Children could not solve a problem that required more working memory than they could muster.

It is clear that young children do not do as well as older children on tasks that directly measure aspects of working memory. One of the most basic, often-replicated findings is that older children are able to repeat back verbatim a longer list of words than younger children; that is, they have a higher "memory span" (for a review see Dempster 1981). However, we still must ask, what is the basis of developmental differences in working memory such as this one? Do they reflect a developmental increase in working memory capacity, or perhaps of the persistence of working memory across time? Do they instead just reflect the use of better knowledge and strategies in older children?

Before examining these developmental questions, however, it is important to ask how working memory operates in general. This is a complicated, unresolved issue that involves many different processes. There are multiple views of how working memory operates, and they have implications for what type of developmental change is theoretically possible. As a result of this unresolved debate, I believe, there has not been a recent comprehensive review of what we know about working memory development. Baddeley (1986) provided a review of working memory from one theoretical vantage point, and Gathercole and Baddeley (1993) updated it from a similar perspective, with more developmental information included. This chapter will cover some of the same material but will place greater emphasis on highlighting some controversial issues that arise from a comparison of opposing theoretical viewpoints. A single chapter on this issue cannot be fully comprehensive, but this chapter will at least surf across a wide range of relevant topics in an attempt to organize and explain them.

Theoretical views of working memory

The traditional view of working memory (Baddeley 1986) has been that it depends in part on an older concept, "short-term storage." The concept of short-term storage states that there is a part of the mind that is capable of holding a small amount of information for a limited period of time. It is contrasted with "long-term storage," the vast store of information accumulated throughout one's life.

In order to use short-term storage within a working memory system, the right information must be placed in the store, kept active in the store until it is needed, and then retrieved in a timely fashion. For example, to remember a phone number until it can be dialed, according to Baddeley's (1986) model, one would save the phonetic sequence corresponding to the digits in short-term storage; keep the phonetic sequence active as long as necessary by silently rehearsing it (i.e., repeating it to oneself); and then mentally read out the contents of the short-term store while dialing. In an arithmetic problem, the same working memory mechanisms might be used. One might, for example, need to store the phonetic sequence "carry a one" in short-term storage; keep it active in this memory store for as long as needed using covert verbal rehearsal; and then retrieve it when the operation is to be carried out.

Recently, though, some researchers have questioned whether working memory does have to depend on a short-term store after all. The essential defining property of a short-term store is that information in the store has a limited capacity, which theoretically might occur either because it can only hold so many items at once (see G. A. Miller 1956) or because whatever information it holds decays over time (see Baddeley 1986). An alternative possibility described by Cowan (1995: Ch. 4) and Ericsson and Kintsch (1995) is that information in long-term memory has properties that just make it *seem* as if a short-term store is involved. According to that view, chunks of information are stored in memory with contextual markers that point out the situations in which the information is relevant. New information concerning the problem one is presently working on would be stored with the most relevant contextual markers, and therefore would be, for the time being, easier to retrieve than most other information in memory.

According to this description of "virtual short-term memory" (Cowan 1995) or "long-term working memory" (Ericsson & Kintsel 1995), the information would not decay over time. However, it could become harder to retrieve over time for two other reasons: (a) because the context does not remain the same as it was, and (b) because subsequent information may interfere with retrieval. For example, suppose you wanted to carry out an addition problem (42 + 39) in your head. Suppose further that the numbers represented the dollar prices of items to be purchased, and you wanted to figure out the sum while standing in the store's checkout line. This requires having the numbers available in memory while carrying out the operation. Even if you were able to meet this requirement with no problem, it might be impossible for you to report the numbers or their sum a few minutes later, while driving away from the department store. According to the view in which there is no special short-term storage, the reason might be that the sights and sounds of the store helped you remember how much each item cost. Without that context, the sensory information corresponding to the price tags might be harder to retrieve from memory. Still another reason might be that, in the meantime, you have thought of the prices of several other items that you wish to buy in another store, or that you decided not to buy. These numbers in your memory are stored with contextual cues similar to the ones in the addition problem, and when you try to retrieve those numbers again the new numbers might interfere. This is just one example of how a change in context and inter-item interference can reduce the chance of correct recall. We do not know what all of the relevant contextual markers and aspects of interference really are. If the contextual changes and interference occurred quickly and strongly enough, there might be enough forgetting to make it look as if information must have been lost from a quickly decaying short-term store.

So, despite many reliable findings in the working memory literature, different theoretical views still remain viable. As an analogy to these possibilities, we might consider libraries with several different types of organization.

First, in a library with a decaying short-term memory, you can telephone in a request for a book and it will be retrieved from the stacks and held at the checkout desk (the short-term store) for you. You can request as many books as you want; the library will find a way to accommodate you. However, each book will be held for only a certain period of time (say, 1 week) and then will be reshelved.

Second, in a library with a capacity-limited short-term memory, the books you request are held indefinitely, provided that there are not too many books requested. When the holding area is full, though, the older requests that have not yet been picked up are sent back to be reshelved. The holding time will depend on the demand for the space. If there is an extremely heavy book-holding demand, your book might not even be held for an entire day, and you might not have time to pick it up!

Third, in a library without a short-term store, the books you request are not moved from their original storage locations, but a little flag is placed sticking out of the book, making it easier to retrieve when you arrive. The flag is color-coded for the date, day of the week, season, and year. So if you come in soon or recall exactly what flag was used on that day, the retrieval process could be easy. That will be true especially if not many books received similar flags. However, if you wait too long (so that the flag that was used is no longer exactly clear to you) or if too many books were tagged at around the same time, retrieval will be difficult.

One should not take the analogy too literally. It breaks down, for example, in that memories may not exist in discrete locations like books but rather may be distributed across large, overlapping areas of the cortex, and almost certainly would not disappear from their long-term memory locations when they were placed in short-term storage. However, the analogy can help to clarify how different working memory systems might operate.

Let us now examine the evidence for and against a distinct short-term memory in a little more detail, on the basis of some of the relevant research.

The basis of short-term forgetting, part 1: Is there decay?

The fundamental question of whether "short-term memory storage" really exists as a separate entity is an old one (Conrad 1967, McGeoch 1932; Melton 1963), but it is more alive in the field today than some popular summaries would lead one to believe. An opposing view, the "unitary memory" view, is that the same rules of learning apply to all memory tasks, from those lasting a few seconds to those lasting hours or days (Crowder 1993).

According to the "dual-storage" view, which states that the human mind includes separate short- and long-term storage mechanisms, the basic distinguishing property of short-term storage is that it is based on a temporary memory representation that deteriorates or decays within, say, a minute or less. Long-term storage would be subject to forgetting from contextual changes and interference, but not decay. The unitary memory view holds that memory in any task is not susceptible to decay, just retrieval failures owing to other factors (contextual shifts, interference).

Some of the evidence that used to be viewed as strongly in favour of a short-term memory store has had to be reinterpreted in light of more recent evidence. In one classic study, Peterson and Peterson (1959) presented three spoken consonant letters on each trial and then imposed a distracting task, counting backward by three or four from a particular number, lasting between 3 and 18 seconds. After that distraction, the participant was to recall the letters. Even though it did not seem likely that there would be much interference from the numbers, the recall of the consonants fell off dramatically as the period of distraction lengthened. It was assumed that consonants could not be rehearsed during the distracting period and that the short-term memory representation of those consonants decayed during that time.

Keppel and Underwood (1962) re-examined performance in Peterson and Peterson's procedure, and found something disturbing to the view that the dropoff of memory performance as a function of the distractor period resulted from short-term memory decay. They found that there was very little forgetting in the first trial or so, regardless of the distractor period. It was only after several trials that long distractor periods within a trial hurt performance much. This suggested that long-term memory was involved in the task, and that memory loss occurred only if there was the possibility of interference from the letters presented on previous trials. The dual-storage theorists still could suggest that the distractor period was effective because it allowed short-term memory decay, and that this decay would hurt performance only if there was enough interference from previous trials to prevent a more durable type of memory storage from forming. However, the unitary memory theorists could explain the results without decay, by suggesting that good recall depends upon remembering the context in which the last set of consonants was presented, and that a distractor period reduces the distinctiveness in memory of that most recent set of consonants, allowing its consonants to become more easily confused with consonants presented on previous trials. It is as if one is standing near the last telephone pole in a row, which would look very large and distinct in comparison to poles farther down in the row. As one moves away from the row of poles (i.e., as the duration of the distracting period increases), the last pole appears to merge closer to the other ones (i.e., distinctiveness of the most recent consonant set in memory decreases).

Another classic type of evidence for short-term storage came from "free recall" procedures, in which a list of words was presented in either written or spoken form on each trial and was to be repeated with the words in any order that the participant found convenient. That type of procedure results in a U-shaped recall function, with much better recall of the words presented near the beginning and end of the list, and poorer recall of words presented in the middle. The superior recall at the beginning of the list, or "primacy effect," was thought to occur because the first few words can be attended and rehearsed without competition from other items. In contrast, the superior recall at the end of the list, or "recency effect," was thought to occur because the short-term memory representation of the last few words has not yet decayed much by the time of recall. Seeming to support this interpretation, Glanzer and Cunitz (1966) found that a distracting task interposed between the end of the list and the participant's recall attempt left the primacy effect unaltered, but greatly reduced the magnitude of the recency effect.

Bjork and Whitten (1974) carried out a procedure that challenged the dual-store explanation of the recency effect in free recall, much as Keppel and Underwood's (1962) study challenged the dual-storage explanation of Peterson and Peterson's (1959) study. Bjork and Whitten presented pairs of words with a distracting period before and after each pair. The final distracting period occurred just before the recall test and was long enough (12–42 seconds) that it should have allowed the short-term memory representation of the list to be eliminated, or nearly so. Nevertheless, a recency effect emerged. It could be attributed to the greater temporal distinctiveness of the last few pairs of items, given that they were separated by distracting periods. It is as if the poles in a row were greatly separated, which would allow one to stand further back from the end pole without losing a sense of its special distinctiveness from the other poles.

This "continual distractor procedure" that Bjork and Whitten used has been extended to a situation with distractor periods between individual items rather than item pairs (e.g. Koppenaal & Glanzer 1990), again resulting in the "long-term recency effect." The procedure also has been extended to produce long-term analogs to other effects that previously had been taken as indices of short-term memory at work, including an advantage of memory for words presented in a spoken as compared to a printed modality (Gardiner & Gregg 1979) and a disruptive effect of an interfering spoken word, or "suffix," placed directly after a spoken list to be recalled (Glenberg 1984). All of these findings opened up the possibility that a unitary memory account could explain the basic short-term memory findings (forgetting across distractor periods; recency, modality, and suffix effects in free recall) without any need to make reference to a decaying short-term store. The principle that the temporal distinctiveness of an item in memory aids its recall would be sufficient.

Nevertheless, there are findings in the research literature that seem difficult to account for without the notion of memory decay (for reviews see Cowan 1988, 1993, 1994, 1995; Healy & McNamara 1996). Perhaps foremost among them, Reitman (1974) tested memory for lists of five monosyllabic nouns (presented visually and read aloud by the participant) that were followed by a distracting period filled only with tones to be detected in noise, and included an elaborate system for finding out if a particular participant was likely to have been rehearsing the words while carrying out the detection task. There was little forgetting of words in participants who rehearsed, but there was considerable forgetting in those who did not rehearse. It is possible that the rehearsal

168

just served to counteract interference from the intervening noise and tones, but they are so unlike the verbal items to be remembered that it seems more likely that the rehearsal served to counteract decay. There was little in the intervening stimulation that could have interfered with the items, so this suggests that the rehearsal process prevented words from decaying in memory. (For other evidence that appears to pose a problem for unitary memory theories, see Conrad 1967; Cowan et al. 1994b; Craik 1970; Craik & Birtwistle 1971; Vallar & Baddeley 1982; Watkins et al. 1973; Wingfield & Byrnes 1972).

There also is recent physiological evidence of neural aftereffects of tone stimulation in the temporal lobe lasting several seconds, which is easy to explain on the basis of memory decay but might be difficult to explain without decay (e.g. Lu et al. 1992; Mäntysalo & Näätänen 1987; Sams et al. 1993). It has been assumed that these neural responses are related to behavioral components of memory, and there is evidence to support that. For example, the "mismatch negativity" component of the event-related potential occurs basically for any physical change in a repeated sound that participants would be able to detect if they were listening, even though the mismatch negativity is recorded while the participants ignore the sounds. Thus, it has been assumed that the mismatch negativity occurs when a sensory trace of a standard sound is compared to a deviant sound in the brain and found to differ from the standard (Näätänen 1992). However, the mismatch negativity does not occur if the sounds are further apart than about 10 seconds (Sams et al. 1993).

Cases of neurological damage also seem to support the notion of memory decay (Squire et al. 1993). One relevant phenomenon is damage to the hippocampus, an area embedded within each temporal lobe of the brain, and to closely surrounding areas (typically through strokes, disease, or operations to cure severe epilepsy). This does not affect performance on short-term memory tasks (or memory for about a 10- to 30-second period), but in severe cases of bilateral damage it prevents the patient from learning anything new in a way that can be deliberately, consciously recalled later. In contrast, damage to certain other areas of the brain can severely impair short-term memory for a particular type of information (e.g. spoken verbal information). That also has the effect of impairing long-term memory for the same kind of information, presumably because the information does not get a chance to be encoded well in long-term memory; but it does not produce a general long-term memory impairment. Thus, different types of brain injury selectively impair short- versus long-term memory.

Still, objections could be raised. For example, a unitary memory theorist might argue that the hippocampus is needed to link an event to its context for the sake of memory encoding. It would have to be assumed that within a matter of seconds, the context has changed and the event therefore no longer can be consciously retrieved (though it has left a mark on memory that can affect procedural or indirect tests of memory). However, proposing that a contextual change depends on a fixed brief period seems somewhat arbitrary.

A final type of evidence for memory decay is an indirect one, having to do with Baddeley's (1986) notion of a verbal "articulatory loop," a system in which verbal information is presumably held temporarily and, until it decays from storage, can be refreshed from time to time through covert verbal rehearsal. A strong impetus for the formation of this theory was research on the word length effect by Baddeley et al. 1975. They found that immediate memory for sets of short words was superior to memory for sets of longer words. They also conducted a separate task in which participants received short subsets of the items that had appeared in the memory test, either in spoken or in written form, and were to read or repeat these items as quickly as possible. This task was meant as an estimate of the rate at which covert verbal rehearsal could take place. It was found that there was a linear relation between the rate at which items of a particular type could be repeated and immediate memory for those items. Specifically, it seemed that people remembered about as much of a particular type of item as they could repeat in about 1.8 seconds. This relation between rapid speech rate and immediate memory performance has been replicated many times, with diverse means of varying the repetition rate including manipulations of word length, individual differences, age differences, or differences between one language and another (Baddeley et al. 1975; Cowan et al. 1994; Gathercole et al. 1994; Hulme et al. 1984; Naveh-Benjamin & Ayres 1986; Nicolson 1981; Schweickert & Boruff 1986; Standing 1980; Stigler 1986). This relationship is illustrated schematically in Figure 7.1.

The explanation (Baddeley 1986) has been as follows. The phonological representation in each word in a list to be recalled is saved in a short-term memory

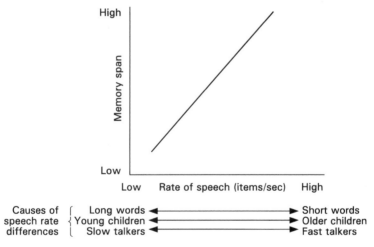

Figure 7.1 A schematic illustration of the linear relationship that has been observed between the maximal rate at which words can be pronounced and the memory span for sets composed of those words. As shown, the variations in pronunciation rate and span have been obtained either by manipulating the length of the words or by varying the characteristics of the participant groups' abilities.

store, or "buffer." In order to be retained in the store, each item must be rehearsed before it is totally lost from storage through decay. Assuming that overt repetition and covert rehearsal can take place at about the same rates (not a bad assumption; see Landauer 1962), it seems that one can recall as much as can be rehearsed in about 1.8 seconds. This suggests that the persistence of information in the buffer without rehearsal is only about that long – about 1.8 seconds.

An alternative theory is that more slowly rehearsed words hurt performance not because they allow more decay, but because they cause more interference with memory. One problem with that account is that it does not explain the 1.8-second constant. When rehearsal speeds up, the rate of interference also speeds up (at least in terms of the number of phonemes rehearsed per second). Therefore, the memory performance should not go up with rehearsal speed. It does just that.

Nevertheless, the relation between speech rate and memory span is just a correlation. We do not know the true cause of the correlation, so the unitary memory account cannot be ruled out definitively.

In sum, for the sake of the simplicity and parsimony of theory, it has seemed attractive to some investigators to have a unitary theory of memory with as few explanatory principles as possible and no concept of memory decay. However, there are important aspects of the evidence that the unitary memory theorists have yet to explain. These types of evidence seem to be more readily explainable using the concept of memory decay. Still, this is a fundamental unresolved question in need of further evidence.

The basis of short-term forgetting, part 2: Is there a capacity limit?

A possibility that requires more attention is that memory is limited not by time *per se*, but by the quantity of information. G. A. Miller (1956) was an early proponent of this view when he observed that short-term recall in many circumstances seemed to be limited to about seven items (plus or minus two).

If there is such a limit, its nature is still in question. The old interpretation is that there is a limited number of fixed "slots" in short-term storage and when too many items are presented, some items are bumped out of the slots they occupy. A unitary memory theorist might argue that the limit occurs because of interference between items in memory generally, not in a special short-term store. Perhaps more than seven or so items presented in immediate succession cannot all be remembered because they are not distinct enough from one another, having been presented close to one another in time and with little opportunity for very meaningful, coherent encoding.

Some researchers have proposed that there is a capacity limit in short-term memory, but that it is inflated by other contributions. There can be recall from long-term memory even in what is viewed as a short-term memory task; and recall can be enhanced by mnemonic processing strategies, such as covert verbal rehearsal, that help one to hold more items than would be possible through effortless, automatic processing alone. Techniques in which rehearsal is minimized and the performance levels are corrected for the presumed contribution of long-term memory have resulted in the revised estimate that two to four items can be held passively in memory (e.g. Glanzer & Razel 1974; W⁻ tkins 1974).

Time and capacity limits considered jointly

One important question that has not been answered yet by research in the field is how the short-term memory time limit that Baddeley et al. (1975) observed is related to the capacity limit that other have observed. Zhang and Simon (1985) suggested that both limits exist. They examined short-term memory in Chinese, for sets of monosyllabic characters, disyllabic words, and idioms consisting of four syllables. In terms of the number of units, the average observed memory spans were 6.6 characters, 4.6 words, and 3.0 idioms. However, consider that this amounts to 6.6 syllables for the character spans, 9.2 syllables for the word spans, and 12.0 syllables for the idiom spans. To account for these results, they developed a model in which there was a time limit in recall (similar to the model of Baddeley 1986) but in which this limit consisted of a constant amount of time to retrieve each unit plus an extra amount of time to unpack the unit into its syllables and process them individually.

Even if one accepts Zhang and Simon's proposal, a remaining question is whether the capacity and time constraints operate similarly. Specifically, assuming that the phonetic information is lost over time, is there information in a limited number of nonphonetic "slots" that remains until it is bumped out by additional information, or is the nonphonetic information lost through the passage of time, as well? The answer to this question may depend on exactly what "capacity limits" are. They could reflect a limit in automatically held information. Indeed, that seems to be the spirit in which researchers such as G. A. Miller (1956) thought of short-term memory slots. In this case, it seems reasonable that these automatically held slots might be susceptible to memory decay, in addition to the severe interference from additional information. Theories of memory have rarely considered the possibility of a form of memory representation that has both capacity limits and time limits.

Alternatively, the capacity limit that has been observed (just two to four items, according to the literature we have discussed) could reflect the amount that can be held in awareness or the "focus of attention" at any one time. It does not seem that attention to an item just fades away; it is maintained on the item or items for a while and then abruptly shifts to other matters depending on such things as task demands and the person's motivation.

A working model of working memory

The purpose of the discussion above was to make the point that we still do not really know exactly what the limits on memory are. In a situation like that, in which much basic research remains to be done, it often reduces confusion if one assumes that a particular tentative or "working" model of the processing system is correct. People tend to hold to such models implicitly, even if they are not fully aware of doing so; and stating a model explicitly may just bring one's assumptions out in the open.

One simple model of memory was suggested by Cowan (1988, 1993, 1995). The essence of this model is reproduced in Figure 7.2. In it, only a subset of the vast information in an individual's memory is in an activated state at any one time, making that information easy to access if it should be needed. The activated information can be sensory, phonological, or semantic in nature. Moreover, only a subset of this activated information is in the individual's current focus of attention. The attentional focus is controlled in part by the central executive, which represents the individual's voluntary processing strategies, and in part by shifts of attention to abrupt changes in the stimulus (e.g. loud noises, color changes) and possibly pertinent words in it that sometimes appear to be analyzed automatically (e.g. one's own name spoken by someone trying to get one's attention).

According to this model, any amount of information could be activated at once, but the information decays. Based on various types of evidence, it has been suggested that the decay is most severe for about 2 seconds and continues at a continually decreasing rate for about 15 or 20 seconds (Cowan 1984, 1988). In contrast, information in the focus of awareness does not decay, but there is a capacity limit on how much information can be in the focus. Thus, in this model, the time and capacity limits apply to different aspects of short-term memory. Retrieval of information of both kinds also might be affected by interference.

Not shown in Figure 7.2, there could be differences between types of activated memory (e.g. the separate verbal versus spatial stores described by Baddeley 1986). However, the simplicity of the diagram is meant to suggest that these different modules could operate in a similar manner. It also is meant

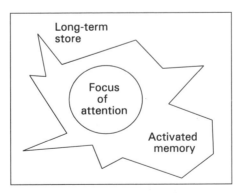

Figure 7.2 A simplified diagram of the relationship between memory faculties suggested by Cowan (1988). The focus of attention is only a subset of the activated elements in memory because there is also the possibility of automatic activation of memory elements.

to suggest that we do not yet know all of the relevant subdivisions of memory. For example, are tone and speech memory handled together, or by separate modules? It is not yet clear (Jones & Macken 1993).

If one removes the time limit on activation, the model shown in Figure 7.2 also would turn into one version of the unitary memory model. Unitary theorists do not deny that there is a capacity-limited focus of attention; they deny only that there is a time-limited aspect of memory.

Thus, although there are many theoretical possibilities that have not been ruled out, Figure 7.2 can serve as a device to simplify our perspective as we move on to other issues. It is similar in spirit to the prior model suggested by Baddeley (1986), except that the "active memory" of the present figure is a short-term storage device that includes any type of processed information (e.g. sensory, phonological, or semantic information), and thus is more inclusive than the distinct phonetic and visuospatial short-term stores depicted in Baddeley's model.

There are some neurophysiological findings with positron emission tomography in humans (Awh et al. 1996) and individual neural cell recordings in monkeys (E. K Miller & Desimone 1994) that provide general support for a model like Baddeley's (1986) or the model shown in the figure. These studies show that there are separate areas of the brain that are involved in the passive, automatic retention of information for a short time (e.g. in the temporal lobe), versus the active, effortful processing that can be used to prolong short-term memory (e.g. in the frontal lobe).

Developmental changes in working memory

Working memory can be involved in various ways in almost any mental task, ranging from memory to problem-solving to comprehension. It would be overwhelming to try to summarize developmental changes in each of these tasks individually. Instead, the following discussion focuses on what the underlying changes in the processing system may be. There are some changes that clearly do occur, and others that are still tentative.

Focusing on the basic processes that appear to change is important for two reasons. First, it can lead to a better appreciation of development in general. Secondly, the developmental changes can be relevant to the theoretical model of working memory that is favoured. In turn we will consider apparent developmental changes in (a) knowledge, (b) processing strategies, (c) processing speed, (d) the use of attention and processing capacity, (e) passive memory loss over time, and (f) passive memory storage capacity.

Changes in knowledge

Since the beginning of cognitive psychology, it has been clear that knowledge aids in immediate memory tasks, in which the participant tries to recall a list of items presented on each trial. G. A. Miller (1956) discussed the short-term memory limit in terms of "chunking," which is a grouping together of items on the basis of knowledge. For example, one can remember and repeat back a list of nine unrelated letters (e.g. "sdc-rqb-ltz") only with great difficulty. In contrast, it is easy to repeat back a list of nine letters that can be grouped into three meaningful three-letter chunks (e.g. "usa-cia-bbc"). In the latter case, the relevant real-world knowledge greatly helps to reduce the load on memory.

If there is one mental attribute that is sure to increase with age, it is knowledge. However, it is often difficult to decide if a developmental improvement in the use of working memory occurs because of an increase in knowledge, or because of other reasons. Ordinarily, the developmental change in knowledge is also accompanied by a developmental change in the brain and an improvement in other aspects of mental functioning. Therefore, it is difficult to know what improvements are due to knowledge *per se*.

Some work of Chi (1978) occurred in a special situation in which the effects of knowledge are evident. They tested memory for chessboard setups in adults who were relative novices at chess, and in children who were experts. In this test, each participant inspected the chessboard and then had to reproduce the setup without looking at the original board. Other short-term memory skills also were tested. In general, the children's short-term memory was inferior. When it came to legitimate chess game setups, however, the expert children were superior to the novice adults. The children's knowledge of chess presumably allowed them to chunk the board into larger configurations of pieces that were easier to remember.

In general, knowledge aids working memory because it reduces the effective memory load. To the extent that one has the knowledge to link items together into a meaningful pattern, and to the extent that these patterns are in fact noticed, the stimuli no longer have to be remembered as separate, arbitrary elements.

Some studies have been useful in distinguishing knowledge contributions from other contributions to working memory. For example, Roodenrys et al. (1993) studied the development of memory span for words (of which one can have lexical knowledge) and nonword strings of sounds (of which one cannot have such knowledge). Older children's short-term recall benefitted from the lexical factor more than younger children. This finding will be discussed in greater detail later on, when the aim will be to distinguish knowledge from other possible sources of development in working memory.

Changes in processing strategies

The way in which a person approaches a working memory task, or any other task for that matter, is far from automatic or consistent. Instead, individuals have various choices of processing methods or "strategies" from which they can choose. This topic is not totally separate from the previous topic, knowledge, because the use of a better strategy may depend partly on the individual's knowledge of which strategy is best (and partly on the individual's ability to use the strategy effectively when that knowledge is present).

To illustrate strategy use, consider a child's means of solving a simple addition problem such as 9 + 3 (Geary 1990, 1993). If the child knows the answer, the fastest way to solve the problem is usually to retrieve it from long-term memory. If the child does not know it (or, at least, does not know it with sufficient confidence), another method will be preferred. The child might rearrange the numbers. By transferring 1 from the second number to the first, it can be seen that they are equivalent to 10 + 2, which the child may recognize as 12. If the child cannot decompose the numbers in this way, a third method is to start at 9 and count up to 12. If that ability is not present, the child may have to count all the way from 1 to 12. Sometimes, especially for problems with sums less than 10, fingers are used as a working memory aid. A problem such as 5 + 3 can be solved by the child uplifting five fingers on one hand and three fingers on the other, and counting the uplifted fingers.

A child may not use a developmentally new strategy consistently at first. Instead, work by Siegler (1994) has shown that the use of strategies varies from trial to trial. A new strategy may be used only on a small proportion of the trials, and that proportion tends to grow as the value of the strategy becomes clear and the child becomes better at using it effectively. All the while, the older, less desirable strategy becomes less and less frequent.

Strategies that are used to assist in a memory task are termed "mnemonic strategies." One might think of general, commonsense guidelines such as writing down the information or ignoring potential distractions as mnemonic strategies. However, most mnemonic strategies would fall under the rubric of "rehearsal," or going over the information in one's mind. Rehearsal, in turn, can be subdivided into "rote" and "elaborative" rehearsal. Rote rehearsal means going over the information exactly, whereas elaborative rehearsal means forming new, meaningful connections between items to be remembered.

When the material permits elaborative rehearsal, it is by far the more effective means of remembering. However, the ability to carry out elaborative rehearsal is more a reflection on the knowledge structure and inventiveness of individuals than of their working memory capacity *per se*. Therefore, tasks that are intended to measure working memory capacity are often designed in such a way that it is difficult to carry out elaborative rehearsal. For example, in memory span tasks, often the items are drawn from the same small set on every trial and do not form a meaningful pattern. This is the case, for instance, in the digit span task used in tests of intelligence. The participant hears a short sequence of digits and repeats it back, and the sequence length is made longer until the participant makes an error on several trials in a row. The longest length successfully repeated is one estimate of the participant's span. Without intensive training, it would be very difficult to do more than rote rehearsal in this type of task. There is not much time to make up a story about the sequence of numbers.

The use of the strategy of rote rehearsal is one that is known to improve with development. This topic is examined in much more detail by Bjorklund and Douglas (Ch. 8 in this volume), so it will just be briefly summarized here. Flavell (1966) examined children's lip movements during a delay between a short list of items and the memory test, relying on the observation that, in young children, even "covert" rehearsal could not be entirely covert but would produce movements of the lips. It was found that the lip movements did become more frequent in older children, who remembered more. Subsequent studies have shown that the absence of rehearsal is not just a matter of knowledge that this strategy would be useful; very young children can be instructed to rehearse at the age of about 5, but it still does not improve their recall. Older children benefit more from rehearsal, and that is at least partly because they come to rehearse in a more useful, cumulative fashion in which more items in a row are strung together in rehearsal. This plays an important role in the development of short-term memory. For example, Cowan et al. (1987) found that a rehearsal-blocking task in adults (whispering the alphabet while listening to a spoken list of words to be recalled) resulted in short-term recall levels very similar to what 5-year-olds ordinarily attain without any rehearsal-blocking task.

There also is a developmental trend in the tendency to use rehearsal spontaneously. Even though young children's performance sometimes benefits from instructions to rehearse, they typically do not continue to rehearse when they are no longer explicitly instructed to do so. Ornstein et al. (1975) and Naus et al. (1977) found that sixth-grade children rehearsed spontaneously whereas second- and third-grade children did not. This might be accounted for on the grounds that rehearsal is more effortful, and therefore probably more aversive, in younger children. Guttentag (1984) showed this using a secondary probe task in which children were to tap repeatedly on a plastic key connected to a computer while engaging in a memory task with instructed cumulative rehearsal. The logic of the experiment was that the more effort is needed for the rehearsal process, the less effort will be available for tapping, which therefore will be slowed relative to a control condition in which tapping is carried out by itself. It was indeed found that there was more interference in younger children, amounting to a tapping slowdown of 41 per cent in second-graders, 31 per cent in third-graders, and only 17 per cent in sixth-graders. All ages managed to rehearse in sets of about three items together in a rehearsal cycle. (They were to include the word just presented along with at least two words presented previously. For example, while hearing the list *car, bear, house, desk*, a child in compliance might be heard to repeat, "car . . . bear, car . . . house, bear, car . . . desk, house, car . . ." and so on). This rehearsal set of three was no higher than the normal, spontaneous rehearsal sets of older children when simply asked to rehearse out loud, whereas the younger children spontaneously rehearsed in smaller sets of one or two items in a cycle.

It is not really known whether "cumulative rehearsal" is exactly the way that words are rehearsed silently when overt rehearsal is not required; it could be, for example, that people are able to covertly rehearse several words at once in a parallel fashion, which of course they are unable to do in overt rehearsal.

In sum, it seems certain that working memory strategies improve with development. What is less clear is why they improve. There is evidence of improvements in (a) the knowledge or understanding of what strategies would be useful; (b) the ability to implement the strategies; (c) the ability to use the strategy without expending undue effort; and (d) the ability to use better versions of the strategy. These changes come at different points in development, making the entire developmental sequence a complex and fascinating one.

Changes in processing speed

Until this point, we have discussed developmental changes in knowledge and strategy use, both of which are very complex and must involve the acquisition of additional information in older children. The next type of change, in speed of processing, could occur more directly because of the maturation of brain tissue. Brain maturation is completed gradually, with some changes occurring as late as adolescence (Rabinowicz 1980). Some of this maturation, for example, involves completion of the myelin layer that serves as insulation for some nerve cells and speeds up the transmission of impulses. It is perhaps for this reason that various processing speeds increase with development (Hale & Jansen 1994; Kail & Salthouse 1994). This speedup can have important implications for how working memory operates.

Theoretically, there are at least two ways in which processing speed could matter. One way is simply that faster processing could allow a task to be completed more quickly. This could be especially important because a task that takes too long may be discouraging, and a child may give up before completing it. Faster processing minimizes the chances of that happening.

Secondly, faster processing is especially important if information is lost over time. This could occur either if the premise of "memory decay" is correct, or if the situation is one in which there is continuing interference that is imposed as a function of time. By speeding up processing, it becomes more likely that the necessary processing will be completed before the information upon which that processing must operate becomes unavailable.

As we have seen, one process that depends on speed is just what we considered in the strategy section, covert verbal rehearsal. According to Baddeley's (1986) model, faster rehearsal is more effective because it allows more items to be refreshed in short-term storage before they are lost from storage, and therefore allows more items to be held in short-term storage at the same time. As discussed above and depicted in Figure 7.1, a great deal of research has suggested that the rate at which the to-be-remembered items can be pronounced is important. Older children not only know their words, letters, and numbers better, but also can pronounce these items faster than younger children, and therefore might reactivate items in short-term storage through rehearsal at a faster rate (Baddeley 1986).

More recent research has suggested, though, that this cannot be the entire story. Based on the earlier research by Flavell et al. (1966), Henry (1991), and many others, children as young as 4 or 5 years of age do not use rehearsal at all, so "the speed of rehearsal" would not be a meaningful parameter for these children. Sure enough, when one looks at pronunciation speed and memory span in individuals within an age group, rather than averaged across individuals, one finds that the correlation holds up fairly well for older children (e.g. 8-year-olds) and adults, but not for younger children (Cowan et al. 1994a; Gathercole et al. 1994). This, then, leads to a puzzle. Rehearsal speed might explain why there is a linear relationship between speaking rate and memory span in children 8 or older, but it does not explain why the same relationship holds across age group means including even younger children. One possibility is that the speaking rate correlates with some important property of cognition in addition to covert rehearsal speed. For example, the sophistication of the rehearsal strategy might be correlated with the rate of speech, as both of these things improve with age. It will take some very careful analyses of individual differences to determine the full reason why speech rate and memory span are correlated.

Research in my laboratory (Cowan 1992; Cowan et al. 1994b) has discovered another process that is faster in children with a better memory span and speeds up with development. We measured the timing of children's correct repetitions of lists of words in a memory span task, using a computer program that is capable of measuring individual segments of speech and pauses. The duration of words in the response did not differ depending on the memory ability or age of the child; at least between the ages of 4 and 8, the age range of children in these studies, words are spoken at a relatively constant rate regardless of how fast the child *could* pronounce individual words. What varied much more, however, was the duration of silent pauses between words in the responses. These silent pauses were shorter in older and mnemonically more advanced children.

These inter-word pauses in the spoken responses also were longer for longer lists, which helps to clarify what process may be occurring during the pauses. During these periods, the child may be trying mentally to sift through the words in the entire list to determine which word to pronounce next; the words were to be pronounced in the order in which they were presented. This process could be termed "memory search" and has been discussed in related studies in adults (Sternberg et al. 1978, 1980). For correctly repeated lists of an approximately fixed length (about 3 to 3.5 items), 4-year-olds produced an average inter-word pause of 0.38 seconds, whereas 8-year-olds produced an average pause of only 0.23 seconds.

If these inter-word pauses do reflect memory search, as we suspect, then it is important that there are converging reasons to believe that memory search changes with age. This kind of result has been obtained in the simple procedure developed by Sternberg (1966). In this procedure, participants receive a list and then a probe item, the task being to indicate whether the probe comes from the list or not. In adults, each item in the list adds an additional 20 to 40 milliseconds to the reaction time, suggesting that participants mentally search for the probe in their mental representation of the list items, in a rapid manner. However, this search process is several times slower in young children (e.g. Keating et al. 1980). It also is intriguing that Sininger et al. (1989) found much slower than normal memory search in children with language impairment.

Is there an explicit explanation of why memory search rates would be expected to affect memory span, similar to speaking rates? Perhaps the reason itself is similar. Information can be lost from short-term storage while either speech articulation processing or a rapid memory search are ongoing, and the faster these were to be conducted the less time there would be for short-term memory loss to take place. Thus, it appears that the speeds of at least two processes, speech and memory search, contribute to working memory. (Our ongoing work suggests, moreover, that they are not highly related to one another.)

Nevertheless, a possibility that must be considered carefully is that some factor that changes with development, other than processing speeds, may be responsible for the correlation between processing rates and memory span. This remains possible because we only have correlations between processing speeds and memory span, which is not the same as an experimental demonstration that processing speeds determine span. For example, it is theoretically possible that the causal factor is knowledge. Older children and adults know words better than younger children, and this may allow them both to process the words faster and to recall more of them than younger children. In fact, Case et al. (1982) supported this possibility. They showed that adults who were to repeat nonsense words could do so only at a rate that was equivalent to 6-year-olds producing words, and that the levels of recall for these two situations were comparable also.

There is no way to rule out such an explanation definitively at this point, but at least one recent study (Roodenrys et al. 1993) did address it. This study examined memory for sets of short, medium, and long words, and also for sets of short, medium, and long nonwords (e.g. "glof" is short, "spigdub" is medium, and "prelafoon" is long). When one plots memory versus speeded speaking rate for words of different lengths, one finds that they are linearly related; sets of shorter words can be pronounced more quickly and recalled better than sets of longer words, as shown in Figure 7.1. The same is true for nonwords, but these do not fall on the same line as words. They fall at a lower level of recall for a particular speech rate. This suggests that recall may be affected by speech rate and word knowledge separately, with speech rate determining the slope of the relation between word length and memory span, and word knowledge affecting the intercept or overall height of the line depicting that relation (Hulme et al. 1991). Roodenrys et al. (1993) used this technique with children aged 6 and 10 years old. The difference between performance on words versus nonwords was greater in the older children, so they appear to have benefitted more from word knowledge. However, a more striking effect was that if one drew a straight line through all of the word data in a plot comparable to the present Figure 7.1, younger children would be lower down on that line than older children (with slower speech and smaller spans). The same is true for nonwords. So there is a speech rate change that seems separate from the word knowledge change. More work on this topic is needed.

Until now, the types of developmental changes that have been pointed out could be consistent with almost any reasonable theory of working memory. The theories all could attribute importance, for one reason or another, to knowledge, strategies, and processing speed. However, that may not be the case for the possible changes to be considered below. Theories of working memory that do not emphasize the role of attention and how it is employed would not predict that differences in the allocation of attention would lead to different working memory ability. Theories with no decay would not predict what looks like decay differences across ages, and those without a memory capacity limit would not predict a developmental difference in that limit. The findings of the relevant studies therefore may be of use in helping to determine what theory of working memory is most apt.

Changes in the use of attention and processing capacity

In the model of Cowan (1988, 1995) shown in Figure 7.2, one important aspect of working memory is the focus of attention. There could be developmental differences in the functioning of this focus of attention that would be seen as working memory differences. For example, there could be a difference in how much material can be subsumed within the focus of attention at one time. This amount of useful information in the focus of attention can be termed "processing capacity," under the assumption that a larger amount of attended information permits a larger amount of information processing. There also could be a difference in how efficiently attention is kept focused on the relevant stimuli and tasks. Finally, there could be a difference in how well attention can be used to prevent the activation of irrelevant information. That is, there could be a difference in the inhibitory function of attention. All of these will be discussed in turn.

Attention as processing capacity One possible individual difference in the focus of attention has been proposed by Just and Carpenter (1992). In their model of working memory, there are individual differences essentially in how much information can be in the focus of attention at any one time. They use a slightly different terminology, however, stating that there are differences in the amount of memory that can be activated at any one time. When they use the term "activation," though, they mean "kept active by attention," without considering a role for information that might be activated automatically, without attention.

Daneman and Carpenter (1980) developed a measure of working memory span that seems closely related to this emphasis on attentional limits. The measure is based on the idea that there are two separable aspects of working memory: storage and processing. Daneman and Carpenter suggested that adequate performance in complex tasks requires that storage and processing be used together, and their measure was developed to stress both of these. On each trial, a participant must do two things. The first is to comprehend a series of sentences, and the second is to repeat the last word of each of the sentences after the sequence of sentences is completed. This requires that the subject hold the sentence-final words in mind throughout the time that the comprehension task is being conducted. Given adequate comprehension, the number of sentence-final words that can be remembered serves as the measure of "working memory span." This working memory span correlates rather well with performance on verbal comprehension and reasoning tasks; much better, for example, than does a simple memory span. Turner and Engle (1989) have shown that this finding is not specific to the use of sentential material. One can use a working memory span measure in which the processing portion of the task is arithmetic instead of sentence comprehension, and the results still correlate with performance on verbal tasks.

Some correspondence between working memory span tasks and the focus of attention seems likely, even though the exact correspondence is still uncertain. If one individual is found to have a higher working memory span than another, the explanation could be that the first individual is able to keep more information in the focus of attention at any one time. That might help the individual to store more information during the working memory task, and it also might help the individual to attend to the processing that needs to be done despite the load on memory.

What I have described is the notion that attention or its usefulness in performing tasks (processing capacity) has to be shared between storage and processing. This idea has been proposed before (Case et al. 1982) and will be examined a little later on. Case et al. suggested that an important difference between younger and older children is that the older ones can do processing more efficiently, leaving them more processing capacity to use for storing items.

There have been at least a few developmental studies with this type of working memory span task. Swanson et al. (1993) tested third- and fourth-grade children's ability to solve word problems and collected a number of other measures including working memory span. A small (less than 0.30) but significant correlation between working memory span and problem solving ability was obtaineds. Walczyk and Raska (1992) studied children in second, fourth, and sixth grades and, not surprisingly, found an increase in working memory span across those ages. Within each age group, working memory span correlated with high-level reading skills including the detection of errors in reading and the ability to draw inferences about the reading. These correlations were substantial, generally in a range of about 0.4 to 0.6. Swanson (1996) carried out a wide range of working memory, intelligence, and achievement measures on individuals from 5 to 19 years of age and found correlations between measures in a range of magnitudes similar to Walczyk and Raska. Verbal and visual/spatial measures of working memory were found to be correlated with each other and both correlated with the same intelligence and achievement measures, suggesting that it is a very general resource that develops.

Whether this developmental difference in active processing can account for differences in short-term memory is another question. It should do so if memory storage relies on the same pool of attention or processing capacity that active processing does. To examine this, Case et al. (1982) used a "counting span task," which is similar to the working memory span task of Daneman and Carpenter (1980). In the counting span task, participants counted the number of items on each card and then tried to recall the series of card totals. The longest series resulting in correct serial recall is the counting span. According to the theoretical framework of Case et al., older children's better counting span is to be explained on the grounds that they used less processing capacity for counting, leaving more capacity for the storage of the totals.

Towse and Hitch (1995: Experiment 2) reported results of a study with a modification of the counting task that run counter to this processing capacity account of Case et al. (1982). The participants were children 5 to 11 years old. The counting task was modified so that the targets on each card could or could not be identified by a color feature. In either case, the targets to be counted were blue squares. When they shared a card with orange triangles, the targets could be identified on the basis of either color or shape. However, when they shared a card instead with blue triangles, the targets could be identified by shape only. (The latter were called "conjunction" cards based on the notion that the combination of shape and color was relevant, but all objects on these cards were blue so that only shape was useful as a cue.) The latter cards produced far more errors in counting and were slower to be counted than the cards that provided a color cue. According to the processing capacity account, therefore, these uniform-color cards should take more capacity away from storage, which should result in lower counting spans. This is in fact was found, in all age groups.

However, Towse and Hitch noted that there was an alternative hypothesis to be considered. Because the more difficult counting task took longer, it allowed more time for memory of the totals to be lost before the recall task. To control for the effect of time, they included a third condition in which the color cue was present, but in which more time was needed anyway (roughly comparable to the time needed in the uniform-color condition) because the number of targets per card was higher than in the other two conditions. Even though there were far fewer counting errors in this third condition than in the uniform-color condition, it produced a counting span that was about as low as in the uniform-color condition. This suggested that it was the amount of time taken by counting that was important for counting span, not the amount of attention, processing capacity, or effort.

Another possible reason for the counting span to be reduced in the third condition (the one with a color cue but more targets per card) is that it involves memory for higher numbers, which are well known to be more difficult to process than lower numbers. A figure in which the counting time was matched across conditions (Towse & Hitch 1995: Fig. 5) does show the counting span decreasing markedly as a function of the time taken in counting, but it also suggests that memory was nevertheless poorer in the uniform-color (conjunction) condition than in the other two conditions. There may be separate effects of both the amount of time and the processing capacity used in the task. One might well expect this, if counting span is based on a system in which there is both passive storage and active processing of the material to be recalled (Baddeley 1986; Cowan 1988). It remains possible that developmental changes in either the passive persistence of information across time or the efficient use of attention and processing capacity accounts for the developmental change in counting span.

Halford et al. (1994: Experiment 3) modified the card counting span task in an interesting way. Instead of having to remember the total for each card, a series of numbers was presented first as a memory "preload." Next the cards were presented for counting, and then the preload was to be recalled. The results were consistent with those of Towse and Hitch (1995) in that memory declined as a function of the number of cards counted.

If the same processing capacity were shared between the memory load and the counting task, then the cost of counting should be greater in younger children because they would have to expend more processing capacity in order to count. However, Halford et al. (1994) found that the decline in memory as a function of the number of cards counted was very comparable for children who were 5, 8–9, and 12 years old. This, along with other results of this study, suggested that the main source of forgetting was the result of interference or decay of the representation of items in memory, with only a very small effect of the difficulty of the processing task that was carried out along with the memory task.

So, in sum, although it is clear that older children use attention better than younger ones, this does not translate into a commensurately large gain in short-term memory, as Case et al. (1982) would have expected. There is a developmental gain in short-term memory ability in these tasks, but it does not seem to have very much to do with a developmental change in processing capacity or processing efficiency.

This, in turn, leads to a puzzle. If, in working memory span and counting span tasks, the span does not depend much on the difficulty of processing, then why does working memory span correlate with performance in comprehension and problem-solving tasks more highly than ordinary memory span does? One answer is that it could be the ability to carry out two tasks concurrently that is the critical variable distinguishing among individuals and changing with age. This ability to manage different concurrent streams of information would depend upon how adeptly the focus of attention could be switched between tasks, or perhaps split between tasks. This ability probably is closely related to what Baddeley (1986) has termed the "central executive" function (see also Engle & Oransky, in press). Individual differences in working memory span apparently do not have much to do with varying *amounts* of information in the focus of attention, however. Clearly, more work on this important topic is needed.

Maintaining the focus of attention A pioneering study conducted by Maccoby and Hagen (1965) illustrates well that changes in maintaining the focus of attention do affect memory performance. They studied first-, third-, fifth-, and seventh-grade children, using both intentional and incidental memory tasks. On each trial, the child saw a series of colored cards with a picture of an animal or common object on each card. The task that the child was instructed to carry out (the intentional task) was to remember the sequence of colors. After all of those trials were completed, however, a surprise (incidental) memory task was administered. In it, the child was to identify which pictures had been presented with which colors. This was incidental in the sense that the children had not been asked to remember the pictures or their relation to the background colors at the time that the cards were seen. Whereas performance on the intentional task increased with age, performance on the incidental task actually decreased; it was lower in seventh-grade children than in the younger children. The older children apparently had learned to focus attention on the relevant aspects of the materials to be remembered, and to ignore distractions, more effectively than younger children did. A similar followup study by Hagen (1967) suggested that the tendency of older children to shut out the irrelevant information increased when an additional distracting task, listening for a deviant low tone within a high-pitched melody, was to be carried out concurrent with the intentional memory task. It appears, then, that older children are more able to focus attention on relevant information, which may increase the likelihood that this relevant information is encoded adequately and recalled.

How would this developmental difference in the deployment of attention contribute to working memory performance? Possibly in a very simple, straightforward way. Within the model shown in Figure 7.2, it is assumed that some of the correct answers that a participant produces on a working memory task are made possible precisely because the information was held in the focus of attention throughout the duration of the test trial. If a child's attention wanders away from the task-relevant material, fewer of those correct answers can be produced.

Attention and inhibition Attention is used not only to activate relevant elements of memory, but also to suppress or inhibit irrelevant aspects, which sometimes appear to become activated automatically and could cause the focus of attention to wander from the relevant information or topic. In the experiment by Maccoby and Hagen (1965), inhibition might have been needed to suppress the urge to attend to the pictures on the cards, which would have detracted from learning of the relevant stimulus dimension (which was the card color). Along these lines, Hasher and Zacks (1989) suggested that working memory may be less efficient when some of the available storage space is taken up by irrelevant information that was not inhibited adequately. They applied this view to changes that occur in aging, but Bjorklund and Harnishfeger (1990) discussed how the same principles might be extended to child development.

There is good reason to suspect that the ability to inhibit irrelevant information would change with age. For example, maturation of the frontal lobe of the brain is not complete until adolescence (Yakovelev & Lecours 1967). Judging from the behavior patterns of individuals with frontal lobe damage, some areas of the frontal lobe are essential for brain operations in which one holds information in mind and inhibits irrelevant information (Fuster 1989; Goldman-Rakic 1992).

One additional type of procedure illustrates that older children do use inhibition more effectively within working memory. It is a variety of the test used to examine Jean Piaget's notion of "object permanence." In the simplest version of the object permanence test, an object such as a toy is covered with a cloth or other obstruction. Infants who are advanced enough to be physically capable of moving the obstruction still will not do so in order to retrieve the toy, presumably because the memory of the toy has faded. Infants who are advanced enough to pass this test still will fail to retrieve the object in another, slightly more sophisticated task with two containers, A and B. After the desirable object has been hidden and retrieved from Container A a few times, the object is moved to Container B. Even though the infant sees the adult place the object under B, often the infant will still search for it under A. Apparently, the short-term memory representation of the object under Container B is weak enough that the influence of this memory is overwhelmed by the recently learned habit of looking for the object under Container A. This is termed the "A not B" error.

How do we know that inhibition is involved in this type of error? Consider a situation in which the Containers A and B are transparent (e.g. clear drinking glasses). In this situation, infants sometimes still make the error (Butterworth 1977). In this situation, it appears that the learned habit can be stronger than even the perception of the object under the obstruction. With age, there is a greater tendency to inhibit the irrelevant response, allowing the current correct perception or memory to control the response.

Then how do we know that working memory is really involved? There are two reasons to believe that it is. First, far fewer errors are made when the obstruction is transparent than when it is opaque. At least some of the errors have to do with memory of the object being weaker than perception of the object. Secondly, in one experiment (Diamond 1985) the obstructions were opaque but a delay was imposed between the time when the object was hidden and the time when the infant was allowed to find it. In this situation, more errors were made at longer delays. Apparently the memory of the hidden object became weaker during the delay, allowing the learned habit of searching at A to predominate more and more as the delay increased. Moreover, this increase in errors with delay time was greater for the younger children. The mean delay at which the A-not-B error first occurred was about 2 seconds in 7.5-month-old infants, and it increased steadily to about 10 seconds by 12 months of age.

This pattern suggests that as the short-term memory of the object in Container B fades, at some point the learned habit of looking in Container A becomes more compelling, and that control of behavior by the learned habit occurs at shorter delays for younger infants. It is still not clear, however, if the developmental change that accounts for this pattern is an increase in short-term memory persistence or an increase in the ability to inhibit the inappropriate learned habit.

We have focused on an example of inhibition in infancy, but it seems likely that the use of inhibition continues to improve throughout childhood (Bjorklund & Harnishfeger 1990). An experiment by Tipper et al. (1989) demonstrates this in an interesting way, using a task known as "negative priming." The basic task comes from Stroop's (1935) procedure in which color words are presented in conflicting colors of ink. (For example, the word "blue" might be presented in red ink.) The task is to name the color of ink, but there is a tendency to want to read the word aloud instead, which slows down the color naming and results in errors. The children in the study by Tipper et al. (1989) were susceptible to this effect also, though they were slower and made over twice as many errors as the adults.

In the negative priming procedure, Stroop's task was modified further through a relationship between one trial and the next. The irrelevant word of one trial was used as the relevant color of the next trial. For example, if the irrelevant word was "blue" on trial n, the relevant color and correct response would be "blue" on trial n+1. Previous research with adults had shown that this condition results in even slower color-naming than for Stroop's procedure. The explanation offered was that people inhibited responses to the irrelevant word on each trial. In the case of negative priming, the word that was just inhibited in one trial had to be brought back out of inhibition for the very next trial, which presumably took extra time. However, Tipper et al. found that second-grade children responded differently. Unlike the adults, the children were not slowed down further in the negative priming condition than in the Stroop condition. It is as if the children did not carry out as much inhibition in this circumstance, and so neither reaped the reward nor suffered the consequence of this inhibition.

Although it thus does appear that there are important developmental changes in inhibition, more work is needed to determine how this developmental change affects various working memory tasks. More work is needed also to determine if this change in inhibition is specific, or if it is just one example of a more general developmental trend toward a more efficient control of the focus of attention through central executive functioning.

Changes in passive memory loss over time

We have reviewed evidence that there are many developmental changes in knowledge, strategies, and the use of attention that may affect the way in which working memory tasks are carried out. In scientific thinking, it is always wise to begin with the simplest theory possible, and then to complicate the theory only insofar as the evidence demands. It is simpler to believe, for example, that there are at least some aspects of working memory that do not change developmentally. It is in this context that researchers often have suggested that there does not appear to be a developmental change in the period for which of information is passively held by the brain; that is, information of the type referred to by Cowan (1988) and in Figure 7.2 as "activated memory," or the kinds referred to by Baddeley (1986) as the "passive phonological buffer" and the "visuospatial sketch pad." However, there is no evidence that this memory remains fixed with age; there just has been no evidence that it changes. A change in this type of memory would be important simply because it would mean that older children could hold information in memory longer without even trying.

There is evidence that it is not only the frontal lobes that matures slowly during childhood; there also are appreciable changes in other lobes of the brain (Rabinowicz 1980) that are likely to be involved in the passive storage of information.

Two studies have shown that at least for auditory stimuli, there in fact *is* a change in how long information remains in short-term storage. Keller and Cowan (1994) examined participants' ability to compare two different tones and determine if they are the same or different in pitch. There was a silent period between tones that could vary from trial to trial, and the actual difference between tone frequencies could vary. ("Frequency" is the primary tone characteristic that determines the pitch that one hears.) In order to make the task sufficiently difficult, the tone frequencies were rather close together, generally less than a musical note apart. In this situation, correct performance depends on whether the participant still remembers the first tone in the pair in sufficient detail at the time when the second tone is presented, so that the two tones can be compared. Performance in this situation declines as the inter-tone interval increases from a fraction of a second to about 20 seconds, usually leveling off by that time. The hypothesis under investigation was that younger children would lose tone pitch memory more quickly over time. Participants in three age ranges were tested: 6–7 years, 10–12 years, and adults.

The developmental difference in tone pitch memory loss over time can be examined fairly only if the age groups are not different at all inter-tone intervals. If, for example, older children are better no matter what the interval, then differences in the loss of information across intervals could be explained with the uninteresting hypothesis that memory loss can be observed better at some levels of performance than at others. To rule out that uninteresting type of explanation, Keller and Cowan adjusted the difference between the tone frequencies for each individual, in order that each age group would perform at about the same proportion correct (0.84) when there were about 2 seconds between tones. However, then the groups were tested also with longer inter-tone intervals using these same tone differences. It was found that the younger children performed at a particular fixed level of performance (0.71) with 8 seconds between the tones on the average. The older children, however, could perform at this same level with about 10 seconds between the tones, and the adults could do so with about 12 seconds between them.

One interpretation of this age difference is that older participants' brains automatically preserved the tone memory longer, but another possibility is that older participants were better able to use attention to continue to preserve the tones. To examine this, Keller and Cowan conducted a second experiment using only adults. In one condition they were allowed to think about the first tone during the inter-tone interval, just as in the previous experiment. In a second condition, however, they were required to imagine a familiar melody during the inter-tone interval and to mark the contour of the melody. Even though there was ample evidence from the contour marks that the adults were faithfully imagining melodies, they did about equally well in the tone comparison task under these two conditions. It appears that memory for the exact tone pitch is held in the brain rather automatically, and is not influenced much by what the participant does intentionally to remember it. Therefore, it seems unlikely that active mnemonic strategies during the inter-tone interval could account for the superior performance of older participants in this procedure. There instead appears to be an age difference in how long tone memories persist automatically before they fade away.

There is one way in this conclusion could be questioned. Our musical imagery task effectively prevented rehearsal, but it could not totally control the way in which the tones were encoded in the first place. Perhaps older children and adults are more attentive at the time that the first tone is presented, and this in some way results in a memory trace that is more persistent over time.

Another recent experiment (Saults & Cowan 1996: Experiment 2) helps to rule out that possibility because the sounds were ignored at the time that they were presented. Participants, who were first-grade children, third-grade children, and adults, played a silent video game that involved matching each picture in the center of the computer screen to one of four surrounding pictures, whichever one had a name that rhymed with that of the central picture. Meanwhile, random repetitions of the four words *bee*, *tea*, *bow*, and *toe* were presented at irregular intervals over headphones. Once in a while, without warning, the video game was suddenly replaced by pictures of the four items that had been heard over headphones. The task then was to select (with a mouse click) the item that had been presented most recently. This most recent item had been presented 1, 5, or 10 seconds ago.

The speed and accuracy on the video game could be monitored, and they were found to be the same in this dual-task situation as when no sounds were presented at all, which suggests that the sounds did not take attention away from the video game. Also, in another control condition in which participants were to pay attention to the spoken words and identify them, all age groups did extremely well on these words. However, there was an interesting pattern of memory for ignored words. At a 1-second test delay, all groups did about equally well. Nevertheless, the amount of forgetting across test delays was greater in younger children. This was the case no matter whether one looks at recall of the correct word as a whole, recall of the correct initial consonant (*b* vs. *t*), or recall of the correct vowel (*ee* vs. *o*). Figure 7.3 shows the results for the vowels, which seem particularly interesting. By a 5-second test delay, extreme memory loss had occurred in the youngest group only. By a 10-second delay, considerable loss occurred in the older children also, but little forgetting had yet occurred in adults.

There still are ways in which one might account for these findings on the basis of subtle shifts of attention that we were unable to measure. At this point, however, the likelihood that there is a developmental difference in passive memory storage seems much greater than it once did. We intend to continue to pursue this avenue of research until it is clear if passive memory loss changes with development or not.

Changes in passive memory storage capacity
Another way in which passively held memory storage theoretically could change with development is that it could increase in amount. In the terms of

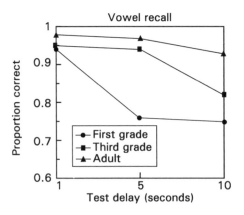

Figure 7.3 Recall of the correct vowel in memory for ignored speech at three different silent test delays, for first-graders, third-graders, and adults. (Data from Saults & Cowan 1996.)

Figure 7.2, there could be a limit to how much activated memory one can have at any one time, and that limit could increase with age in childhood.

That kind of idea has been proposed by Pascual-Leone (1970), who has conducted a number of experiments in which the number of items that must be kept in mind are varied, under circumstances that would discourage rehearsal. The amount that can be kept in mind, termed the "M-space" in the theory, is found to increase with age. However, alternative explanations of such findings are certainly possible. The main alternative has been the notion of Case et al. (1982) that the efficiency of mental operations increases with age. If the efficiency increases, this could leave more room for the storage of information, even if M-space does not change with development. It is going to be difficult to separate these two hypotheses.

Changes in complex tasks

The previous discussion is organized around basic processes within working memory that could change with development. To proceed with this discussion, we have had to assume that particular tasks that have been used are indicative of these specific processes. In reality, most tasks are not pure and a particular task could indicate more than one process.

This point can be illustrated with a discussion of one task that has played an important role in the recent literature. Gathercole and Baddeley (1989, 1990) have developed a task in which young children (e.g. 3-, 4-, and 5-year-olds) hear a multisyllabic nonsense word on each trial and are to repeat it. As long as they succeed, progressively longer and more complex nonwords are given. Older children are able to repeat longer and phonologically more complex nonwords than younger children. This task is clearly interesting because it predicts the acquisition of vocabulary and reading in preschool children; children with better-than-average nonword repetition scores generally acquire vocabulary words and begin reading faster than other children. What process is involved?

Theoretically, it could be any of the six types of process we have examined. First, it could be a difference in knowledge. Older children's superior knowledge of English could make it more likely that a nonword would sound like a word, which would ease the phonological memory load. However, this possibility has been addressed by Gathercole (1995). She divided the nonwords in her experiment into those judged more versus less word-like. It was the less word-like nonwords that best predicted vocabulary acquisition and reading ability. Still, knowledge could play a role in a different way. The more advanced children may have better knowledge of English phonological rules, which could allow them to divide the nonwords into fewer, larger, multiphonemic chunks to be stored in memory.

Second, nonword repetition could depend upon strategies. Older or more advanced children may be more likely to rehearse the nonword while it is being presented, making recall more likely. This would be expected according to the research of Flavell et al. (1966), Henry (1991), and others.

191

Third, nonword repetition may depend upon speed. For example, older children may be able to rehearse nonwords faster, helping to prevent rapid memory loss until the word can be repeated. This would be expected according to the theory of Baddeley (1986). If this is the case, one might expect tests of articulation speed to predict vocabulary acquisition. Perhaps they will.

Fourth, nonword repetition could depend on the versatility of attention. Perhaps older children can begin to plan their articulatory responses while still listening to the nonword stimuli, which would ease the demand on memory. Younger children may be less able to do so because it is a type of dual task.

A fifth possibility is that it is a difference in the rate of passive memory loss. Younger children may be more likely to lose phonological information from the passive store before they get a chance to repeat it.

Sixth, and finally, older or more advanced children may simply have more room in phonological memory for multiple phonemes to be held simultaneously. This was the hypothesis that first came to mind when I read about the nonword repetition task, but there is no firm evidence for it.

Thus, as in this illustration, any of the six bases of change in working memory development that have been discussed above remain possible. Any of the six may account for developmental changes in a complex task. It should be clear that more research is needed to determine which of these processes is relevant in particular situations of special importance.

Implications for working memory and its development

The research we have discussed has important theoretical and practical implications. Studies of the development of working memory processes may have implications for what theoretical interpretations of working memory tasks are correct even in adults. For example, we mentioned that the studies showing a limit in memory span (approximately equal to the number of items that the individual can pronounce in 2 seconds) may be difficult to explain if the unitary memory theorists are correct in asserting that there is no specific time limit to memory, only the results of interference and retrieval conditions. The finding of age differences in the persistence of memory for ignored speech may also prove to be awkward to explain from a unitary memory standpoint.

The recent research also has important theoretical implications for memory development in general. It now seems likely that working memory changes in more ways than any of the current theories have proposed, and this changes the way in which memory development is viewed. The recently discovered factors, such as changes in the persistence of memory and the rate of memory search seem likely to be strongly rooted in biological maturation and not very amenable to training, unlike the factors that were most often discussed previously in the field, such as changes in knowledge and strategy use. However, it still is unclear how much of a role training plays. For example, could the rate of memory search or rehearsal be increased through training? Results so far are mixed (Hulme & Muir 1985; McCauley et al. 1976).

Although we have focused on the development of working memory in childhood, there also are important developmental changes in working memory in the aging process (e.g. Pratt et al. 1989; Tun et al. 1991). A comparison of the bases of development in children and in aging can be of considerable use because there must be both similarities and differences between the two. The efficiency of processing in the brain is likely to be below the normal young adult in both children (because of immaturity) and in elderly people (because of the deterioration of brain processes), and in this way they are similar. However, a big difference is that the experience and knowledge of an elderly individual should be, in many ways at least, as good or better than that of a young adult, whereas children have less experience and knowledge. If a child does not carry out a mnemonic strategy that young adults use, it is not clear if that is because the strategy is too difficult or because the child did not know the strategy (or did not have enough specific knowledge to use it well). When an elderly adult does not use a strategy that young adults use, that seems more likely to be because the strategy is too difficult given the deterioration in brain processes (though a strategy might be forgotten with disuse).

Similarities in results obtained with children and the elderly suggest that some very similar processes are important in both cases. In particular, much of the deviation from young adults can be explained on the basis of slower brain processes (Baddeley 1986; Cowan 1994; Hale & Jansen 1994; Kail & Salthouse 1994; Salthouse 1994). Relative slowness in brain processes may make it difficult to carry out as effectively many of the strategies that young adults use, and it may permit more memory loss before the individual's mental task at hand is completed.

Finally, there are important practical implications of the development of working memory in childhood for various types of cognitive delay and impairment. Types of task that measure various short-term and working memory processes have been found to be related broadly, across many different situations, to the rate of language acquisition and comprehension ability (Gathercole & Baddeley 1989, 1990; Gilian et al. 1995; Lincoln et al. 1992; Montgomery 1995); the quality and complexity of language production (Adams & Gathercole 1995; Blake et al. 1994) and reading ability (Apthorp 1995; Farmer & Klein 1995; Siegel 1994). The relation between verbal short-term memory and intellectual functioning is further illustrated in that one type of short-term memory task, the spoken digit span, is included in intelligence tests and is related to verbal intelligence (Cantor et al. 1991). If we gain a better understanding of working memory tasks and their development, we may be better able to diagnose, interpret, predict, and eventually treat serious cognitive developmental problems.

References

Adams, A.-M. & S. E. Gathercole 1995. Phonological working memory and speech production in preschool children. *Journal of Speech and Hearing Research* **38**, 403–14.

Apthorp, H. S. 1995. Phonetic coding and reading in college students with and without learning disabilities. *Journal of Learning Disabilities* **28**, 342–52.

Awh, E., J. Jonides, E. E. Smith, E. J. Schumacher, R. A. Koeppe, & S. Katz 1996. Dissociation of storage and rehearsal in verbal working memory: Evidence from positron emission tomography. *Psychological Science* **7**, 25–31.

Baddeley, A. D. 1986. *Working memory*. Oxford: Clarendon.

Baddeley, A. D., N. Thomson, & M. Buchanan 1975. Word length and the structure of short-term memory. *Journal of Verbal Learning and Verbal Behavior* **14**, 575–89.

Bjork, R. A. & W. B. Whitten 1974. Recency-sensitive retrieval processes in long-term free recall. *Cognitive Psychology* **6**, 173–89.

Bjorklund, D. F. & K. K. Harnishfeger 1990. The resources construct in cognitive development: Diverse sources of evidence and a theory of inefficient inhibition. *Developmental Review* **10**, 48–71.

Blake, J., W. Austin, M. Cannon, A. Lisus, & A. Vaughan 1994. The relationship between memory span and measures of imitative and spontaneous language complexity in preschool children. *International Journal of Behavioral Development* **17**, 91–107.

Bowers, P., R. Steffy, & E. Tate 1988. Comparison of the effects of IQ control methods on memory and naming speed predictors of reading disability. *Reading Research Quarterly* **23**, 304–19.

Butterworth, G. 1977. Object disappearance and error in Piaget's Stage IV task. *Journal of Experimental Child Psychology* **23**, 391–401.

Cantor, J., R .W. Engle, & G. Hamilton 1991. Short-term memory, working memory, and verbal abilities: How do they relate? *Intelligence* **15**, 229–46.

Case, R., D. M. Kurland, & J. Goldberg 1982. Operational efficiency and the growth of short-term memory span. *Journal of Experimental Child Psychology* **33**, 386–404.

Chi, M. T. H. 1978. Knowledge structures and memory development. In *Children's thinking: What develops?*, R. Siegler (ed.). Hillsdale, NJ: Erlbaum.

Conrad, R. 1967. Interference or decay over short retention intervals? *Journal of Verbal Learning and Verbal Behavior* **6**, 49–54.

Cowan, N. 1984. On short and long auditory stores. *Psychological Bulletin* **96**, 341–70.

Cowan, N. 1988. Evolving conceptions of memory storage, selective attention, and their mutual constraints within the human information processing system. *Psychological Bulletin* **104**, 163–91.

Cowan, N. 1992. Verbal memory span and the timing of spoken recall. *Journal of Memory and Language* **31**, 668–84

Cowan, N. 1993. Activation, attention, and short-term memory. *Memory and Cognition* **21**, 162–7.

Cowan, N. 1994. Mechanisms of verbal short-term memory. *Current Directions in Psychological Science* **3**, 185–9.

Cowan, N. 1995. *Attention and memory: An integrated framework*. New York: Oxford University Press.

Cowan, N., C. Cartwright, C. Winterowd, & M. Sherk 1987. An adult model of preschool children's speech memory. *Memory and Cognition* **15**, 511–17.

Cowan, N., T. Keller, C. Hulme, S. Roodenrys, S. McDougall, & J. Rack 1994a. Verbal memory span in children: Speech timing clues to the mechanisms underlying age and word length effects. *Journal of Memory and Language* **33**, 234–50.

Cowan, N., N. L. Wood, & D. N. Borne 1994b. Reconfirmation of the short-term storage concept. *Psychological Science* **5**, 103–6.

Craik, F. I. M. 1970. The fate of primary memory items in free recall. *Journal of Verbal Learning and Verbal Behavior* **9**, 143–8.

Craik, F. I. M. & J. Birtwistle 1971. Proactive inhibition in free recall. *Journal of Experimental Psychology* **91**, 120–3.

Crowder, R. G. 1993. Short-term memory: Where do we stand? *Memory and Cognition* **21**, 142–5.

Daneman, M. & P. A. Carpenter 1980. Individual differences in working memory and reading. *Journal of Verbal Learning and Verbal Behavior* **19**, 450–66.

Dempster, F. N. 1981. Memory span: Sources of individual and developmental differences. *Psychological Bulletin* **89**, 63–100.

Diamond, A. 1985. Development of the ability to use recall to guide action, as indicated by infants' performance on A–B. *Child Development* **56**, 868–83.

Engle, R. W. & N. Oransky, in press. The evolution from short-term to working memory: Multi-store to dynamic models of temporary storage. In *The concept of cognition*, R. Sternberg (ed.).

Ericsson, K. A. & W. Kintsch 1995. Long-term working memory. *Psychological Review* **102**, 211–45.

Farmer, M. E. & R. M. Klein 1995. The evidence for a temporal processing deficit linked to dyslexia: A review. *Psychonomic Bulletin and Review* **2**, 460–93.

Flavell, J. H., D. H. Beach, & J. M. Chinsky 1966. Spontaneous verbal rehearsal in a memory task as a function of age. *Child Development* **37**, 283–99.

Fuster, J. M. 1989. *The prefrontal cortex: Anatomy, physiology, and neuropsychology of the frontal lobe*. New York: Raven.

Gardiner, J. M. & V. H. Gregg 1979. When auditory memory is not overwritten. *Journal of Verbal Learning and Verbal Behavior* **18**, 705–19.

Gathercole, S. E. 1995. Is nonword repetition a test of phonological memory or long-term knowledge? It all depends on the nonwords. *Memory and Cognition* **23**, 83–94.

Gathercole, S. E., A.-M. Adams, G. J. Hitch 1994. Do young children rehearse? An individual-differences analysis. *Memory and Cognition* **22**, 201–7.

Gathercole, S. E. & A. D. Baddeley 1989. Evaluation of the role of phonological STM in the development of vocabulary in children: A longitudinal study. *Journal of Memory and Language* **28**, 200–13.

Gathercole, S. E. & A. D. Baddeley 1990. Phonological memory deficits in language disordered children: Is there a causal connection? *Journal of Memory and Language* **29**, 336–60.

Gathercole, S. E. & A. D. Baddeley 1993. *Working memory and language*. Hove, UK: Erlbaum.

Geary, D. C. 1990. A componential analysis of an early learning deficit in mathematics. *Journal of Experimental Child Psychology* **49**, 363–83.

Geary, D. C., C. C. Bow-Thomas, L. Fan, & R. S. Siegler 1993. Even before formal instruction, Chinese children outperform American children in mental arithmetic. *Cognitive Development* **8**, 517–29.

Gillam, R. B., N. Cowan, & L. S. Day 1995. Sequential memory in children with and without language impairment. *Journal of Speech and Hearing Research* **38**, 393–402.

Glanzer, M. & A. R. Cunitz 1966. Two storage mechanisms in free recall. *Journal of Verbal Learning and Verbal Behavior* **5**, 351–60.

Glanzer, M. & M. Razel 1974. The size of the unit in short-term storage. *Journal of Verbal Learning and Verbal Behavior* **13**, 114–31.

Glenberg, A. M. 1984. A retrieval account of the long-term modality effect. *Journal of Experimental Psychology: Learning, Memory and Cognition* **10**, 16–31.

Goldman-Rakic, P. S. 1992. Working memory and the mind. *Scientific American* September, 111–17.

Guttentag, R. E. 1984. The mental effort requirement of cumulative rehearsal: A developmental study. *Journal of Experimental Child Psychology* **37**, 92–106.

Hagen, J. W. 1967. The effect of distraction on selective attention. *Child Development* **38**, 685–94.

Hale, S. & J. Jansen 1994. Global processing-time coefficients characterize individual and group differences in cognitive speed. *Psychological Science* **5**, 384–9.

Halford, G. S., M. T. Maybery, A. W. O'Hare, & P. Grant 1994. The development of memory and processing capacity. *Child Development* **65**, 1338–56.

Hasher, L. & R. T. Zacks 1989. Working memory, comprehension, and aging: A review and a new view. In *The psychology of learning and motivation, Vol. XXII*, G. H. Bower (ed.). Orlando, FL: Academic Press.

Healy, A. F. & D. S. McNamara 1996. Verbal learning and memory: Does the modal model still work? *Annual Review of Psychology* **47**, 143–72.

Henry, L. A. 1991. Development of auditory memory span: The role of rehearsal. *British Journal of Developmental Psychology* **9**, 493–511.

Hulme, C., S. Maughan, & G. D. A. Brown 1991. Memory for familiar and unfamiliar words: Evidence for a long-term memory contribution to short-term memory span. *Journal of Memory and Language* **30**, 685–701.

Hulme, C. & C. Muir 1985. Developmental changes in speech rate and memory span: A causal relationship? *British Journal of Developmental Psychology* **3**, 175–81.

Hulme, C., N. Thomson, C. Muir, & A. Lawrence 1984. Speech rate and the development of short-term memory span. *Journal of Experimental Child Psychology* **38**, 241–53.

Jones, D. M. & W. J. Macken 1993. Irrelevant tones produce an "irrelevant speech effect": Implications for phonological coding in working memory. *Journal of Experimental Psychology: Learning, Memory and Cognition* **19**, 369–81.

Just, M. & P. A. Carpenter 1992. A capacity theory of comprehension: Individual differences in working memory. *Psychological Review* **99**, 122–49.

Kail, R. & T. A. Salthouse 1994. Processing speed as a mental capacity. *Acta Psychologica* **86**, 199–255.

Keating, D. P., A. H. Keniston, F. R. Manis, & B. L. Bobbitt 1980. Development of the search-processing parameter. *Child Development* **51**, 39–44.

Keller, T. A. & N. Cowan 1994. Developmental increase in the duration of memory for tone pitch. *Developmental Psychology* **30**, 855–63.

Keppel, G. & B. J. Underwood 1962. Proactive inhibition in short-term retention of single items. *Journal of Verbal Learning and Verbal Behavior* **1**, 153–61.

Koppenaal, L. & M. Glanzer 1990. An examination of the continuous distractor task and the "long-term recency effect." *Memory and Cognition* **18**, 183–95.

Landauer, T. K. 1962. Rate of implicit speech. *Perceptual and Motor Skills* **15**, 646.

Lincoln, A. J., P. Dickstein, E. Courchesne, R. Elmasian, & P. Tallal 1992. Auditory processing abilities in non-retarded adolescents and young adults with developmental receptive language disorder and autism. *Brain and Language* **43**, 613–22.

Lu, Z.-L., S. J. Williamson, & L. Kaufman 1992. Physiological measures predict behavioral lifetime of human auditory sensory memory. *Science* **258**, 1668–70.

Maccoby, E. E. & J. W. Hagen 1965. Effects of distraction upon central versus incidental recall: Developmental trends. *Journal of Experimental Child Psychology* **2**, 280–9.

Mann, V. A. 1984. Review: Reading skill and language skill. *Developmental Review* **4**, 1–15.

Mäntysalo, S. & R. Näätänen 1987. The duration of a neuronal trace of an auditory stimulus as indicated by event-related potentials. *Biological Psychology* **24**, 183–95.

McCauley, C., G. Kellas, J. Dugas, & R. F. DeVellis 1976. Effects of serial rehearsal training on memory search. *Journal of Educational Psychology* **68**, 474–81.

McGeoch, J. A. 1932. Forgetting and the law of disuse. *Psychological Review* **39**, 352–70.

Melton, A. W. 1963. Implications of short-term memory for a general theory of memory. *Journal of Verbal Learning and Verbal Behavior* **2**, 1–21.

Miller, E. K. & R. Desimone 1994. Parallel neuronal mechanisms for short-term memory. *Science* **263**, 520–2.

Miller, G. A. 1956. The magical number seven, plus or minus two: Some limits on our capacity for processing information. *Psychological Review* **63**, 81–97.

Montgomery, J. W. 1995. Sentence comprehension in children with specific language impairment: The role of phonological working memory. *Journal of Speech and Hearing Research* **38**, 187–99.

Näätänen, R. 1992. *Attention and brain function.* Hillsdale, NJ: Erlbaum.

Naus, M. J., P. A. Ornstein, & S. Aivano 1977. Developmental changes in memory: The effects of processing time and rehearsal instructions. *Journal of Experimental Child Psychology* **23**, 237–51.

Naveh-Benjamin, M. & T. J. Ayres 1986. Digit span, reading rate, and linguistic relativity. *Quarterly Journal of Experimental Psychology* **38A**, 739–51.

Nicolson, R. 1981. The relationship between memory span and processing speed. In *Intelligence and learning*, M. Friedman, J. P. Das, & N. O'Connor (eds.), 179–184. New York: Plenum.

Ornstein, P. A., M. J. Naus, & C. Liberty 1975. Rehearsal and organizational processes in children's memory. *Child Development* **46**, 818–30.

Pascual-Leone, J. 1970. A mathematical model for the transition rule in Piaget's developmental stages. *Acta Psychologica* **32**, 301–45.

Peterson, L. R. & M. J. Peterson 1959. Short-term retention of individual verbal items. *Journal of Experimental Psychology* **58**, 193–8.

Pratt, M. W., C. Boyes, S. Robins, & J. Manchester 1989. Telling tales: Aging, working memory, and the narrative cohesion of story retellings. *Developmental Psychology* **25**, 628–35.

Rabinowicz, T. 1980. The differentiate maturation of the human cerebral cortex. In *Human growth, Vol. III, Neurobiology and nutrition*, F. Falkner & J. M. Tanner (eds.).

New York: Plenum.

Reitman, J. S. 1974. Without surreptitious rehearsal, information in short-term memory decays. *Journal of Verbal Learning and Verbal Behavior* **13**, 365–77.

Roodenrys, S., C. Hulme, & G. Brown 1993. The development of short-term memory span: Separable effects of speech rate and long-term memory. *Journal of Experimental Child Psychology* **56**, 431–42.

Salthouse, T. A. 1994. The aging of working memory. *Neuropsychology* **8**, 535–43.

Sams, M., R. Hari, J. Rif, & J. Knuutila 1993. The human auditory sensory memory trace persists about 10 sec: Neuromagnetic evidence. *Journal of Cognitive Neuroscience* **5**, 363–70.

Saults, J. S. & N. Cowan 1996. The development of memory for ignored speech. *Journal of Experimental Child Psychology* **63**, 239–61.

Schweickert, R. & B. Boruff 1986. Short-term memory capacity: Magic number or magic spell? *Journal of Experimental Psychology: Learning, Memory, and Cognition* **12**, 419–25.

Siegel, L. S. 1994. Working memory and reading: A life-span perspective. *International Journal of Behavioral Development* **17**, 109–24.

Siegler, R. S. 1994. Cognitive variability: A key to understanding cognitive development. *Current Directions in Psychological Science* **3**, 1–5.

Sininger, Y. S., R. L. Klatzky, & D. M. Kirchner 1989. Memory scanning speed in language-disordered children. *Journal of Speech and Hearing Research* **32**, 289–97.

Sipe, S. & R. W. Engle 1986. Echoic memory processes in good and poor readers. *Journal of Experimental Psychology: Learning, Memory, and Cognition* **12**, 402–12.

Squire, L. R., B. Knowlton, & G. Musen 1993. The structure and organization of memory. In *Annual review of psychology* **44**, L. W. Porter & M. R. Rosenzweig (eds.), 453–95.

Standing, L., B. Bond, P. Smith, & C. Isely 1980. Is the immediate memory span determined by subvocalization rate? *British Journal of Psychology* **71**, 525–39.

Sternberg, S. 1966. High-speed scanning in human memory. *Science* **153**, 652–4.

Sternberg, S., S. Monsell, R. L. Knoll, & C. E. Wright 1978. The latency and duration of rapid movement sequences: Comparisons of speech and typewriting. In *Information processing in motor control and learning*, G. E. Stelmach (ed.). New York: Academic.

Sternberg, S., C. E. Wright, R. L. Knoll, & S. Monsell 1980. Motor programs in rapid speech: Additional evidence. In *Perception and production of fluent speech*, R. A. Cole (ed.). Hillsdale, NJ: Erlbaum.

Stigler, J. W., S.-Y. Lee, & H. W. Stevenson 1986. Digit memory in Chinese and English: Evidence for a temporally limited store. *Cognition* **23**, 1–20.

Stroop, J. R. 1935. Studies of interference in serial verbal reactions. *Journal of Experimental Psychology* **18**, 643–62.

Swanson, H. L. 1996. Individual and age-related differences in children's working memory. *Memory and Cognition* **24**, 70–82.

Swanson, H. L., J. B. Cooney, & S. Brock 1993. The influence of working memory and classification ability on children's word problem solution. *Journal of Experimental Child Psychology* **55**, 374–95.

Tipper, S. P., T. A. Bourque, S. H. Anderson, & J. C. Brehaut 1989. Mechanisms of attention: A developmental study. *Journal of Experimental Child Psychology* **48**, 353–78.

Towse, J. N. & G. J. Hitch 1995. Is there a relationship between task demand and storage space in tests of working memory capacity? *Quarterly Journal of Experimental Psychology* **48A**, 108–24.

Tun, P., A. Wingfield, & E. A. Stine 1991. Speech-processing capacity in young and older adults: A dual-task study. *Psychology and Aging* **6**, 3–9.

Turner, M. L. & R. W. Engle 1989. Is working memory capacity task dependent? *Journal of Memory and Language* **28**, 127–54.

Vallar, G. & A. D. Baddeley 1982. Short-term forgetting and the articulatory loop. *Quarterly Journal of Experimental Psychology* **34A**, 53–60.

Walczyk, J. J. & L. J. Raska 1992. The relation between low- and high-level reading skills in children. *Contemporary Educational Psychology* **17**, 38–46.

Watkins, M. J. 1974. Concept and measurement of primary memory. *Psychological Bulletin* **81**, 695–711.

Watkins, M. J., O. C. Watkins, F. I. M. Craik, & G. Mazuryk 1973. Effect of nonverbal distraction of short-term storage. *Journal of Experimental Psychology* **101**, 296–300.

Wingfield, A. & D. L. Byrnes 1972. Decay of information in short-term memory. *Science* **176**, 690–2.

Yakovlev, P. I. & A. R. Lecours 1967. The myelinogenetic cycles of regional maturation of the brain. In *Regional development of the brain in early life*, A. Minkowski (ed.). Oxford: Blackwell.

Zhang, G. & H. A. Simon 1985. STM capacity for Chinese words and idioms: Chunking and acoustical loop hypotheses. *Memory and Cognition* **13**, 193–201.

Acknowledgements

This work was supported by NIH grant HD–21338. I thank Scott Saults for reading an earlier draft.

CHAPTER 8

The development of memory strategies

David F. Bjorklund and Rhonda N. Douglas

Sometimes memory is easy, like when you're driving down the road and recognize a street corner and just "know" that there's a *Baskin Robbins* store on the next block, or when you're watching *Jeopardy* and blurt out "Who was Captain Cook" in response to "The first European explorer to set foot on Hawaii," and being surprised that you knew that piece of trivia. Other times memory is difficult, like when you're trying to learn and later recall the causes and consequences of the French Revolution, or when, while walking up and down the aisles of the supermarket, you try to reconstruct the grocery list you left on the kitchen table. It is the development of the latter type of explicit, often difficult, memory that is the focus of this chapter, specifically children's use of *strategies*, or *mnemonics*, to acquire and later retrieve information.

Strategies: Their definition, importance to memory development, and history

Strategies as effortful and controllable processes

Memory strategies are a particular type of cognitive process. Although strategies have been defined slightly differently by different researchers, they are generally conceived of as mentally effortful, goal-directed processes that are adopted to enhance memory performance. Strategies are controllable and are implemented deliberately by the individual and are potentially available to consciousness (see Harnishfeger & Bjorklund 1990a; Naus & Ornstein 1983; Pressley et al. 1985; Pressley & McCormick 1995). Strategies are used to help acquire information, such as the study skills children learn in school to help them master new materials or to learn their lines for a play. They are also used to retrieve information from long-term memory (that is, recall the information that one spent so much time learning). Strategies co-exist with other cognitive operations and are influenced by many factors. And, above all, strategies develop. Age differences are observed both in the number of strategies children of different ages have available to them and in the efficiency with which they use those strategies.

David Geary (1995) has suggested that cognitive processes can be classified into one of two broad categories: biologically primary abilities and biologically secondary abilities. Biologically primary abilities are those that have been selected in evolution and are found in similar forms across cultures. Biologically secondary abilities are those that are shaped by one's particular culture, especially formal schooling. The memory strategies discussed in this chapter are clearly biologically secondary abilities. They are not found universally, but are acquired through practice, and some may develop only as a result of formal schooling. We should not expect children to spontaneously use most memory strategies without some instruction. However, we can expect children to sometimes *discover* strategies while performing memory tasks. High levels of performance on some memory tasks, such as those encountered in school, can only be achieved when strategies are used, and children may learn this and discover or invent strategies for these tasks.

Understanding strategy development is important for understanding memory development. The lives of many children, especially those growing up in information-age societies such as ours, require the deliberate acquisition, retention, and retrieval of information. The significance of strategy development to memory development in general is reflected by the number of studies published on this topic since the 1960s. Beginning in the 1960s and continuing into the 1980s, strategy research dominated the study of memory development. Since that time, it has become obvious that there is more to memory development than strategies. Some processes that look to be strategic may actually reflect the relatively automatic activation of relations in semantic memory (Bjorklund 1985), and much of what children learn and remember is acquired and retrieved without the need of specific, effortful plans, but rather occurs without apparent intention and awareness (see Fivush & Hudson 1990; Schneider & Bjorklund 1997). This new insight, reflected in the current volume, does not make strategies less important, but merely recognizes the complexity of the developing memory system. An examination of memory strategy development provides a look at how children learn to control aspects of their mental lives. Not all important aspects of cognition are controllable by the individual or subject to conscious evaluation; but much of what we consider to be central to human intelligence is intentionally implemented and available to self-awareness, and a look at children's strategies provides a window to this important aspect of cognitive development.

A little history
Strategies as verbal mediators The modern era of memory development research can trace its beginnings to a paper published in 1966 by Flavell, Beach, and Chinsky. (For a more in-depth review of the history of strategy development research, see Harnishfeger & Bjorklund 1990a.) In this study, Flavell and his colleagues noted that older children who rehearsed sets of pictures during an interval between studying and recalling the pictures named the pictures to

themselves more so than did younger children. This led to research examining the role of the strategy of rehearsal in children's memory development. (The Flavell et al. study will be discussed in greater detail on p. 208 in this chapter.)

Upon reading this seminal paper, one is struck by the fact that it was *not* designed as a study of memory development. Rather, Flavell and his colleagues were following a tradition stemming from the neo-behaviorists, which emphasized the relation between stimuli and responses (*S-R* psychology). It became obvious to many psychologists, however, that what intervened between the environmental stimulus and a person's response (that is, what went on in the head) could not be ignored if one wished to develop a serious psychology of human behavior. One response to this was to propose *covert verbal mediators* (that is, little *s-r* connections intervening "in the head" between the overt *S*s and *R*s). For example, in discrimination-learning problems in which one of a pair of stimuli is designated as "correct," older children can learn a rule such as "the big one is always right," regardless of the particular shape any stimulus happened to be. In the vernacular of mediational (neo-behaviorist) theorists of the time, these children can generate the verbal mediators that will guide their problem-solving behavior; younger children fail to learn similar problems because they do not generate such verbal mediators. Neo-behaviorists did not use the term "strategy," although their descriptions of "intervening verbal mediators" came close to current conceptualizations of strategies.

Strategy deficiencies: Mediation, production, and utilization deficiencies
Research in strategy development has focused as much on what children *cannot* do as what they can do. For example, it was recognized that, for some problem-solving tasks, many young children could not benefit from a strategy even when one was demonstrated to them. Reese (1962) originally described this as a *mediation deficiency*. The implication was that children do not have the conceptual ability to use a strategy. Most research in memory strategy development, however, has not been concerned with mediation deficiencies, but rather with *production deficiencies* (Flavell 1970). A production deficiency is inferred when children who do not spontaneously use a strategy can use one when instructed and experience some benefit from its use. That is, their "deficiency" is in terms of producing the strategy, not in benefiting from its use. Despite changes in theoretical models (that is, from neo-behaviorism to information processing), the terms *mediation* and *production deficiencies* have stayed with developmental psychologists, and there have been substantial research efforts trying to determine why it is that children fail to use a strategy when it would seemingly be in their best interests to do so.

A relative newcomer to the "strategy deficiency" list is *utilization deficiency*, described by Patricia Miller (1990, 1994). Miller has suggested that a utilization deficiency represents an early phase in strategy acquisition when children spontaneously acquire a strategy but experience little or no benefit from it. Unlike mediation deficiencies, children produce the strategy themselves; and unlike production deficiencies, when they use the strategy they experience little or no enhancement of their task performance (see Bjorklund & C yle 1995; Miller 1994; Miller & Seier 1994).

Contemporary research in strategy development is concerned not only with these "deficiencies," but with the factors that cause children to use strategies in the first place and the conditions under which children will benefit from the strategies they use. Although early research assumed that young children (2- and 3-year-olds) did not use strategies, more recent research acknowledges that even they are strategic to a certain degree. Also, contemporary researchers emphasize that there is not a single path to effective strategy use. For example, whereas most research in the past has examined the development of a particular memory strategy (for example, rehearsal), contemporary research is more apt to look at the variety of different strategies children may use on a single task. This complicates the picture considerably. Modern research has shown more variability in strategy use, both within and between children, than we once thought existed. Moreover, there is mounting evidence that strategies do not always facilitate children's memory performance. The picture is not always a neat and clean one, but rather is a panorama of the multiple factors and multiple ways that children of different ages go about remembering.

The training study   With the emphasis that researchers have placed on strategy "deficiencies," it should not be surprising that the principal research paradigm involves training children to use strategies. Many studies of strategy development follow a three-step process: (1) find a strategy that older children use but younger children do not; (2) train young children to use the strategy and assess the effects of training; and (3) evaluate the extension, or transfer, of training by letting children perform a similar memory task again "any way they want."

Following this paradigm, successful training implies a production deficiency. However, most training studies are done not just to demonstrate that training is possible (that is, to illustrate a production deficiency), but are theoretically motivated. Experimental manipulations are performed to provide some insight into the mechanisms that underlie normal development. When training or transfer "work," one can infer something about the processes of natural development. If the experiment was designed to manipulate children's metacognitive awareness, background knowledge, or processing load, the results of the study suggest how these processes may contribute to age differences in memory performance in groups of nontrained children. Similar inferences are made when evaluating the transfer of training. Unsuccessful training and transfer can also be informative. For example, if children's memory performance increases during training but falls back to baseline levels on a transfer task, what does it say about the role of the factors being trained?

In the remainder of this chapter, we will look at research and theory into children's strategy development. Having defined memory strategies, we will first look at their existence in young children, and pose the question, "What are production deficient children doing?" This will be followed by a lengthy section examining the development over childhood of some of the different memory strategies that have been studied since the 1960s. We will then review some of the factors that have been shown to influence both developmental and individual differences in children's strategy use. Included in this section will be the factors of processing efficiency, the knowledge base, metamemory, encoding, motivation, and intelligence. This will be followed by a look at two "new" issues in strategy development – utilization deficiencies and children's multiple and variable strategy use. We will conclude the chapter with a brief overview of where strategy development research has been and where it is likely going in the future.

Strategic behavior in young children (or, what are production deficient children doing?)

Memory can be assessed in a variety of ways. Strategic memory is customarily evaluated in tests of *recall*. *Free recall* is the most difficult type of memory test, with children having to retrieve information to only a general request (for example, tell me the names of all your cousins). Levels of performance are generally higher when more specific prompts, or cues, are provided (for example, tell me the names of all your cousins on your father's side, starting with the children of Uncle Joe, etc.). This later type of memory test is referred to as *cued recall*. Age differences are quite large for free recall, with preschool children showing especially low levels of performance. However, when more specific prompts are provided, levels of performance increase, often substantially. The interpretation of this finding is that young children are not very good at searching their memories (e.g. Ceci et al. 1980; Emmerich & Ackerman 1978). Stated another way, young children do not possess, or do not use, memory strategies either to acquire information or to retrieve what information they have acquired. That their memory performance can be quite good given specific prompts (see Fivush & Hudson 1990; Schneider & Bjorklund 1997; Schneider & Pressley 1989) indicates that they are able to use retrieval strategies effectively; they just do not use them spontaneously. This is the classic demonstration of a production deficiency.

If young children are not using strategies (unless we train them), what are they doing? It appears that, at least under some situations, they actually *are* using strategies, just not the ones we think they should be using. The strategies they use are often very simple and frequently not very effective, but preschool children do do things to help them remember, and we feel comfortable calling these things strategies (see Wellman 1988).

A simple strategy used by some 3- and 4-year-olds involves selectively attending to items that they are trying to remember (Baker-Ward et al. 1984; Yussen 1974). This includes frequently re-attending to the stimuli, which is a form of visual rehearsal (Wellman et al. 1975). Preschool children have also been observed to spontaneously name items they are asked to remember, but this strategy, although associated with higher levels of memory performance for school-aged children, is ineffective for 4-year-olds (Baker-Ward et al. 1984).

One potentially useful strategy involves the use of external memory cues. For example, Heisel and Ritter (1981) asked 3- to 9-year-old children to hide an object in 1 of 196 containers, arranged in a 14 × 14 grid, so that they could remember the location. An effective strategy would be to hide objects in distinctive positions, such as the corners of the display, which is what children 5 years of age and older did. The youngest children, however, did not use such techniques, although some children attempted to hide the objects in the same location on all trials. This is a good idea and reflects a controllable behavior executed to facilitate performance (that is, a strategy). Unfortunately, 3-year-olds rarely chose distinctive locations to hide objects, making the strategy an ineffective one.

Other research using similar designs has found that 3-year-olds will use retrieval cues to aid their recall only under optimal conditions (Blair et al. 1978; Geis & Lange 1976; Schneider & Sodian 1988; Sophian & Wellman 1983). For example, in a study by Ritter et al. (1973), 3- to 5-year-old children were given six pictures of people (for example, a soccer player) and six small toys (for example, a soccer ball). Each of the six toys was related to one of the six people. Each person was hidden in one of six houses in front of the children. They were then asked to show a "twin" of each person where to find his or her "partner" and were told that they could use the toys to help them remember the correct locations if they wished. Under these very explicit conditions, a majority of the preschoolers used the toys as retrieval cues (for example, placing the soccer ball outside of the house containing the soccer player). However, only 20 per cent of the 3-year-olds used retrieval cues in a second task where the picture cards had to be turned around in order to serve as cues. In contrast, 75 per cent of 5-year-olds used toys as cues in this situation. In other words, 3-year-olds will use a retrieval strategy, but only when the conditions make its use highly obvious or when they are specifically instructed to do so (Whittaker et al. 1985).

One reason why strategies are rarely observed in young children may be because they perceive the memory tasks they are asked to perform as being irrelevant and meaningless. By the time children from our culture are in first grade, they have learned that many of the tasks that adults, such as teachers, ask them to do may have no immediate consequences to their lives. That is, these tasks are performed "out of context." Formal schooling in general takes education out of the homes, streets, and fields, where children in more traditional societies are educated, and moves it into the classroom. Perhaps

206

preschool children will show more goal-directed and strategic behavior when the task is embedded in a more relevant context.

This approach was taken by Somerville et al. (1983) in a study that evaluated 2- to 4-year-old children's *prospective memory* for everyday activities. Prospective memory is the ability to plan ahead, such as being able to remember to perform a particular activity. Children were asked to carry out a specific task in the near future. Some tasks were highly appealing, such as getting candy, whereas others were of less inherent interest to young children, such as getting the wash out of the dryer. Children of all ages remembered to perform many of the activities, although memory was better for the more interesting event. Although we cannot specify what, if any, strategies children used to perform these prospective memory tasks, the results suggest that even 2-year-olds are capable of intentional memory, at least when given an interesting event to remember.

In other research, young children's memory for the location of hidden objects was assessed in a naturalistic setting – their homes (DeLoache & Brown 1983; DeLoache et al. 1985). These experimenters used a hide-and-seek-game format, something that even the 18- to 24-month-old children in their studies were familiar with. A toy (Big Bird) was hidden in one of several locations in a child's home, and children were told to remember the location so they could find the toy later. After waiting several minutes, children were permitted to search for the hidden toy. Despite being distracted during the waiting interval, many children showed signs of mnemonic activity. For example, children sometimes checked the hiding place to see if the toy was indeed still hidden there, stated the name of the hidden toy, or stared or pointed at the hiding location during the delay interval.

As this brief overview of research indicates, it is not appropriate to classify preschool children as astrategic. Under highly constrained, highly motivated, and naturalistic conditions, they do indeed implement what appear to be intentional, goal-directed behaviors. Sometimes these strategies work, and other times they are what Wellman (1988) described as "faulty strategies" – strategic behaviors that do not help remembering. Wellman (1988) goes so far as to make the claim that preschoolers' strategies are every bit as goal-directed and influential as are the strategies of older children. We make a more cautious interpretation of the research findings. Young children's memory activities tend to be fragile and restricted to limited domains (Brown et al. 1983). There has been a tendency in developmental psychology over the past several decades to redress previous overstatements about what infants and young children *cannot do* and instead emphasize what they can do. This trend can be seen in the study of memory strategies. However, while noting that preschoolers are not as deficient in strategic abilities as we once believed they were, we should not overlook the fact that their mnemonic abilities are substantially less than those of older school-aged children, who display strategies in a wide range of situations, including school-like and laboratory tasks.

The development of strategies

The following sections discuss specific types of memory strategies that have been frequently investigated in developmental psychology. Strategies can be executed either at time of learning—at *input*—or at time of retrieval—at *output*. The input strategies discussed include *rehearsal*, which involves the repetition of target information, *organization*, which involves the combination of different items into categories, and *elaboration*, which involves the association of two or more items through the creation of a representation which connects them. Additionally, input strategies for studying more complex materials, such as texts, are discussed. The output strategies we discuss are called simply retrieval strategies, which include the processes of accessing and bringing information into consciousness.

Rehearsal

In 1966, the publication of an innovative study conducted by John Flavell and his colleagues (discussed briefly earlier in the chapter) described the development of rehearsal between the ages of 5 and 10. Kindergarten, second-, and fifth-grade children were asked to play some games, during which they wore space helmets with translucent visors. The children observed a set of pictures of familiar objects as an experimenter pointed to three of the pictures in succession. Immediately after presentation and following a 15-second delay, children viewed the set of pictures arranged in a different, random order and were asked to point to the three pictures in the sequence that had been demonstrated earlier by the experimenter (a serial recall task). Young children talk to themselves by moving their lips. In this experiment, the children pulled their space helmet visors down during the 15-second delay so that they could not see the to-be-remembered items during the study period. An experimenter, who was trained to identify lip movements corresponding to the target words, then observed the children's mouths in order to record frequency of rehearsal.

Flavell et al. (1966) reported age-related increases in both the amount of rehearsal and levels of recall. More specifically, 85 per cent of fifth-graders produced some spontaneous rehearsal in comparison to only 10 per cent of the kindergartners. Furthermore, within each grade, levels of recall for children who exhibited more rehearsal were generally higher than those of children who rehearsed less. Based on these results, Flavell and his colleagues concluded that verbal rehearsal serves to mediate memory and that the more children rehearse, the more they remember.

This study served as a catalyst for developmental psychologists, and several studies on children's rehearsal were published in the following years (Hagen et al. 1973; Keeney et al. 1967; Kingsley & Hagen 1969). However, it was not until almost a decade later that Flavell's frequency hypothesis was seriously questioned (Cuvo 1975; Ornstein et al. 1975). For example, in a study by Ornstein and his colleagues, third-, sixth-, and eighth-grade children were presented a series of words for recall with an interval of several seconds between each successive word. Children were instructed to repeat aloud the last word presented at least once and were told that they may repeat any of the other words as well during each rehearsal set. Thus, in this *overt-rehearsal procedure*, rehearsal was mandatory, and the experimenters were able to determine the exact nature of their rehearsal.

Similar to the findings of Flavell and his colleagues, age-related increases in recall were found. In contrast to Flavell's study, however, the overt-rehearsal procedure did *not* reveal age-related differences in the frequency of rehearsal. Younger children rehearsed just as much as older children. Ornstein and his colleagues explained these findings in terms of differences in the quality, or style, of children's rehearsal. More specifically, younger children's rehearsal style was characterized as *passive* because they repeated each word with only one or two other words during the inter-stimulus interval. In contrast, the older children rehearsed the target word with many other words during the inter-stimulus interval, a style labeled *active*, or *cumulative*. This led Ornstein and his colleagues to conclude that the primary developmental change in rehearsal concerns style rather than frequency (see also Cuvo 1975; Guttentag et al. 1987; Kellas et al. 1975).

Training studies provided additional evidence for a causal relationship between rehearsal style and memory performance. For example, young children trained to use a cumulative rehearsal style exhibit increased levels of recall, especially for items presented early in lists (those represented in the primacy portion of the serial-position curve) (B. C. Cox et al. 1989; Kingsley & Hagen 1969; Naus et al. 1977; Ornstein et al. 1977). Thus, although age differences are rarely eliminated, training young children to use a more effective rehearsal strategy benefits their memory performance. These findings led to the conclusion that a critical developmental difference concerns children's inclination to implement a particular strategy rather than their ability to use it. That is, younger children are production deficient in that they have access to a strategy that would facilitate their performance but fail to rehearse when it would prove beneficial to do so.

Organization

Ornstein and Naus (1978) suggested that active rehearsal benefits memory performance by facilitating the recognition of conceptual relations among items that are rehearsed together. Indeed, one of the most frequently studied encoding strategies involves the organization of stimulus materials such as pictures or words into meaningful categories. For example, memory for items that must be purchased at the grocery store is enhanced if the shopper organizes the items into categories (dairy products, meats, or vegetables) or meals (breakfast, lunch, or dinner items).

Studies examining the effects of organization on recall usually involve the random presentation of items that can be organized into categories, such as animals, tools, or fruits. Such studies are designed to detect whether or not children remember items from the same category together even though they were presented randomly, a phenomenon referred to as *clustering*. Results indicate that adults who demonstrate high levels of clustering in their recall generally remember more than adults who demonstrate lower levels of clustering (Bower 1970; Mandler 1967). Developmental trends in clustering and recall indicate that preschoolers perform at chance levels and that clustering and recall increase with age (Arlin & Brody 1976; Furth & Milgram 1973).

A more direct measurement of organization in memory is obtained through the use of *sort-recall tasks*, in which children are provided with the opportunity to sort items into categories in the interval between presentation and recall. Similar to findings of clustering studies, sort-recall experiments demonstrate that younger children rarely organize (that is, sort) information by meaning spontaneously; however, older children are more likely to do so and experience greater memory performance as a result.

Young children's reluctance to use an organizational strategy in sort-recall tasks is illustrated in a study conducted by Salatas and Flavell (1976). In their study, first-grade children were given 16 pictures which could be organized into four distinct categories (animals, clothing, toys, and tools). After naming each picture and each of the four categories, the experimenter placed the pictures randomly on a table in front of the children. The children were then told that they would be asked to remember the pictures later and that they should put the pictures together in a way that would help them remember. Free recall was tested 90 seconds later. Despite instructions that would seemingly lead children to physically sort the pictures into categories, only 27 per cent did so. Other studies using similar instructions report that even 8-year-olds often fail to organize items into meaningful categories. Older children are more likely than younger children to categorize items according to their meaning and to use such organization during study. As a result, they produce higher levels of clustering and recall (Best & Ornstein 1986; Corsale & Ornstein 1980; Hasselhorn 1992; Schneider 1986).

However, even preschoolers use organizational strategies and demonstrate enhanced levels of memory performance when instructions are modified to emphasize the importance of grouping items according to their meaning (Corsale & Ornstein 1980; Lange & Jackson 1974; Sodian et al. 1986), when slight changes in stimulus presentation procedures are made (Guttentag & Lange 1994), or when children are explicitly trained to use organizational strategies (Black & Rollins 1982; Carr & Schneider 1991; Lange & Pierce 1992; Moely et al. 1969). In other words, the organizational abilities of preschoolers, kindergartners, and young elementary school children resemble their rehearsal abilities in that they demonstrate a production deficiency. Young children are capable of organizing information for recall, but they typically fail to do so without training. Additionally, training rarely eliminates age differences, and young children transfer organization to new situations only after extensive training (Carr & Schneider 1991; D. Cox & Waters 1986). Even so, higher levels of organization do not necessarily lead to high levels of recall, providing evidence for utilization deficiencies in organization for preschoolers and elementary school children (Bjorklund et al. 1992; Lange & Pierce 1992; Lange et al. 1990; see discussion of utilization deficiencies later on pp. 229–32 of this chapter). Spontaneous and effective use of organizational strategies is typically not found until 10 or 11 years of age (Frankel & Rollins 1985; Hasselhorn 1992; Schneider 1986).

Elaboration

Elaboration is similar to organization in that both strategies involve the imposition of semantic relations upon items to be remembered. More specifically, in elaboration, an association between two or more items is formed by the creation of a representation, such as an image, sentence, or word, that links the items. For example, if you needed to remember to pickup your dry cleaning on the way home from work, you could imagine your car wearing a sports coat. When you saw your car, the ridiculous image of it wearing a coat would increase your chances of stopping at the cleaners.

Elaboration research has typically concentrated on its effects upon *paired-associate task* performance. In paired-associate tasks, participants learn pairs of unrelated items and are asked upon presentation of one item to recall the other. Research indicates that children do not spontaneously generate elaborations until adolescence (Pressley & Levin 1977; Rohwer et al. 1977), although school-age children can be trained to do so, reflecting a production deficiency (Pressley 1982; Rohwer 1973; Siaw & Kee 1987). Often, even adults need instructions to elaborate on paired-associate tasks (Rohwer 1980). However, older children are still more likely than younger children to spontaneously produce elaborations, to retrieve them in order to facilitate recall, and to transfer them to other tasks (Beuhring & Kee 1987; Pressley & Dennis-Rounds 1980; Rohwer 1973). Additionally, when younger children generate elaborations, they tend to be less effective in aiding performance than those produced by older children, reflecting a utilization deficiency (Reese 1977).

Strategies for studying complex materials

Although most of the research on strategy development discussed to this point has emphasized processes that facilitate rote recall of words or pictures, strategies are also beneficial for understanding, storing, and retrieving more complex and meaningful information, such as texts. Developmental trends indicate that spontaneous strategic activities involved in extracting meaning from text are rarely observed in elementary school children. More specifically, research conducted by Ann Brown and her colleagues revealed that processes such as identifying, underlining, and summarizing the main ideas of text passages develop during the high school years (Brown et al. 1983).

Although strategies for studying complex materials are acquired later,

211

Schneider and Bjorklund (1997) note that the qualitative developmental trend found between sixth grade and twelfth grade parallels the pattern found for rote-recall memory strategies between first and sixth grades. The trend indicates intermittent strategic activity, followed by more frequent and effective applications in a broader variety of learning contexts. As with the previous strategies discussed, production deficiencies and poor performance characterize children's initial use of strategies for understanding and remembering texts. Proficient strategy use can be observed only after extensive practice.

Training experiments reveal that complicated text processing strategies can be taught to normal elementary school children (Gaultney 1995; Paris & Oka 1986; Pressley et al. 1988). Instructional programs that include reading strategy components are beneficial for poor readers as well (Palincsar & Brown 1984; Short & Ryan 1984). However, although training promotes the use of complicated text processing strategies, their spontaneous production is the exception rather than the rule. Thus, traditional accounts of strategy development that focus on rote recall seem to underestimate age-related variability in natural strategic competence. That is, although simple strategies can be observed in early childhood, more complex strategies often cannot be observed even in adults (Pressley & Van Meter 1993).

Retrieval

Retrieval strategies can be described as deliberate operations that individuals perform in order to access information from long-term memory. In recognition tasks, the occurrence of the original stimulus prompts retrieval. In recall tasks, retrieval is more complex. Howe et al. (1985) stated that the critical developmental change in memory performance concerns age-related increases in retrieval ability rather than age-related increases in storage ability (see also Morrison & Lord 1982). Kobasigawa (1977) suggested three retrieval deficits that younger children may experience: (a) failure to recognize the value of internal or external memory cues as memory aids; (b) underdeveloped strategies for locating information in memory; and (c) inexperience with problems, which leads to poor evaluation of searching processes.

Young children's retrieval deficits appear to reflect their dependence on the original encoding context and their difficulty to generalize. For example, Ackerman (1985a, b) presented children with a set of cues (for example, *rose* and *tulip*) associated with a target word (for example, *lily*). At recall, children were presented with some or all of the cues, or with an extra-list cue that could have been associated with the target to be recalled, but was not paired with it at the initial presentation (for example, *flower* for *lily*). They were then asked to recall the target words associated with the cue words. Results indicated that 7-year-olds required more items from the original encoding environment to be reinstated in order to correctly recall target words than did older children and adults. Thus, young children can access information stored in long-term

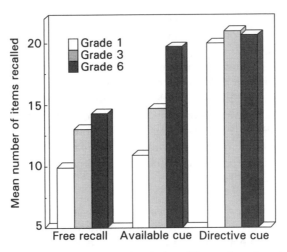

Figure 8.1 Children's mean level of recall by grade and retrieval condition (based on data from Kobasigawa 1974).

memory, but their successful retrieval requires more explicit cues in comparison to older children.

A classic demonstration of age differences in retrieval and younger children's deficiencies in using external memory cues was provided by Kobasigawa (1974). In his procedure, first-, third-, and sixth-grade children were presented with sets of categorizable pictures to remember and with cue cards for classifying the pictures. For example, a picture of a zoo served as the cue card for classifying pictures of animals. This procedure required the children to use categorical information as they encoded the items. There were three retrieval conditions in this experiment: free-recall, in which children were asked to remember the items in any order; available-cue, in which children were asked to recall the items in any order using the cue cards that had been paired with the items earlier, if they wished; and directive-cue, in which children were shown each cue card one at a time, told how many items had been paired with it, and then asked to recall as many of those items as they could before going on to the next category.

Results from the experiment are illustrated in Figure 8.1. Levels of performance were generally low in the free-recall condition, with the sixth-graders recalling more than the first- and third-grade children. Recall was elevated in the available-cue condition only for the sixth-graders, who made use of the cues to guide their recall. Only very few first-graders used the available cues to guide their recall, although 75 per cent of the third-graders did so. However, third-graders' performance indicated that, although they were aware of the cues, they used them poorly and their recall was not significantly higher than for children in the free-recall condition. The directive-cue condition produced high levels of performance for all children and minimized developmental

213

differences. This finding indicates that first- and third-graders stored just as much information about the stimuli as sixth-graders; their difficulty was getting it out of memory.

Other studies using similar procedures have also reported considerable reductions in younger children's recall deficits under directive-cue conditions (Kee & Bell 1981; Williams & Goulet 1975), and when children are asked to recall information from stories or personal experiences (Fivush & Hamond 1990; Hudson 1990). These studies suggest that younger children benefit more from the presentation of retrieval cues than older children, who may spontaneously generate retrieval plans (Hasselhorn 1990; Mistry & Lange 1985; Schmidt & Schmidt 1986).

Encoding versus retrieval strategies as determinants of memory development

Several studies have attempted to determine whether developmental differences in memory performance are due to age differences in storage ability, retrieval ability, or an interaction between the two. For example, Brian Ackerman and his colleagues (summarized in Ackerman 1987) conducted studies that examined developmental differences in children's dependency on identical encoding and retrieval contexts, using a paired-associate learning task. Their findings suggest that orienting questions at encoding (e.g. for example, for the word pair knife-axe, "Are these weapons?") generate a memory trace that is optimally retrieved by comparable orienting cues at recall (for example, "Is this a weapon?"). These results are supported by the research on retrieval cues discussed above, which demonstrated that younger children are more dependent on comparable encoding and retrieval cues. Similar findings have been obtained using different memory tasks (Ceci & Howe 1978; Emmerich & Ackerman 1978). These studies seem to indicate the critical role of age differences in retrieval ability in explaining developmental differences in memory development.

However, other research examining organizational strategies using sort-recall tasks showed that variations in behaviors during encoding, but not during retrieval, produced differences in memory performance (Black & Rollins 1982; Schneider 1986; Schneider et al. 1986). Thus, the question concerning whether encoding or retrieval processes drive memory development is not easily answered. In reviewing the relevant research, Brainerd (1985) concluded that the relative contributions of encoding and retrieval development upon memory performance may be task-specific.

Factors that influence children's use of memory strategies

From the research presented in the previous sections, it is clear that strategies develop. After describing some of these changes, the next question is, "How?",

214

or more precisely, "What are the factors that contribute to developmental and individual differences in memory strategies?" The list of contributing factors can become quite long, and, of course, any factor does not have its effect independent of others. Moreover, although some of these factors may have a greater influence than others, it is not possible to point to any single factor as "the" principal cause of strategy development. Any factor may have a different affect on strategy performance as a function of the age, background knowledge, and ability level of the child, as well as the strategy in question. In this section, we examine some of the most important and most studied influences on children's memory strategies. Included in our survey are efficiency of cognitive processing, knowledge base, encoding, metamemory, motivation, and intelligence.

Efficiency of cognitive processing: Strategies and mental effort

By definition, strategies are effortful mental processes, consuming some portion of a person's limited mental resources for their execution. One hypothesis concerning age differences in strategy use revolves around age differences in the efficiency of cognitive processing. Younger children must use more of their limited mental resources to execute a strategy than older children. Because of this difference, younger children are less likely to use a strategy, or less likely to use one effectively (Bjorklund 1987; Kee 1994). That is, strategy use has a cost in terms of mental effort. Young children use so much of their limited resources executing the strategy that they do not retain sufficient mental capacity to perform other aspects of the task efficiently (Case 1985).

How can one test this hypothesis? One technique that has been used is the *dual-task paradigm*, which is based on the simple idea that it is difficult to do two things at once. The degree of this difficulty is reflected by the amount of interference that doing one task has on doing another. For example, Bjorklund and Harnishfeger (1987) used a dual-task paradigm to assess the degree of mental effort required to execute a memory strategy for third- and seventh-grade children. In their study (Experiment 2), children tapped the space bar of a microcomputer as rapidly as they could: (a) alone (baseline); (b) during a free-recall task with categorically related words (free recall); and (c) during a free-recall task in which they were trained to use an organizational memory strategy (trained recall). Changes in tapping rate between the free- and trained-recall sessions, all relative to baseline tapping rate, reflect the differences in the mental effort requirements of the two tasks. It was expected that the trained task, on which children were required to use an organizational strategy, would be more effortful than the free-recall task. Also assessed were changes in levels of recall and clustering, the latter of which served as the measure of strategy use.

Levels of recall, clustering, and percentage interference in tapping rate for the third and seventh graders on the free- and trained-recall tasks are shown in Table 8.1. As can be seen, both the third- and the seventh-graders experienced more interference in tapping rate for the trained- than for the free-recall task, and both demonstrated significant improvements in clustering. These findings indicate that both groups of children learned the instructed organization strategy and that using this strategy was significantly more effortful than not using it. However, only the older children also experienced a significant increase in recall on the trained trial. The third-grade children, despite successfully using the trained strategy (as reflected by the higher clustering scores), did not show a corresponding increase in recall. Bjorklund and Harnishfeger (1987) interpreted these findings as reflecting the fact that the younger children expended too much of their limited mental resources on executing the strategy and thus had too few resources remaining to devote to retrieving individual items.

Similar interpretations have been reached by other researchers. For example, Guttentag (1984) trained second-, third-, and sixth-grade children to use a cumulative rehearsal strategy, all while tapping their index finger as fast as possible. Guttentag reported that even the youngest children learned the cumulative rehearsal strategy, but that the cost in terms of mental effort varied with age. Younger children demonstrated more interference (that is, slowed down their tapping rate more) than older children, indicating that they allocated more mental effort to execute the strategy than older children. Similar findings and interpretations have been reported for both simpler attentional strategies (Miller et al. 1991a) and a more complex elaboration memory strategy (Kee & Davies 1990).

Strategies are effortful. Developmental research has consistently found that young children process information more slowly (Kail 1993) and less efficiently (Case 1985) than older children. As a result, they are less likely to use a strategy spontaneously and less likely to benefit from the imposition of a strategy.

Knowledge base

Differences in efficiency of cognitive processing certainly have a profound effect on strategic memory. Moreover, because speed of processing, which is

Table 8.1 Mean recall, clustering and percentage interference scores for free recall (baseline) and trained recall for third and seventh grade children (from Bjorklund & Harnishfeger, 1987, experiment 2).

	Free recall	Trained recall
Third grade		
Percent interference	17.31	21.29 (p< .01)
Clustering (ARC)	.14	.53 (p< .001)
Recall	4.60	5.07 (ns)
Seventh grade		
Percent interference	18.07	23.53 (p< .01)
Clustering (ARC)	.09	.80 (p< .001)
Recall	5.89	7.73 (p<.01)

the single best indicator of efficiency of processing, varies reliably with age and is presumably under endogenous control (Kail 1993), it is tempting to think that cognitive efficiency is therefore under strict maturational control and is relatively uninfluenced by other factors. This is not the case, however. Speed and efficiency of processing are also influenced substantially by one's *knowledge base* – the background information a person has about a particular topic. For instance, memory span and working-memory span, which are often used as measures of information-processing capacity (see Ch. 7 in this volume), are influenced by a child's knowledge base for the to-be-remembered information (Chi 1978; Dempster 1978; Schneider et al. 1993). For example, in the classic study by Chi (1978), the memory span of chess-expert children for chess pieces on a chessboard was superior to that of a group of non-chess-expert adults. The pattern was reversed when digits were used as stimuli. Do these children have greater *capacity* for chess pieces than for digits? Yes and no. The interpretation that most psychologists prefer is that one's *actual* capacity does not change, but that one's *functional capacity* does vary as a function what is being remembered; people use their limited information-processing capacity more efficiently when dealing with information for which they have detailed knowledge (Bjorklund 1987; Chi & Ceci 1987; Kee 1994; Ornstein et al. 1988; Schneider 1993).

Knowledge has a significant impact on all types of memory, not just strategic memory. For example, events are more easily encoded and remembered when they occur in a familiar context (see Ch. 6 in this volume), texts dealing with familiar content are more easily comprehended than texts dealing with less familiar content (Recht & Leslie 1988; Schneider et al. 1989), and specific names or items are more easily recalled, apparently independent of any strategy, when they are highly familiar versus less familiar (Chechile & Richman 1982; Ghatala 1984; Richman et al. 1976). Also, in some cases, children may have such well-developed knowledge bases that organized retrieval can be achieved without the need of a deliberate strategy. For example, Bjorklund and Zeman (1982, 1983) reported that first- through fifth-grade children recalled the names of their current school classmates in highly organized orders (for example, by seating arrangement, reading groups, or sex), yet seemed unaware that they were following any particular scheme. Rather, because their classmates' names constituted a well-established knowledge base, the recall of one name automatically activated the recall of another, without the need of a deliberate plan. They speculated that this process of nonstrategic organization could sometimes lead to strategic organization. In the process of retrieving names via the relatively automatic activation of semantic-memory relations, children may reflect upon what they have done and discover a strategy in the process ("Hey, all these kids sit together. Maybe I'll remember the rest of the class that way."). In this case, an elaborated knowledge base might indirectly lead to better strategy use (see Bjorklund & Jacobs 1985 for a demonstration of this). As this paragraph indicates, the influence of knowledge on memory and its development is broad and by no means limited to strategic functioning. However, the remainder of our discussion of the role of knowledge will be restricted to strategic memory.

In an influential review, Kee (1994) stated that "most researchers acknowledge that strategic processing is *dependent* on the availability and accessibility of relevant knowledge" (1994: 9), and that the reason for this is that having a detailed, or elaborated, knowledge base results in faster processing, which in turn results in more efficient processing. According to Bjorklund et al.,

> the primary effect that an elaborated knowledge base has on cognitive processing is to increase speed of processing for domain-specific information. Individual items can be accessed more quickly from the long-term store, as can relations among related items in the knowledge base ... faster processing is equated with more efficient processing, which results in greater availability of mental resources. These mental resources can then be applied to retrieving specific items (item specific effects ...), to domain-specific strategies, or to metacognitive processes (Bjorklund et al. 1990: 95).

Bjorklund et al. developed an information-processing model to capture these relations, and this is presented in Figure 8.2.

There have been many demonstrations of both developmental and individual differences in strategy use and memory performance as a function of knowledge base. For example, when children are given sets of category-typical items to remember (for example, for the category CLOTHING, *shirt, dress, coat*) as opposed to sets of category-atypical items (for example, for the category CLOTHING, *hat, socks, belt*), both levels of strategy use (usually clustering)

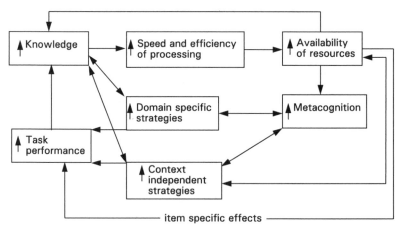

Figure 8.2 A model of the effects of knowledge on strategic memory (from Bjorklund et al. 1990).

and memory performance are greater for the category-typical sets of items (Bjorklund 1988; Rabinowitz 1984). In other research, young children perform well when sets of highly associated items serve as stimuli (for example, *dog, cat, horse, cow*), but not when equally familiar but less strongly associated category items are used as stimuli (for example, *tiger, elephant, cow, pig*). Older children perform well for both sets of materials (e.g. Bjorklund & Jacobs 1985; Frankel & Rollins 1985; Lange 1973; Schneider 1986). The apparent reason for this pattern is that highly associated words become well established early in life (Bjorklund & Jacobs 1984), whereas well-developed relations among the less strongly related category items are not established until later in development. Other research has shown that children acquire strategies more readily, both spontaneously and through training, and generalize a learned strategy to new contexts more successfully when familiar and well-integrated sets of items (such as highly associated words or category-typical items) as opposed to less familiar and well integrated sets of items (such as low associated words or category-atypical items) are used as stimuli (Best 1993; Bjorklund & Buchanan 1989).

The relation between knowledge, strategy use, and efficiency of processing is illustrated in an experiment by Kee and Davies (1990). They used a dual-task procedure (tapping their index finger while performing a memory task) with 10- and 11-year-old children who were instructed in the use of an elaboration strategy (generating relations between pairs of items to facilitate memory; see our earlier discussion). Two types of lists were used. One was comprised of what they called "accessible" pairs (for example, *stairs-tower, cowboy-ranch, pig-mud*). They believed that because children would have substantial background knowledge for the relations between the items, they should be able to generate elaborations for the pairs with relative ease. The other list consisted of "inaccessible" pairs (for example, *ticket-knee, frog-chair, cake-valley*). Although the words were equally familiar, children would not be likely to have any pre-established associations between the pairs. This would make the generation of elaborations more effortful (see Kee & Guttentag 1994 for evidence of this).

Children remembered fewer of the inaccessible than the accessible pairs, revealing the effect of knowledge base on memory performance. More critically, however, was the differential expenditure of mental effort between the two conditions. Children's tapping rate slowed down significantly more when trying to remember the inaccessible than the accessible pairs. In other words, it was mentally more difficult for children to use the elaboration strategy for the inaccessible (and thus less familiar) than for the accessible (and thus more familiar) word pairs.

Although the impact of knowledge base on children's strategic memory seems incontrovertible, there is one peculiar finding that deserves attention. When comparing the memory performance on strategic memory tasks of experts and novices on materials in the experts' area of specialty, the experts always remember more than the novices. The surprising finding, however, is that this memory advantage is not always mediated by strategies. For example, several free- and sort-recall experiments have contrasted the memory performance of expert children (in soccer or baseball) with those of novices. The typical result is significantly greater memory performance for the experts when the list consists of categories and items from the experts' area of expertise (for example, baseball equipment, types of baseball plays). Yet, few or no differences are found between the experts and novices for strategy use (for example, clustering or sorting) (Gaultney et al. 1992; Schneider & Bjorklund 1992; Schneider et al. 1996). These findings suggest that the enhanced performance on strategic tasks for expert children are primarily mediated by item-specific effects associated with their more elaborated knowledge base rather than through more effective use of strategies (Bjorklund & Schneider 1996).

The evidence for a potent role of knowledge base on children's strategic memory cannot be denied. In fact, it seems that there is no other single factor that has such an effect on children's memory performance. In studies that have assessed the impact of a variety of factors on children's free recall, including intelligence, metamemory, and knowledge base, more of the differences in memory performance can be attributed to differences in knowledge base than to any other factor (Alexander & Schwanenflugel 1994; Hasselhorn 1992).

Encoding

Encoding is the process of representing information. Even a simple event, such as a word, can be encoded in a variety of ways. For example, the word *dog* can be described in terms of a set of features. A dog is an animal, a mammal, a pet; it has certain physical characteristics, engages in certain behaviors, and makes certain sounds; it is related to other concepts such as *cat*, *wolf*, and *fire hydrants*. The word *dog* may bring to mind a particular image, or perhaps a set of images. When presented with the word *dog*, any combination of these various features may be encoded.

Encoding is usually thought of as a relatively automatic operation that occurs without conscious awareness. However, the manner in which information is encoded will affect how, or whether, that information will later be remembered. Younger children tend to encode items with fewer features than older children (Ackerman 1984; Ceci 1980; Ceci & Howe 1978). As a result, they recall fewer items, in part because individual items that are more elaboratively encoded are more easily activated and retrieved than less elaboratively encoded items.

Age differences in encoding can also influence strategic memory. For instance, when adults are presented a word, for example *apple*, activation of that word spreads in semantic memory (the long-term repository of language terms) to related concepts, for example *orange*, *pear*, and *pie*. Research by Howe et al. (1985) showed that although second- and sixth-grade children encoded words in terms of their categorical features (for example FRUIT for the word *apple*), unlike adults, there was little spread of activation to other similarly encoded words (for example *orange*) by either age group. That is, despite knowing the categorical features of sets of words, the children were less likely to use those features to identify categories of items. Rather, they are encoding and presumably trying to remember words on an item-by-item basis, ignoring the relations among the items (Bjorklund & Hock 1982). On a task where organization on the basis of categorical relations is the most effective strategy, this failure will severely limit the likelihood and effectiveness of children's strategic memory.

Metamemory

The role of metamemory in children's memory warrants a chapter of its own (see Ch. 10 in this volume). In this section, we briefly outline the development of metamemory and then look more closely at the role metamemory plays in strategic memory.

Metamemory can be described as knowledge an individual possesses regarding the functioning and contents of his or her memory. Two general types of metamemory are usually distinguished: *declarative metamemory* and *procedural metamemory*. Declarative metamemory refers to explicit, conscious, and factual knowledge concerning person and task characteristics and memory strategies. Person characteristics include, for example, a child's ideas about his or her memory strengths and weaknesses (that is, a child's mnemonic self-concept), whereas task characteristics include information regarding factors that influence task difficulty, such as item familiarity, list length, or study time. Memory strategy knowledge includes information regarding the effectiveness and deficiencies of one's strategy use. Procedural metamemory refers to knowledge concerning when memory activity, such as the use of a strategy, is required, as well as assessments of how well one is doing on any particular memory task (memory monitoring) (Brown et al. 1983; Paris & Lindauer 1982). In general, research conducted over the past two decades reveals that metamemory knowledge increases with age, following a pattern that is similar to that reported for actual memory behavior (for reviews see Cavanaugh & Perlmutter 1982; Schneider 1985; Schneider & Pressley 1989; Wellman 1983).

Developmental differences in metamemory   A common method used for determining what children know about their memories is simply to ask them. In an early and extensive study of children's metamemory, Kreutzer et al. (1975) examined kindergartners', first-, third-, and fifth-graders' declarative metamemory by interviewing them about their memories. Third- and fifth-grade children realized that there are situational and individual differences in memory skills. Kindergarten and first-grade children were much less likely to have this knowledge and many of these younger children believed, for example, that they never forgot things, that a delay would not affect their memory, and that remembering pairs of unrelated words (for example, Mary-walk) is as easy or easier than remembering sets of related words (for example, boy-girl).

Other research confirmed that young children are generally out of touch with their memory abilities, demonstrating, for example, that they vastly over-estimate their memory abilities (Flavell et al. 1970; Yussen & Levy 1975), allocate their study time poorly (Masur et al. 1973), and fail to realize that recall of gist is easier than verbatim memory (Rogoff et al. 1974). Despite these substantial metamemory difficulties, young children do know something about their memories. For example, even 3- and 4-year-olds know that remembering a large number of items is more difficult than remembering a small number of items (Yussen & Bird 1979), and 4-year olds attend to information more when they are given instructions to remember rather than when they are told just to look or to play with the items (Acredolo et al. 1975; Baker-Ward et al. 1984; Yussen 1974).

Simply asking children to tell you about their memory has some obvious problems. Young children's verbal reports can be highly inaccurate, and children may have a good deal more knowledge of their memories than they can articulate. Justice (1985) developed a procedure to get around this difficulty. She showed children videotaped examples of other children using different strategies (for example, looking, naming, rehearsing, and grouping). Children were then presented with each strategy paired with each other one, one pair at a time, and asked which of the two strategies was better suited for remembering. This and similar studies (Justice 1986; Schneider 1986; Schneider et al. 1987) have produced a consistent picture of children's developing strategy knowledge. Kindergarten and young elementary-school children recognized differential effectiveness only when strategies produced substantial differences in performance (for example, grouping versus looking), whereas older children were more likely to detect subtle differences in strategy effectiveness. These experiments corroborate the results of the interview studies. Taken together, they demonstrate that young children are often unaware of the existence or effectiveness of simple memory strategies such as rehearsal and organization, at least in the context of school-like memory tasks.

Memory monitoring More immediately pertinent to the topic of strategy development is the metacognitive process of *memory-monitoring*. Memory- (or self-) monitoring can be described as a bottom-up process that involves keeping track of one's progress towards goals concerning understanding and remembering (Schneider & Bjorklund 1997). Several researchers have provided evidence that memory-monitoring training guides the effectiveness and maintenance of strategy training (e.g. Ghatala et al. 1986; Paris et al. 1982). For example, Ringel and Springer (1980) trained first-, third-, and fifth-graders in using an organizational strategy. In comparison to a baseline phase, all participants demonstrated increases in memory performance as a result of training. After completing training, but before beginning a third memory task designed to assess transfer of training, some participants were given explicit feedback regarding their improved performance on the task and others were not. Fifth-graders demonstrated successful transfer of the organizational strategy in both conditions, whereas first-graders failed to demonstrate any significant transfer. However, third-graders who received feedback concerning their memory performance transferred the organizational strategy to the third task, whereas those who did not receive feedback failed to demonstrate any significant transfer. Thus, information regarding their memory performance affected third-graders' generalization of a strategy. The older children did not appear to need feedback, presumably because they were capable of assessing their own progress, and the younger children were either incapable of transferring the strategy or insufficiently trained. This study is consistent with the findings of other researchers who note that transfer of strategy training is most effective when training includes a significant metamemory component (Ghatala et al. 1986; Leal et al. 1985; Lodico et al. 1983; Paris et al. 1982).

Metamemory–memory relations Cavanaugh and Borkowski (1980) examined the relation between metamemory and actual memory behaviors by interviewing first-, third-, and fifth-graders. They reported age-related increases in both metamemory knowledge and memory performance, but, within each grade, the two factors were only weakly related. Subsequent research demonstrated that the strength of the memory–metamemory relation varies with both the nature of the memory task and with age (Cantor et al. 1985; Schneider 1985).

Concerning organization and elaboration tasks, strong relations between children's metamemory and memory does not emerge until children reach elementary school (Lange et al. 1990), and is not stable until age 10 (Hasselhorn 1992). However, when simpler tasks and metamemory questions that are highly related to successful task performance are used, the relations between metamemory knowledge and memory behavior is significant even for preschoolers. For example, Schneider and Sodian (1988) asked 4- and 6-year-olds to remember 10 objects that they placed in each of 10 playhouses. Each playhouse was associated with pictures of people who could be identified by their occupations (for example, a doctor, a farmer, a soccer player, a sailor). Some of the objects could be associated with the people (for example, a syringe, a tractor, a soccer ball, a ship), whereas others could not (for example, a comb, a letter, a flower, a lamp). Both age groups recognized the importance of pairing the objects with the people and performed well on the memory test. Thus, the relation between metamemory and memory is significant for 4-year-olds when tasks are simplified and metamemory questions are directly related to the memory behavior. (More will said of the influence of metamemory on strategic memory on p. 227.

The research presented above implies a dynamic, bidirectional relationship between metamemory knowledge and memory performance (Borkowski 1988; Brown 1978; Schneider 1985). More specifically, memory knowledge can increase memory performance, which, in turn, facilitates further memory knowledge. However, the nature of this relationship varies as a function of age and task variables.

Motivation

One obvious influence on children's strategy use is motivation (Guttentag 1995; Paris 1988; Renninger et al. 1992). Strategies are effortful and goal-directed procedures, and it makes sense that they should be used more frequently and more effectively only when the potential payoff is high.

Early studies assessed the effects of extrinsic rewards on children's strategy use (Cuvo 1974; Kunzinger & Witryol 1984). For example, Kunzinger and Witryol (1984) gave 7- and 8-year-old children sets of words to rehearse and remember. Some words were identified as 10-cent words. Children would receive a dime for every one of these words they remembered. Other words were designated as 1-cent words. Children would receive only a penny for each of these words they recalled. Children rehearsed the 10-cent words twice as much as the 1-cent words. These findings indicate that young children can be sensitive to differences in "payoff" and modify their strategic behavior and recall according to extrinsic incentives.

Other research has investigated the effects of rewards on study time (Guttentag 1995; O'Sullivan 1993). For example, O'Sullivan (1993) provided 4-year-olds with either a highly valued toy (a box of crayons) or a less-valued toy (a pencil) for "good" memory performance. She reported that children used more sophisticated strategies and paid more attention to the memory task when they were expecting the highly valued toy for a reward. Similar results were reported by Guttentag (1995) for third-grade children. (Interestingly, in both of these experiments, the more strategic behaviors for children in the high-incentive condition did *not* result in higher levels of recall, reflecting a utilization deficiency.)

Other researchers have examined the effect of *intrinsic* motivation on children's strategic memory behavior. For example, several theorists have proposed that children who attribute their success to the use of effortful strategies should be more motivated to put in the effort required for success than children who attribute success to factors such as task difficulty or luck (Kurtz 1990; Paris 1988). Some researchers have reported such a pattern, although in general, the magnitude of the effects are small (Fabricius & Hagen 1984; Kurtz & Borkowski 1984; Schneider et al. 1986) and sometimes nonexistent (Kurtz & Weinert 1989). For example, Schneider et al. (1986) found that correlations between measures of attribution and intrinsic motivation and strategy use in a sort-recall task were mostly significant but did not exceed 0.30. Other research has investigated the relation between mastery motivation and children's memory strategies (Guttentag & Lange 1994; Lange et al. 1989, 1990). Mastery motivation has been described as children's "general inclinations to be independent, spontaneously active, self-directed, and mastery-oriented when interacting with people and objects in everyday environments" (Lange et al. 1989: 774). Although research has found a connection between measures of mastery motivation and memory performance, these relations are apparently not mediated through strategies. Relations between mastery motivation and strategy use are low and often nonsignificant (Lange et al. 1989).

Although the relation between intrinsic motivation and children's strategy use is weak, it is premature to assume that this relation may not be important in some contexts. For instance, related to the concept of intrinsic motivation is that of *interest*. Children are more apt to spend time on tasks that they are interested in than tasks they are not, which results in higher levels of memory performance (see Renninger et al. 1992; Tobias 1994). With respect to strategies, contemporary researchers have emphasized the importance of interest to strategy instruction (Pressley et al. 1992). When tasks are designed to increase interest, strategies are more likely to be acquired.

The influence of intelligence/aptitude on strategic memory

Not all factors that influence children's strategic memory have to be developmental in nature. Some factors may vary independently of developmental level, and are studied under the term *individual differences*.

A convenient dimension of individual differences is intelligence as measured by IQ tests, and differences in strategic memory between children of different IQ levels have been studied extensively. Memory differences between children of different academic aptitudes (e.g. giftedness; reading ability; learning disabilities) have also been studied (e.g. Bjorklund & Schneider 1996; Borkowski & Turner 1990; Schneider & Weinert 1990). In general, children with higher IQs remember more than children with lower IQs (e.g. Borkowski & Peck 1986; Bray & Turner 1986), and children with academic disabilities, such as poor readers, remember less than children without disabilities (e.g. Bauer 1979; Worden 1983). It is not enough merely to note differences between high- and low-ability children, however, but one must look for the cognitive reasons behind these differences. Many of the factors that influence the *development* of strategic memory also contribute to *individual differences* in strategic memory among children of the same age, including knowledge base, efficiency of processing, and metamemory.

Knowledge base   As in the development of memory strategies, knowledge base has been shown to play a substantial role in individual differences in children's strategic memory performance (see Bjorklund & Schneider 1996). This is illustrated in a study reported by Bjorklund and Bernholtz (1986). They asked 13-year-old good and poor readers to make typicality judgments of items selected from 12 natural language categories (for example, TOOLS, BIRDS, CLOTHING). The ratings of the good readers were more similar to those of adults than those of the poor readers for each of the 12 categories. In fact, the typicality judgments of the poor readers were similar to those of a normative sample of third-graders, indicating a retardation for the poor readers with respect to knowledge of natural language categories.

The good and poor readers were next given two categorized free-recall tasks. Lists for both tasks consisted of two categories of typical items and two other categories of atypical items. In the adult-generated condition, the typicality of the items were based on adult ratings. In the self-generated condition, the lists was based on each child's individually generated ratings. Thus, differences in category knowledge of the list words between the good and poor readers should have been eliminated, or at least greatly minimized, in the self-generated condition. The good readers had significantly greater recall than the poor readers when the adult-generated lists served as stimuli. There were no significant differences between the two groups, however, when they remembered the self-generated lists. These findings suggest that the differences on strategic memory tasks typically found between good and poor readers is due to the greater knowledge base of the good readers for the things they are asked to remember, not to differences in underlying memory abilities.

In research using the expert/novice paradigm, soccer-expert children had better memory for a story about soccer than soccer-novice children, and this effect was independent of IQ or school abilities (Schneider et al. 1989; see also Recht & Leslie 1988; Walker 1987). This implies that having detailed knowledge about a topic can fully compensate for the effects of low IQ. Story recall seems not to involve deliberate and effortful strategies to the same extent as categorized recall, however. Contrasts of high- and low-IQ soccer experts and novices on sort-recall tasks yielded a different pattern of results. In these experiments, soccer experts still remembered more than soccer novices, but the effect of IQ was not eliminated. Rather, high-IQ children in each expertise group remembered more words than low-IQ children (Schneider & Bjorklund 1992; Schneider et al. 1997). Schneider and his colleagues concluded that knowledge can apparently fully compensate for the effect of low IQ on tasks requiring little in the way of memory strategies for their success (text recall), but not on more strategically demanding tasks (sort recall).

Gifted/nongifted differences and the role of nonstrategic factors in strategic memory   Gifted children generally perform better on strategic memory tasks and demonstrate greater use of strategies than do nongifted children (Borkowski & Peck 1986; Wong 1982; but not always, see Harnishfeger & Bjorklund 1990b; Scruggs & Mastropieri 1988). However, there is some evidence that strategies have a greater consequence on the performance of nongifted than gifted children (Gaultney et al. 1996). For example, Gaultney and her colleagues reported that strategic nongifted seventh-grade children had significantly higher recall than nonstrategic nongifted children; the strategic–nonstrategic difference was much smaller for a group of gifted children. The gifted seventh-graders in this study had relatively high levels of recall regardless of whether they used memory strategies or not. In contrast, strategies seemed necessary for the nongifted children to demonstrate high levels of memory.

The results of Gaultney et al. (1996) suggest that some of the advantage that gifted children enjoy over nongifted children on strategic memory tasks cannot be attributed to the use of strategies. If not strategies, then what is their superior performance attributed to? Knowledge base is one obvious possibility. Gifted children know more about the things they are asked to remember and have more detailed semantic memories than nongifted children (Harnishfeger & Bjorklund 1990b). Another nonstrategic factor that has been suggested is speed or efficiency of processing. Gifted children are consistently faster in processing a wide range of information than nongifted children (Cohn et al. 1985; Jensen et al. 1989). This effect is found even when differences in knowledge base are eliminated (Kranzler et al. 1994). The faster processing of gifted children may make retrieval of individual items easier, the execution of strategies more efficient, and may even make the use of strategies for some tasks unnecessary.

Metamemory   Speed of processing and related basic-level mechanisms represent one extreme of the information-processing continuum. These are "bottom-up" processes that are performed without conscious awareness and are apparently not easily amenable to modification "at will." At the other extreme are the "top-down," potentially available-to-consciousness processes, such as metamemory. We should not be surprised to find that differences in metamemory have been found between children of different intellectual and aptitude levels.

Although differences in metamemory have consistently been found between retarded and nonretarded children (e.g. Brown et al. 1979), more research interest has focused on differences in metamemory between high-IQ (often gifted) and low-IQ (but not retarded) children (see Alexander et al. 1995). Generally, gifted and high-IQ children have better metamemory knowledge on strategic memory tasks than nongifted children (Borkowski & Peck 1986; Carr et al. 1991; Schneider et al. 1987). Gifted children are more likely to generalize an acquired strategy to a new context (Borkowski & Peck 1986) and to recognize the benefit of (and adopt sooner) an effective strategy than nongifted children (Gaultney et al. 1996). Other studies, however, report small or no differences in metamemory between high- and low-IQ children (Alexander & Schwanenflugel 1994; Kurtz & Weinert 1989; Scruggs & Mastropieri 1988).

In a review of the literature, Alexander and her colleagues (1995) concluded that the type of metacognitive task is an important factor in predicting whether IQ effects would be found or not. Gifted children typically show an advantage when declarative metacognition is assessed (for example, "Which strategy would be best for this task?"). They are less likely to be better than average or low-IQ children on tasks involving cognitive monitoring (for example, "How well am I doing on this task?"). Alexander et al. (1995) also noted that gifted children are most likely to have an advantage for transfer of training effects. Gifted and high-IQ children are more aware of the benefits of strategy training and are better able to generalize those strategies than nongifted and lower-IQ children.

Strategies and schooling   We noted at the beginning of this chapter that, following Geary's (1995) classification, memory strategies are biologically secondary abilities in that they are highly dependent upon cultural experience. In fact, some of the memory strategies discussed in this chapter are found almost exclusively in schooled cultures. This is not to say that people from more traditional cultures do not use strategies, merely that the intellectual demands of their environment are different from those for us growing up in information-age societies and that the out-of-context-type of memory strategies that develop so predictably in our culture may not develop in the same manner in theirs.

Parents may do some teaching themselves and children may pick up a strategy on their own in some contexts, but memory strategies are primarily useful to children in school, and it is in school where they learn them. Strategies, however, do not need to be specifically "taught." They can be imitated, or simply discovered in the process of performing tasks that require them for successful completion. But one factor that may influence both developmental and individual differences in strategy use and efficiency is the degree to which they are taught in school.

Barbara Moely and her colleagues have conducted several studies examining strategy instruction in American schools, and they report that there is substantial variability among teachers (Moely et al. 1986, 1992, 1995; see also Folds et al. 1990; Kurtz 1990). Specific strategy instruction was generally low in most classrooms they observed, with instruction varying with subject matter (for example, strategies were more likely to be taught for solving math problems). Children from classrooms where strategies were taught more often seemed to garner some advantage from their experience, showing higher levels of achievement (Moely et al. 1995).

Differences in strategy instruction in school and in the home may also account for some cross-cultural differences in memory performance. For example, research comparing German and American children on sets of strategic memory tasks reported a consistent advantage for the German children as young as 7 years of age (Carr et al. 1989; Kurtz et al. 1990; Schneider et al. 1986). The apparent reason for the German children's superior performance was found in instructional practices in their schools and homes. Questionnaires completed by children's teachers and parents revealed that the German teachers taught more strategies in schools than the American teachers, and that the German parents engaged in more games requiring strategies with their children than did the American parents.

Some educators have emphasized the importance of teaching strategies effectively to schoolchildren. Michael Pressley, John Borkowski, and their colleagues have developed the "Good Information Processing" model to provide an account of how children can be taught effective thinking skills in schools; and strategies play a central role in the Good Information Processing model (Borkowski et al. 1990; Pressley 1994, 1995; Pressley et al. 1987, 1989; Schneider & Pressley 1989).

Pressley and Borkowski emphasize the importance of metamemory in

228

effective strategy use. They conceive of metamemory as involving several interacting and dependent processes. The process of knowledge acquisition is characterized by the following steps: (1) *Specific strategy knowledge*: Children are taught by parents or teachers to use a strategy, and with practice, they learn about the attributes and advantages of the strategy. If children's environments at home and in the school are stimulating, more strategies will be encountered, leading to expanded specific strategy knowledge. (2) *Relational knowledge*: Teachers show children the similarities and differences of various strategies, and allow the children to structure strategies based on their common features. (3) *Metacognitive acquisition procedures*: Children now recognize the general benefits of being strategic. They thus learn to attribute their successes to the effort they put into using strategies and acquire higher-order metacognitive skills such as selecting and monitoring strategies appropriate for the task.

The Good Information Processing model is not just a description or a theoretical account of strategy development, but a general formula for strategy instruction. It recognizes the important role parents and teachers play in strategy development and provides procedures for enhancing children's strategic memory. Research by Pressley and colleagues illustrates that these goals can be accomplished (see Pressley 1994, 1995).

How important are strategies? The case of utilization deficiencies

Perhaps the reason the study of strategies dominated the field of memory development for so long was the belief that strategies improved children's performance and were the principal cause of age-related changes in memory. After all, by definition, strategies are used to enhance task performance. Beginning in the 1980s, however, researchers began to realize that children's memory performance was *not* always helped by using strategies (e.g. Bjorklund & Bjorklund 1985; Bjorklund & Harnishfeger 1987; Miller et al.

Figure 8.3 Apparatus used in studies of children's attentional strategies by Patricia Miller and her colleagues (thanks to Patricia Miller).

1986) As we mentioned earlier in this chapter, Miller (1990, 1994) labeled this phenomenon a *utilization deficiency*.

In her initial research, Miller and her colleagues assessed children's use of a selective-attention strategy to facilitate memory for target items (DeMarie-Dreblow & Miller 1988; Miller et al. 1986; Woody-Ramsey & Miller 1988). In these experiments, children, usually ranging in age between 3 and 8 years of age, were shown two rows of six boxes each. On top of each box was a door. Each door also had a picture on it, corresponding to the type of object that was in the box (see Figure 8.3). Half the doors had pictures of cages, meaning that the box contained an animal. On the remaining doors were pictures of a house, meaning that those boxes contained household objects. Children were told that their task was to remember the location of objects from one of the two categories – either animals or household objects – and they could open any doors they wished during a study period. The most effective strategy is to open only those doors that have a picture of the target category on it.

Miller has described a four-phase sequence of strategy development on this task. In the initial phase, young children use no apparent strategy. They usually open all the doors on the top first, then all the doors on the bottom, ignoring which pictures are on the doors. This is followed by a phase in which children use the selective-attention strategy, but only partially, opening many irrelevant doors. In the third phase, children use the most effective strategy, but their later memory for the target items is not enhanced; they do not remember the location of the items any better than same-age children who do not use the strategy. This is a utilization deficiency. Finally, in the fourth phase, children use the strategy and their memory performance improves accordingly.

Utilization deficiencies are not limited to preschool children nor to the simple strategies evaluated by Miller and her colleagues. More recent research has demonstrated utilization deficiencies for school-aged children for more complicated strategies such as organization in free- and sort-recall tasks (Bjorklund et al. 1992; Coyle & Bjorklund 1996) or strategies involved in reading comprehension (Gaultney 1995). And despite the fact that utilization deficiencies have only recently been discovered, the phenomenon is not a new one. In a review of the strategy development literature extending over a 20-year period, Miller and Seier (1994) evaluated studies in which levels of memory performance and strategy use were assessed independently. They reported that 95 per cent of all cases yielded partial or strong evidence of utilization deficiencies across a variety of tasks, strategies, and ages.

The evidence for utilization deficiencies has been available for nearly as long as memory strategies have been studied, but because the pattern of results did not fit well with conventional wisdom, researchers usually dismissed the findings as "random error" and rarely discussed them in their papers (see Bjorklund & Coyle 1995). Current research makes it clear, however, that children using and not benefiting from strategies is neither an exception nor experimental error, but a part of the typical pattern of strategy development.

How can the counterintuitive finding of utilization deficiency be explained? Some of the same factors that have been found to influence children's strategy development in general (for example, efficiency of processing, knowledge base, metamemory) have also been proposed to affect the incidence of utilization deficiencies (Bjorklund & Coyle 1995; Miller 1994). The most commonly offered explanation suggests that the amount of mental effort that children must expend to execute a strategy is so great that they have too few additional resources remaining to devote to the actual retrieval of target information (Bjorklund & Harnishfeger 1987; Miller et al. 1991a, b). This has been demonstrated in several experiments in which children use a strategy but gain little or no benefit from it in situations in which their information-processing resources are taxed (Miller et al. 1991a, b). For example, Miller, Seier, Probert, and Aloise (1991) used a dual-task procedure in which children had to tap their finger as rapidly as they could while performing the selective-attention task. They reported that strategic 5- and 6-year-olds experienced more interference than older children and became utilizationally deficient as a result of executing the secondary task, a clear indication of the relation between mental effort and utilization deficiencies.

Other factors have been found to influence utilization deficiencies. For example, children with more detailed knowledge of the to-be-remembered material are more likely to produce a strategy in the first place and less likely to show a utilization deficiency (e.g. Gaultney 1995; Miller et al. 1994). Miller and her colleagues (1994) have also shown that utilization deficiencies may result because of children's difficulties integrating one strategy with another. Age differences in metamemory may also contribute to utilization deficiencies. For example, older children with good metamemory awareness may continue to use an ineffective strategy in the belief that, with practice, it will eventually "work." Younger children, however, may actually benefit from poor metamemory. They may be unaware that the strategy they are using is not helping them. As a result, they continue to use the strategy, and the increased practice eventually results in enhanced performance. A more metacognitively aware child might have realized the cost of using the strategy and desisted from using it accordingly. Evidence in support of this possibility comes from multitrial experiments in which children demonstrate utilization deficiencies on early trials but show improvements in recall on later trials (Bjorklund et al. 1992). Another possible reason for utilization deficiencies is related to young children's difficulties in inhibiting the execution of previously acquired, but relatively ineffective, strategies (see Bjorklund & Harnishfeger 1990; Harnishfeger 1995). According to Miller, children "who must use capacity to inhibit a less mature strategy as well as produce the more mature strategy may be disadvantaged with respect to recall" (Miller 1994: 295–6). Another reason that has been proposed for why children may use strategies that do not seem to work is related to a preference for novelty. Using a new, even ineffective, strategy may have some merit from using a

231

"tried-and-true" strategy, simply for the sake of experimentation (Bjorklund & Coyle 1995; Siegler & Jenkins 1989).

The occurrence of utilization deficiencies adds a new twist to understanding strategy development. Strategies are effortful operations and, as we have seen, they are not always beneficial to task performance. This, by itself, may not be so surprising. But that this failure to facilitate task performance is so common indicates that a serious rethinking about the causes and consequences of being strategic is needed.

Utilization deficiencies are not the only recent discovery to challenge the conventional wisdom of strategy development. Robert Siegler (1994, 1995) and his colleagues have emphasized that the canonical view of strategy development as progressing smoothly from less to more efficient strategies is more wishful thinking than fact. Rather, children use a variety of different strategies on any given task, making developmental change more complicated.

Multiple- and variable-strategy use

Working in the area of the development of arithmetic skills in young children, Siegler began to question the conventional wisdom of the stage-like development of addition strategies (Siegler 1987; Siegler & Jenkins 1989). Instead, Siegler noted that there was substantial variability in the strategies children used, both between children of a given age (*inter*child variability) and within a single child over repeated trials on a problem (*intra*child variability). Rather than viewing the development of strategies as progressing in a step-like fashion, Siegler proposed the *strategy-choice model*, in which children have available to them and use a variety of strategies at any one time; what changes in development is the frequency with which these various strategies are used. This is exemplified in his "overlapping wave" model of development, shown in Figure 8.4. Different strategies compete with one another for use, depending on the learning context and the general cognitive abilities of the child. Over time, children will generally use more efficient strategies with increasing frequency, but both simple and inefficient and complicated and efficient strategies co-exist in a child's cognitive repertoire at the same time and compete for use.

Although most research on strategy variability, competition, and selection has been done with arithmetic strategies, some research based on this framework also has been done with memory strategies. For example, McGilly and Siegler (1989, 1990) asked kindergarten, second-grade, and fourth-grade children to remember a list of digits in exact order over repeated trials (a serial-recall task). Consistent with the strategy-choice model, they found that children used a variety of different strategies and that any given child used a combination of strategies over repeated trials. That is, multiple strategy use was the rule and not the exception. Other research, examining performance on

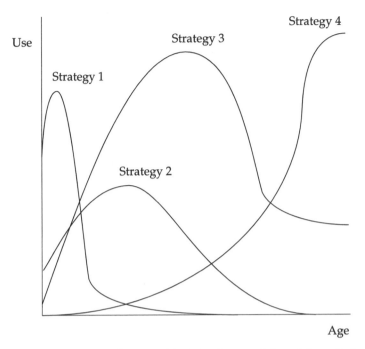

Figure 8.4 Siegler's strategy-choice model of development (adapted from Siegler 1995; thanks to Robert Siegler).

free-recall tasks, has found that children as young as 4 years of age will use different combinations of strategies (for example, rehearsal, sorting, category naming), and that older children tend to use more different strategies than younger children (Coyle & Bjorklund 1997; Lange & Pierce 1992). Other researchers have reported that third-grade children instructed to sort words by meaning not only improved their memory performance but also used more sophisticated rehearsal techniques (B. C. Cox et al. 1989). That is, improvements in one strategy (organization) lead to improvements in another strategy (rehearsal), which in turn lead to enhanced memory performance.

Siegler (1994, 1995) believes that variability enhances learning, at least when children are first mastering a task. By generating a variety of alternative strategies, children can discover which ones work well and which ones do not. However, Siegler notes that strategies are not always selected because they produce the best performance. As we suggested in our discussion of utilization deficiencies, sometimes children use a strategy because it is novel – "just for the fun of it" – and this may lead to less than optimal performance.

Conclusion

The modern era of memory development began with the study of strategies. Strategies are what children use to learn and later to retrieve information. Strategies develop, with children using more effective strategies as they age. Our view of the role of strategies has changed somewhat since the early days of memory development research. Strategies are still important, especially for people growing up in information-age societies. But much of what is important and interesting in memory development is not highly effortful or planned, and this volume represents many other aspects of memory development that deserve serious attention. Moreover, memory strategies do not develop in as straightforward a way as we once thought. Strategies do not always help performance, at least not immediately, and simple and inefficient strategies reside alongside more sophisticated and efficient ones, competing for use. The process of strategy development is not one of simply replacing the ineffective with the effective.

What is the future of strategy research? First of all, we expect that the issue of strategy variability will become more important. For example, what is the relation between strategy variability, age, and strategy effectiveness? Are children who show more variability in strategy use different in any important way from less variable children? Second, we expect that researchers will take closer looks at strategies that develop in more naturalistic contexts, that is, not in school or for school-specific tasks. What role do parents and peers play in fostering children's use of simple learning and memory strategies? Do these real-world strategies generalize to school? Third, as we learn more about the processes of strategy development, researchers will be asking themselves what is universal and typical of all members of the species with respect to strategy development and what is tied to specific cultural contexts. Cross-cultural studies, examining both developmental and individual differences, will be done in order to answer these questions. And fourth, more still needs to be learned about school-type strategies. When is the best time to teach various strategies to children? Is earlier always better, or might it be desirable to wait until children's general cognitive abilities are better developed before beginning some instruction? How can we best teach strategies, especially to low-achieving children?

Research into memory strategies has changed over the decades, as any vital research topic must change. The questions that scientists are now asking reflect the diversity of factors that affect children's strategy use and the insight that there is no single developmental pathway that all children in a culture must follow to become effective rememberers.

References

Ackerman, B. E. 1984. Item specific and relational encoding effects in children's recall and recognition memory for words. *Journal of Experimental Child Psychology* **37**, 426–50.

Ackerman, B. E. 1985a. Children's retrieval deficit. In *Basic processes in memory development: Progress in cognitive development research*, C. J. Brainerd & M. Pressley (eds.). New York: Springer-Verlag.

Ackerman, B. P. 1985b. Constraints on retrieval search for episodic information in children and adults. *Journal of Experimental Child Psychology* **40**, 152–80.

Ackerman, B. P. 1987. Descriptions: A model of nonstrategic memory development. In *Advances in child development and behavior, Vol. XX*, H. W. Reese (ed.). Orlando, FL: Academic.

Acredolo, L. P., H. L. Pick, & M. G. Olsen 1975. Environmental differentiation and familiarity as determinants of children's memory for spatial location. *Developmental Psychology* **11**, 495–501.

Alexander, J. M., M. Carr, & P. J. Schwanenflugel 1995. Development of metacognition in gifted children: Directions for future research. *Developmental Review* **15**, 1–37.

Alexander, J. M. & P. J. Schwanenflugel 1994. Strategy regulation: The role of intelligence, metacognitive attributes, and knowledge base. *Developmental Psychology* **30**, 709–23.

Arlin, M. & R. Brody 1976. Effects of spatial presentation and blocking on organization and verbal recall at three grade levels. *Developmental Psychology* **12**, 113–18.

Baker-Ward, L., P. A. Ornstein, & D. J. Holden 1984. The expression of memorization in early childhood. *Journal of Experimental Child Psychology* **37**, 555–75.

Bauer, R. H. 1979. Memory, acquisition, and category clustering in learning-disabled children. *Journal of Experimental Child Psychology* **27**, 365–83.

Best, D. L. 1993. Inducing children to generate mnemonic organizational strategies: An examination of long-term retention and materials. *Developmental Psychology* **29**, 324–36.

Best, D. L. & P. A. Ornstein 1986. Children's generation and communication of mnemonic organizational strategies. *Developmental Psychology* **22**, 845–853.

Beuhring, T. & D. W. Kee 1987. The relationships between memory knowledge, elaborative strategy use and associative memory performance. *Journal of Experimental Child Psychology* **44**, 377–400.

Bjorklund, D. F. 1985. The role of conceptual knowledge in the development of organization in children's memory. In *Basic processes in memory development: Progress in cognitive development research*, C. J. Brainerd & M. Pressley (eds.). New York: Springer-Verlag.

Bjorklund, D. F. 1987. How age changes in knowledge base contribute to the development of children's memory: An interpretive review. *Developmental Review* **7**, 93–130.

Bjorklund, D. F. 1988. Acquiring a mnemonic: Age and category knowledge effects. *Journal of Experimental Child Psychology* **45**, 71–87.

Bjorklund, D. F. & J. E. Bernholtz 1986. The role of knowledge base in the memory performance of good and poor readers. *Journal of Experimental Child Psychology* **41**, 367–93.

Bjorklund, D. F. & B. R. Bjorklund 1985. Organization versus item effects of an elaborated knowledge base on children's memory. *Developmental Psychology* **21**, 1120–31.

Bjorklund, D. F. & J. J. Buchanan 1989. Developmental and knowledge base differences in the acquisition and extension of a memory strategy. *Journal of Experimental Child Psychology* **48**, 451–71.

Bjorklund, D. F. & T. R. Coyle 1995. Utilization deficiencies in the development of memory strategies. In *Memory performance and competencies: Issues in growth and development*. F. E. Weinert & W. Schneider (eds.). Hillsdale, NJ: Erlbaum.

Bjorklund, D. F., T. R. Coyle, & J. F. Gaultney 1992. Developmental differences in the acquisition and maintenance of an organizational strategy: Evidence for the utilization deficiency hypothesis. *Journal of Experimental Child Psychology* **54**, 434–48.

Bjorklund, D. F. & K. K. Harnishfeger 1987. Developmental differences in the mental effort requirements for the use of an organizational strategy in free recall. *Journal of Experimental Child Psychology* **44**, 109–25.

Bjorklund, D. F. & K. K. Harnishfeger 1990. The resources construct in cognitive development: Diverse sources of evidence and a model of inefficient inhibition. *Developmental Review* **10**, 48–71.

Bjorklund, D. F. & H. S. Hock 1982. Age differences in the temporal locus of memory organization in children's recall. *Journal of Experimental Child Psychology* **32**, 347–62.

Bjorklund, D. F. & J. W. Jacobs 1984. A developmental examination of ratings of associative strengths. *Behavior Research Methods, Instruments and Computers* **16**, 568–9.

Bjorklund, D. F. & J. W. Jacobs 1985. Associative and categorical processes in children's memory: The role of automaticity in the development of organization in free recall. *Journal of Experimental Child Psychology* **39**, 599–617.

Bjorklund, D. F., J. E. Muir-Broaddus, & W. Schneider 1990. The role of knowledge in the development of strategies. In *Children's strategies: Contemporary views of cognitive development*. D. F. Bjorklund (ed.). Hillsdale, NJ: Erlbaum.

Bjorklund, D. F. & W. Schneider 1996. The interaction of knowledge, aptitudes, and strategies in children's memory performance. In *Advances in child development and behavior, Vol. XXV*, H. W. Reese (ed.). San Diego, CA: Academic.

Bjorklund, D. F. & B. R. Zeman 1982. Children's organization and metamemory awareness in the recall of familiar information. *Child Development* **53**, 799–810.

Bjorklund, D. F. & B. R. Zeman 1983. The development of organizational strategies in children's recall of familiar information: Using social organization to recall the names of classmates. *International Journal of Behavioral Development* **6**, 341–53.

Black, M. M. & H. A. Rollins 1982. The effects of instructional variables on young children's organization and free recall. *Journal of Experimental Child Psychology* **33**, 1–19.

Blair, R., M. Perlmutter, & N. A. Myers 1978. Effects of unlabeled and labeled picture cues on very young children's memory for location. *Bulletin of Psychonomic Society* **11**, 46–8.

Borkowski, J. G., M. Carr, E. A. Rellinger, & M. Pressley 1990. Self-regulated strategy use: Interdependence of metacognition, attributions, and self-esteem. In *Dimensions of thinking: Review of research*, B. F. Jones (ed.). Hillsdale, NJ: Erlbaum.

Borkowski, J. G., M. Milstead, & C. Hale 1988. Components of children's metamemory: Implications for strategy generalization. In *Memory development: Universal changes and individual differences*, F. E. Weinert & M. Perlmutter (eds.), Hillsdale, NJ: Erlbaum.

Borkowski, J. G. & V. A. Peck 1986. Causes and consequences of metamemory in gifted children. In *Conceptions of giftedness*, R. J. Sternberg & J. C. Davidson (eds.). Cambridge: Cambridge University Press.

Borkowski, J. G. & L. A. Turner 1990. Transituational characteristics of metacognition. In *Interactions among aptitudes, strategies, and knowledge in cognitive performance*, W. Schneider & F. E. Weinert (eds.). Hillsdale, NJ: Erlbaum.

Bower, G. H. 1970. Organizational factors in memory. *Cognitive Psychology* 1, 18–46.

Brainerd, C. J. 1985. Model-based approaches to storage and retrieval development. In *Basic processes in memory development*, C. J. Brainerd & M. Pressley (eds.). New York: Springer.

Bray, N. W. & L. A. Turner 1986. The rehearsal deficit hypothesis. In *International review of research in mental retardation, Vol. XIV*, N. R. Ellis & N. W. Bray (eds.). New York: Academic.

Brown, A. L. 1978. Knowing when, where, and how to remember: A problem of metacognition. In *Advances in instructional psychology*, R. Glasser (ed.). Hillsdale, NJ: Erlbaum.

Brown, A. L., J. D. Bransford, R. A. Ferrara, & J. C. Campione 1983. Learning, remembering, and understanding. In *Handbook of child psychology, Vol. 3*, J. H. Flavell & E. M. Markman (eds.). New York: Wiley.

Brown, A. L., J. C. Campione, & C. R. Barclay 1979. Training self-checking routines for estimating test readiness: Generalization from list learning to prose recall. *Child Development* 50, 501–12.

Cantor, D. S., C. Andreassen, & H. S. Waters 1985. Organization in visual episodic memory: Relationships between verbalized knowledge, strategy use, and performance. *Journal of Experimental Child Psychology* 40, 218–32.

Carr, M., J. G. Borkowski, & S. E. Maxwell 1991. Motivational components of underachievement. *Developmental Psychology* 27, 108–18.

Carr, M., B. E. Kurtz, W. Schneider, L. A. Turner, & J. G. Borkowski 1989. Strategy acquisition and transfer among American and German children: Environmental influences on metacognitive development. *Developmental Psychology* 25, 765–771.

Carr, M. & W. Schneider 1991. Long-term maintenance of organizational strategies in kindergarten children. *Contemporary Educational Psychology* 16, 61–72.

Case, R. 1985. *Intellectual development: Birth to adulthood*. New York: Academic.

Cavanaugh, J. C. & J. G. Borkowski 1980. Searching for metamemory–memory connections: A developmental study. *Developmental Psychology* 16, 441–53.

Cavanaugh, J. C. & M. Perlmutter 1982. Metamemory: A critical examination. *Child Development* 3, 11–28.

Ceci, S. J. 1980. A developmental study of multiple encoding and its relationship to age-related changes in free recall. *Child Development* 51, 892–5.

Ceci, S. J. & M. J. A. Howe 1978. Semantic knowledge as a determinant of developmental differences in recall. *Journal of Experimental Child Psychology* 26, 230–45.

Ceci, S. J., S. E. G. Lea, & M. J. A. Howe 1980. Structural analysis of memory traces in children from 4 to 10 years of age. *Developmental Psychology* 16, 203–12.

Chechile, R. A. & C. L. Richman 1982. The interaction of semantic memory with storage and retrieval processes. *Developmental Review* 2, 237–50.

Chi, M. T. H. 1978. Knowledge structure and memory development. In *Children's thinking: What develops?*, R. Siegler (ed.). Hillsdale, NJ: Erlbaum.

Chi, M. T. H. & S. J. Ceci 1987. Content knowledge: Its role, representation, and restructuring in memory development. In *Advances in child development and behavior, Vol. XX*, H. W. Reese (ed.). Orlando, FL: Academic.

Cohn, S. J., J. S. Carlson, & A. R. Jensen 1985. Speed of information processing in academically gifted youths. *Personality and Individual Differences* 6, 621–9.

Corsale, K. & P. A. Ornstein 1980. Developmental changes in children's use of semantic information in recall. *Journal of Experimental Child Psychology* 30, 231–45.

Cox, B. C., P. A. Ornstein, M. J. Naus, D. Maxfield, & J. Zimler 1989. Children's concurrent use of rehearsal and organizational strategies. *Developmental Psychology* 25, 619–27.

Cox, D. & Waters, H. S. 1986. Sex differences in the use of organization strategies: A developmental analysis. *Journal of Experimental Child Psychology* 41, 18–37.

Coyle, T. R. & D. F. Bjorklund 1996. The development of strategic memory: A modified microgenetic assessment of utilization deficiencies. *Cognitive Development* 11, 295–314.

Coyle, T. R. & D. F. Bjorklund 1997. Age differences in, and consequences of, multiple- and variable strategy use on a multitrial sort-recall task. *Developmental Psychology*.

Cuvo, A. J. 1974. Incentive level influence on overt rehearsal and free recall as a function of age. *Journal of Experimental Child Psychology* 18, 167–81.

Cuvo, A. J. 1975. Developmental differences in rehearsal and free recall. *Journal of Experimental Child Psychology* 19, 265–78.

DeLoache, J. S. & A. L. Brown 1983. Very young children's memory for the location of objects in a large scale environment. *Child Development* 54, 888–97.

DeLoache, J. S., D. J. Cassidy, & A. L. Brown 1985. Precursors of mnemonic strategies in very young children's memory. *Child Development* 56, 125–37.

DeMarie-Dreblow, D. & P. H. Miller 1988. The development of children's strategies for selective attention: Evidence for a transitional period. *Child Development* 59, 1504–13.

Dempster, F. N. 1978. Memory span and short-term memory capacity: A developmental study. *Journal of Experimental Child Psychology* 26, 419–31.

Emmerich, H. J. & B. P. Ackerman 1978. Developmental differences in recall: Encoding or retrieval? *Journal of Experimental Child Psychology* 25, 514–25.

Fabricius, W. V. & J. W. Hagen 1984. The use of causal attributions about recall performance to assess metamemory and predict strategies memory behavior in young children. *Developmental Psychology* 20, 975–87.

Fivush, R. & N. R. Hamond 1990. Autobiographical memory across the preschool years: Toward reconceptualizing childhood amnesia. In *Knowing and remembering in young children*, R. Fivush & J. A. Hudson (eds.). Cambridge: Cambridge University Press.

Fivush, R. & J. A. Hudson 1990. *Knowing and remembering in young children*. Cambridge: Cambridge University Press.

Flavell, J. H. 1970. Developmental studies of mediated memory. In *Advances in child development and behavior*, H. W. Reese & L. P. Lipsitt (eds.). New York: Academic.

Flavell, J. H., D. R. Beach, & J. H. Chinsky 1966. Spontaneous verbal rehearsal in a memory task as a function of age. *Child Development* 37, 283–99.

Flavell, J. H., A. G. Friedrichs, & J. D. Hoyt 1970. Developmental changes in memorization processes. *Cognitive Psychology* **1**, 324–40.

Folds, T. H., M. Footo, R. E. Guttentag, & P. A. Ornstein 1990. When children mean to remember: Issues of context specificity, strategy effectiveness, and intentionality in the development of memory. In *Children's strategies: Contemporary views of cognitive development*, D. F. Bjorklund (ed.). Hillsdale, NJ: Erlbaum.

Frankel, M. T. & H. A. Rollins 1985. Associative and categorical hypotheses of organization in the free recall of adults and children. *Journal of Experimental Child Psychology* **40**, 304–18.

Furth, H. & N. Milgram 1973. Labeling and grouping effects in the recall of pictures by children. *Child Development* **44**, 511–18.

Gaultney, J. F. 1995. The effect of prior knowledge and metacognition on the acquisition of a reading comprehension strategy. *Journal of Experimental Child Psychology* **59**, 142–63.

Gaultney, J. F., D. F. Bjorklund, & D. Goldstein 1996. To be young, gifted, and strategic: Advantages for memory performance. *Journal of Experimental Child Psychology* **61**, 43–66.

Gaultney, J. F., D. F. Bjorklund, & W. Schneider 1992. The role of children's expertise in a strategic memory task. *Contemporary Educational Psychology* **17**, 244–57.

Geary, D. C. 1995. Reflections of evolution and culture in children's cognition: Implications for mathematical development and instruction. *American Psychologist* **50**, 24–37.

Geis, M. F. & G. Lange 1976. Children's cue utilization in a memory-for-location task. *Child Development* **47**, 759–66.

Ghatala, E. S. 1984. Developmental changes in incidental memory as a function of meaningfulness and encoding condition. *Developmental Psychology* **20**, 208–11.

Ghatala, E. S., J. R. Levin, M. Pressley, & D. Goodwin 1986. A componential analysis of the effects of derived and supplied strategy-utility information on children's strategy selection. *Journal of Experimental Child Psychology* **41**, 76–92.

Guttentag, R. E. 1984. The mental effort requirement of cumulative rehearsal: A developmental study. *Journal of Experimental Child Psychology* **37**, 92–106.

Guttentag, R. E. 1995. Mental effort and motivation: Influences on children's memory strategy use. In *Research on memory development: State of the art and future directions*, F. E. Weinert & W. Schneider (eds.). Hillsdale, NJ: Erlbaum.

Guttentag, R. E. & G. Lange 1994. Motivational influences on children's strategic remembering. *Learning and Individual Differences* **6**, 309–30.

Guttentag, R. E., P. A. Ornstein, & L. Seimens 1987. Children's spontaneous rehearsal: Transitions in strategy acquisition. *Cognitive Development* **2**, 307–26.

Hagen, J. W., S. Hargrave, & W. Ross 1973. Prompting and rehearsal in short-term memory. *Child Development* **44**, 201–4.

Harnishfeger, K. K. 1995. The development of cognitive inhibition: Theories, definitions, and research evidence. In *New perspectives on interference and inhibition in cognition*. F. Dempster & C. Brainerd (eds.). New York: Academic.

Harnishfeger, K. K. & D. F. Bjorklund 1990a. Children's strategies: A brief history. In *Children's strategies: Contemporary views of cognitive development*, D. F. Bjorklund (ed.). Hillsdale, NJ: Erlbaum.

Harnishfeger, K. K. & D. F. Bjorklund 1990b. Memory functioning of gifted and nongifted middle school children. *Contemporary Educational Psychology* **15**,

346–63.

Hasselhorn, M. 1990. The emergence of strategic knowledge activation in categorical clustering during retrieval. *Journal of Experimental Child Psychology* **50**, 59–80.

Hasselhorn, M. 1992. Task dependency and the role of category typicality and metamemory in the development of an organizational strategy. *Child Development* **63**, 202–14.

Heisel, B. E. & K. Ritter 1981. Young children's storage behavior in a memory for location task. *Journal of Experimental Child Psychology* **31**, 350–64.

Howe, M. L., C. J. Brainerd, & J. Kingma 1985. Development of organization in recall: A stages-of-learning analysis. *Journal of Experimental Child Psychology* **39**, 230–51.

Hudson, J. A. 1990. The emergence of autobiographical memory in mother–child conversation. In *Knowing and remembering in young children*, R. Fivush & J. A. Hudson (eds.). Cambridge: Cambridge University Press.

Jensen, A. R., S. J. Cohn, & C. M. G. Cohn 1989. Speed of information processing in academically gifted youths and their siblings. *Personality and Individual Differences* **10**, 29–33.

Justice, E. M. 1985. Categorization as a preferred memory strategy: Developmental changes during elementary school. *Developmental Psychology* **21**, 1105–10.

Justice, E. M. 1986. Developmental changes in judgements of relative strategy effectiveness. *British Journal of Developmental Psychology* **4**, 75–81.

Kail, R. 1993. The role of a global mechanism in developmental change in speed of processing. In *Emerging themes in cognitive development, Vol. I, Foundations*, M. L. Howe & R. Pasnak (eds.). New York: Springer-Verlag.

Kee, D. W. 1994. Developmental differences in associative memory: Strategy use, mental effort, and knowledge-access interaction. In *Advances in child development and behavior, Vol. XXV*, H. W. Reese (ed.). New York: Academic Press.

Kee, D. W. & T. S. Bell 1981. The development of organizational strategies in the storage and retrieval of categorical items in free-recall learning. *Child Development* **52**, 1163–71.

Kee, D. W. & L. Davies 1990. Mental effort and elaboration: Effects of accessibility and instruction. *Journal of Experimental Child Psychology* **49**, 264–74.

Kee, D. W. & R. Guttentag 1994. Resource requirements of knowledge access and recall benefits of associative strategies. *Journal of Experimental Child Psychology* **57**, 211–23.

Keeney, T. J., S. R. Cannizzo, & J. H. Flavell 1967. Spontaneous and induced verbal rehearsal in a recall task. *Child Development* **38**, 953–66.

Kellas, G., C. McCauley, & C. E. McFarland 1975. Developmental aspects of storage and retrieval. *Journal of Experimental Child Psychology* **19**, 51–62.

Kingsley, P. R. & J. W. Hagen 1969. Induced versus spontaneous rehearsal in short-term memory in nursery school children. *Developmental Psychology* **1**, 40–6.

Kobasigawa, A. 1974. Utilization of retrieval cues by children in recall. *Child Development* **45**, 127–34.

Kobasigawa, A. 1977. Retrieval strategies in the development of memory. In *Perspective on the development of memory and cognition*, R. V. Kail & J. W. Hagen (eds.). Hillsdale, NJ: Erlbaum.

Kranzler, J. H., P. A. Whang, & A. R. Jensen 1994. Task complexity and the speed and efficiency of elemental information processing: Another look at the nature of intellectual giftedness. *Contemporary Educational Psychology* **19**, 447–59.

Kreutzer, M. A., C. Leonard, & J. H. Flavell 1975. An interview study of children's knowledge about memory. *Monographs of the Society for Research in Child Development* **40**(159).

Kunzinger, E. L. & S. L. Witryol 1984. The effects of differential incentives on second-grade rehearsal and free recall. *Journal of Genetic Psychology* **144**, 19–30.

Kurtz, B. E. 1990. Cultural influences on children's cognitive and metacognitive development. In *Interactions among aptitudes, strategies, and knowledge in cognitive performance*, W. Schneider & F. E. Weinert (eds.). New York: Springer-Verlag.

Kurtz, B. E. & J. G. Borkowski 1984. Children's metacognition: Exploring relations among knowledge, process, and motivational variables. *Journal of Experimental Child Psychology* **37**, 335–54.

Kurtz, B. E., W. Schneider, M. Carr, J. G. Borkowski, & E. Rellinger 1990. Strategy instruction and attributional beliefs in West Germany and the United States: Do teachers foster metacognitive development? *Contemporary Educational Psychology* **15**, 268–83.

Kurtz, B. E. & F. E. Weinert 1989. Metamemory, memory performance, and causal attributions in gifted and average children. *Journal of Experimental Child Psychology* **48**, 45–61.

Lange, G. 1973. The development of conceptual and rote recall skills among school age children. *Journal of Experimental Child Psychology* **15**, 394–406.

Lange, G., R. E. Guttentag, & R. E. Nida 1990. Relationships between study organization, retrieval organization, and general strategy-specific memory knowledge in young children. *Journal of Experimental Child Psychology* **49**, 126–46.

Lange, G. & P. Jackson 1974. Personal organization in children's free recall. *Child Development* **45**, 1060–7.

Lange, G., C. E. MacKinnon, & R. E. Nida 1989. Knowledge, strategy, and motivational contributions to preschool children's object recall. *Developmental Psychology* **25**, 772–9.

Lange, G. & S. H. Pierce 1992. Memory-strategy learning and maintenance in preschool children. *Developmental Psychology* **28**, 453–62.

Leal, L., N. Crays, & B. E. Moely 1985. Training children to use a self-monitoring study strategy in preparation for recall: Maintenance and generalization effects. *Child Development* **56**, 643–53.

Lodico, M. G., E. S. Ghatala, J. R. Levin, M. Pressley, & J. A. Bell 1983. The effects of strategy-monitoring on children's selection of effective memory strategies. *Journal of Experimental Child Psychology* **35**, 263–77.

Mandler, G. 1967. Organization and memory. In *The psychology of learning and motivation, Vol. I*, K. W. Spence & J. T. Spence (eds.). New York: Academic.

Masur, E. F., C. W. McIntyre, & J. H. Flavell 1973. Developmental changes in apportionment of study time among items in a multitrial free recall task. *Journal of Experimental Child Psychology* **15**, 237–46.

McGilly, K. & R. S. Siegler 1989. How children choose among serial recall strategies. *Child Development* **60**, 172–82.

McGilly, K. & R. S. Siegler 1990. The influence of encoding strategic knowledge on children's choices among serial recall strategies. *Developmental Psychology* **26**, 931–41.

Miller, P. H. 1990. The development of strategies of selective attention. In *Children's strategies: Contemporary views of cognitive development*, D. F. Bjorklund (ed.). Hillsdale, NJ: Erlbaum.

Miller, P. H. 1994. Individual differences in children's strategic behavior: Utilization deficiencies. *Learning and Individual Differences* **6**, 285–307.

Miller, P. H., V. F. Haynes, D. DeMarie-Dreblow, & J. Woody-Ramsey 1986. Children's strategies for gathering information in three tasks. *Child Development* **57**, 1429–39.

Miller, P. H. & W. L. Seier 1994. Strategy utilization deficiencies in children: When, where, and why. In *Advances in child development and behavior, Vol. XXV*, H. W. Reese (ed.). New York: Academic.

Miller, P. H., W. L. Seier, K. L. Barron, J. S. Probert 1994. What causes a memory utilization deficiency? *Cognitive Development* **9**, 77–102.

Miller, P. H., W. L. Seier, J. S. Probert, & P. A. Aloise 1991a. Age differences in the capacity demands of a strategy among spontaneously strategic children. *Journal of Experimental Child Psychology* **52**, 149–65.

Miller, P. H., J. Woody-Ramsey, & P. A. Aloise 1991. The role of strategy effortfulness in strategy effectiveness. *Developmental Psychology* **27**, 738–45.

Mistry, J. J. & G. Lange 1985. Children's organization and recall of information in scripted narratives. *Child Development* **56**, 953–61.

Moely, B. E., S. S. Hart, L. Leal, K. A. Santulli, N. Rao, T. Johnson, & L. B. Hamilton 1992. The teacher's role in facilitating memory and study strategy development in the elementary school classroom. *Child Development* **63**, 653–72.

Moely, B. E., S. S. Hart, K. Santulli, L. Leal, T. Johnson, N. Rao, & L. Burney 1986. How do teachers teach memory skills? *Educational Psychologist* **21**, 55–71.

Moely, B. E., F. A. Olson, T. G. Halwes, & J. H. Flavell 1969. Production deficiency in young children's clustered recall. *Developmental Psychology*, **1**, 26–34.

Moely, B. E., K. A. Santulli, & M. S. Obach 1995. Strategy instruction, metacognition, and motivation in the elementary school classroom. In *Memory performance and competencies: Issues in growth and development*, F. E. Weinert & W. Schneider (eds.). Hillsdale, NJ: Erlbaum.

Morrison, F. J. & C. Lord 1982. Age differences in recall of categorized material: Organization or retrieval. *Journal of Genetic Psychology* **141**, 233–41.

Naus, M. J. & P. A. Ornstein 1983. Development of memory strategies: Analysis, questions and issues. In *Trends in memory development research, Vol. IX, Contributions to human development*, M. T. H. Chi (ed.). Basel: Karger.

Naus, M. J., P. A. Ornstein, & S. Aivano 1977. Developmental changes in memory: The effects of processing time and rehearsal instructions. *Journal of Experimental Child Psychology*, **23**, 237–51.

Ornstein, P. A., L. Baker-Ward, & M. J. Naus 1988. The development of mnemonic skill. In *Memory development: Universal changes and individual differences*, F. E. Weinert & M. Perlmutter (eds.). Hillsdale, NJ: Erlbaum.

Ornstein, P. A. & M. J. Naus 1978. Rehearsal processes in children's memory. In *Memory development in children*, P. A. Ornstein (ed.). Hillsdale, NJ: Erlbaum.

Ornstein, P. A., M. J. Naus, & C. Liberty 1975. Rehearsal and organizational processes in children's memory. *Child Development* **46**, 818–30.

Ornstein, P. A., M. J. Naus, & B. P. Stone 1977. Rehearsal training and developmental differences in memory. *Developmental Psychology* **13**, 15–24.

O'Sullivan, J. T. 1993. Preschoolers' beliefs about effort, incentives, and recall. *Jour-*

nal of Experimental Child Psychology **55**, 396–414.

Palincsar, A. S. & A. L. Brown 1984. Reciprocal teaching of comprehension-fostering and comprehension-monitoring activities. *Cognition and Instruction* **1**, 117–75.

Paris, S. G. 1988. Motivated remembering. In *Memory development: Universal changes and individual differences*, F. E. Weinert & M. Perlmutter (eds.). Hillsdale, NJ: Erlbaum.

Paris, S. G. & B. K. Lindauer 1982. The development of cognitive skills during childhood. In *Handbook of developmental psychology*, B. Wolman (ed.). Englewood Cliffs, NJ: Prentice-Hall.

Paris, S. G., R. S. Newman, & K. A. McVey 1982. Learning the functional significance of mnemonic actions: A microgenetic study of strategy acquisition. *Journal of Experimental Child Psychology* **34**, 490–509.

Paris, S. G. & E. R. Oka 1986. Children's reading strategies, metacognition, and motivation. *Developmental Review* **6**, 25–56.

Pressley, M. 1982. Elaboration and memory development. *Child Development* **53**, 296–309.

Pressley, M. 1994. Embracing the complexity of individual differences in cognition: Studying good information processing and how it might develop. *Learning and Individual Differences* **6**, 259–84.

Pressley, M. 1995. What is intellectual development about in the 1990s? Not strategies! Good information processing, not strategies instruction! Instruction cultivating good information processing. In *Memory performance and competencies: Issues in growth and development*, F. E. Weinert & W. Schneider (eds.). Hillsdale, NJ: Erlbaum.

Pressley, M., J. G. Borkowski, & W. Schneider 1987. Cognitive strategies: Good strategy users coordinate metacognition and knowledge. In *Annals of Child Development, Vol. V*, R. Vasta & G. Whitehurst (eds.), 575–82. New York: JAI.

Pressley, M., J. G. Borkowski, & W. Schneider 1989. Good information processing: What is it and what education can do to promote it. *International Journal of Educational Research* **13**, 857–67.

Pressley, M. & J. Dennis-Rounds 1980. Transfer of a mnemonic keyword strategy at two age levels. *Journal of Educational Psychology* **72**.

Pressley, M., P. B. El-Dinary, M. B. Marks, R. Brown, & S. Stein 1992. Good strategy instruction is motivating and interesting. In *The role of interest in learning and development*, K. A. Renninger, S. Hidi, & A. Krapp (eds.). Hillsdale, NJ: Erlbaum.

Pressley M., D. Forrest-Pressley, & D. J. Elliot-Faust 1988. What is strategy instructional enrichment and how to study it: Illustrations from research on children's prose memory and comprehension. In *Memory development: Universal changes and individual differences*, F. E. Weinert & M. Perlmutter (eds.), Hillsdale, NJ: Erlbaum.

Pressley, M., D. J. Forrest-Pressley, D. J. Elliot-Faust, & G. E. Miller 1985. Children's use of cognitive strategies, how to teach strategies, and what to do if they can't be taught. In *Cognitive learning and memory in children*, M. Pressley & C. J. Brainerd (eds.). New York: Springer.

Pressley, M. & J. R. Levin 1977. Task parameters affecting the efficacy of a visual imagery learning strategy in younger and older children. *Journal of Experimental Child Psychology* **24**, 53–9.

Pressley, M. & C. B. McCormick 1995. *Advanced educational psychology*. New York: Harper Collins.

Pressley, M. & P. Van Meter 1993. Memory strategies: Natural development and use following instruction. In *Emerging themes in cognitive development, Vol. II; Competencies*, R. Pasnak & M. L. Howe (eds.). New York: Springer.

Rabinowitz, M. 1984. The use of categorical organization: Not an all-or-none situation. *Journal of Experimental Child Psychology* 38, 338–51.

Recht, D. R. & L. Leslie 1988. Effect of prior knowledge on good and poor readers' memory of text. *Journal of Educational Psychology* 80, 16–20.

Reese, H. W. 1962. Verbal mediation as a function of age level. *Psychological Bulletin* 59, 502–9.

Reese, H. W. 1977. Imagery and associative memory. In *Perspectives on the development of memory and cognition*, R. V. Kail & J. W. Hagen (eds.). Hillsdale, NJ: Erlbaum.

Renninger, K. A., S. Hidi, & A. Krapp 1992. *The role of interest in learning and development*. Hillsdale, NJ: Erlbaum.

Richman, C. L., S. Nida, & L. Pittman 1976. Effects of meaningfulness on children's free-recall learning. *Developmental Psychology* 12, 460–5.

Ringel, B. A. & C. J. Springer 1980. On knowing how well one is remembering: The persistence of strategy use during transfer. *Journal of Experimental Child Psychology* 29, 322–33.

Ritter, K., B. H. Kaprove, J. P. Fitch, & J. H. Flavell 1973. The development of retrieval strategies in young children. *Cognitive Psychology* 5, 310–21.

Rogoff, B., N. Newcombe, & J. Kagan 1974. Planfulness and recognition memory. *Child Development* 45, 972–77.

Rohwer, W. D., Jr 1973. Elaboration and learning in childhood and adolescence. In *Advances in child development and behavior, Vol. VIII*, H. W. Reese (ed.). New York: Academic Press.

Rohwer, W. D., Jr. 1980. An elaborative conception of learner differences. In *Aptitude, learning, and instruction, Vol. II, Cognitive process analyses of learning and problem*, R. E. Snow, P. A. Federico & W. E. Montague (eds.). Hillsdale, NJ: Erlbaum.

Rohwer, W. D., Jr., J. M. Raines, J. Eoff, & M. Wagner 1977. The development of elaborative propensity during adolescence. *Journal of Experimental Child Psychology* 23, 472–92.

Salatas, H. & J. H. Flavell 1976. Behavioral and metamnemonic indicators of strategic behaviors under remember instructions in first grade. *Child Development* 47, 81–9.

Schmidt, C. R. & S. R. Schmidt 1986. The use of themes as retrieval cues in children's memory for stories. *Journal of Experimental Child Psychology* 42, 237–55.

Schneider, W. 1985. Developmental trends in the metamemory-memory behavior relationship: An integrative review. In *Cognition, metacognition, and human performance, Vol. I*, D. L. Forrest-Pressley, G. E. MacKinnon, & T. G. Waller (eds.). Orlando, FL: Academic.

Schneider, W. 1986. The role of conceptual knowledge and metamemory in the development of organizational processes in memory. *Journal of Experimental Child Psychology* 42, 218–36.

Schneider, W. 1993. Domain-specific knowledge and memory performance in children. *Educational Psychology Review* 5, 257–73.

Schneider, W. & D. F. Bjorklund 1992. Expertise, aptitude, and strategic remembering. *Child Development* 63, 461–73.

Schneider, W. & D. F. Bjorklund 1997. Memory. In *Cognitive, language, and perceptual development*, R. S. Siegler & D. Kuhn (eds.), *Vol. II* of the *Handbook of child psychology*, B. Damon (ed.). New York: Wiley.

Schneider, W., D. F. Bjorklund, & W. Maier-Brückner 1996. The effects of expertise and IQ on children's memory: When knowledge is, and when it is not enough. *International Journal of Behavioral Development*.

Schneider, W., J. G. Borkowski, B. E. Kurtz, & K. Kerwin 1986. Metamemory and motivation: A comparison of strategy use and performance in German and American children. *Journal of Cross-Cultural Psychology* **17**, 315–36.

Schneider, W., H. Gruber, A. Gold, & K. Opwis 1993. Chess expertise and memory for chess positions in children and adults. *Journal of Experimental Child Psychology* **56**, 328–49.

Schneider, W., J. Körkel, & K. Vogel 1987. Zusammenhänge zwischen Meta-gedächtnis, strategischem Verhalten und Gedächtnisleistungen im Grund-schulalter: Eine entwicklungspsychologische Studie [Relationships among meta-memory, strategic behavior, and memory performance in school children: A developmental study]. *Zeitschrift für Entwicklungspsychologie und Pädagogische Psychologie* **19**, 99–115.

Schneider, W., J. Körkel, & F. E. Weinert 1989. Domain-specific knowledge and memory performance: A comparison of high- and low-aptitude children. *Journal of Educational Psychology* **81**, 306–12.

Schneider, W. & M. Pressley 1989. *Memory development between 2 and 20*. New York: Springer.

Schneider, W. & B. Sodian 1988. Metamemory–memory behavior relationships in young children: Evidence from a memory-for-location task. *Journal of Experimental Child Psychology* **45**, 209–33.

Schneider, W. & F. E. Weinert 1990. The role of knowledge, strategies, and aptitudes in cognitive performance. In *Interactions among aptitudes, strategies, and knowledge in cognitive performance*, W. Schneider & F. E. Weinert (eds.). New York: Springer-Verlag.

Scruggs, T. E. & M. Mastropieri 1988. Acquisition and transfer of learning strategies by gifted and nongifted learners. *Journal of the Education of the Gifted* **9**, 105–21.

Short, E. J. & E. B. Ryan 1984. Metacognitive differences between skilled and less skilled readers: Remediating deficits through story grammar and attribution training. *Journal of Educational Psychology* **76**, 225–35.

Siaw, S. N. & D. W. Kee 1987. Development of elaboration and organization in different socioeconomic-status and ethnic populations. In *Imagery and related mnemonic processes: Theories, individual differences, and applications*, M. A. McDaniel & M. Pressley (eds.). New York: Springer-Verlag.

Siegler, R. S. 1987. The perils of averaging data over strategies: An example from children's addition. *Journal of Experimental Psychology: General* **116**, 250–64.

Siegler, R. S. 1994. Cognitive variability: A key to understanding cognitive development. *Current Directions in Psychological Science* **3**, 1–5.

Siegler, R. S. 1995. Children's thinking: How does change occur. In *Research on memory development: State of the art and future directions*, W. Schneider & F. E. Weinert (eds.). New York: Oxford.

Siegler, R. S. & E. Jenkins 1989. *How children discover strategies*. Hillsdale, NJ: Erlbaum.

Sodian, B., W. Schneider, & M. Perlmutter 1986. Recall, clustering, and meta-memory in young children. *Journal of Experimental Child Psychology* **41**, 395–410.

Somerville, S. C., H. M. Wellman, & J. C. Cultice 1983. Young children's deliberate reminding. *Journal of Genetic Psychology* **143**, 87–96.

Sophian, C. & H. M. Wellman 1983. Selective information use and perservation in the search behavior of infants and young children. *Journal of Experimental Child Psychology* **35**, 369–90.

Tobias, S. 1994. Interest, prior knowledge, and learning. *Review of Educational Research*, **64**, 37–54.

Walker, C. H. 1987. Relative importance of domain knowledge and overall aptitude on acquisition of domain-related information. *Cognition and Instruction* **4**, 25–42.

Wellman, H. M. 1983. Metamemory revisited. In *Trends in memory development research*, M. T. H. Chi (ed.). Basel: Karger.

Wellman, H. M. 1988. The early development of memory strategies. In *Memory development: Universal changes and individual differences*, F. E. Weinert & M. Perlmutter (eds.). Hillsdale, NJ: Erlbaum.

Wellman, H. M., K. Ritter, & J. H. Flavell 1975. Deliberate memory behavior in the delayed reactions of very young children. *Developmental Psychology* **11**, 780–7.

Whittaker, S., J. McShane, & D. Dunn 1985. The development of cueing strategies in young children. *British Journal of Developmental Psychology* **3**, 153–61.

Williams, K. G. & L. R. Goulet 1975. The effects of cueing and constraint instructions on children's free recall performance. *Journal of Experimental Child Psychology* **19**, 464–75.

Wong, B. Y. L. 1982. Strategic behaviors in selecting retrieval cues in gifted, normal achieving and learning-disabled children. *Journal of Learning Disabilities* **15**, 33–7.

Woody-Ramsey, J. & P. H. Miller 1988. The facilitation of selective attention in preschoolers. *Child Development* **59**, 1497–503.

Worden, P. E. 1983. Memory strategy instruction with the learning disabled. In *Cognitive strategy research: Psychological foundations*, M. Pressley & J. R. Levin (eds.), New York: Springer-Verlag.

Yussen, S. R. 1974. Determinants of visual attention and recall in observational learning by preschoolers and second graders. *Developmental Psychology* **10**, 93–100.

Yussen, S. R. & J. E. Bird 1979. The development of metacognitive awareness in memory, communication, and attention. *Journal of Experimental Child Psychology* **28**, 300–13.

Yussen, S. R. & V. M. Levy 1975. Developmental changes in predicting one's own span of short-term memory. *Journal of Experimental Child Psychology* **19**, 502–8.

Acknowledgements

We would like to thank Barbara R. Bjorklund, Cynthia Park, Kristina Rosenblum, Elizabeth Kennedy, and Holly Stewart for comments on earlier drafts of this manuscript. This chapter was completed while the first author was supported by National Science Foundation research award SBR–9422177.

CHAPTER 9

Memory development and processing resources

Robert Guttentag

If an act became no easier after being done several times, if the careful direction of conscious attention were necessary to its accomplishment, then no progress could take place in development (William James 1890).

This quote from William James presents a common-sense and fairly widely held view of attention and task performance. The essence of James' idea is that there is an attention-related limitation on some form of processing resource, and that with practice and experience the amount of attention required for task performance declines. When people first learn to drive a car, for example, they must pay close attention to each component of the task (steering, maintaining the proper speed, etc.). With experience, each of these components can be executed with less and less attention, permitting the driver to perhaps even engage in other activities (such as carrying on a conversation) while driving in a safe and proper manner.

Although James focused on the effects of experience on the attentional resource demands of task performance, it is a relatively minor extension of his view to hypothesize general age-related differences in the attentional or processing resource demands of task performance. Indeed, age-related differences in resource demands have at one time or another been suggested as an important factor contributing to age changes in almost every aspect of cognitive functioning, including reasoning and problem solving ability (Case 1985; Chapman 1987; Halford 1982; Halford et al. 1986; Pascual-Leone 1970), reading ability (Curtis 1980; Laberge & Samuels 1974), mental arithmetic skill (Baroody 1984), strategies of early word learning (Liittschwager & Markman 1994), narrative production skills (Case 1991), and even social interaction skills (Bullock 1983; Dodge 1986).

This chapter is concerned with the influence of processing resource limitations, and age differences in the resource demands of task performance, on children's remembering. The chapter begins with a discussion of some general issues in the conceptualization of processing resource limitations, followed by a review of evidence suggesting that age-related differences in resource limitations contribute to age differences in some forms of remembering. Some controversies regarding these findings will then be discussed, with a focus on issues related to the measurement of the resource demands of task execution. The final sections of the chapter will discuss mechanisms through which age differences in resource limitations may manifest themselves as differences in remembering performance.

Conceptualizations of resource limitations

A limitation on the capacity for storing and/or processing information is a central feature of most information processing models. The original three-store model of memory of Atkinson and Shiffrin (1971), for instance, included a limited capacity short-term memory (STM) store. The model proposed that information analysis and control processes (including procedures such as rehearsal that are used to transfer information to long-term memory) could function only on information held in STM. Hence, the limited number of slots available for storing information in STM represented a major capacity limitation of the system. More recent models have generally conceptualized STM as a working memory (Baddeley 1986) whose limited capacity must be shared between storage and processing functions (Case 1985). That is, the limited capacity of working memory not only for holding information for analysis in conscious awareness, but also as a necessary resource for the mental procedures operating on the stored information.

The concept of working memory lends itself most directly to a spatial "workspace" metaphor for capacity limitations (Case 1985). An alternative way of characterizing capacity limitations, however, is as a limitation in energy. Early research on capacity limitations adopted this latter metaphor, based upon the assumption that cognitive operations are fueled by the allocation of some form of energy-like limited capacity mental resource (Welch 1898). The use of an energy metaphor, however, also remains prominent today (Craik & Byrd 1982; Kahneman 1973; R. Kanfer & Ackerman 1989).

In most respects there are few real differences between the energy and spatial views; in each case, it is assumed that there is a limitation in some form of central processing resource that must be shared between different processing operations. One advantage of the energy metaphor, however, is its association with the conceptualization of information processing as requiring mental work or mental effort (Kahneman 1973), thereby forming a potential link between processing limitations and motivational factors affecting cognitive functioning (Kahneman 1973; R. Kanfer & Ackerman 1989). Assuming that we find the exertion of high amounts of mental effort somewhat aversive, an important way in which resource demands may affect task performance is through an effect on the individual's motivation to use a particular mental operation (Guttentag & Lange 1994).

A common feature of these models is the assumption that different mental procedures have different resource demands. That is, the assumption is made that some mental operations require a great deal of mental effort or capacity to be executed, whereas others require much less. Moreover, with the practice of mental operations, and as a consequence of the growth during development of general knowledge, the resource demands of some procedures may decline; indeed, one of the primary effects of practice is thought to be a decline in the resource demands of task performance (as James so astutely observed). In some cases, resource demands may decline so much as a function of practice and other factors that task execution no longer places any demands on the processing capacity limitations of the system at all. Instead, these mental procedures may be executed automatically under appropriate stimulus conditions (Shiffrin & Schneider 1977).

Absolute versus functional growth in processing capacity

There are two possible ways in which the capacity demands of mental operations could change with age (see Figure 9.1). First, the total capacity of the system could increase (McLaughlin 1963; Pascual-Leone 1970), thereby reducing the percentage of total resources required for executing any particular mental operation. According to this view, development during childhood is associated with growth in the absolute capacity of the information processing system, but not necessarily in the absolute resource demands of any particular mental operation. In the illustration of this model in Figure 9.1, for instance, it may be seen that the size of the space required for performing a specific task does not change, but the percentage of the total space does decline as a function of growth in total capacity.

Alternatively, total capacity could remain constant across age, while the absolute amount of that capacity required for most mental operations may decline (Case et al. 1982). Thus, as illustrated in Figure 9.1, the percentage of total capacity required to perform specific tasks declines as a function not of change in total capacity, but rather as a function of a decline in the amount of that capacity required by specific tasks. This, as was discussed above, is presumably what happens as a result of practice (Footo et al. 1988). Other factors, however, have also been proposed to produce a similar effect. For example, growth and/or reorganization of the general knowledge base has been hypothesized to increase the resource efficiency of knowledge access (Bjorklund 1987). In addition, with age children would be expected to learn new, more effective strategies for using mental resources efficiently (Folds et al. 1990).

There is evidence supportive of each of these positions. For example, it has been found that performance on a broad range of tasks improves at generally the same rate during childhood, reaching peak performance in the late teen years (Kail 1991), findings which are supportive of absolute growth models. On the other hand, it is also known that practice and other experiential factors can reduce the resource demands of specific mental operations (Bjorklund

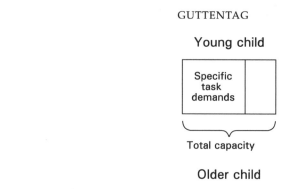

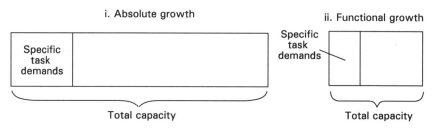

Figure 9.1 Two models of functional growth with age in processing capacity.

1987; Footo et al. 1988), findings which are most consistent with the functional growth perspective.

Complicating the issue, several prominent models of cognitive growth essentially combine elements of the two approaches. In Case's model, for example, while experience (practice, etc.) is proposed as the proximal cause of age changes in the resource demands of mental task execution, there are also presumed to be absolute biological limits on the maximal efficiency of processing that can be achieved, limits which increase with age during childhood (see Fischer & Pipp 1984 for a similar view).

A fuller discussion of the issue of growth in absolute capacity vs. functional capacity growth is beyond the scope of this chapter. Suffice it to say, at present there remains no clear resolution of this issue. With regard to the understanding of the effects of resource limitations on memory development, however, complete resolution of the issue is not of critical importance; the two models make the same prediction, namely, that the percentage of total capacity required for most mental operations, including those involved in remembering, should tend to decrease with age. This can be seen clearly in Figure 9.1; whether the change involves a growth in total capacity on the one hand or whether it involves a decline in the capacity demands of particular mental operations on the other, increased age is associated with a functional increase in attentional or processing capacity.

Single- vs. multiple-resource theories

The models discussed above assume the existence of a single general-purpose resource pool fueling the execution of all nonautomatic mental operations (Kahneman 1973; Posner & Boies 1971). It is possible, however, that instead of a single pool of resources there may be several somewhat independent resource pools (Friedman & Polson 1981; Friedman et al. 1982, 1988; Navon & Gopher 1979, 1980; Wickens 1980, 1984). Most research designed specifically to differentiate between single-resource and multi-resource perspectives has rendered the strong version of single-resource theory untenable (Navon & Gopher 1979). That is, even if there is something to be called general resources, most evidence indicates that there must be a number of independent resource pools as well, and different resource pools have been postulated as a function of: (a) different modalities of stimulus input, (b) processes operating on different internal representational codes (visual vs. verbal), (c) different response modes (manual vs. verbal), and (d) processing in different cerebral hemispheres (Friedman et al. 1982; Hiscock & Kinsbourne 1978; Navon & Gopher 1979, 1980; Wickens 1980, 1984).

In terms of age changes in remembering, the multiple resource perspective raises the interesting possibility that there could be age changes not only in the "how much" of resource demands but also in the "which" of resource demands. That is, age-related changes in remembering could potentially involve a change in which resources are relied upon to support remembering operations. Such a possibility could arise, for example, if subjects at different ages perform remembering tasks in radically different ways or if there are age differences in the structure or organization of the different resource pools; in either case, there could result a difference across age in the pattern of resource-pool use.

At present there exists little empirical evidence on this issue but what scant research does exist has tended to find stable patterns across wide ranges of age in terms of which resources are necessary for problem solving and remembering tasks (see Guttentag 1989 for a review of the relevant literature). Thus, as was the case with the issue of absolute versus functional change in capacity, both perspectives on the multiple versus single resources issue have essentially the same implications for the study of memory development – that with age, the resource demands of remembering operations should decline.

Resource-performance functions

A basic assumption of all resource-limitation models is that the quality of task performance should vary as a function of the amount of processing resources allocated to task execution. Subjects are also assumed to be able to exert some degree of control over resource allocation, deciding, for instance, whether or not to allocate all available resources to task execution or not. The function relating characteristics of process execution to the amount of resources allocated to process execution is called the resource-performance function

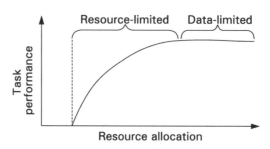

Figure 9.2 The resource-performance function.

(Norman & Bobrow 1975). This function may assume a variety of shapes, within the restriction that an increase in resource allocation to a process will never be associated with a decrease in the quality of process execution. Figure 9.2 presents a typical, albeit simplified, hypothetical resource-performance function.

Reference to resource-performance functions provides a ready definition for the efficiency of task performance; within this context, efficiency is defined as the measure of performance divided by the amount of resources allocated to the task. If one person, or performance in one condition, produces a higher quality of task performance without the allocation of greater resources, then that individual's task execution, or task execution in that condition, is more resource efficient. The slope of the resource-function at any given point defines the marginal resource efficiency of task performance, that is, the gain in task performance resulting from the addition of that resource unit.

There is no fixed shape for resource-performance functions; instead, they may vary from task to task, and the exact shape or slope of the function for a particular task may vary from person to person. Moreover, the general slope of the function is likely to be different at different positions along its curve. Generally, it has been assumed that most functions will have a negatively accelerated shape, such that the marginal efficiency of task performance will decrease with increasing allocation of resources to the task (Norman & Bobrow 1975). Thus for instance, it may be seen in Figure 9.2 that there is a decreasing benefit associated with increases in resource allocation the further one moves along the resource-performance curve.

In addition, for many tasks there is likely to be a section of the upper part of the function where the allocation of further resources will produce no further improvements in task performance, thereby producing a flat portion of the resource-performance curve. Performance under these conditions is said to be data-limited, that is, limited by the task information available to the subject rather than being limited by the amount of resources allocated to the task. In other words, no matter how much harder the subject tries, task performance will not improve. This form of limitation on task performance contrasts with the resource-limited performance which occurs under conditions in which an increase in resource allocation will improve task performance (Norman & Bobrow 1975).

Effects of resource limitations on children's remembering

Performance on many memorization tasks improves dramatically over the course of the elementary school years. Age changes in performance are not, however, found equally on all remembering tasks. Recognition memory performance, for example, has been found to be quite good during early childhood and tends to change relatively little with age, whereas performance on recall memory tasks exhibits dramatic changes with age during the preschool and elementary school years (Schneider & Pressley 1989).

Hasher and Zacks (1979) noted that the tasks on which the largest age changes are observed (e.g. recall of a list of words) tend to be tasks which require the involvement of effortful strategic memorization in order to achieve a high level of task performance. In contrast, those tasks on which the smallest age differences in performance tend to be found are tasks on which automatic processing plays a much more central role. For example, Hasher and Zacks found that, for adults, strategic effort contributes little to memory for the relative frequency of presentation of two pieces of information. Correspondingly, age changes in memory for relative frequency tend to be very small.

These findings are exactly what one would predict if age changes in the resource demands of remembering operations was a primary contributor to age changes in remembering. Specially, one would predict that the most dramatic age differences in remembering would occur on those tasks whose quality of performance is most affected by limitations on processing resources, whereas the smallest age differences would be expected to be found on tasks which are more dependent upon automatic processing operations.

This pattern of results can perhaps be seen most clearly when comparing performance on deliberate versus nondeliberate remembering tasks. Deliberate remembering tasks are those on which subjects are aware, at the time of study, that their memory for the presented information will later be tested. The study of memory development has, until recently, been dominated by studies of deliberate memorization. This research has found that there tend to be large age differences in performance on deliberate memorization tasks, largely resulting from age differences in the use of effortful memorization strategies such as rehearsal (Flavell 1970), organization (Ornstein & Corsale 1979), and elaboration (Pressley 1982).

In the case of rehearsal, for instance, it has been found that older children rehearse more actively than do younger children (that is, they rehearse a larger number of different study items together at one time) and organize the information being rehearsed in more effective ways (Ornstein & Naus 1978). These age differences in rehearsal patterns are closely correlated with age differences in recall performance. The significance of these findings for the issue of resource limitation effects is that age differences in performance are found on precisely the elements of performance which are most resource demanding.

Incidental learning tasks differ from deliberate memorization tasks with respect to the instructions that subjects are given at the time that information is initially presented. Subjects in an incidental learning study might, for example, be presented a list of words, but they would not be told to memorize the words. Instead, subjects would be asked to make some form of judgment about each list item (such as its category membership). Later, memory for the words would be assessed with a surprise recall test. Studies using this general procedure have found that while age differences in recall performance still occur, they tend to be much smaller than the performance differences found with comparable deliberate memorization tasks (Schneider & Pressley 1989). Indeed, some studies have found that very young children actually perform better under incidental than under deliberate memorization conditions (Newman 1990). Thus, when the initial encoding of the information does not depend upon deliberate use of effortful procedures, age differences in recall performance are significantly reduced.

The extreme case of nondeliberate remembering involves implicit remembering. With implicit memory tasks there is neither intent to memorize nor intent to retrieve, thus ruling out effortful strategies as a source of age differences in performance at both encoding and retrieval; indeed, subjects are not necessarily even aware that they are "remembering." For example, subjects in an implicit memory study might be presented a list of words under incidental learning conditions. Later, rather than being presented a recall task for the presented items, subjects would be presented a task which does not require them to recall words from the earlier presentation list but which might nonetheless reveal implicit memory for some of the list items.

A commonly used implicit memory task, for instance, is the word-stem completion task. Subjects are presented three-letter word stems (e.g. hou__ for "house"), some of which can be completed with a word from the incidental learning list. A large number of studies of this type with adults have demonstrated that the presentation of an item on the incidental learning list increases the likelihood that the item will be produced on the implicit memory word-stem completion task, even if subjects have no conscious recollection that the item had been on the original list (Schacter 1992); thus, the task reveals a "memory" effect without subjects being consciously aware that they are remembering.

Similar effects are found even with adults with severe amnesia who may have no conscious memory of the incidental learning task at all (Roediger 1990), and a number of studies have found evidence for robust implicit memory effects with children (Greenbaum & Graf 1989; Naito 1990; Parkin & Streete 1988). Moreover, the developmental studies have generally found that the magnitude of the implicit memory effect remains constant across age,

254

suggesting that when effortful remembering processes are not involved at the time of either encoding or retrieval, age differences in memory are minimal or nonexistent (Ausley & Guttentag 1993; Drummey & Newcombe 1995; Russo et al. 1995).

Resource limitations and mnemonic strategy use

The findings regarding task differences in patterns of age differences in memory functioning suggest that when age differences in remembering do occur, they are often related to mentally effortful elements of the remembering process, and more specifically, are related to age differences in the use of deliberate and effortful encoding and retrieval strategies. This pattern of findings raises the possibility that there might be significant age differences in the resource demands of memory strategy use. That is, if resource limitations constrain the use of remembering strategies, and if these limitations tend to change with age, then one should find that age and individual differences in features of strategy use are related to age and individual differences in resource limitations.

Resource capacity/strategy use correlations

One method used to test this hypothesis has been to measure strategy execution ability in relation to a measure of overall processing capacity. In a study by Pressley et al. (1987b), for example, children aged 6 through 11 years of age were presented a sentence learning task. For adults, a highly effective learning strategy on this task involves the use of mental imagery to encode the to-be-learned sentences. In the Pressley et al. (1987b) study, half of the children at each age were instructed to form mental images of each sentence; the remaining subjects were given no special strategy-use instructions (control condition). A measure was also taken of each subject's overall processing capacity by administering three different types of memory span tasks; a measure of memory span for words, a measure of nonverbal visual memory span, and a measure of memory span for sentences. Significantly, the tasks involved not only storage of information but also some degree of processing of the information, thereby providing a measure of capacity sensitive to both storage and processing functions. It was predicted that because effective use of the mental imagery strategy places high demands on processing resources, the ability of the children to benefit from the imagery strategy instructions should be related to their processing capacity.

Pressley et al. (1987b) found that performance tended to be better in the imagery condition than in the control condition, especially for older children. This finding is consistent with the view that only the older children possessed the processing capacity necessary to utilize an imagery strategy effectively. Pressley et al. (1987b) also found that their measure of processing capacity not only correlated with performance under imagery strategy instructions, but was actually a better predictor of strategy instruction benefit than was age. This finding provides direct support for the view that age differences in processing capacity contribute to age differences in children's ability to utilize an imagery strategy effectively.

A similar pattern of results has been found in the small number of other studies which have used this approach to examine the effects of resource limitations on the use of other strategies. For example, Miller (1990, 1994) found that younger children's effective use of a selective attention strategy on a picture memory task was correlated with age and individual differences in processing capacity.

Dual-task studies of the resource demands of strategy use

The Pressley et al. (1987b) and Miller (1990) studies examined the relation between strategy use and an overall measure of processing capacity. A more direct approach that can be taken to the question of resource limitation effects on strategy use is to measure the resource demands of strategy use itself. With this approach, it is predicted that the capacity demands of strategy should tend to decline with age.

The most commonly used method for assessing resource demands is the dual-task technique (Guttentag 1989; Kerr 1973; Posner & Boies 1971; Welch 1898) . This paradigm is based upon the assumption that when two processes that utilize the same resources are performed concurrently, the processes must compete for resource allocation from the same limited resource supply; consequently, it should be possible to index the resource demands of a task by measuring the extent to which it interferes with the execution of a concurrently performed secondary task. This would be comparable to measuring the attentional demands of driving by requiring the individual to carry on a conversation on a complex topic while driving. Presumably, the skilled driver should have sufficient attention available to converse appropriately; the novice, on the other hand, would be expected either to be unable to converse while driving successfully or to be unable to drive successfully while conversing.

The dual-task technique was first used in 1886 by Loeb (cited in Welch 1898) to measure the attentional demands of mental multiplication. Subjects in Loeb's experiment squeezed a hand-grip as hard as possible while performing the multiplication tasks. Loeb found that increases in the difficulty of the primary mental multiplication task produced corresponding increases in the amount of interference produced by mental multiplication with hand-grip performance; in other words, the harder the multiplication task, the weaker the grip. This effect was attributed by Loeb to the increased amount of attention required to perform the more difficult multiplication problems.

A number of developmental studies have utilized similar dual-task procedures to test for age differences in the resource demands of memory strategy execution. The first of these studies focused on children's use of a cumulative, or multi-item, rehearsal strategy on a free recall task (Guttentag 1984). Research has shown that when children are asked to try to memorize a long list of words, there are systematic changes in their use of rehearsal to accomplish the task. Typically, children younger than age 5 make very little use of rehearsal as a learning aid. Somewhat older children tend to rehearse, but do so in a very simple and relatively ineffective way, repeating over and over each newly presented word alone. In contrast, older children and adults typically group several items together in their rehearsal sets. Children younger than 10 are not, however, totally incapable of multi-item rehearsal; several studies have found that children just 7 years of age can be trained to use the more effective multi-item strategy, resulting in an improvement in their recall performance (Naus et al. 1977; Ornstein & Naus 1978).

Guttentag (1984) instructed children in second, third, and sixth grades to utilize a multi-item rehearsal strategy to memorize a list of words. The children were also required to perform a secondary finger tapping task while memorizing the list; for this task, the children were asked to tap a finger as rapidly as possible while they were rehearsing the to-be-remembered words. Compared with performance under baseline conditions (when subjects performed the finger-tapping task alone), Guttentag found that the amount of interference produced by the primary memory-strategy-use task with the secondary finger-tapping task decreased with age, suggesting an age-related decrease in the resource capacity demands of multi-item rehearsal.

Comparable results have been found when the resource demands of other memory strategies have been examined. Kee and Davies (1988; see also review by Kee 1994), for instance, used a dual-task paradigm to test for age differences in the resource demands of strategy use on a paired associate learning task. This task involves the presentation of word pairs on the study list; at test, subjects are presented the first word from each pair and are asked to recall the other pair member. Kee and Davies found that sixth graders and adults did not differ in the capacity demands of instructed rehearsal (a strategy which sixth-graders are already highly skilled at using). However, when subjects were instructed to utilize an elaboration strategy (generating a sentence inter-relating the two words from each word-pair), the effort demands of strategy use were found to be greater for the children than for the adults.

Similarly, Miller et al. (1991a) used a dual-task procedure to examine the capacity demands of the use of a selective attention strategy by younger children. The primary task in this study required children to try to recall the locations of pictures of members of a particular category (e.g. animals) hidden behind doors. Not all locations, however, were relevant on every trial; instead, half the locations contained items from a different irrelevant category (e.g. household objects). The location of the relevant items, however, was clearly marked by pictures on the doors (e.g. a drawing of a house for household objects, a drawing of a cage for animals). The appropriate strategy, of course, is to examine only those locations containing objects from the relevant category.

The children in Miller et al.'s (1991a) study were instructed to use a selective attention strategy, and were also required to perform a secondary finger-tapping task while they examined the study list pictures. Miller et al. (1991a) found that the amount of finger-tapping interference produced by use of the selective attention strategy was significantly greater for young children (kindergarten and first-grade) than for older children (fourth- and fifth-grade).

In a systematic review of these and other dual-task studies, Guttentag (1989) summarized the findings by noting two patterns of results that have emerged consistently from this line of research: (a) when subjects of different ages utilized the same strategy, age differences have been found in the processing resource demands of strategy use, as indexed by a decrease with age in dual-task interference; (b) in those cases in which dual-task interference has not been found to decline with age, the evidence indicates that older subjects utilized a more complex or more effective form of the strategy than did the younger subjects (e.g. Bjorklund & Harnishfeger 1987). Thus, it has either been found that, in comparison with older children and adults, younger children must allocate a greater percentage of their limited processing resources to execute the same remembering procedures or else younger children must allocate just as high a percentage of their limited resource capacity in order to execute less effective procedures.

These findings seem to provide direct support for the view that age differences in memory strategy use result, in part, from age differences in the resource demands of strategy execution. This conclusion, however, depends very much on the validity of the dual-task methodology used to measure resource demands. In the following section some criticisms of this methodology will be discussed.

Time-sharing ability or resource demands?

Secondary-task interference effects might not be entirely attributable to the resource demands of the primary task. Navon and Gopher (1979) noted that the processes involved in allocating resources to and organizing, coordinating, and scheduling two concurrently performed tasks may themselves require resources. Consequently, there is no way to know, for any particular case of secondary-task interference, how much of that interference reflects the resource requirements of the primary task and how much reflects the more general resource costs of performing two tasks simultaneously. The issue of concern for developmental researchers is whether there might be age differences in the efficiency of these general time-sharing processes, that is, in the basic ability to perform two tasks simultaneously. If age differences in secondary-task interference are to be attributed to age differences in the resource demands of the primary task, the assumption must be made that subjects of different ages do not differ in time-sharing ability *per se*.

The issue of age differences in general time-sharing skill has been addressed in studies utilizing a paradigm in which performance on each of two tasks is measured under both single- and dual-task conditions. Age differences in the combined dual-task costs are then assumed to index age differences in time-sharing skill. In the first studies designed to address the time-sharing issue, Lipps Birch (1976, 1978) measured children's performance on an auditory word processing task and a manual pursuit tracking task (subjects had to move a wand to try to keep it on top of a moving light) under both single-task and dual-task conditions. The subjects ranged in age from 7 to 13 years in the first study and 8 to 13 years in the second. In the first experiment the analysis of time-sharing ability revealed age differences in dual-task costs for the pursuit tracking task but not for the word processing task. However, the presence of age differences in task performance even under single-task conditions raised the possibility that it was age differences in the efficiency of single-task performance, rather than age differences in time-sharing skill, that produced the age differences in dual-task costs. Accordingly, in her second study Lipps Birch provided the younger subjects with extensive practice on the two tasks until their performance matched that of the older subjects under single-task conditions. The elimination of baseline differences in performance in this manner resulted in the elimination of age differences in dual-task costs with each task, suggesting that younger subjects were not deficient at the processes involved in time-sharing the two tasks.

In the only other study conducted specifically to test for age differences during childhood in time-sharing proficiency, Lane (1979) examined the ability of 7-year-olds, 9-year-olds, and college students to time-share auditory and visual serial recall tasks. Lane eliminated baseline differences in task performance by setting the number of items presented on dual-task trials at a constant percentage of each subject's serial recall span measured under single-task conditions. Although dual-task costs were present for each task, no age differences were found in the magnitude of the costs. Thus, Lane's data support Lipps Birch's conclusion that the general ability to time-share tasks does not change with age during the school years. These findings suggest that age differences in dual-task interference effects on memorization tasks are not simply the result of age differences in time-sharing ability; rather, dual-task costs seem to index some feature of skill at executing the primary remembering task.

Resource competition versus response competition explanations
The use of the secondary-task paradigm to assess resource demands entails the assumption that dual-task costs result from competition for shared resources between the primary and secondary tasks. This is not, however, a universally accepted proposition. In Navon and Gopher's (1979) analysis of dual-task costs, for instance, they described several types of "concurrence costs" that result from the mere simultaneous performance of two tasks and that may contribute to dual-task costs independently of resource competition between the two tasks. Indeed, Navon (1984, 1985) has suggested that it may

be possible to account for dual-task costs entirely in terms of concurrence costs, without reference to competition for resources at all.

One potential source of concurrence costs is response competition between the two tasks. In the extreme case, there could be total structural incompatibility between the responses required by the two tasks, as would occur if subjects were required to tap two different, spatially separated, keys with the same finger. In other cases there could be partial incompatibility between required responses, such that it is simply more difficult to generate the responses required by one task while simultaneously performing the other. Navon and Gopher (1979) illustrated the latter phenomenon with the example of response competition between singing a waltz while dancing a tango; neither task is likely to be totally disrupted by concurrence costs, but because of the different tempos required by each task, performance is likely to suffer when they are performed concurrently.

Response competition explanations are most directly relevant to cases in which the primary memorization task required subjects to engage in overt use of a remembering strategy (i.e., studies requiring subjects to rehearse or generate elaborations aloud). For these studies (e.g. Guttentag 1984; Kee & Davies 1988; Kee & Howell, described in Kee 1994), the possibility is present that it may have been solely the motor component of overt strategy use which shared resources with the secondary finger-tapping task (Brainerd & Reyna 1989).

There are, however, several findings which challenge response competition theories as a more general explanation for the findings from dual-task interference studies of children's remembering. In Guttentag's (1984) study, for instance, it was found that greater interference was produced by multi-item than by single-item rehearsal with younger but not older children; if it was only the motor component of overt strategy use which shared resources with finger tapping, it is not clear why more tapping interference was produced by multi- than single-item rehearsal. Moveover, Kee and Howell found that both *silent* rehearsal and *silent* elaboration interfered with finger tapping, and found larger age differences in dual-task interference for elaboration than rehearsal (see Kee 1994).

Although sophisticated versions of response competition theories can handle even the kinds of effects found by Kee and Howell, Guttentag (1989) noted that they do so by defining "resource" in a very narrow way and then by adopting most of the features of a resource model. Indeed, Guttentag (1989) noted that it may be impossible to adjudicate clearly between resource competition and response competition models of dual-task interference. Guttentag also noted, however, that there may be no need to make this distinction. Even response competition models assume that secondary-task interference indexes an important feature of primary task skill; essentially, "resistance to response interference" may be thought of as an index of resource demands. Thus, even response interference models would suggest that in the case of remembering, the evidence suggests that children become more efficient (in terms of resource use) at memory strategy execution with age. Some of the ways in which this difference in strategy skill may translate into differences in remembering performance are discussed in the following sections.

Mechanisms of resource limitation influences on memory strategy use

The evidence from dual-task studies converges with the findings regarding task differences in developmental change in remembering performance to suggest that age differences in memory strategy use and remembering performance result, in part, from age differences in the resource demands of remembering operations. Three different mechanisms that might be involved in translating age differences in resource demands into age differences in remembering performance are discussed below. The first and most direct involves an effect of resource limitations on the ability to execute remembering operations. The second mechanism discussed below focuses on the effects of resource limitations on memory strategy selection. The third mechanism involves an effect of resource limitations on memory monitoring and other metamnemonic processes thought to play a role in the child's learning about the effective use of remembering procedures.

Resource limitation effects on strategy execution

A basic assumption of resource limitation models is that we cannot execute cognitive procedures which require more processing resources than we possess (Norman & Bobrow 1975). Accordingly, age differences in the resource demands of different remembering operations should affect the nature of the strategies that children of different ages are capable of producing and using effectively. A study of children's multi-item rehearsal by Ornstein et al. (1985) illustrates this point. Children in second and sixth grades were instructed to utilize a multi-item rehearsal strategy on a free-recall task. Under the assumption that the retrieval of old list items for rehearsal is a resource demanding procedure, Ornstein et al. (1985) reasoned that age differences in the resource demands of retrieving for rehearsal should manifest themselves as age differences in the number of different items children could rehearse together at each rehearsal opportunity.

The data were consistent with the prediction; even though the younger children utilized a multi-item strategy when instructed to do so (with a corresponding improvement in recall performance), they were not able to rehearse as many items together at each rehearsal opportunity as were the older children. Moreover, when the resource demands of item retrieval for rehearsal were reduced (by maintaining the visible availability of all list items following each item's initial presentation), children at both ages rehearsed with much larger rehearsal sets than they had under the more typical item presentation conditions (see also Guttentag et al. 1987).

Research on the use of elaboration strategies further supports the view that age differences in resource demands contribute to age differences in the ability to execute effective mnemonic strategies (Pressley 1982). In the study by Pressley et al. (1987b) discussed previously, for instance, older children benefitted more than younger children from instructions to use imagery as a learning strategy on a sentence learning task. The correlation found between strategy benefit and processing capacity suggested that only the older children possessed sufficient processing capacity to execute the strategy effectively.

Resource limitation explanations for the differential effect of imagery instructions on younger and older children are also consistent with the finding that young children benefit more from imagery instructions under conditions in which the capacity demands of strategy execution are reduced. For example, young children benefit from instructions to use a prose imagery strategy if they are provided part of the image in the form of a picture before they carry out the strategy (Guttman et al. 1977; Ledger & Ryan 1985); provision of some parts of the images presumably reduces the amount of processing required to produce complete images, thereby permitting younger children to execute the strategy effectively.

In some of the cases discussed above younger children were simply incapable of executing the same strategies that were used by older children. In other cases, however, younger children appeared to be capable of using the same strategies that were used by older children or adults but failed to benefit from strategy use (e.g. Pressley et al. 1989b). In order to explain this latter pattern of findings, Bjorklund and Harnishfeger (1987) have argued that effective memory strategy use requires more than simply the ability to execute the superficial elements of the strategy mechanically. In addition, there are other (sometimes unspecified) encoding and storage procedures which must be executed simultaneously with the more obvious features of the strategy. According to Bjorklund and Harnishfeger, younger children are often unable to execute these latter processes during strategy use because they must allocate so much processing capacity to strategy execution *per se*.

This view suggests that the higher processing demands of strategy execution for younger than older children prevent the younger children from deriving as much benefit from strategy use because, in effect, they are reduced to using a stripped-down version of the strategy – one which superficially resembles the procedure utilized by older children but which lacks certain features which make use of the strategy by older children more effective. An excellent illustration of this kind of effect can be seen in Miller's (1990, 1994) studies examining preschoolers' performance on a selective recall task. Miller not only found age differences in the spontaneous use of a selective looking strategy (looking only behind the doors containing the relevant, to-be-remembered pictures), but also found that when preschool aged children first started to use the strategy spontaneously, they did not derive as much benefit from its use as was the case for older children (DeMarie-Dreblow & Miller 1988; Miller & Harris 1988), a deficit that Miller described as a "utilization" deficiency.

To explain this phenomenon, Miller hypothesized that the high capacity demands of strategy execution for the younger children prevented them from simultaneously performing the selective looking strategy along with other procedures required to make selective looking effective. Several findings support this view; in particular, it has been found that procedures designed to reduce the resource demands of the selective looking strategy improve younger children's recall performance on this task (DeMarie-Dreblow & Miller 1988; Miller et al. 1991b). It has also been found that reduction in the resource capacity demands of selective looking improves performance precisely because it frees capacity to be allocated to other procedures that affect recall performance, particularly rehearsal of the uncovered items (Miller et al. 1991b).

This pattern of results is not limited to studies with very young children. In a study of older children's use of an elaboration strategy, for instance, Kee and Guttentag (1994) found that the use of materials which reduced the resource demands of one component of strategy use freed resources to be allocated to another important strategy component. Consequently, the strategy could be executed with greater effectiveness with the materials which permitted more efficient resource allocation.

Capacity demands and strategy selection

In Guttentag's (1984) study of age differences in the resource demands of multi-item rehearsal, even the second-grade children were capable of executing the strategy effectively when instructed to do so (i.e., their recall benefited from strategy use). Second-graders do not, however, typically use a multi-item strategy spontaneously. This finding is consistent with a large number of studies suggesting that younger children often fail to deploy strategies spontaneously that they can execute (when instructed) with some degree of effectiveness (Flavell 1970). Guttentag also found that use of the strategy was more demanding of cognitive resources for the second-graders than for sixth-graders (an age at which children typically deploy the strategy spontaneously). Moreover, the measure of the resource capacity demands of *instructed* strategy use predicted actual *spontaneous* strategy deployment for children from third to fifth grade. That is, the children who *could* use multi-item rehearsal with least effort (when instructed to do so) tended also to rehearse *spontaneously* with the largest rehearsal sets.

These findings suggest that the high resource demands of strategy execution did not absolutely prevent the younger children from being able to execute the strategy effectively; instead, there seemed to be an influence of the resource demands of strategy use on spontaneous strategy *selection*. Other findings similarly suggest that age differences in the resource demands of strategy execution may affect strategy selection, rather than solely affecting the ability of subjects to execute the strategy effectively. Rohwer and Litrownik (1983), for

263

instance, trained 11- and 17-year old-subjects in the use of an elaboration strategy on two versions of a cued-recall task. The two versions of the task were designed so that use of the strategy would be more capacity demanding with one version (the hard version) than the other (the easy version). Under instructed-strategy-use conditions, subjects at both ages were able to execute the strategy effectively on *both* versions of the task. Age differences emerged, however, on a test of strategy maintenance. Specifically, subjects at both ages maintained their use of the strategy on the easy version of the task, but only the older children maintained strategy use on the harder version.

Thus, in the Rohwer and Litrownik (1983) study, subjects at the younger age were able to utilize the strategy effectively on both versions of the task, but were less likely than the older subjects to exhibit strategy maintenance on the more capacity demanding version. The older subjects were presumably able to execute the strategy on the difficult task with less effort than was the case for the younger subjects; consequently, the older subjects maintained use of the strategy with both versions of the task (Rohwer & Litrownick 1983). These findings, then, further implicate age differences in the processing resource demands of strategy use in the process of strategy selection.

Motivational influences on strategy selection

A likely reason why strategy selection is affected by the resource demands of strategy use is that resource demands may affect the *motivation* to use a particular strategy. A model from the adult literature explicitly relating concepts of processing resource demands to motivational processes was presented by R. Kanfer and Ackerman (1989). Their model is based upon Kahneman's (1973) mental effort conceptualization of processing resource capacity limitations; according to this view, the greater the percentage of total processing capacity that must be allocated to task performance, the more cognitively effortful will be the task. R. Kanfer and Ackerman (1989) further assume that humans seek economy of mental effort. That is, they assume that individuals seek the greatest payoff (in terms of levels of task performance) for the least effort.

The Kanfer and Ackerman model proposes that the intensity of effort (i.e., proportion of total capacity) and persistence of effort over time that a subject is willing to devote to the execution of task procedures involves a weighing of the subjective benefits and costs of the use of different procedures. The benefit to be derived from use of a procedure is the subjective value of expected improvements in task performance. The primary cost is the mental effort demands of procedure execution. For any particular task, therefore, subjects are presumed to base their strategy selection upon a subjective effort-utility function for each procedure. Consequently, subjects may select a less effective (but less effortful) procedure if the increment in task performance that would result from the application of the more effective strategy is not deemed to be worth the additional effort.

A study by Rabinowitz (1988) supports this view. The adult subjects in this

264

study were instructed to utilize an organizational strategy to memorize a list of words. The nature of the lists, however, varied across subject groups; the three groups received lists containing either all high-typicality category members (e.g. apple, peach, for the category fruit), all moderate-typicality items (e.g. cherries, pear, for the category fruit), or all low-typicality items (e.g. lime, coconut, for the category fruit). As expected, subjects receiving high- and moderate-typicality items rated the use of the strategy as less effortful than did subjects in the group receiving low-typicality items. The most significant finding from the study involved an examination of performance on a subsequent recall task, when subjects in all three groups received a list of moderate-typicality items. Rabinowitz found that subjects initially given the low-typicality list (who rated the strategy as highly effortful) made less use of the organizational strategy on the transfer task than did subjects initially given the moderate- or high-typicality lists. Apparently, the subjective expectation by subjects in the low-typicality group that use of the strategy would be highly effortful resulted in a reduced motivation to deploy the strategy on the final free recall task.

The idea that strategy selection involves a weighing of costs, in terms of mental effort, and benefits, in terms of subjective valuation of levels of performance, can also be found in a number of conceptualization of children's memory strategy use. Paris (1988), for instance, proposed that children's strategy selection involves judgments about the subjective expected utility (SEU) of various strategy options; SEU is assumed to vary positively as a function of the subjectively perceived effectiveness of strategy deployment and negatively as a function of the perceived mental workload of strategy execution. Thus, according to Paris, age-related changes in spontaneous strategy selection may be influenced by interactions among children's changing judgments of the effort demands of various strategies (costs) and their perceptions of the relative effectiveness of the strategies and the importance placed upon high levels of performance (benefits).

These assumptions form the basis for a model of memory strategy selection proposed by Guttentag and Lange (1994), illustrated in Figure 9.3. The first element of this model is strategy access. One factor influencing the likelihood that use of a strategy will even be considered is the subject's relevant task and strategy knowledge (Wellman 1983). There is considerable evidence, however, that strategy access can also be influenced by seemingly minor features of the task structure and by the exact nature of the task materials, factors which may operate to help cue access to particular strategies (e.g. Guttentag & Lange 1994; Rohwer et al. 1982).

For strategies which are accessed, subjects are hypothesized to engage in a costs/benefits analysis involving the other three components of the model. The primary cost of strategy use considered by this analysis is the amount of mental effort required for strategy execution. The primary benefit of strategy use, on the other hand, is the subjective expected value of the use of any particular strategy for achieving the goals of the task. The weighing of these

265

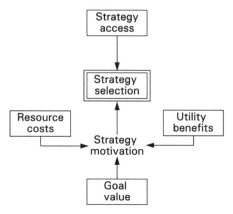

Figure 9.3 A model of memory strategy selection.

two factors will also be influenced by the individual subject's level of motivation to achieve various levels of performance on the task at hand. When, for instance, motivation to achieve a high level of task performance is very high, subjects are assumed to be willing to invest a large amount of mental effort in the use of a believed-to-be effective strategy. In contrast, when task motivation is low and/or when a less effortful (but still effective) alternate strategy is also accessed, the motivation to invest effort in the use of the initial strategy will be low.

One implication of this model is that age differences in the resource demands of memory strategy use should translate into higher *perceived costs* for younger than for older children. Consequently, even when younger children are able to utilize a strategy effectively, they may be unwilling to expend the large amount of mental effort required for strategy execution. For instance, second-graders may be less willing than sixth-graders to rehearse several different items together (Guttentag 1984), and early adolescents may be less motivated to maintain use of a highly effortful elaboration strategy than are older adolescents (Rohwer & Litrownick 1983).

In addition, children should not be willing to exert large amounts of mental effort on memory strategy use if they do not believe that their efforts will lead to improved recall performance (Borkowski et al. 1990). Partial support for this position derives from training studies demonstrating that children will not transfer a trained strategy if they do not *attribute* improved performance during training to the use of the strategy (e.g. Fabricius & Hagen 1984). Further, cross-cultural research has demonstrated that variations in remembering activities may be associated with cultural differences in the perceived importance of investing resources in the use of effortful strategies (Schneider et al. 1986).

Perceived benefits of strategy use should also be affected by the subjective value children place on the goal of recalling a large amount of information (Paris 1988). In particular, any feature of a task which increases, or minimizes, the individual's motivation to remember a large amount of information should affect willingness to invest resources in the use of an effortful remembering strategy.

Consistent with this view, research with adults has demonstrated that the manipulation of extrinsic rewards may affect resource allocation for remembering (Loftus & Wickens 1970). Only one directly relevant study has been conducted with children, but the findings were also generally consistent with the Guttentag and Lange model. In this study, third-grade children were presented a picture name recall task (Guttentag & Lange 1994). Prior to task presentation the children were shown an attractive prize and were told either that the prize required a high (although attainable) level of recall performance (recall-contingent prize condition) or that the prize was the child's to keep no matter how few pictures were remembered on the recall task (non-contingent prize condition). A measure was also taken of general academic ability based upon teacher ratings.

Guttentag and Lange (1994) found an effect of prize contingency on recall performance, but only for children above the mean in overall academic ability. An examination of the children's study and recall behaviors revealed that when the prize was made contingent upon recall performance, the high academic ability children, but not the lower academic ability children, studied the pictures longer, engaged in more self-testing during study, and were more persistent in trying to recall more items at retrieval. Thus, consistent with predictions, the high academic ability children were willing to invest more resources in effortful study and retrieval procedures when a high level of recall was required to obtain an attractive reward. The failure of the lower academic achievement children to show such an effect was interpreted as a possible reflection of a lack of knowledge on their part of how to translate higher goal motivation into effective remembering behaviors.

Resource limitation effects on metacognitive procedures

A full understanding of the development of strategic competence requires that the discussion of the resource requirements of remembering procedures be supplemented by a parallel treatment of the demands placed by metacognitive procedures. Most accounts of memory development assume that strategy acquisition and deployment are governed to some extent by a broad set of higher level processes (e.g. Pressley et al. 1987a). Examples of these metacognitive processes include the abilities to monitor ongoing cognitive procedures and to assess the effectiveness of strategic efforts, as well as the tendency to refer to existing metamnemonic knowledge at the time of strategy selection.

In R. Kanfer and Ackerman's (1989) model of mental effort and motivation, metacognitive procedures are assumed to be capacity-dependent, and to the extent that they must be executed during strategy deployment they will compete with strategy execution for the allocation of the subject's limited processing capacity. Support for this position is provided by a study with adults designed to examine the resource demands of self-regulatory activities during memory task performance (F. H. Kanfer & Stevenson 1985). Subjer in the study performed a continuous paired-associate task; in addition, some partici- pants were instructed to provide responses to self-monitoring, self-evaluation, and self-reaction questionnaires at regular intervals during list presentation. It was found that the subjects who were required to engage in self-regulatory activities performed more poorly on the paired-associate task than did those who were given standard memorization instructions. Indeed, subjects given the self-regulatory instructions performed as poorly as a group of subjects required to solve mental arithmetic problems during list presentation. These findings suggest that the self-regulatory processes were mentally effortful, and that they affected memory task performance by competing for scarce processing resources.

Research on strategy acquisition has amply demonstrated age differences in the use of self-regulatory procedures. Pressley et al. (1984a), for instance, provided 13-year-olds with practice using two different strategies for foreign language vocabulary learning. Performance with a keyword technique was objectively far superior to that associated with use of a repetition strategy. Nonetheless, the children were not aware of the relative effectiveness of the two strategies unless they were given explicit performance feedback on each of the practice trials. Other research has shown that even when children are aware of the relative effectiveness of two strategies, they may not appropriately refer to this knowledge to guide their strategy selection (Ghatala et al. 1986; Pressley et al. 1984b). Indeed, in a study of children's recall of classmates names, Bjorklund and Zeman (1982) found that children in first grade through fifth grade were often not even aware of the strategies they were using, reflecting a dramatic failure on their part to monitor their own goal-directed behaviors.

Children's failure to monitor and evaluate their strategy use may be related, in part, to the relatively high resource demands of strategy use for younger children (Paris & Myers 1981). The execution of the strategies may consume so much of the children's limited resources that there are too few resources left over for monitoring and other metacognitive activities. Alterna- tively, just as there are age differences in the processing resource demands of memory strategy use (Guttentag 1989), there may be age differences in the resource demands of self-regulatory activities themselves. In either case, one would predict that younger children would exhibit deficiencies in memory monitoring and other metacognitive activities. This, of course, has been found to be the case.

Conclusions

The view that human cognitive abilities are constrained by some form of cog- nitive resource limitation has a long history, and remains central to our understanding of cognitive functioning today. There has been a similarly lengthy history to the view that age-related change in the resource demands of many cognitive procedures represents a major mechanism of cognitive growth. Research discussed in this chapter provides evidence supportive of this view with regard to age changes in conscious remembering.

There are currently, however, several challengers to the predominance of the resource perspective. A number of prominent theorists have proposed that evidence regarding age changes in resource demands may reflect instead age changes in response competition mechanisms (Brainerd & Reyna 1989). Recent theorizing has also seen a resurgence of interest in the role of age changes in inhibitory mechanisms as a way of explaining many of the same findings previously discussed in terms of resource limitations (Dempster 1992; Harnishfeger & Bjorklund 1994).

Whether these challenges represent truly alternative perspectives regarding explanations of cognitive growth is not yet clear. Indeed, in terms of the issues of importance for the field of memory development, determining whether the basic underlying mechanism is one of age changes in resources or whether it is resistance to interference or the ability to inhibit may be less important than understanding the way in which age changes in these basic mechanisms affect the acquisition, selection, use, and effectiveness of the procedures involved in effective remembering. It is in terms of these latter questions that the major challenges still lie for any basic process-based explanation of the development of memory.

References

Atkinson, R. C. & R. M. Shiffrin 1971. The control of short-term memory, *Scientific American* **225**, 82–90.

Ausley, J. & R. E. Guttentag 1993. Developmental studies of intentional and nonintentional remembering. In *Emerging themes in cognitive development*, R. Pasnak & M. Howe (eds.). Lincoln, NB: University of Nebraska Press.

Baddeley, A. D. 1986. *Working memory*. Oxford: Oxford University Press.

Baroody, A. J. 1984. The case of Felicia: A young child's strategies for reducing memory demands during mental addition. *Cognition and Instruction* **1**, 109–16.

Bjorklund, D. F. 1985. The role of conceptual knowledge in the development of organization in children's memory. In *Basic processes in memory development*, C. J. Brainerd & M. Pressley (eds.). New York: Springer-Verlag.

Bjorklund, D. F. 1987. How changes in knowledge base contribute to the development of children's memory: An interpretive review. *Developmental Review* **7**, 93–130.

Bjorklund, D. F. & K. K. Harnishfeger 1987. Developmental differences in the mental effort requirements for the use of an organizational strategy in free recall. *Journal of Experimental Child Psychology* **44**, 109–25.

Bjorklund, D. F. & B. R. Zeman 1982. Children's organization and metamemory awareness in their recall of familiar information. *Child Development* **53**, 799–810.

Borkowski. J. G., M. Carr, E. Rellinger, & M. Pressley 1990. Self-regulated cognition: Interdependence of metacognition, attributions, and self-esteem. In *Dimensions of thinking and cognitive instruction*, B. F. Jones & L. Idol (eds.). Hillsdale, NJ: Erlbaum.

Brainerd, C. J. & V. F. Reyna 1989. Interference and resource interpretations of dual-task deficits in memory development. *Journal of Experimental Child Psychology* **47**, 1–18.

Bullock, D. 1983. Seeking relations between cognitive and social-interactive transitions. *New Directions for Child Development* **21**, 97–108.

Cariglia-Bull, T. & M. Pressley 1988. Short-term memory as a determinant of imagery strategy effectiveness during reading. In *Attentional and capacity constraints on strategy utilization: Developmental and individual differences*, F. Dempster (chair), Symposium presented at the meeting of the American Educational Research Association, New Orleans.

Case, R. 1985. *Intellectual development: Birth to adulthood*. New York: Academic.

Case, R. 1991. *The mind's staircase: Exploring the conceptual underpinnings of children's thought and knowledge*. Hillsdale, NJ: Erlbaum.

Case, R., D. M. Kurland, & J. Goldberg 1982. Operational efficiency and the growth of short-term memory span. *Journal of Experimental Child Psychology* **33**, 386–404.

Chapman, M. 1987. Piaget, attentional capacity, and the functional implications of formal structure. In *Advances in child development and behavior, Vol. XX*, H. W. Reese (ed.), 289–334. Orlando, FL: Academic.

Craik, F. I. M. & M. Byrd 1982. Aging and cognitive deficits: The role of attentional resources. In *Aging and cognitive processes*, F. I. M. Craik & S. E. Trehub (eds.). New York: Plenum.

Curtis, M. E. 1980. The development of components of reading skill. *Journal of Educational Psychology* **72**, 656–69.

DeMarie-Dreblow, D. & P. H. Miller 1988. The development of children's strategies for selective attention: Evidence for a transitional period. *Child Development* **59**, 1504–13.

Dempster, F. N. 1992. The rise and fall of inhibitory mechanism: Toward a unified theory of cognitive development and aging. *Developmental Review* **12**, 45–75.

Dodge, K. A. 1986. A social information processing model of social competence in children. In *Minnesota symposium on child psychology, Vol. XVIII*, M. Perlmutter (ed.). Hillsdale, NJ: Erlbaum.

Drummey, A. B. & N. Newcombe 1995. Remembering versus knowing the past: Children's explicit and implicit memories for picgtures. *Journal of Experimental Child Psychology* **59**, 549–65.

Fabricius, W. V. & J. Hagen 1984. The use of causal attributions about recall performance to assess metamemory and predict strategic memory behavior in young children. *Developmental Psychology* **20**, 975–87.

Fischer, K. W. & S. L. Pipp 1984. Processes of cognitive development: Optimal level and skill acquisition. In *Mechanisms of cognitive development*, R. J. Sternberg (ed.), New York: Freeman.

Flavell, J. H. 1970. Developmental studies of mediated memory. In *Advances in child development and behavior*, H. W. Reese & L. P. Lipsitt (eds.), 181–211. New York: Academic.

Folds, T. H., M. Footo, R. E. Guttentag, & P. A. Ornstein 1990. When children mean to remember: Issues of context specificity, strategy effectiveness and intentionality in the development of memory. In *Children's strategies: Contemporary views of*

270

cognitive development, D. F. Bjorklund (ed.). Hillsdale, NJ: L. Erlbaum Associates.

Footo, M., R. E. Guttentag, & P. A. Ornstein 1988. Capacity demands of strategy execution: Effects of training and practice. In *Attentional and capacity constraints on strategy utilization: Developmental and individual differences*, F. Dempster (chair), Symposium presented at the meeting of the American Educational Research Association, New Orleans.

Friedman, A. & M. C. Polson 1981. The hemispheres as independent resource systems: Limited-capacity processing and cerebral specialization. *Journal of Experimental Psychology: Human Perception and Performance* 7, 1031–58.

Friedman, A., M. C. Polson, & C. G. Dafoe 1988. Dividing attention between the hands and head: Performance trade-offs between rapid finger tapping and verbal memory. *Journal of Experimental Psychology: Human Perception and Performance* 14, 60–8.

Friedman, A., M. C. Polson, C. G. Dafoe, & S. J. Gaskill 1982. Dividing attention within and between hemispheres: Testing a multiple resources approach to limited-capacity information processing. *Journal of Experimental Psychology: Human Perception and Performance* 8, 625–50.

Ghatala, E. S., J. R. Levin, M. Pressley, & D. Goodwin 1986. A componential analysis of the effects of derived and supplied strategy-utility information on children's strategy selection. *Journal of Experimental Child Psychology* 41, 76–92.

Greenbaum, J. L. & P. Graf 1989. Preschool period development of implicit and explicit remembering. *Bulletin of the Psychonomic Society* 27, 417–20.

Guttentag, R. E. 1984. The mental effort requirement of cumulative rehearsal: A developmental study. *Journal of Experimental Child Psychology* 37, 92–106.

Guttentag, R. E. 1989. Age differences in dual-task performance: Procedures, assumptions, and results. *Developmental Review* 9, 146–70.

Guttentag, R. E. 1996. Mental effort and motivation: Influences on children's memory strategy use. In *Research on memory development: State of the art and future directions*, F. Weinert & W. Schneider (eds.). Hillsdale, NJ: L. Erlbaum.

Guttentag, R. E. & G. Lange 1994. Motivational influences on children's strategic remembering. *Learning and Individual Differences* 6, 309–30.

Guttentag, R. E., P. A. Ornstein, & L. Siemens 1987. Children's spontaneous rehearsal: Transitions in strategy acquisition. *Cognitive Development* 2, 307–26.

Guttman, J., J. R. Levin, & M. Pressley 1977. Pictures, partial pictures, and young children's oral prose learning. *Journal of Educational Psychology* 69, 473–80.

Halford, G. S. 1982. *The development of thought*. Hillsdale, NJ: Erlbaum.

Halford, G. S., M. T. Maybery, & J. D. Bain 1986. Capacity limitations in children's reasoning: A dual-task approach. *Child Development* 57, 616–27.

Harnishfeger, K. K. & D. F. Bjorklund 1993. The ontogeny of inhibition mechanisms: A renewed approach to cognitive development. In *Emerging themes in cognitive development: Foundations, Vol. I*, M. L. Howe & R. Pasnak (eds.). New York: Springer-Verlag.

Harnishfeger, K. K. & D. F. Bjorklund 1994. A developmental perspective on individual differences in inhibition. *Learning and Individual Differences* 6, 331–56.

Hasher, L. & R. T. Zacks 1979. Automatic and effortful processes in memory. *Journal of Experimental Psychology: General* 108, 356–88.

Hiscock, M. & M. Kinsbourne 1978. Ontogeny of cerebral dominance: Evidence from time-sharing asymmetry in children. *Developmental Psychology* 14, 321–9.

Hiscock, M., M. Kinsbourne, M. Samuels, & A. E. Krause 1985. Effects of speaking

271

upon the rate and variability of concurrent finger tapping in children. *Journal of Experimental Child Psychology* **40**, 486–500.

James, W. 1890. *Principles of psychology.* New York: Henry Holt.

Kahneman, D. 1973. *Attention and effort.* Englewood Cliffs, NJ: Prentice-Hall.

Kail, R. 1986. Sources of age differences in speed of processing. *Child Development* **57**, 969–87.

Kail, R. 1991. Development of processing speed in childhood and adolescence. In *Advances in child development and behavior, Vol. XXIII*, H. W. Reese (ed.). San Diego, CA: Academic Press.

Kanfer, F. H. & Stevenson, M. K. 1985. The effects of self-regulation on concurrent cognitive processing. *Cognitive Therapy and Research* **9**, 667–84.

Kanfer, R. & P. L. Ackerman 1989. Dynamics of skill acquisition: Building a bridge between intelligence and motivation. In *Advances in the psychology of intelligence, Vol. V*, R. J. Sternberg (ed.). Hillsdale, NJ: Erlbaum.

Kee, D. W. 1994. Developmental differences in associative memory: Strategy use, mental effort, and knowledge-access interactions. In *Advances in child development and behavior, Vol. XXV*, H. W. Reese (ed.). New York: Academic.

Kee, D. W. & L. Davies 1988. Mental effort and elaboration: A developmental analysis. *Contemporary Educational Psychology* **13**, 221–8.

Kee, D. W. & L. Davies 1990. Mental effort and elaboration: Effects of accessibility and instruction. *Journal of Experimental Child Psychology* **49**, 264–74.

Kee, D. & R. E. Guttentag 1994. Resource requirements of knowledge access and recall benefits of associative strategies. *Journal of Experimental Child Psychology* **57**, 211–23.

Kerr, B. 1973. Processing demands during mental operations. *Memory and Cognition* **1**, 401–12.

Laberge, D. & S. J. Samuels 1974. Toward a theory of automatic information processing in reading. *Cognitive Psychology* **6**, 292–323.

Lane, D. M. 1979. Developmental changes in attention deployment skills. *Journal of Experimental Child Psychology* **28**, 16–29.

Ledger, G. W. & Ryan, E. B. 1985. Semantic integration: Effects of imagery, enaction, and sentence repetition training on prereaders' recall for pictograph sentences. *Journal of Experimental Child Psychology* **39**, 531–545.

Liittschwager, J. C. & E. M. Markman 1994. Sixteen- and 24-month-olds' use of mutual exclusivity as a default assumption in second-label learning. *Developmental Psychology* **30**, 955–68.

Lipps Birch, L. 1976. Age trends in children's time-sharing performance. *Journal of Experimental Child Psychology* **22**, 331–45.

Lipps Birch, L. 1978. Baseline differences, attention, and age differences in time-sharing performance. *Journal of Experimental Child Psychology* **25**, 505–13.

Loftus, G. R. & T. D. Wickens 1970. Effect of incentive on storage and retrieval processes. *Journal of Experimental Psychology* **85**, 141–7.

McLaughlin, G. H. 1963. Psycho-logic: A possible alternative to Piaget's formulation. *British Journal of Educational Psychology* **33**, 61–7.

Miller, P. H. 1990. The development of strategies of selective attention. In *Children's strategies: Contemporary views of cognitive development*, D. F. Bjorklund (ed.). Hillsdale, NJ: Erlbaum.

Miller, P. H. 1994. Individual differences in children's strategic behavior: Utilization deficiencies. *Learning and Individual Differences* **6**, 285–307.

Miller, P. H. & Y. R. Harris 1988. Preschoolers' strategies of attention on a same-different task. *Developmental Psychology* 24, 628–33.

Miller, P. H., W. L. Seier, J. S. Probert, & K. L. Ayers 1991a. Age differences in the capacity demands of a strategy among spontaneously strategic children. *Journal of Experimental Child Psychology* 52, 149–65.

Miller, P. H., J. Woody-Ramsey, & P. A Aloise 1991b. The role of strategy effortfulness in strategy effectiveness. *Developmental Psychology* 27, 738–45.

Naito, M. 1990. Repetition priming in children and adults. *Journal of Experimental Child Psychology* 50, 462–84.

Naus, M. J., P. A. Ornstein, & S. Aivano 1977. Developmental changes in memory: The effects of processing time and rehearsal instructions. *Journal of Experimental Child Psychology* 23, 237–51.

Navon, D. 1984. Resources: A theoretical soupstone? *Psychological Review* 91, 216–34.

Navon, D. 1985. Attention division or attention sharing? In *Attention and performance, Vol. XI*, M. I. Posner & O. S. M. Marin (eds.), 133–46. Hillsdale, NJ: Erlbaum.

Navon, D. & D. Gopher 1979. On the economy of the human processing system. *Psychological Review* 86, 214–55.

Navon, D. & D. Gopher 1980. Task difficulty, resources, and dual-task performance. In *Attention and performance, Vol. VIII*, R. S. Nickerson (ed.), 297–315. Hillsdale, NJ: Erlbaum.

Newman, L. S. 1990. Intentional and unintentional memory in young children: Remembering vs. playing. *Journal of Experimental Child Psychology* 50, 243–58.

Norman, D. A. & D. G. Bobrow 1975. On data-limited and resource-limited processes. *Cognitive Psychology* 7, 44–64.

Ornstein, P. A. & K. Corsale 1979. Organizational factors in children's memory. In *Memory, organization, and structure*, C. R. Puff (ed.), 219–257. New York: Academic.

Ornstein, P. A., R. G. Medlin, B. P. Stone, & M. J. Naus 1985. Retrieving for rehearsal: An analysis of active rehearsal in children's memory. *Developmental Psychology* 21, 633–41.

Ornstein, P. A. & M. J. Naus 1978. Rehearsal processes in children's memory. In P. A. Ornstein (ed.). *Memory development in children*, 69–99. Hillsdale, NJ: Erlbaum.

Paris, S. G. 1988. Motivated forgetting. In *Memory development: Universal changes and individual differences*, F. E. Weinert & M. Perlmutter (eds.). Hillsdale, NJ: Erlbaum.

Paris, S. G. & N. A. Myers 1981. Comprehension monitoring memory and study strategies of good and poor readers. *Journal of Reading Behavior* 13, 5–22.

Parkin, A. J. & S. Streete 1988. Implicit and explicit memory in young children and adults. *British Journal of Psychology* 79, 361–9.

Pascual-Leone, J. 1970. A mathematic model for the transition rule in Piaget's developmental stages. *Acta Psychologia* 32, 301–45.

Posner, M. I. & S. J. Boies 1971. Components of attention. *Psychological Review* 78, 391–408.

Pressley, M. 1982. Elaboration and memory development. *Child Development* 53, 296–309.

Pressley, M., J. G. Borkowski, & C. J. Johnson 1987a. The development of good strategy use. In *Imagery and related mnemonic processes*, M. A. McDaniel & M. Pressley (eds.). New York: Springer-Verlag.

Pressley, M., T Cariglia-Bull, S. Deane, & W. Schneider 1987b. Short-term memory, verbal competence, and age as predictors of imagery instructional effectiveness. *Journal of Experimental Child Psychology* **43**, 194–211.

Pressley, M., J. R. Levin, & E. S. Ghatala 1984a. Memory strategy monitoring in adults and children. *Journal of Verbal Learning and Verbal Behavior* **23**, 270–88.

Pressley, M., K. A. Ross, J. R. Levin, & E. S. Ghatala 1984b. The role of strategy utility knowledge in children's strategy decision making. *Journal of Experimental Child Psychology* **38**, 491–501.

Rabinowitz, M. 1988. On teaching cognitive strategies: The influence of accessibility of conceptual knowledge. *Contemporary Educational Psychology* **13**, 229–35.

Roediger, H. L. 1990. Implicit memory: Retention without remembering. *American Psychologist* **45**, 1043–56.

Rohwer, W. D., Jr. & J. Litrownik 1983. Age and individual differences in the learning of a memorization procedure. *Journal of Educational Psychology* **75**, 799–810.

Rohwer, W. D., Jr, M. Rabinowitz, & N. F. Dronkers 1982. Event knowledge, elaborative propensity, and the development of learning proficiency. *Journal of Experimental Child Psychology* **33**, 492–503.

Russo, R., P. Nichelli, M. Gibertoni, & C. Cornia 1995. Developmental trends in implicit and explicit memory: A picture completion study. *Journal of Experimental Child Psychology* **59**, 566–78.

Schacter, D. L. 1992. Understanding implicit memory. *American Psychology* **47**, 81–9.

Schneider, W., J. G. Borkowski, B. E. Kurtz, & K. Kerwin 1986. Metamemory and motivation: A comparison of strategy use and performance in German and American children. *Journal of Cross-Cultural Psychology* **17**, 315–36.

Schneider, W. & M. Pressley 1989. *Memory development between 2 and 20*. New York: Springer-Verlag.

Shiffrin, R. M. & W. Schneider 1977. Controlled and automatic human information processing: II. Perceptual learning, automatic encoding, and a general theory. *Psychological Review* **84**, 127–90.

Sternberg, R. J. & R. K. Wagner 1982. Automatization failure in learning disabilities. *Topics in Learning and Learning Disabilities* **2**, 1–11.

Welch, J. C. 1898. On the measurement of mental activity through muscular activity and the determination of a constant of attention. *American Journal of Physiology* **1**, 283–306.

Wellman, H. M. 1983. Metamemory revisited. In *Trends in memory development research*, M. T. H. Chi (ed.), 31–51. Basel: Karger.

White, N. & M. Kinsbourne 1980. Does speech output control lateralize over time? Evidence from verbal-manual time sharing tasks. *Brain and Language* **10**, 215–23.

Wickens, C. D. 1980. The structure of attentional resources. In *Attention and performance VIII*, R. S. Nickerson (ed.). Hillsdale, NJ: Erlbaum.

Wickens, C. D. 1984. Processing resources in attention. In *Varieties of attention*, R. Parasuraman & R. Davies (eds.), 63–101. New York: Academic Press.

Woody-Ramsey, J. & P. H. Miller 1988. The facilitation of selective attention in preschoolers. *Child Development* **59**, 1497–503.

Acknowledgement

The writing of this chapter was supported by a Research Council Grant from the University of North Carolina at Greensboro.

274

CHAPTER 10

Metamemory development

Mary Holland Joyner and Beth Kurtz-Costes

After participating in a dance rehearsal featuring children of different ages, 6-year-old Lydie said to her mother, "You know why our dance isn't as long as the big girls' dance? Well, the big girls have bigger brains than we do, so they can remember more dance steps than we can!" Whether or not Lydie's explanation was correct, her statement illustrates what psychologists refer to as "metamemory" – understanding about how memory processes work. As you will see in this chapter, children's metamemory is related to individual differences in strategy use and performance on memory tasks, and develops steadily across early and middle childhood. In this chapter, we first summarize how theorists have described and measured metamemory, and discuss research that shows relationships among metamemory, strategy use and memory performance. Next we discuss the development of metamemory. Finally, we give an overview of some recent new directions in research in this area.

Metamemory theory

Historical origins

The *concept* of metamemory, or people's awareness of their own memory processes, has been with us for some time. As early as 1907, Kuhlmann investigated subjects' knowledge about their memory for pictures of familiar objects. Half a century later, several investigators became interested in individuals' "feeling-of-knowing" – that is, of evaluations that information was stored in long-term memory but was not accessible (e.g. R. Brown & McNeill 1966; Hart 1965). The term "metamemory" was first introduced by John Flavell (1971; Flavell & Wellman 1977). Flavell used the term "meta" to indicate the higher-level aspect of the phenomenon: Thus "metacognition" is "thinking about thinking," or "knowing about knowing." Metamemory, one type of metacognition, refers to the knowledge that individuals have about memory processes.

Flavell and his colleagues argued that metamemorial knowledge encompasses at least three areas: person, task, and strategy knowledge. Metamemory about *person variables* includes knowledge about how, when, and why one remembers or forgets. A child's knowledge about person variables might include the recognition that math concepts are easier to remember than foreign languages, or that Mommy will remember the lunch box if the child forgets it. For Flavell, the person category included intra-individual differences in memory functioning (e.g. I can remember "X" more easily than I can remember "Y"), interindividual differences (e.g. my friend is better at this memory task than I), and universals (e.g. people learn information more quickly when they are awake and alert).

Metamemory about *task variables* comprises knowledge about task influences on memory performance. For example, shorter lists are generally easier to remember than longer lists, and familiar names are easier to remember than unfamiliar ones. Task-related metamemory includes knowledge about task characteristics, how those characteristics are likely to influence performance, and ways to maximize performance given specific task demands. Thus a child is likely to learn that some memory goals are more difficult than others (for instance, learning the gist of a story is easier than learning it word-for-word), and that different goals require different strategies (e.g. gist-learning might be accomplished by reading a story through once, while rote memorization would probably require multiple readings and rehearsal).

Strategy knowledge encompasses knowledge about the use of strategies on memory tasks, and of the benefits of such use for performance. The knowledge that writing down items on a grocery list will aid recall of those items is an example of metamemory about strategies. Although Flavell (1971) distinguished among these three categories, he argued that most metamemory knowledge is actually a combination of two or three categories. For example, you might believe that you (in contrast to your brother) should drink plenty of coffee and stay up late cramming (rather than getting a good night's sleep) when preparing for a psychology (versus a math) examination.

As these examples illustrate, metamemorial knowledge is a subset of the general knowledge base, including both procedural knowledge about "how to" (e.g. how best to prepare for a class presentation in order not to forget the main points) and declarative knowledge "that" (e.g. my boyfriend is incapable of remembering the anniversary of when we met). Although metamemory is viewed primarily as enhancing memory performance, Flavell also argued that, like other knowledge, metamemory might be inaccurate, might not be activated when needed, and might not be beneficial when activated. As we review later in the chapter, these metamemory "failures" are especially likely to occur for younger children.

Memory knowledge and memory monitoring

Ann Brown and her colleagues (e.g. A. L. Brown 1978; A. L. Brown et al. 1983) elaborated upon Flavell's work by focusing on an aspect of metamemory that Flavell and Wellman (1977) had called "here and now memory monitoring." This regulatory component of metamemory is responsible for selecting and implementing strategies, monitoring their usefulness, and modifying them when appropriate. For instance, after reading your class notes several times in preparation for an exam, you might ask a friend to quiz you over the material. In this case, the monitoring component of your metamemory had indicated to you that you might be ready for a practice test.

As A. L. Brown et al. (1983) argued, the two aspects of metamemory (i.e., the knowledge component and the regulatory component) complicate its definition. That is, while the two components are closely related, they are fundamentally different in nature. On the one hand, the knowledge component of metacognition is primarily statable, stable, late-developing, and fallible. The regulatory component, in contrast, is not necessarily statable, is somewhat unstable, is relatively age independent, and is task and situation dependent. As we discuss in greater detail below, measurement and theory have further differentiated the knowledge and regulatory components of metacognition.

Pressley and his colleagues (Pressley et al. 1984, 1985, 1987) made significant theoretical contributions to our understanding of meta-memory through their elaboration of the Good Strategy User Model, and later the Good Information Processor Model (Pressley 1995; Pressley et al. 1989a). According to this model, sophisticated metamemory is integrally related with the learner's strategy use, motivational orientation, general knowledge about the world, and automated use of efficient learning procedures. The contributions of these authors to our understanding of the linkages between knowledge about memory and the learner's efficient use of strategies are further explored below in the section on metamemory and strategy use. First we turn to a discussion of how metamemory has been measured.

The measurement of metamemory

Interview assessments

Most assessments of metamemory have utilized interviews or questionnaires that feature questions about memory processes. One of the earliest and best-known batteries was developed by Kreutzer et al. (1975), who interviewed children in kindergarten, first, third, and fifth grades about memory processes. These investigators used an interview technique that was aimed at measuring children's knowledge about everyday memory phenomena relevant for their own lives, including planning for future events (e.g. remembering to bring ice skates to school the next day) and recalling past events (e.g. remembering how long one has had a dog). Interview questions assessed children's knowledge about person variables (e.g. Can you remember better than your friends, or do they remember better than you?), strategies (e.g. If you lost your jacket at school, how would you go about finding it? Think of everything possible you could do to try and find it.), and task demands (e.g. These two sets of pictures are exactly alike except that one set is in color, and the other is black and white. If I asked you to learn them, would one list be easier for you to learn?).

Children's responses to Kreutzer et al.'s (1975) interview questions indicated that even kindergartners and first-graders possessed a fairly sophisticated understanding of memory concepts such as the idea that information decays rapidly from short-term memory, and that memory performance is affected by study time and familiarity of items. However, their results indicated that third- and fifth-graders had more sophisticated metamemory than younger children.

Much of the subsequent developmental research in metamemory used portions of the Kreutzer et al. (1975) battery, with some attempts to assess the validity and reliability of items (e.g. Belmont & Borkowski 1988; Cavanaugh & Borkowski 1980; Kurtz et al. 1982; Schneider 1986; Schneider et al. 1986). This subsequent work made three contributions to the measurement of metamemory. First, refinements in items resulted in a battery with established internal consistency, construct validity, and test-retest reliability (cf. Cavanaugh & Borkowski 1980; Kurtz et al. 1982). Secondly, an important addition to the original battery was an attempt to measure the regulatory aspect of metamemory. For example, in an item originally used by Levin and his colleagues (1977), children are asked to predict how many items they will remember on a memory task; next children perform the task, and are told how many items they correctly remembered, then are finally asked how many items they would remember if given another, similar task. While children in the middle elementary grades readily adjust their estimates according to their actual performance on the first task, 6-year-olds apparently fail to monitor, and thus continue to report unrealistically high expectations for future recall in spite of feedback about their actual performance (Levin et al. 1977). This procedure has been frequently used as a measure of children's memory monitoring.

A third contribution toward the measurement of metamemory was the development of group tests (e.g. Belmont & Borkowski 1988; Schneider 1986). Although group assessment could not be used with children younger than first grade, the development of group tests greatly facilitated subsequent meta-memory research.

Metamemory has also been assessed through concurrent measurement of memory and metamemory. In this case, individuals are asked to perform a memory task and to simultaneously (or immediately afterwards) report their knowledge about how they performed the task and about factors that may have influenced their performance. This concurrent assessment has taken the form either of a series of probe questions, or of a "think aloud" procedure, in which the participant says out loud everything that comes to mind while performing a memory task. Although concurrent assessment has been found to yield significant relationships between memory performance and metamemory, it is inherently tied to the task the individual is performing while thinking aloud. Therefore metamemory information obtained through such concurrent think-aloud procedures probably cannot be easily generalized to other types of memory tasks.

Problems in metamemory assessment and new measurement techniques

One of the main problems in metamemory assessment has been the reliance on self-report (cf. A. L. Brown et al. 1983; Schneider & Pressley 1989). Meta-memory – particularly the knowledge component – is cognitive in nature rather than behavioral. Therefore, like all mental processes, it cannot easily be measured through direct observation. Instead, individuals are usually asked questions (either open-ended or forced-choice) about memory processes. Think- aloud procedures similarly rely on verbal self-report.

Several problems arrive from this reliance on verbal report. First, not all cognitive processes are accessible to the individual. In fact, this concern pinpoints a theoretical issue at the heart of metamemory theory: Whether or not metamemory knowledge is necessarily verbalizable. Most theorists have argued that metamemory is at least potentially verbalizable; yet cognitive developmentalists widely agree that one hallmark of mature cognition is automaticity – or the ability for cognitive processing to take place *without* conscious attention (cf. Shiffrin & Schneider 1977). For example, students who are adept at text processing will spontaneously slow when reading difficult passages and may read a particularly difficult passage a second time without consciously noting their use of monitoring and strategy adjustment. Because strategy selection and monitoring frequently occur without conscious awareness, the reliance on self-report in metamemory assessment may be problematic.

A second problem associated with the reliance on self-report is that it puts young children at an unfair disadvantage. Young children are notoriously poor at verbalizing. Therefore, it cannot be concluded with confidence that the poor performance of young children on metamemory measures is due to a lack of understanding of memory processes; rather, poor language skills might be responsible for these age differences. Researchers working in this area have noted that young children often do not answer direct questions or will respond with "yes" or "no" when greater elaboration is appropriate. Even older children who have better verbalization skills than younger children may still lack the vocabulary necessary to explain how they can remember or what strategy they used. An additional complication is that young children may be puzzled by requests to report information that they believe is obvious to the interviewer. Some metamemory researchers have attempted to address these measurement problems by using extensive probes following-up questions to young children (e.g. What else? Can you tell me any other things you would do? Tell me everything you can think of.).

Metamemory researchers have also tried to redress the problems inherent in verbal self-report through the use of illustrations or videotapes. For instance, Wellman (1977, 1978) and Yussen and Bird (1979) developed a procedure in which children were presented pictures of actors engaged in various memory tasks. The children were asked about the effects of age, time, hair color, and clothing on memory. Importantly, children were asked to select pictures indicating their responses rather than giving a verbal response. Using this procedure, researchers were able to note developmental differences in metamemory that were not dependent on expressive language skills. Similarly, consistent data were found by Justice (1985, 1986) through the use of videotapes. Children were shown videotapes of another child using several memory strategies (looking, naming, rehearsing, and categorizing) and were asked to rank the strategies from best to worst.

Another assessment procedure designed to overcome some of the problems in self-report is peer tutoring. Best and Ornstein (1986) taught a memory strategy to a target child who was then asked to teach the strategy to another child. The first child's instructions were analyzed to provide a measure of metamemory. Although this procedure presupposes adequate verbal skills, peer tutoring is likely to be more motivating to young children than interviews, and also bypasses the problems of children responding to an adult (whom the child may suppose to be knowledgeable and not in need of the information requested).

While ideally these methods appear to alleviate some of the problems associated with verbal self-report, other problems arise with these assessment techniques. In many of the studies involving illustrations, children are asked to put three or more pictures in order of best to worst performance. Like verbal interviews, this task may be easier for older children than younger children for reasons other than differences in metacognitive knowledge: In this case, older children are probably more familiar with classification tasks than younger children. The unique approach of peer-tutoring certainly reveals information about strategy use, because children are more likely to use their metamemory knowledge in such a setting than to report it to an adult. However, child tutors do not necessarily use all the metamemory knowledge at their disposal in a single tutoring setting, and therefore this procedure is also not infallible as a measurement tool. Researchers continue to experiment with different ways to assess metamemory; however, it should be noted that some of the problems related to the measurement of metamemory are linked to ambiguities in its definition. In other words, theorists are not in agreement regarding whether information must be conscious and verbalizable to be considered part of the child's metacognitive repertoire, nor to what extent regulatory processes such as comprehension monitoring may be automatic and yet be considered metacognitive.

Given the aforementioned problems in measuring metamemory, you may ask yourself, "Why do people even bother to study metamemory?" Problems aside, metamemory research provides valuable insight into the minds of children, their memory skills, and what they know about and do with the skills they have. One of the main reasons for studying metamemory is because of its presumed relationship to memory performance. It is logical that possessing accurate knowledge about the conditions under which one best remembers, the types of information one can easily remember, and efficient strategies, should enable the learner to maximize memory performance. But although this connection seems plausible, strong correlations between children's metamemory knowledge and memory performance have not always been found. The next section discusses research in the relationship between metamemory and memory performance.

The memory–metamemory connection

In theory, rich and accurate knowledge about memory tasks and strategies should aid memory performance. Early research in this area showed anticipated differences in metamemory knowledge among children of different ages and skill levels (Borkowski & Cavanaugh 1979; A. L. Brown et al. 1983; Kail & Hagen 1977); however, across-group differences in metamemory knowledge and memory performance did not always translate into within-group associations between metamemory and memory. The late 1970s and early 1980s evidenced an explosion of studies that examined this relationship.

Metamemory knowledge and memory performance
The first studies investigating the relationship between metamemory knowledge and memory performance yielded mixed results. Early studies by Kelly et al. (1976) and by Salatas and Flavell (1976) found no clear evidence for a reliable relationship between metamemory and memory performance. In contrast, studies by Levin et al. (1977) and Yussen and Berman (1981) provided evidence of a much stronger link: In both of these studies, metamemory–memory correlations were in the range of $r = 0.60$ or 0.70.

Early studies also yielded inconsistencies in *patterns* of results. For instance, Cavanaugh and Borkowski (1980) examined metamemory, strategy use, and memory performance in kindergarten, first-, third-, and fifth-grade children. Although many of the metamemory–memory correlations were significant, findings were not consistent either across the three memory tasks used, or across the four age groups. Similarly, Yussen et al. (1979) illustrated that while fifth-graders were more likely than first- and third-graders to understand that the presence of semantic categories enhances recall, children's metamemory knowledge did not lead to higher recall.

In their review of early literature in this area, Cavanaugh and Perlmutter (1982) were pessimistic: The low-to-moderate correlations between memory performance and metamemory knowledge combined with theoretical and methodological weaknesses in the area led these authors to conclude that "metamemory has little value" (Cavanaugh & Perlmutter 1982: 22). These authors argued that both measurement and conceptual issues were responsible for the failure of researchers to establish strong, reliable relationships between memory performance and memory knowledge.

In contrast to Cavanaugh and Perlmutter's (1982) discouraging analysis, a much more optimistic view was provided soon after by Wellman (1983), who argued that the memory–metamemory connection was alive and flourishing. Upon closer examination, the reason for these discrepant views was clear: Whereas Cavanaugh and Perlmutter (1982) had focused on studies that examined children's verbalizable knowledge about organizational strategies, Wellman had concentrated primarily on studies of monitoring, the regulatory aspect of metacognition. This contrast was further elaborated by Schneider (1985), who conducted an extensive review and meta-analysis of literature assessing the metamemory–memory connection in children. Results of his meta-analysis confirmed a stable relationship between memory performance and metamemory that averaged $r = 0.41$ across studies. Importantly, Schneider's excellent summary and analysis pinpointed the discrepancies between the two earlier reviews. In particular, in studies where children were measured on how they sorted items into categories and later recalled the items, weak correlations were found between memory knowledge and memory performance. However, in studies where children were questioned about how they monitored their own memories, more positive results were found, even with kindergartners and preschoolers.

Although much of the metamemory research since the mid-1980s has substantiated Schneider's (1985) conclusions, positive relationships are not always found between metamemory and memory performance. On the one hand, children sometimes have knowledge of their own memory processes and of effective strategies but fail to use that information. Alternatively, children may possess accurate metamemory and may use this knowledge to apply a task-appropriate strategy, yet not show performance benefits from that use. These two phenomena, production deficiencies and utilization deficiencies, are discussed in greater detail in Bjorklund (Ch. 8 in this volume). In both cases, we would not expect a strong correlation between metamemory knowledge and memory performance. In the next section we discuss the relationship between metamemory and strategy use.

Metamemory and strategy use

One of the main reasons memory researchers became interested in metamemory was because of its potential relationship to children's use of strategies (cf. Borkowski 1985; Pressley 1995). The efficient and appropriate use of memory strategies improves memory performance; accurate metamemory knowledge about strategies would presumably be a prerequisite to effective strategy use.

Pressley et al. (1985, 1987) called this knowledge "metamemory about strategies" or "MAS." MAS is presumed to be directly related to strategy use, and appropriate strategy use enhances performance. For example, a student's knowledge about how best to memorize concepts for a psychology test demonstrates MAS. The student may recognize that simply reading the textbook a few times is not a particularly effective way to learn the new concepts, but that organizing the information into meaningful units, integrating it with other information the learner knew before, and performing a self-test of the material will enhance recall on next week's test. The more knowledge one has about different strategies and their potential applications, the easier it will be to select the optimal strategy, modify it to meet the demands of a particular task, and monitor performance, changing the strategy if necessary (Pressley et al. 1985).

Pressley et al. (1985) argued that two important aspects of MAS that good learners possess is general strategy knowledge (i.e., the recognition that it takes effort to apply strategies, but that if properly applied, strategies enhance learning) and specific strategy knowledge concerning when, where, and how to apply each particular strategy. Thus, metamemory was viewed by these authors as an integral part of a strategic approach to memory tasks.

Most investigations of the relationship between metamemory and strategy use have been in training studies, which attempted to move beyond simple correlations in order better to understand the cause and effect relationships operating among metamemory, strategy use, and memory performance. In one of the simpler designs, children are given baseline memory and metamemory assessments, then are instructed in the use of one or more memory strategies, and later perform a post-test assessment of memory performance and strategy use. Investigators have frequently used "transfer" tasks that assess the child's use of the instructed strategy in a task or setting that differs from the instructional one. An assumption guiding much of this work was that children who possessed richer metamemory knowledge would be more facile than their peers at learning new strategies and at transferring them to other tasks. In fact, the failure of strategy instructional programs to achieve transfer across tasks and settings has driven much of the research and theory in metacognition (cf. Borkowski 1985; Butterfield & Nelson 1989).

Strategy training studies have differed in whether or not metacognitive information about the strategies was included as part of the instruction. Most strategy instructional studies prior to 1980 did not include more than minimal information about how to execute the strategy (see Pressley et al. 1985 for a discussion of this point). Later investigations more often gave the learners specific information identifying those situations for which the strategy was especially suited, describing ways the strategy might be modified to fit other tasks, and noting that performance monitoring is a critical part of successful strategy use. Three examples of these later studies will be described here to give a flavor of this chapter in metamemory research.

In one of the first studies to include metacognitive feedback as part of the training procedures, Borkowski et al. (1976) trained 4- through 7-year-old children in the use of an elaboration strategy with a paired-associates task. Half of the children were also given metacognitive information about the potential value of the strategy in enhancing recall. Children who received additional information about the value of the strategy were more likely than children who received only strategy instruction to use the strategy on a maintenance task 2 weeks after training (Borkowski et al. 1976).

Ringel and Springer (1980) instructed first-, third-, and fifth-graders in the use of a sort recall strategy. After a pretest that was used to place children in four groups (one control and three treatment groups) matched on free recall, children in the treatment groups received instruction in how to sort the pictures semantically for future recall. Children in Groups 3 and 4 were given feedback about their improved performance in the instructional setting, and children in the fourth group were also told that their improved performance was due to use of the strategy. In a final session, strategy use and recall were measured on transfer tasks. Clear age differences were noted in the effects of training: Fifth-graders showed enhanced recall with or without feedback as part of the instruction. However, for third-graders, only children who received feedback about performance gains continued to use the strategy on transfer tasks in the final session. First-graders benefited from strategy instruction, but did not show clear gains due to feedback.

Another example of a strategy training study that incorporated meta-memory information was conducted by Paris et al. (1982). In this study, 7- and 8-year-olds were shown pictures on 5 consecutive days and were assessed on recall. On the first 2 days, the children simply practised with the materials. On Day 3, the children were given information about sorting pictures into similar groups, labeling the groups, using cumulative rehearsal, and performing self-tests. Half of the students were also told why the strategies were effective. In Days 4 and 5, strategy maintenance was assessed. Results indicated that the children who heard rationales for strategy use recalled more words, studied more strategically, and displayed more metamemory knowledge of strategies than the children who did not hear the rationale.

All of the above examples demonstrated that metacognitive information about the value of being strategic (i.e., what Pressley et al. 1985 termed "general strategy knowledge") increased the probability that children would learn the strategy and later use it. Paris et al. (1982) demonstrated that strategy instruction alters metamemory, and Ringel and Springer's (1980) results provided an additional glimpse of how metamemory and strategies develop in tandem: While fifth-graders did not need feedback to be persuaded of the strategy's utility (and to apply it successfully), third-graders only showed strategy transfer if they had received metamemory feedback. First-graders, who were generally poor in metamemory knowledge, did not benefit from feedback.

Most instructional studies that have incorporated metamemory information have tied that instruction fairly closely to the instructed strategy. An exception was a study conducted by Kurtz and Borkowski (1984), who provided children with general metacognitive information about the value of being strategic, the concept that strategies should match the task, and of the importance of monitoring and strategy modification. First- and third-graders were assigned to three groups: One group received strategy instruction appropriate to each of three memory tasks, a second received general metacognitive instructions, and the third received both strategy and metacognitive instructions. Results indicated that whereas strategy instructions were generally beneficial for all children who received them, children who received general metacognitive instruction in conjunction with the strategy instruction did not show an additional advantage on maintenance and generalization tasks. However, pretest metamemory was significantly correlated with strategy use on the generalization task only for children who had received both strategy and metacognitive instructions, leading the authors to conclude that children who were high in metamemory benefited most from the metacognitive training (Kurtz & Borkowski 1984).

Three conclusions may be drawn from the results of the above studies (as well as from the dozens of other instructional studies that have been conducted since the early 1980s). First, the relationship between metamemory and strategy use is bidirectional: Better metamemory leads to more efficient strategy use, and use of strategies leads to richer metamemory (e.g. Best 1993; Paris et al. 1982). Second, children's knowledge about memory processes is probably acquired across a wide variety of tasks and settings, and a large increase in metamemory knowledge resulting from a single instructional encounter is unlikely to occur (cf. Kurtz & Borkowski 1984). Third, metacognitive instructions to children are most likely to be effective when they are closely geared to a specific memory task and strategy (e.g. Cornoldi et al. 1991; Fatal & Kaniel 1992; Rao & Moely 1989). This may particularly be the case for young children, who require greater scaffolding to see the linkages between a newly instructed strategy or meta-cognitive concept and their prior knowledge about tasks and strategies. The next section explores in depth some of the differences noted among children of different ages with regard to their knowledge and regulation of memory processes.

The development of metamemory

We have discussed *what* the concept metamemory is, *how* it is measured, and *why* it is studied. Now we turn to a discussion of the *development* of metamemory. Although a comprehensive discussion of age-related changes in children's metamemory is beyond the scope of this chapter, we will provide an overview of research in four areas: preschoolers' knowledge and regulation of memory processes, children's metamemory about task variables, age differences in children's strategy knowledge, and the development of memory monitoring.

Preschoolers' knowledge and regulation of memory processes
At first glance, preschoolers appear to have only a very limited understanding of the concept of memory and, more importantly, of how their own memory systems work. For example, most young children do not recognize the limits to their memory capacities. In Kreutzer et al.'s (1975) monograph study, 5- and

6-year-olds reported that they always remembered better than their friends, and some said they never forgot anything! Further, if young children are presented with a list of pictures to be remembered and are asked to predict their performance, preschoolers and kindergartners will considerably overestimate their performance (Flavell et al. 1970). These young memory stars continue to make this optimistic prediction even after attempting recall of a target list and actually remembering a relatively small number of items. Flavell et al. (1970) found that only by age 7 could children reliably assess their memory span accurately. However, two points should be noted here. First, Flavell et al. found substantial individual differences in their results: About one-third of younger children were accurate in predicting their memory spans. Secondly, although preschoolers lack awareness regarding memory span, in other ways 4-year-olds possess accurate, though rudimentary, ideas about memory and ways to remember.

One area in which preschoolers have elementary metamemory knowledge is regarding the usefulness of a strategic approach to remembering. For instance, Justice (1989) found that 4-year-olds were able to identify an effective strategy for finding a hidden object. Participating children were first familiarized with a task in which a colored chip was hidden in a movable display. Next the children watched a videotape that showed actors either looking away when the hiding place was rotated or marking the place with a colored chip. The 4-year-olds in this study were able to identify the marking strategy as the more effective memory technique.

Beal (1985) demonstrated that preschoolers have a basic but incomplete understanding of strategy use as a memory aid. In her study, 4-year-olds, kindergartners, and third-graders were asked several questions regarding how they could locate a penny that they had observed being hidden under one of many identical cups. All children understood that a retrieval cue (marking the cup with a paper clip) should be associated with the target (the cup with the penny underneath). However, younger children did not fully comprehend the problems of multiple retrieval cues and how they may present problems in identifying the target item in the future. For example, half the 4-year-olds believed that the paper-clip marker would help them even with three other markers present. Thus, these younger children realized that the strategy of marking the target cup was effective, but did not recognize that ambiguous cues would interfere with accurate retrieval.

Another aspect of metamemory that young children do understand is the effect of effort on remembering. O'Sullivan (1993) investigated 4-year-olds' knowledge about the effects of effort and incentives on recall performance. Participating children viewed pictures of children exhibiting high and low levels of effort to remember 10 toys placed in front of them. The participating children had just performed an identical task. While viewing the pictures, children were asked how many items each child would remember. A similar procedure was used to compare the effects of a "good" reward (crayons) versus a "poor" reward (a pencil). Results indicated that the majority of children believed that an increase in effort or incentive would lead to an increase in recall. Further, they believed that the "good" reward would cause the children to try harder (exert more effort) and that this effort would lead to better recall. These results indicate that preschoolers can and do understand the relationships among effort, incentives, and performance. O'Sullivan (1993) suggested that pre-schoolers have much experience in the areas of effort and its effect on recall performance. Thus, everyday activities contribute to their growing under-standing of memory processes.

Although these studies and others demonstrate that young children cer-tainly have a basic understanding of memory, more sophisticated understand-ing does not develop until later. One such area is knowledge about the limitations of short-term memory. Kreutzer et al. (1975) asked children whether it would make a difference if they got a drink of water between being told their friend's phone number and actually phoning the friend. About half the kindergartners and two-thirds of the first graders in the sample recognized that getting a drink might interfere with remembering. In contrast, 95 per cent of the third- and fifth-graders had this awareness. In the following section we de-scribe research examining the development of children's understanding of task characteristics that influence memory performance.

Children's metamemory about task variables

As noted above, 5- and 6-year-olds in Kreutzer et al.'s (1975) study were less likely than older children to recognize limitations of their short-term memory capacity. In that study, older children had more sophisticated metacognitive understanding than younger children across a number of tasks. For instance, in one subtest children were shown a set of 20 colored drawings and were asked who would remember more: a child who studied for 1 minute or a child who studied for 5 minutes. Although three-fourths of kindergartners predicted that studying for 5 minutes would be more beneficial, only one-third of the kindergartners (in contrast to all the third- and fifth-graders) provided ad-equate justifications of their responses. Similarly, whereas kindergartners and first-grade children frequently said that eight words embedded in a story would be easier to remember than a simple listing of the same words, only third- and fifth-graders could explain *why* the story was easier to remember (Kreutzer et al. 1975).

Another task variable explored by Kreutzer et al. (1975) was understanding how familiarity or prior learning of material can facilitate recall performance. Whereas kindergartners and fifth-graders alike were able to anticipate that relearning a list would be easier than learning it for the first time, older children were better able to explain why. These results highlight one of the measurement issues described earlier: In these studies, the inability of young children to ex-plain their responses may have been due to insufficient meta-memory, or it may have been because of poor verbal skills or an immature concept of causality.

Levin, Yussen, and their colleagues have explored individuals' awareness of the difference between recognition and recall memory capacity. Although cognitive psychologists are well aware of the substantial performance differences found between recall and recognition memory, older children and adults seem to be unaware of the enormous capacity of their recognition memory. Because young children usually overestimate their memory performance, Levin et al. (1977) hypothesized that young children would show greater prediction accuracy for a recognition task than young adults. These authors confirmed this hypothesis in a study of first-graders, third-graders, and college students. On the one hand, prediction of recall performance was increasingly accurate with age. In contrast, the overestimation of young children and the lack of awareness of adults of their large recognition capacity actually led to greater recognition prediction accuracy for young children. Not surprisingly, the relationship between metamemory and memory performance for recognition tasks was weak for both children and adults (Levin et al. 1977; Yussen & Berman 1981).

One task variable that has received much attention from metamemory researchers is whether or not to-be-remembered items are related. Older children are more likely than younger children to notice relationships among items, and are also more likely to understand that if items "go together" in some meaningful way, they will be easier to learn (e.g. Hasselhorn 1990). Further, when presented with a memory task, older children are more likely to sort items into taxonomic categories – either spontaneously, or following instruction (e.g. Sodian et al. 1986).

Kreutzer et al. (1975) showed children two lists of word pairs; one list was composed of pairs of opposites (e.g. hard-easy) and the other of random pairs (e.g. Mary-walk). Whereas third- and fifth-graders accurately noted that opposite pairs would be easier to learn, 5- and 6-year-olds did not show this awareness. Similarly, Moynahan (1973) found that when learning categorized and noncategorized picture lists, third- and fifth-graders were better able than first graders to explain that recall is easier for related items. These findings were further extended by Yussen et al. (1979), who had children predict recall for three types of lists: lists with semantic categories, lists with physical (shape) categories, and random lists. In this study, first-, third-, and fifth-graders all recognized that semantically organized lists would be easier to remember than random lists, but only the fifth-graders rated semantic organization as more beneficial than physical organization.

In another study, Schneider (1986) presented second- and fourth-grade children with clusterable lists that differed in the degree of inter-item association and category relatedness. He found that second-graders were more likely to cluster highly associated items than low-associated items, whereas the strategic behavior of fourth graders did not differ on this dimension. Importantly, correlations between clustering behavior and metamemory indicated that the clustering of second-graders was unrelated to awareness of its potential value as a memory strategy, in contrast to fourth-graders, for whom study clustering was related to metamemory.

The results of the above studies seem robust: Either young children do not recognize that items in categorized lists fall into related groups, or they do not realize that categorical organization may enhance recall. However, these results should not obscure the fact that young children *do* possess some accurate information about how task variables influence memory processes. For instance, Yussen and Bird (1979) found that even 6-year-olds were able to recognize that noise would make learning and memorizing a list of words more difficult. However, task-related memory knowledge is usually not as comprehensive and accurate in young children as in older children, and is less likely in younger children to translate into appropriate strategy use and enhanced recall. In the next section we discuss children's knowledge about strategies.

Age differences in children's strategy knowledge

When simply asked to name strategies they would use in a memory task, children show a steady increase in sophistication across the elementary years. For instance, Kreutzer et al. (1975) asked children how they could help another child remember which Christmas he got his dog. Whereas most kindergartners could not arrive at any possible solutions, all of the fifth-graders offered viable strategies. These included taking trips through the mind in an effort to "relive" each Christmas or trying to remember other things about the dog that might spark some memories. Similarly, although kindergartners in the Kreutzer et al. (1975) study were able to produce some strategies when asked how they would remember to take their skates to school the next day, their responses were not as numerous, varied, or practical as those proposed by older children.

In addition to their difficulty in spontaneously naming potentially useful strategies, young children are also less knowledgeable than older children about the relative effectiveness of various strategies. Justice (1986) found a clear developmental progression in children's judgments of strategy effectiveness on a sort-recall task. Second-, fourth-, and sixth-graders judged the usefulness of four memory strategies (looking, naming, rehearsing, and categorizing) either before or after studying and recalling sets of stimuli. Children at all age levels judged rehearsal and categorization as more effective than looking or naming; however, only fourth-graders who had made strategy judgments prior to recalling items and sixth-graders in both conditions preferred categorization over rehearsal.

While most researchers have tended to view the development of declarative knowledge about memory and especially about strategies as complete by the age of 11 or 12, some researchers have noted that even college students frequently fail to be strategic, and are unaware of the most efficient strategies to use for particular tasks. Adults also fail to monitor performance and change their strategy use when it would be appropriate to do so (e.g. Shaughnessy

1981). In the next section we further explore developmental differences in monitoring.

Development of memory monitoring

The aspect of memory regulation that has received the most attention from developmental researchers is children's monitoring of their memory performance. This monitoring may take the form of initial strategy selection, of evaluation of the efficacy of the strategy being used, or an estimation of how much has been learned. Most of the research investigating memory monitoring examines children's prediction of their memory performance or children's allocation of effort in memory tasks.

As noted above, young children have difficulty estimating their memory abilities. In particular, young children usually overestimate the amount of material they are capable of remembering. In one of the classic studies in this area, children were asked to predict how many pictures they could recall in the correct order (Flavell et al. 1970). Preschoolers, kindergartners, second-, and fourth-graders were shown increasingly longer sets of pictures of objects and were asked if they could remember the order of the sequences. This procedure continued until the child indicated that she could not recall the long sequence correctly. As a comparison, each child's actual memory span was assessed using the same method. Results demonstrated that most of the younger children (preschoolers and kindergartners) believed they could recall a sequence of 10 pictures. In contrast, only 25 per cent of the older children (second and fourth graders) predicted they could remember a 10-item sequence. Although both groups overestimated their memory abilities, the gap between actual and predicted span for the older children was smaller than that of the younger children.

Why is it that younger children are not better able to predict and monitor their own memories? Schneider (1985) presents two hypotheses regarding this problem. First, perhaps the tasks used in these prediction studies are unfamiliar to young children, and thus they have difficulty accurately predicting their performance level in these novel situations. For example, if you were asked how many hieroglyphic symbols you could recall in the correct sequence, you might not be able to predict your memory span accurately due to your lack of experience. According to this hypothesis, predictions would be expected to be more similar across age groups for tasks that are relatively abstract for both younger and older children.

The other hypothesis offered by Schneider (1985) proposes that young children are unable to correctly estimate their memory span capacities because they rarely think about their own memories. However, Schneider points out that the evidence in support of this hypothesis is mixed at best (see Schneider 1985 for a review). Nevertheless, older children do appear to understand the limits of their memories better and are better judges of their memory span than younger children. Thus, knowledge of how best to monitor one's own memory appears to develop with increasing age.

The other area of research investigating age differences in memory monitoring centers around the amount of effort and attention children allocate for memorization. Ann Brown and her colleagues have studied children's attention allocation while "reading for remembering." In this paradigm, children are given a reading task with the goal of remembering the text for later recall. Because both comprehension and learning are required in order to successfully remember what has been read, the successful reader/learner monitors performance while reading. For example, if a paragraph is confusing or difficult to understand, the reader will slow down and might re-read. As Baker and Brown (1981) outlined, several steps are associated with reading for remembering. First, readers must differentiate between important and unimportant information. Then, the reader must decide if he or she has understood the material that was read. Finally, the reader selects a strategy to use if comprehension failure has occurred (e.g. re-read, ask for help). Certainly this complex skill requires much experience with various types of text to develop fully and function effectively.

A. L. Brown and Smiley (1978) tested the hypothesis that older readers would use these complex skills and additional time to increase their knowledge and understanding of the themes of a text. These researchers believed that older students, compared to younger students, would realize that more attention should be given to critical story themes and thus would spend more time and effort on such passages. Results indicated that while fifth-graders' knowledge of story themes did not increase with extra study time, seventh-graders and older students dramatically increased their understanding of story themes. In addition, younger children were more likely to include extraneous, unimportant ideas in their recall protocols than were older children, whose recall generally focused on phrases that the authors had established as more important. Thus, Brown and Smiley (1978) concluded that younger children were not able to use extra study time efficiently because of their failure to distinguish between important and unimportant ideas in the text.

Although knowledge of one's own memory span and knowledge of how much time to allot to studying are skills that develop with age, task difficulty and experience also factor in to the equation. For example, young children are more likely to demonstrate their memory monitoring abilities efficiently with tasks that are relatively easy and familiar to them. In fact, older children and even adults sometimes fail to monitor their performance if given a difficult, unfamiliar task. Thus, while age differences in memory monitoring are apparent, it is important to remain aware of the role of context in monitoring behavior and development.

Recent trends and future directions

A review of the literature revealed that although most early metamemory research was conducted by developmental psychologists who worked with children, much of the current work on metamemory comes from cognitive psychologists who focus on metacognitive processes in adults (e.g. Metcalfe & Shimamura 1994; Nelson 1996). Because the focus of this volume is development, we will limit our summary of recent work to developmental studies. However, we note in passing that research since the mid-1980s has considerably enriched our understanding of metacognitive processing in adults, and we look forward to the eventual application of this work to children.

We identified four new trends in metamemory research that we will discuss here. Whereas early research focused on measurement issues, the effect of metamemory and strategy instruction on recall performance, and age differences in metamemory, recent research has focused on the relationship between metamemory and school performance (e.g. Fusco 1996; Geary et al. 1989), domain differences in metamemory (e.g. Short et al. 1993; Weed et al. 1990) parents' fostering of metamemory development (e.g. Carr et al. 1989), and the relationship between metamemory and attributional beliefs. Each of these topics will be investigated in turn, and directions for future research and implications will be presented.

Metamemory and school performance

One new area of metamemory research involves applications of metacognitive theory to educational settings (e.g. Butterfield & Nelson 1989; Moely et al. 1986, 1995; Osman & Hannafin 1992; Pressley et al. 1989b). Both Pressley and Moely, with their colleagues, have undertaken very ambitious programs of evaluating effective instructional programs in public school systems. Pressley's work was conducted first in the Benchmark School, and then in the public schools in a Maryland county (e.g. Pressley et al. 1991, 1992). Results of these investigations nicely complement the theorizing that has taken place in the field of metamemory and strategy instruction since the mid-1970s.

Pressley et al. found that effective teachers in both studies regularly incorporated strategy instruction and metacognitive information about effective strategy selection and modification as a part of daily instruction. Strategy instruction was not conducted in isolation, but was viewed as an integral part of the curriculum, and thus was taught as *part* of language arts, mathematics, science, and social studies. Effective teachers did not emphasize the use of single strategies, but rather, the flexible use of a range of routines that corresponded to subject matter, time restraints, and other task demands. Much strategy instruction occurred in groups, with the teacher or children modeling effective learning techniques for other children. The work of both Pressley and Moely has greatly illuminated our understanding of strategy and metacognitive instruction in the classroom. These researchers' careful documentation of excellent instruction methods provides a valuable illustration of the interface between metamemory and strategies in children's everyday learning.

Other investigators have focused on the relationship between traditional measures of metamemory and children's school performance. For instance, Geary et al. (1989) investigated the relationship between metamemory and academic performance in second- and fourth-graders. Learning-disabled children comprised part of the sample. Students were administered a metamemory battery with five subtests: memory estimation, organized list, preparation object, study time for paired associates, and study time for circular recall. Although fourth-graders performed better than second-graders, children with learning disabilities did not perform differently from academically normal children. A modest link between metamemory skills and academic achievement was established for both second- and fourth-graders in this group assessment. For the younger children, scores on the preparation object subtest were moderately correlated with language, reading, and math achievement scores. For the fourth-graders, only a composite metamemory score was consistently correlated with achievement test performance.

Fusco (1996) conducted an interesting investigation of adolescents' metacognitive processing in the context of mathematical word problems. In this study, ninth-graders were asked to think aloud while solving a nonroutine math problem. Both think-aloud protocols and students' problem-solving behavior were used to identify metacognitive activities such as planning and exploration. Fusco found that students who attributed successful performance to the use of strategies were more likely to monitor and regulate their problem solving than other students. Her results with an academic task (i.e., a mathematical word problem) substantiate both the link between metacognition and strategy use, and the link between metacognition and attributional beliefs. The latter relationship is discussed in greater detail below.

Domain differences in metamemory

A second area of recent research in metamemory has focused on domain differences. The critical question driving most of this research is whether relationships among metamemory, strategy use, and memory performance vary across different types of metamemory knowledge. Several researchers (e.g. Lange et al. 1990; Short et al. 1993; Weed et al. 1990) have investigated the relationships between general metamemory (i.e., that in which assessment is not linked to a particular memory task) and task-specific metamemory. These investigators have hypothesized that task-specific metamemory would be more strongly related to memory performance than general metamemory, and that the relationship between task-specific metamemory and performance would appear at an earlier point developmentally than the relationship between general metamemory and memory.

Short et al. (1993) examined whether memory could be predicted by measuring the task-specific and general metamemory of average and low-achieving second, fourth, and sixth graders. These researchers found that average learners acquired task-specific knowledge more quickly than less-skilled learners. As the authors had hypothesized, regression analyses indicated that task-specific metamemory (e.g. "What did you do to help yourself remember the numbers in the game?") was a stronger predictor of memory performance than general metamemory.

A similar study conducted by Weed et al. (1990) also investigated task-specific and general metamemory as they relate to recall performance and academic causal attributions. Fourth graders were shown two lists of seven letters each and then were asked to recall the lists one letter at a time. Students were subsequently given instructions on strategy use, monitoring, both strategy and monitoring instructions, or no instructions. After an uninstructed post-test, students repeated a similar task using nonsense syllables in place of letters (i.e., near-transfer task), then in seven far-transfer trials, children were asked to locate the position in which a probe letter had been presented. Weed et al. found that whereas both general and task-specific metamemory were significantly related to recall on the near-transfer task, task-specific metamemory was more important for far-transfer performance.

Parents' fostering of metamemory development

A third new and exciting area of metamemory research involves the role that parental instruction plays in children's metamemory development. Carr and her colleagues (1989) examined cultural differences in the amount of instruction that German and American parents provided to their children at home. In addition, this study investigated the effects of parents' metacognitive instruction on children's skills. Third-graders participated in six sessions including a sort-recall memory task, a metacognitive test, strategy instructions, post-test memory and strategy assessment, and a six-month follow-up assessment of strategy maintenance. Participating parents completed questionnaires that assessed their fostering of children's flexible use of strategies and meta-cognitive development.

Carr et al. (1989) found that German parents, in contrast to US parents, reported more instruction of strategies, checked homework more often, and used games that promoted strategic thinking. These cultural differences in home instruction were accompanied by superior strategy use of German children on the memory tasks. Further, German parents' reported instruction correlated with their children's memory performance across tasks, whereas US parents' behaviors correlated only with the long-term recall of their children. Carr et al. concluded that parental instruction is an important avenue for children's metamemory development.

Metamemory and children's beliefs about effort

A fruitful area of research for both developmental and educational psychologists interested in children's cognitive performance has been attributional beliefs – the beliefs that children hold about their success and failure. As the classic work of Dweck (1975) and Weiner (1979) have illustrated, children's beliefs are adaptive when success is ascribed to stable, internal factors such as ability, and when failure is blamed on lack of effort or task difficulty. Children who consistently attribute failure to a lack of ability or success to chance are likely to show learned helpless behavior, giving up in the face of difficult tasks (Dweck & Elliott 1983).

As noted above, Borkowski, Pressley, and their colleagues (e.g. Borkowski 1990; Pressley et al. 1989a) have argued that attributional beliefs are integrally related to metacognition. One direction that metamemory research has gone since the mid-1980s is to further delineate the relationship between attributional beliefs about task outcomes and children's more general meta-memory knowledge. A number of the studies previously mentioned in this chapter included assessments of children's attributional beliefs (e.g. Fusco 1996; Kurtz & Borkowski 1984; Weed et al. 1990). In general, those studies indicate that children who are more successful on memory tasks and who possess richer metamemory knowledge are relatively more likely than peers to believe that their success is due to effort. However, as Pressley et al. (1987) have argued, effortful use of a task-appropriate strategy is the key to success; thus, instructing children to "try hard" in the face of failure will be helpful only if accompanied by appropriate strategy instruction. In fact, many of the most successful instructional efforts have incorporated information about the value of effort – therefore resulting in altered attributional beliefs.

In summary, the studies described in this section represent recent trends in metamemory research. Whereas the first decade of metamemory research focused on the metamemory–memory relationship, children's strategy use, and the value of metamemory in training studies, recent research has investigated links to academic performance, task-specific metamemory, parental instruction, and children's beliefs about effort. More work in these and other areas will further enrich our understanding of children and the ways in which they use experiences and exposure to different environments to enhance their own understanding of their mental processes.

Summary and conclusions

Metamemory is knowledge about and regulation of memory processes. The knowledge component of metamemory includes both declarative knowledge about memory functioning, and procedural knowledge about how to remember information. Metamemory has typically been assessed with interviews or questionnaires. Given the problems inherent in self-report measures, especially those that rely heavily on verbal report from young children, a number of investigators have developed metamemory measures that use picture stimuli, videotapes, or peer tutoring to assess children's knowledge.

While early reports on the metamemory–memory relationship were not overly optimistic, a careful examination of the area has indicated stable

295

memory–metamemory connections, especially for monitoring and perform-ance prediction. Metamemory has been a particularly useful construct when studying children's strategy use, and many investigators have incorporated metamemory information into training programs designed to enhance chil-dren's strategy use and memory performance.

Although preschoolers know less about memory processes than older chil-dren, they have been shown to have rudimentary knowledge about effort allo-cation and a strategic approach to remembering. Some specific ways in which metamemory changes across the elementary school years are in children's knowledge about tasks characteristics that influence performance, knowledge about and sophisticated use of strategies, and monitoring.

Metamemory research since the mid-1980s has examined the educational implications of metamemory theory, distinctions between general and task-specific metamemory, parental influences on children's metamemory devel-opment, and children's understanding of the role of effort in determining task outcomes. Future research may further illuminate the course of children's metamemory development, how home and school influences intermingle to shape that development, and how individual differences emerge in children's metamemory as their brains get bigger.

References

Baker, L. & A. L. Brown 1981. Metacognition and the reading process. In *A handbook of reading research*, D. Pearson (ed.). New York: Plenum.

Beal, C. R. 1985. Development of knowledge about the use of cues to aid prospec-tive retrieval. *Child Development* **56**, 631–42.

Belmont, J. M. & J. G. Borkowski 1988. A group test of children's metamemory. *Bulletin of the Psychonomic Society* **26**, 206–8.

Best, D. L. 1993. Inducing children to generate mnemonic organizational strategies: An examination of long-term retention and materials. *Developmental Psychology* **29**, 324–36.

Best, D. L. & P. A. Ornstein 1986. Children's generation and communication of mnemonic organizational strategies. *Developmental Psychology* **22**, 845–53.

Borkowski, J. G. 1985. Signs of intelligence: Strategy generalization and meta-cognition. In *The growth of reflection in children*, S. Yussen (ed.), 105–44. New York: Academic.

Borkowski, J. G., M. Carr, E. Rellinger, & M. Pressley 1990. Self-regulated cognition: Interdependence of metacognition, attributions, and self-esteem. In *Dimensions of thinking and cognitive instruction, Vol. I*, B. F. Jones & L. Idol (eds.), 53–92. Chicago: Association for Supervision and Curriculum Development.

Borkowski, J. G. & J. C. Cavanaugh 1979. Maintenance and generalization of skills and strategies by the retarded. In *Handbook of mental deficiency*, 2nd edn., N. R. Ellis (ed.), 569–618. Hillsdale, NJ: Erlbaum.

Borkowski, J. G., S. R. Levers, & T. M. Gruenenfelder 1976. Transfer of mediational strategies in children: The role of activity and awareness during strategy acquisition. *Child Development* **47**, 779–86.

Borkowski, J. G., V. Peck, M. K. Reid, & B. Kurtz 1983. Impulsivity and strategy transfer: Metamemory as mediator. *Child Development* **54**, 459–73.

Brown, A. L. 1978. Knowing when, where, and how to remember: A problem of metacognition. In *Advances in instructional psychology*, R. Glaser (ed.), 77–165. Hillsdale, NJ: Erlbaum.

Brown, A. L., J. D. Bransford, R. A. Ferrara, & J. C. Campione 1983. Learning, remembering, and understanding. In *Handbook of child psychology: Cognitive development*, P. H. Mussen (ed.), 77–166. New York: Wiley.

Brown, A. L. & S. S. Smiley 1978. The development of strategies for studying texts. *Child Development* **49**, 1076–88.

Brown, R. & D. McNeill 1966. The "tip of the tongue" phenomenon. *Journal of Verbal Learning and Verbal Behavior* **5**, 325–37.

Butterfield, E. C. & R. P. Ferretti 1987. Toward a theoretical integration of cognitive hypotheses about intellectual differences among children. In *Cognition in special children: Comparative approaches to retardation, learning disabilities, and giftedness*, J. G. Borkowski & J. D. Day (eds.), 195–233. Norwood, NJ: Ablex.

Butterfield, E. C. & G. D. Nelson 1989. Theory and practice of teaching for transfer. *Educational Technology Research and Development* **37**, 5–38.

Carr, M., B. E. Kurtz, W. Schneider, L. A. Turner, & J. G. Borkowski 1989. Strategy acquisition and transfer among American and German children: Environmental influences on metacognitive development. *Developmental Psychology* **25**, 765–71.

Cavanaugh, J. C. & J. G. Borkowski 1979. The metamemory–memory "connection": Effects of strategy training and maintenance. *Journal of General Psychology* **101**, 161–74.

Cavanaugh, J. C. & J. G. Borkowski 1980. Searching for metamemory–memory connections: A developmental study. *Developmental Psychology, 16*, 441–53.

Cavanaugh, J. C. & M. Perlmutter 1982. Metamemory: A critical examination. *Child Development* **53**, 11–28.

Cornoldi, C., C. Gobbo, & G. Mazzoni 1991. On metamemory–memory relationship: Strategy availability and training. *International Journal of Behavioral Development* **14**, 101–21.

Dweck, C. S. 1975. The role of expectations and attributions in the alleviation of learned helplessness. *Journal of Personality and Social Psychology, **31***, 674–85.

Dweck, C. S. & E. S. Elliott 1983. Achievement motivation. In *Handbook of child psychology, Vol. III*, P. Mussen & E. M. Heatherington (eds.), 643–91. New York: Wiley.

Dweck, C. S. & N. D. Reppucci 1973. Learned helplessness and reinforcement responsibility in children. *Journal of Personality and Social Psychology, **25***, 109–16.

Fatal, S. & S. Kaniel 1992. The influence of metamemory on transfer and durability of memory tasks. *Learning and Individual Differences* **4**, 91–102.

Flavell, J. H. 1971. First discussant's comments: What is memory development the development of? *Human Development* **14**, 272–8.

Flavell, J. H., A. Friedrichs, & J. Hoyt 1970. Developmental changes in memorization processes. *Cognitive Psychology* **1**, 324–340.

Flavell, J. H. & H. M. Wellman 1977. Metamemory. In *Perspectives on the development of memory and cognition*, R. V. Kail, Jr. & J. W. Hagen (eds.), 3–33. Hillsdale, NJ: Erlbaum.

Fusco, D. R. 1996. *Beyond effort: A look at strategy attributions in the domain of math-*

ematical problem solving. Paper presented at the annual meeting of the American Educational Research Association, New York.

Geary, D. C., I. H. Klosterman, & K. Adrales 1989. Metamemory and academic achievement: Testing and validity of a group-administered metamemory battery. *Journal of Genetic Psychology* **151**, 439–50.

Hart, J. T. 1965. Memory and the feeling-of-knowing experience. *Journal of Educational Psychology* **56**, 208–16.

Hasselhorn, M. 1990. The emergence of strategic knowledge activation in categorical clustering during retrieval. *Journal of Experimental Child Psychology* **50**, 59–80.

Justice, E. M. 1985. Categorization as a preferred memory strategy: Developmental changes during elementary school. *Developmental Psychology* **21**, 1105–10.

Justice, E. M. 1986. Developmental changes in judgments of relative strategy effectiveness. *British Journal of Developmental Psychology*, **4**, 75–81.

Justice, E. M. 1989. Preschoolers' knowledge and use of behaviors varying in strategic effectiveness. *Merrill-Palmer Quarterly* **35**, 363–77.

Kail, R. V., Jr. & J. W. Hagen (eds.) 1977. *Perspectives on the development of memory and cognition*. Hillsdale, NJ: Erlbaum.

Kelly, M., E. K. Scholnick, S. H. Travers, & J. W. Johnson 1976. Relations among memory, memory appraisal, and memory strategies. *Child Development* **47**, 648–59.

Kreutzer, M. A., C. Leonard, & J. H. Flavell 1975. An interview study of children's knowledge about memory. *Monographs of the Society for Research in Child Development* **40** (1, serial no. 159).

Kuhlmann, F. 1907. On the analysis of memory consciousness for pictures of familiar objects. *American Journal of Psychology* **18**, 389–420.

Kurtz, B. E. & J. G. Borkowski 1984. Children's metacognition: Exploring relations among knowledge, process, and motivational variables. *Journal of Experimental Child Psychology* **37**, 335–54.

Kurtz, B. E., M. K. Reid, J. G. Borkowski, & J. C. Cavanaugh 1982. On the reliability and validity of children's metamemory. *Bulletin of the Psychonomic Society* **19**, 137–40.

Lange, G., R. E. Guttentag, & R. E. Nida 1990. Relationships between study organization, retrieval organization, and general and strategy-specific memory knowledge in young children. *Journal of Experimental Child Psychology* **49**, 126–46.

Levin, J. R., S. R. Yussen, T. M. DeRose, & M. Pressley 1977. Developmental changes in assessing recall and recognition memory capacity. *Developmental Psychology* **13**, 608–15.

Metcalfe, J. & A. Shimamura 1994. *Metacognition: Knowing about knowing*. Cambridge, MA: Bradford.

Moely, B. E., S. S. Hart, L. Leal, K. Santulli, N. Rao, T. Johnson, & L. B. Hamilton 1992. The teacher's role in facilitating memory and study strategy development in the elementary school classroom. *Child Development* **63**, 653–72.

Moely, B. E., S. S. Hart, K. Santulli, L. Leal, T. Johnson, N. Rao, & L. Burney 1986. How do teachers teach memory skills? *Educational Psychologist* **21**, 55–71.

Moely, B. E., K. A. Santulli, & M. S. Obach 1995. Strategy instruction, metacognition, and motivation in the classroom. In *Memory performance and competencies*, F. E. Weinert & W. Schneider (eds.), 301–21. Mahwah, NJ: Erlbaum.

Moynahan, E. D. 1973. The development of knowledge concerning the effect of categorization upon free recall. *Child Development* **44**, 238–46.

Nelson, T. O. 1996. Consciousness and metacognition. *American Psychologist* **51**, 102–16.

Osman, M. E. & M. J. Hannafin 1992. Metacognition research and theory: Analysis and implications for instructional design. *Educational Technology Research and Development* **40**, 83–99.

O'Sullivan, J. T. 1993. Preschoolers' beliefs about effort, incentives, and recall. *Journal of Experimental Child Psychology* **55**, 396–414.

Paris, S. G., R. S. Newman, & K. A. McVey 1982. Learning the functional significance of mnemonic actions: A microgenetic study of strategy acquisition. *Journal of Experimental Child Psychology* **34**, 490–509.

Pressley, M. 1995. What is intellectual development about in the 1990s? Good information processing. In *Memory performance and competencies*, F. E. Weinert & W. Schneider (eds.), 375–404. Mahwah, NJ: Erlbaum.

Pressley, M., J. G. Borkowski, & J. T. O'Sullivan 1984. Memory strategy instruction is made of this: Metamemory and durable strategy use. *Educational Psychologist* **19**, 94–107.

Pressley, M., J. G. Borkowski, & J. T. O'Sullivan 1985. Children's metamemory and the teaching of memory strategies. In *Metacognition, cognition, and human performance*, *Vol. I*, D. L. Forrest-Pressley, G. E. McKinnon, T. G. Waller (eds.), 111–54. New York: Academic.

Pressley, M., J. G. Borkowski, & W. Schneider 1987. Cognitive strategies: Good strategy users coordinate metacognition and knowledge. In *Annals of Child Development*, *Vol. V*, R. Vasta & G. Whitehurst (eds.), 89–129. Greenwich, CT: JAI.

Pressley, M., J. G. Borkowski, & W. Schneider 1989a. Good information processing: What it is and what education can do to promote it. *International Journal of Educational Research* **13**, 857–67.

Pressley, M., I. W. Gaskins, E. A. Cunicelli, N. J. Burdick, M. Schaub-Matt, D. S. Lee, & N. Powell 1991. Strategy instruction at Benchmark School. *Learning Disability Quarterly* **14**, 19–48.

Pressley, M., F. Goodchild, J. Fleet, R. Zajchowski, & E. D. Evans 1989b. The challenges of classroom strategy instruction. *Elementary School Journal* **89**, 301–42.

Pressley, M., T. Schuder, J. L. Bergman, & P. B. El-Dinary 1992. A researcher–educator collaborative interview study of transactional comprehension strategies instruction. *Journal of Educational Psychology* **84**, 231–46.

Rao, N. & B. E. Moely 1989. Producing memory strategy maintenance and generalization by explicit or implicit training of memory knowledge. *Journal of Experimental Child Psychology* **48**, 335–52.

Ringel, B. A. & C. J. Springer 1980. On knowing how well one is remembering: The persistence of strategy use during transfer. *Journal of Experimental Child Psychology* **29**, 322–33.

Salatas, H. & J. H. Flavell 1976. Behavioral and metamnemonic indicators of strategic behaviors under remember instructions in first grade. *Child Development* **47**, 81–9.

Schneider, W. 1985. Developmental trends in the metamemory–memory behavior relationship: An integrative review. In *Cognition, metacognition, and human performance*, *Vol. I*, D. L. Forrest-Pressley, G. E. McKinnon & T. G. Waller (eds.), 57–109. New York: Academic.

Schneider, W. 1986. The role of conceptual knowledge and metamemory in the development of organizational processes in memory. *Journal of Experimental Child Psychology* **42**, 318–36.

Schneider, W., J. G. Borkowski, B. E. Kurtz, & K. Kerwin 1986. Metamemory and motivation: A comparison of strategy use and performance in German and American children. *Journal of Cross-Cultural Psychology* **17**, 315–36.

Schneider, W. & M. Pressley 1989. *Memory development between 2 and 20*. New York: Springer-Verlag.

Shaughnessy, J. J. 1981. Memory monitoring accuracy and modification of rehearsal strategies. *Journal of Verbal Learning and Verbal Behavior* **20**, 216–30.

Shiffrin, R. M. & W. Schneider 1977. Controlled and automatic human information processing. II. Perceptual learning, automatic attending, and a general theory. *Psychological Review* **84**, 127–90.

Short, E. J., C. W. Schatschneider, & S. E. Friebert 1993. Relationship between memory and metamemory performance: A comparison of specific and general strategy knowledge. *Journal of Educational Psychology* **85**, 412–23.

Sodian, B., W. Schneider, & M. Perlmutter 1986. Recall, clustering, and metamemory in young children. *Journal of Experimental Child Psychology* **41**, 395–410.

Waters, H. S. 1982. Memory development in adolescence: Relationships between metamemory, strategy use, and performance. *Journal of Experimental Child Psychology* **33**, 183–95.

Weed, K., E. B. Ryan, & J. Day 1990. Metamemory and attributions as mediators of strategy use and recall. *Journal of Educational Psychology* **82**, 849–55.

Weiner, B. 1979. A theory of motivation for some classroom experiences. *Journal of Educational Psychology* **71**, 3–25.

Wellman, H. M. 1977. Preschoolers' understanding of memory relevant variables. *Child Development* **48**, 1720–23.

Wellman, H. M. 1978. Knowledge of the interaction of memory variables: A developmental study of metamemory. *Developmental Psychology* **14**, 24–9.

Wellman, H. M. 1983. Metamemory re-visited. In *Trends in memory development research: Contributions to human development*, M. T. H. Chi (ed.), 31–51. Basel: Karger.

Yussen, S. R. & L. Berman 1981. Memory predictions for recall and recognition in first-, third-, and fifth-grade children. *Developmental Psychology* **17**, 224–9.

Yussen, S. R. & J. E. Bird 1979. The development of metacognitive awareness in memory, communication, and attention. *Journal of Experimental Child Psychology* **28**, 300–13.

Yussen, S. R., J. R. Levin, L. Berman, & J. Palm 1979. Developmental changes in the awareness of memory benefits associated with different types of picture organization. *Developmental Psychology* **15**, 447–9.

Yussen, S. R. & V. M. Levy 1977. Developmental changes in knowledge about different retrieval problems. *Developmental Psychology* **13**, 114–20.

CHAPTER 11

Children's eyewitness testimony: Memory development in the legal context

Jianjian Qin, Jodi A. Quas, Allison D. Redlich, and Gail S. Goodman

In June 1994, the New Jersey Supreme Court ruled that a defendant can request a taint hearing to assess the reliability of a child's testimony (*New Jersey v. Michaels* 1994). If, during the course of the taint hearing, a judge decides that the investigative interviews were seriously defective, the judge can exclude the child from testifying at trial and deny admission of the child's out-of-court statement (e.g. the child's statements to the police; Rosenthal 1995). When a case relies heavily on a child's eyewitness memory, as is often the situation when a child is the victim of sexual assault or attempted murder, the prosecution may not be able to proceed without the child's testimony. Children in New Jersey, apparently, are to be considered a special class of witnesses whose eyewitness memory is particularly suspect.

The New Jersey Supreme Court ruling mirrors several often-held beliefs: One is that children are more suggestible than adults; a second is that children's memory can be irrevocably distorted or even destroyed by suggestive interviews. For example, in their Amicus Brief for defense attorneys in the case of *New Jersey v. Michaels*, Bruck and Ceci wrote "in a variety of conditions, young children are more suggestible than adults with preschoolers being more vulnerable than any other age group" (1995: 273).

In the appeals of Michaels' original conviction, judges raised another often-held belief, one that concerns the use of protective measures in court to shield child witnesses from face-to-face confrontation. At the trial the children did not have to face the defendant because they testified via closed-circuit TV. The appeals court judges feared that the use of closed-circuit TV might have fostered inaccuracies in the children's testimony and biased the jurors to over-believe the child witnesses. Are these beliefs and concerns justified in light of contemporary research on children's eyewitness memory?

Developmental differences in eyewitness memory and suggestibility

Age differences in children's eyewitness memory and suggestibility are a common finding in child witness research, at least when young children are included in the studies. With some noted exceptions (e.g. Duncan et al. 1982; Flin et al. 1992), ample evidence has shown that in general, young children (e.g. 3-year-olds) tend to be less complete in their reports of experienced events and more suggestible than older children and adults (e.g. Goodman & Aman 1990; Goodman & Reed 1986; see Ceci & Bruck 1993; Saywitz & Goodman 1996 for reviews). For example, in a study conducted by Goodman and Aman (1990), 3- and 5-year-old children experienced a social interaction with a male confederate. About a week later, the children were tested under one of four recall conditions: re-enactment with anatomically detailed dolls, re-enactment with regular dolls, free recall with visual reminders ("cues") of the event, or free recall without visual cues. The children were also asked a variety of specific and misleading questions, some of them dealing with acts associated with child abuse. The results indicated that overall, 3-year-olds were more suggestible than 5-year-olds. That is, the younger children were more likely than the older children to acquiesce (e.g. say "yes") to questions that contained false information (misleading questions). In another study in which the subjects included victims of child maltreatment, 3- to 15-year-olds were asked questions about a medical examination they experienced 3 days earlier (Eisen et al. 1995). The proportion of correct answers was significantly lower for 3- to 5-year-olds than for 6- to 10-year-olds and 11- to 15-year-olds in response to all question types, including misleading questions and misleading abuse-related questions (e.g. "How many times did the doctor kiss you?"), indicating poorer memory performance and higher suggestibility in young children.

Despite age differences, most children nevertheless possess the cognitive capacity necessary for accurate testimony. Even 3-year-olds can provide accurate accounts of personally significant events, including their own victimization (Jones & Krugman 1986). Children's memory for salient, meaningful, and personally significant events can be quite good over a relatively long interval (Baker-Ward et al. 1993; Goodman et al. 1991b). Moreover, results concerning developmental trends in eyewitness memory and suggestibility are not always consistent. Age differences may diminish or even disappear under certain conditions. If an event is particularly salient or personally meaningful to children, the event may become highly memorable, and then even younger children can be quite resistant to suggestions about the main actions involved (Goodman et al. 1990). In the first scientific study to investigate children's memory for genital contact (the type of contact of particular concern in child sexual assault cases), Saywitz et al. (1991) examined children's memory for a physical check-up during which half of the 5- and 7-year-old children experienced genital touch. Age effects in children's free recall (i.e., to an open-ended question about what happened) and anatomically detailed doll demonstration were significant only for children in the nongenital condition. Moreover, age differences in memory and suggestibility can be the result of omission errors (i.e., children failing to report something that did indeed occur) or commission errors (i.e., children falsely reporting something that did not actually happen) (Saywitz et al. 1991), with the two types of errors having very different legal and psychological implications.

Mechanisms of age effects

Nearly all developmental theories would predict age differences in children's eyewitness memory and suggestibility, but many of the theories differ in predictions about children's ability to serve as reliable witnesses. Piagetian theory conceptualizes cognitive development as the acquisition of general cognitive competencies (Piaget 1983). Thus, according to this view, children must acquire a general cognitive ability before they can apply it to a specific domain. Based on this view, preschool- and even elementary-aged children were thought to be incompetent witnesses because of their illogical thinking and insufficient understanding of the moral implications of testimony. Information-processing theory has also been used to assert that children cannot remember events well. This view was based largely on the evidence that young children often perform poorly on certain laboratory-based memory tasks (e.g. remembering words and sentences) and that young children infrequently use memory strategies spontaneously (see Kail 1990 for review).

Neo-Piagetian theories such as that of Fischer (1980) would paint a less simplistic picture of children's eyewitness abilities. In Fischer's theory (1980), cognitive development is characterized as the development of various skills defined in terms of children's actions together with task situations. The skills in different domains develop fairly independently and thus often unevenly, although the highest level of ability a child can reach at any one point in time is constrained by developmental factors. In other words, children's cognitive ability can be significantly more advanced in certain domains than in others. According to this theory, children's memory performance may depend on the nature of the to-be-remembered event and the context of the situation. It can be inferred from this theory that, if the to-be-remembered event is familiar, meaningful, and personally significant, children may well be able to provide accurate memory reports, especially if the questions asked are simple and understandable, the child is not too upset, and the interviewers are supportive. Likewise, contextual approaches to cognitive development taken by developmentalists such as Vygotsky (see Flavell et al. 1993) and Nelson (1986) would make similar predictions.

To set the stage for understanding what might account for developmental trends in children's eyewitness memory and suggestibility, it is important to understand the mechanisms underlying the "misinformation effect." The misinformation effect refers to the phenomenon that introducing post-event misleading information may reduce subjects' (adults' or children's) performance on a subsequent memory test about the original event as compared to the performance of control subjects who receive neutral post-event information (e.g. Loftus 1979; Loftus et al. 1978). For example, if a child interacted with a person wearing a blue T-shirt (the original event) but was later asked a question such as "When you played with that person who was wearing a red T-shirt, what games did you play?", the misleading post-event information would be the false suggestion that the person was wearing a red T-shirt. A control subject might be asked instead "When you played with that person who was wearing a T-shirt, what games did you play?", a neutral question that contains no misinformation. Sometimes the misinformation or neutral information is presented not in a question but instead in the form of a post-event narrative read to or by the subjects, under the guise of reminding the subject about what happened. In either case, the subject would later either be asked to recall what the person was wearing or to indicate which of two pictures (one of a red T-shirt and one of a blue T-shirt) showed what was seen in the original event (Goodman et al. 1991; Loftus 1979). A certain percentage of subjects exposed to the misleading post-event information err on this final test, indicating that they actually experienced the misinformation in the original event.

One explanation for the misinformation effect is the memory impairment hypothesis: Post-event misleading information and original event information either "blend" together in memory (Loftus 1977), or misleading post-event information "over-writes" or replaces the memory for the original event, so that the memory for the original event is irrevocably lost (e.g. Loftus 1979; Loftus et al. 1978). Other researchers argue that misinformation effects could occur without post-event information affecting a person's ability to remember the original event (McCloskey & Zaragoza 1985; Zaragoza et al. 1987; Zaragoza & Koshmider 1989). For example, a misinformation effect could occur because of retrieval competition between post-event information and event information (e.g. subjects remember both the original and misleading information but the misleading information is stronger in memory because it is more recent and thus more accessible; Belli 1989; Bowers & Bekerian 1984), use of post-event information to fill in a memory gap (e.g. subjects fail to encode part of the original event and thus fill in the gap in their memory with the misinformation; McCloskey & Zaragoza 1985), or the power of demand characteristics (e.g. social influence factors that lead subjects to agree with the interviewer's false suggestion even though they remember the original event accurately; McCloskey & Zaragoza 1985). More recent studies generally point to the multi-mechanism nature of misinformation effects, that is, a confluence of all or several of the above mechanisms. However, at least under certain conditions such as long retention intervals, memory impairment (e.g. actual memory change) may occur as the result of misinformation (Belli et al. 1992, 1994).

The concept of memory trace, which relates closely to the memory impairment explanation of the misinformation effect, has attracted the attention of some developmental psychologists. A memory trace can be conceptualized as a set of integrated features that result from the processing activities carried out at the time of encoding (Brainerd & Reyna 1988). The features that represent the original event may become loose or disintegrated over time, which would allow easier incorporation or coexistence of post-event features. Thus, the post-event misinformation effect can vary as a function of the trace strength of the original information (Loftus 1979). According to some memory trace theorists, semantic or "gist"-like memory traces are more resistant to featural disintegration and consequently to the intrusion of suggested information than verbatim perceptual memory traces (Brainerd et al. 1990).

Thus, developmental differences in memory and suggestibility could arise if children are more likely to encode weaker and also more verbatim memory traces. A prediction based on the notion of trace strength is that if children's memory trace for an event is particularly strong (e.g. when young children's knowledge of a particular subject excels that of older children and adults, thus permitting stronger and more gist-like encoding), the developmental trend could diminish or even reverse (e.g. Duncan et al. 1982). However, more recent studies seem to suggest that the relation between children's suggestibility and trace strength may be more complex than originally thought. For example, Howe (1991) found that the misinformation effect is not directly related to the degree of memory strength. Furthermore, some researchers contend that memory impairment (e.g. incorporation of suggested post-event features into the trace of the original event) could occur as a function of the interaction between trace strength of the original event and the strength of the suggested information (Ceci & Bruck 1993; Howe 1991). Thus, memory impairment is more likely to occur when erroneous suggestion is particularly strong (e.g. through repeated suggestions) (Leichtman & Ceci 1995).

Another possible mechanism of the misinformation effect is failure to discriminate between different sources of memories (Belli et al. 1994; Zaragoza & Lane 1994). For example, in the study by Belli et al. (1994), adult subjects were asked free-recall questions about a witnessed event. They were warned that the post-event information included misleading information, and they were instructed to report both the information they witnessed and the information they received in the post-event narrative. The results showed that subjects not only performed poorer on misled items than on control items, but also misidentified the sources of their memory. Thus, even when subjects remember both original event information and post-event misinformation, confusion between the sources of their memories may still lead to a misinformation effect.

How do people identify the source of their "memories"? The reality monitoring model proposes that the reality status of a memory (i.e., real or imagined) is determined by a decision-making process which utilizes information about the memory itself (Johnson & Raye 1981). Johnson et al. (1993) extended the model into a framework for understanding the cognitive process by which people identify the sources of their memories. According to Johnson et al., source monitoring is based upon qualities of experience resulting from both perceptual and reflective processes. These qualities of experience (e.g. amount of perceptual detail in the memory) drive attributions as to whether the memory reflects an experienced event or one's imagination. The attribution process can either be conscious or unconscious. Like memory itself, source monitoring is subject to error and disruption. Thus under certain conditions, subjects may attribute imagined or suggested information to memory of experienced events.

The relation between young children's source monitoring abilities and suggestibility is difficult to examine because young children have difficulty understanding source monitoring questions (Poole & Lindsay 1995). However, it is conceivable that developmental differences in suggestibility may result if young children are less proficient than older children or adults in monitoring the sources of their memories. Generally, the ability to monitor memory sources improves with increasing age, but it may also be affected by other factors. Young children are found to be more likely to confuse different sources of their memories (Parker 1995). Ackil and Zaragoza (1995) compared first-, third-, and fifth-graders' and college students' abilities to monitor accurately the source of suggested information. Subjects viewed a short film and then listened to a summary that included information not in the film. The results showed that the first-graders made more source confusion errors (i.e., claiming to remember seeing suggested items) than third- and fifth-graders who, in turn, made more errors than college students. Young children also performed worse at remembering sources of actions they actually performed versus actions they only imagined themselves performing compared to older children and adults (Foley & Johnson 1985; Parker 1995). Trying to explain why source judgments are particularly difficult for young children, Lindsay et al. (1991) speculated that young children may be particularly vulnerable to the effects of source similarity. In a series of experiments, they demonstrated that although both children and adults are more likely to confuse sources when sources are highly similar (e.g. being asked to remember two female voices), source monitoring improves during the preschool and childhood years.

In summary, young children are, in general, less accurate in their witness reports and more susceptible to suggestion than older children and adults. The mechanism for the developmental differences in memory and suggestibility is likely to be multi-faceted. Despite their greater suggestibility, young children can be accurate in their reports and resistant to suggestion under a variety of conditions.

Children's developing event memory

Memory development is often described in terms of the development of memory strategies, metamemory, and knowledge (Flavell et al. 1993). Young children are less proficient memory strategy users than older children and adults. They are less likely to spontaneously produce memory strategies, such as mental rehearsal of an event, and even if they do (e.g. under instructions), they are less likely to benefit from memory strategies because using memory strategies *per se* may consume too much of their cognitive capacity (Case 1991). Children are also quite deficient in terms of metamemory. They often have undue confidence in their own memory. Preschoolers and first-graders believe that memory is invulnerable to suggestion (O'Sullivan et al. in press). When asked to make predictions about their own memory performance, young children often grossly overestimate the number of items they will be able to remember (Flavell et al. 1970).

Children's knowledge also influences their memory. The development of children's knowledge and memory for real-life events is closely related to their testimony and suggestibility because forensic interviews and court testimony are ultimately tests of children's memories for events (Brainerd & Ornstein 1991). In general, a stronger memory of the event should lead to more accurate testimony and greater resistance to suggestions (Goodman & Reed 1986), short of attempts of a witness to lie.

Ample studies have shown that children are capable of remembering simple components of event information very early in life. Meltzoff (1988) found evidence in 9-month-olds of deferred imitation of simple actions with novel objects. Mandler (1990) has shown that 11- to 13-month-olds can reproduce two- and three-action sequences that they only observed but did not perform days ago. The presence of deferred imitation suggests conscious recall in preverbal children (Bauer 1996; Mandler 1990). Evidence also indicates that even 16- and 20-month-old children can retain information about specifics of events and have the capacity to form distinct event memories (Bauer & Dow 1994). Furthermore, preverbal children's recall shares important characteristics with that of older children (Bauer & Mandler 1989). Specifically, preverbal infants can include temporal order information in their recall. They can also use order information to organize their recall and benefit from causal relationships between actions (Bauer & Mandler 1989, 1992). However, later in childhood and adulthood, long-term memory for events experienced in infancy and toddlerhood remains elusive. For instance, adults are unlikely to remember events experienced before the age of 2 to 3 years (Usher & Neisser 1993), a phenomenon called "infantile amnesia."

As children's linguistic ability develops, verbal recounting of their past experiences begins. With the assistance of adults' cuing and probing, 2- and 3-year-olds can provide accounts of episodes that they experience (Nelson 1992). Even without cuing or probing, young children at times provide spontaneous memory reports. Nelson (1991) described observations of a 2-year-old girl who recounted extensive and well-organized memories of ordinary everyday episodes from her daily life as pre-sleep monologues (i.e., talking to herself while falling asleep). At the age of 4, children can recall their trips to DisneyWorld experienced over one year ago (Hamond & Fivush 1991). Evidence also suggests that these young children's recall shares much of the structural organization evidenced in recall by older children and adults. For example, recall of routine real-life events by children as young as 3 years of age maintains much of the correct temporal order (Nelson 1986).

Despite young children's impressive performance, their event memory endures significant changes during preschool years. Although children around 2 or 3 years do have memories of past events, their memories are often fragmentary. Unlike older children or adults, who would consistently recall the core components (e.g. who, where, when, what) when asked to recall an event, children around age 2 tend to report different information across interviews and thus show greater inconsistencies (Fivush & Hamond 1990). These young children also appear to lack a general plan or scheme for memory probing, thus extensive cuing and probing by others is often necessary to elicit their memories. Adults', especially parents', guidance plays an important role in children's event memory development (Fivush & Hamond 1990; Goodman et al. 1994).

Children's knowledge increases steadily over the preschool years (Flavell et al. 1993). A particularly important and useful type of knowledge is called a "script," which is an abstract and generic description about the temporal and causal sequences of recurring events (Farrar & Goodman 1990, 1992; Nelson 1986). A script is a set of mental expectations that contains slots for agents, actors, and actions for the events. When a real-life event is encountered, the slots are instantiated (i.e., filled in) by specific episodes of the event. Once a script is activated, script-consistent information is often blended into a general representation, while script-inconsistent information is stored separately and often becomes more memorable. Thus, script knowledge about recurring events (e.g. What happens when one goes to McDonald's) helps children retain memory for specific events. Studies show that even young children are able to form scripts and utilize script knowledge, but they are often less efficient in forming scripts compared to older children and adults and show more merging of or confusion between related script information (Farrar & Goodman 1990, 1992). There is also evidence that young children are more likely than older children to recall generic script information in place of the specifics of their one-time experiences (e.g. Fivush 1984). This could potentially lead to errors in children's testimony about a specific event even though they may still be accurate about the general recurring event pattern or gist. A more serious error can occur when part or all of the script has been suggested by adults who provide misinformation and when the child then recounts such information as if it were part of an experienced event (Poole & Lindsay 1995).

In regard to children's knowledge and scripts, it is important to note that most young children lack precise sexual knowledge or scripts for sexual acts (Gordon et al. 1990). Thus, they tend to lack the knowledge base needed to make false reports of such acts as sexual abuse on their own (but see Boat & Everson 1994, regarding cultural differences in children's sexual knowledge). Nevertheless, at least by the age of 4 or 5 years, children seem to recognize the inappropriateness of sexual acts, and such realization may help bolster their resistance to abuse-related false suggestions compared to suggestions about more trivial events (Goodman et al. 1990; Rudy & Goodman 1991).

In summary, children develop event memory very early in their lives. Although such memories may still be fragile and although children often need adults' guidance in organizing and probing memory, children of very young age (e.g. 3- to 4-year-olds) are capable of providing accurate memory of events they experienced before, although certain types of errors can also occur.

Repeated interviews and questions

Multiple interviews and repetition of questions within interviews are common experiences for child witnesses in the American legal system (Whitcomb 1992). Repeated interviewing of child witnesses could lead to many deleterious effects, such as increases in the stress children experience during legal involvement (Goodman et al. 1992), heightened suggestibility (Poole & Lindsay 1995), and greater opportunities for inconsistencies in their reports (Fivush & Shukat 1995). However, under certain conditions, repeated interviews can have beneficial effects on children's eyewitness performance. One prominent finding from traditional laboratory studies of memory is that repeated testing often leads to improved memory performance. It is possible, at least theoretically, that repeated interviews and repetition of questions could improve children's eyewitness memory (Brainerd & Ornstein 1991). Repetition preserves memory against forgetting. Thus, providing that the initial memory is accurate, repeated recall is likely to enhance retention. In addition, information not reported in earlier interviews can sometimes be successfully recalled later. In a experiment by Dent and Stephenson (1979, but see Poole & White 1995), 10- and 11-year-olds viewed a film depicting a theft. They were then either interviewed on four different occasions, on one occasion, or received no interview before the final interview two months later. In every interview, children were asked to provide a free-recall recounting of the film. The results showed that children who received prior interviews recalled more correct information than those who did not, but the amount of incorrect information did not differ among conditions. In another study (Goodman et al. 1991a), 3- to 4-year-olds' and 5- to 7-year-olds' memory for inoculations was examined. They were interviewed about the inoculation either once after a 4-week delay or twice, following 2- and 4-week delays. Although repeated interviews did not affect free recall, children who received an interview at the 2-week delay were more accurate on specific questions about the person and room, and on abuse-related questions. A study by Warren and Lane (1995) also showed that initial neutral questioning can reduce susceptibility to leading questions in later interviews for both adults and children, although adults benefited more from prior questioning.

What if initial interviews include misleading questions? Will misleading information be incorporated into later answers? In a study conducted by Cassel and Bjorklund (1995), 6-year-olds, 8-year-olds, and adults received either negative leading questions (suggesting an incorrect answer), positive leading questions (suggesting a correct answer), or neutral questions 1 week after they viewed a videotaped event. They were tested again 1 month from the original event. The results revealed no effect of prior leading questions on free recall 1 month later; the patterns of both correct and incorrect recall were the same among conditions for all ages groups. However, responses to specific leading questions were affected by prior exposure to leading questions. The results of this study suggest that a single exposure to leading questions may not necessarily bias subjects' subsequent recollections, and that free recall is particularly immune from detrimental effects of leading questions.

Repeated exposure to misleading information, however, can lead to serious effects on children's eyewitness reports (Lewis et al. 1995). When suggestions are repeated, their strength is likely to increase. In the study by Warren and Lane (1995), for example, children who experienced two interviews of suggestive questioning made significantly more errors even in their free recall than children who had only one interview of suggestive questioning. In the "Sam Stone" study by Leichtman and Ceci (1995), 3- to 6-year-old children received four bi-weekly interviews under one of four conditions after an uneventful, brief visit by a stranger named Sam Stone: no suggestion, no stereotype (control condition); stereotype but no suggestion; suggestion but no stereotype; and suggestion plus stereotype. Ten weeks after Sam's visit, all children received a final interview in which open-ended questions were asked. Children in both the stereotype condition and suggestion condition provided some false reports about Sam's action, but children who were in the suggestion plus stereotype condition made the highest portion of false reports. However, despite repeated interviews (without suggestion), children in the control group provided accurate accounts of Sam's visit.

Repetition of free recall questions can also facilitate children's eyewitness performance (Poole & White 1995). However, when specific questions are repeated within interviews, both adult and child witnesses may perceive a pressure to change their answers or to speculate about missing information, and young children are more susceptible to this effect. In a study by Poole and White (1991), adults and 4-, 6-, and 8-year-olds first observed an event. They were then asked open-ended questions, specific yes-no questions, and questions that could be answered only by speculation. All the questions were repeated three times in succession. The results indicated that repetition of general open-ended questions did not increase the amount of incorrect information. However, in response to specific yes-no questions, 4-year-old children were less consistent than older children and adults, indicating a greater tendency to shift their answers. A more dramatic example is provided by an experiment conducted by Warren et al. (1991), in which they repeated suggestive questions two times. After subjects answered the first round of questions, they were given explicit negative feedback ("You did not get all of those questions exactly right. Let's try it again."). Both adults and children shifted their answers on the second trial, but children were significantly more likely to change their answers.

In sum, multiple interviews and repetition of questions can have both beneficial and detrimental effects on children's eyewitness performance. Repeated interviews and questions *per se* do not appear to negatively affect children's memory and suggestibility, providing that prior interviews are competently conducted. However, repeated exposure to misleading questions can lead to significant increases in incorrect responses, especially among young children.

Stress, trauma, and memory

An important factor to consider when evaluating children's eyewitness capabilities is the effect of stress on memory. Children typically testify about stressful events involving their own victimization. Throughout the history of psychology, different theories have been put forth to explain the relation between stress and memory (Christianson 1992; Easterbrook 1959; Freud 1938; Rapaport 1942). These theories include clinically based explanations originally proposed at the turn of the century, such as Freud's idea that traumatic events can be repressed and Janet's (Putnam 1989) idea that trauma may cause a dissociative state in which traumatic memories are stored separately from other memories (Terr 1991). These ideas have witnessed a strong comeback in recent decades. Unfortunately, empirical research has yet to demonstrate unequivocal support for any one theory.

Three theories
Three theories concerning the relation between stress and memory have received considerable attention: repression, dissociation, and the flashbulb memory hypothesis. Repression was originally put forth by Freud as one of several defense mechanisms that serve to protect a person's ego from unacceptable information. Specifically, Freud proposed that when a person encounters a trauma, he or she may engage in an automatic, unconscious process of forcing the traumatic information out of conscious awareness (Freud 1915/1957). Although the repressed information is not consciously accessible to the person,

it may "leak out" and express itself indirectly through dreams, behaviors, neuroses, and other psychological difficulties. Freud originally proposed that one important type of trauma that adults often repress is past experience of child sexual abuse. Later, Freud modified his view to emphasize the role of child sexual fantasy. However, more recent theory and research has focused attention again on actual traumas in relation to repressed memory (e.g. Briere & Conte 1993; Herman & Schatzow 1987; Williams 1994, 1995). Thus, repression theories would predict that a negative relation exists between trauma and memory with extremely stressful events that are unacceptable to consciousness being inaccessible to memory, though not forgotten. In addition, according to this theory, repressed memories can gain access to consciousness under certain conditions (e.g. in emotionally supportive, therapeutic situations). In a number of controversial legal cases, adults claimed to have recovered formerly repressed memories of child abuse or murder. Although scientific evidence suggests that some traumatic childhood events, such as sexual abuse, can be forgotten by the time adulthood is reached (Williams 1994, 1995), there is also reason to believe that false memories of childhood trauma can be induced in a certain percentage of the adult population (Bottoms et al. 1996; Hyman et al. 1995; Loftus & Pickerell 1995; Qin et al. in press; but see Pezdek & Chantal 1994).

Dissociation theories are similar to repression theories in asserting that traumatic childhood events can become lost to consciousness. However, the mechanism differs. Dissociative responses are believed to arise as a coping mechanism for trauma. Pretending to be somewhere else during an inescapable traumatic event would be an example of a dissociative reaction. Proponents of this view believe that, when dissociation occurs, a separate memory can be formed for the traumatic event, that is, a memory that is not linked to normal consciousness. Thus, lost memory of a childhood trauma can result. Although dissociative tendencies do appear to be linked to childhood abuse (Putnam et al. 1993), at present, there are no adequate tests of dissociation as a mechanism for memory loss.

In contrast to the above two notions, the "flashbulb memory" hypothesis makes an opposite prediction about the relation between stress and memory. The flashbulb memory hypothesis, originally outlined by Brown and Kulik (1977), posits that highly charged emotional events form picture-like representations in memory. The memories contain vivid and durable information about specific circumstances surrounding the event, such as the time of day, the location, any ongoing activity, what clothes the person was wearing, and his or her affective experiences (Bohannon 1988; Bohannon & Symons 1993; Brown & Kulik 1977). According to this view, not only are significant details remembered quite vividly, but also the memories are quite resistant to forgetting, even over lengthy retention intervals. Thus, according to flashbulb memory notions, extreme stress can have a positive effect on memory by helping to create durable, picture-like representations of stressful events.

Despite the intuitive appeal of these theories, there are shortcomings to them all. First, whether repression exists is still heavily debated (e.g. Loftus 1994). In addition, it is often impossible to determine whether a flashbulb or recovered repressed or dissociated memory is accurate or not. Furthermore, not everyone agrees that flashbulb memories are impervious to forgetting (McCloskey 1993). Nor are the mechanisms that control repression, dissociation, or the formation of picture-like representations well described or empirically tested, and some propose that special memory mechanisms for traumatic events are not necessary at all (Hembrook & Ceci 1995). Finally, none of these theories makes direct predictions about moderate levels of stress. Rather they are concerned with highly traumatic or shocking information. Therefore, although the theories make interesting predictions, testing the theories' predictions has proven much more difficult.

Research on stress and memory in children

Conducting sound empirical research on stress and memory is a challenging task. For obvious ethical reasons, researchers cannot induce high levels of stress in subjects, especially children. Developmentalists have therefore taken advantage of naturally occurring stressors in children's lives, such as medical experiences or natural disasters, and examined children's memories for these events.

Some research has revealed a beneficial effect of stress on children's recall (e.g. Goodman et al. 1991b, Study 3; Oates & Shrimpton 1991). For example, Goodman et al. (1991b) examined children's memory for doctor visits. A positive relation between stress and memory was uncovered. In this study, the researchers compared memory reports of children who received an inoculation to those of a group of children who had a design rubbed on their arms instead of the inoculation. Children who were inoculated recalled less incorrect information than children who only had designs put on them.

Other research has uncovered a negative relation between stress and memory (Bugental et al. 1992; Merritt et al. 1994; Peters 1991). In one study, children were asked to recall a woman who had entered their classroom when either a fire alarm sounded or a radio was turned on (Peters 1991). Children who heard the alarm were worse at identifying the woman than children who heard the radio. Merritt et al. (1994) examined children's memory for a medical procedure, called voiding cystourethrogram fluoroscopy (VCUG), that involves invasive genital contact (i.e., children received urethral catheterization). The procedure, prescribed by physicians to identify kidney problems, is often frightening, painful, and embarrassing. Merritt et al. (1994) found that observers' ratings of children's stress levels during the procedure were negatively associated with children's later memory.

Still other research has failed to find any relation between stress and memory (Eisen et al. 1995; Goodman et al. 1991b, Study 1; Howe et al. 1995). For example, even in the Merritt et al. (1994) study of children's memory for VCUG just described, although observer ratings of children's stress were negatively associated with children's recall, children's salivary cortisol levels (often taken as a biological indicator of stress) were not related to memory performance. Likewise, Goodman et al. (1991b, Study 1) rated children's stress levels as they were getting blood drawn and failed to find any relation between stress and later memory for the venipuncture.

One explanation for discrepancies across the stress and memory research relies on the Yerkes-Dodson law (Yerkes & Dodson 1908) and on the centrality of information in relation to the stressor (Christianson 1992; Easterbrook 1959). The Yerkes-Dodson law posits that an inverted "U" relation exists between arousal and performance such that increases in arousal benefit performance up to a point, but that further increases in arousal inhibit performance. In regard to stress and memory, Easterbrook (1959) also proposed that an inverted "U" relation exists between stress and memory, but Christianson (1992) further specified that this relation applied only to peripheral information. Specifically, as stress begins to increase, memory is enhanced. But once stress increases beyond an optimal level, attentional focus narrows such that peripheral information is omitted. According to Christianson, central information directly related to the stressor is retained well in memory even at extremely high stress levels.

Easterbrook's (1959) proposal about an inverted "U" relation along with Christianson's (1992) extension about the narrowing of attentional focus provide a partial explanation for some contradictory findings across the stress and memory literature. For example, in the study described earlier in which children were worse at remembering a woman if a fire alarm sounded than if a radio was turned on (Peters 1991), the woman was unrelated to the cause of the stress (i.e., the fire alarm). Therefore, the negative relation between stress and memory may have been because the to-be-remembered event was a peripheral component of the stressful event. On the other hand, the positive relation between stress and memory observed in Goodman et al.'s (1991b) study may have been due to the to-be-remembered event also being the source of stress. Additionally, in another of Goodman et al.'s (1991b) studies, the researchers compared children's memory for central information (e.g. whether the person who gave them a shot was a man or woman) and peripheral information (e.g. whether pictures were on the wall in the exam room) about the inoculation they experienced. Children recalled central information better than peripheral information, but this trend occurred regardless of stress level.

However, not all stress and memory results can be explained in terms of centrality of the to-be-remembered information (Vandermaas et al. 1993). Vandermaas et al. asked children central and peripheral questions about what happened during a dental visit. Contrary to Christianson's (1992) proposal, children who were more stressed during the dental exam did *not* evidence worse recall of peripheral information than children who were less stressed. As has been the case with the Yerkes-Dodson law, it is difficult to determine the optimal stress level for memory, and thus a variety of findings could be interpreted as support for the theory. For example, a positive relation between stress and memory could mean that the stress was at a low level, and a negative relation could indicate that the stress was at a high level, but such interpretations quickly become *post hoc* and circular. Additionally, what is central and peripheral for children may vary considerably from what is central and peripheral for adults. Therefore, although a distinction between central and peripheral information may be useful at times, research to date indicates that the effects of stress on children's memory are not adequately explained by this dichotomy.

Individual differences

The lack of consistent findings across the stress and memory literature has led some developmentalists to look in new directions and answer the question "What *affects* the relation between stress and memory", rather than the question "What *is* the relation between stress and memory." This recent line of research is concerned with identifying individual difference variables that affect both how stressed children become during a particular experience and how well they recall that experience (e.g. Goodman et al. 1994; Stein & Boyce 1995; Steward 1993). Some potentially important factors include children's temperament (Merritt et al. 1994), children's physiological reactivity (Stein & Boyce 1995), and parent-child interaction styles (Goodman et al. 1994).

Both parent–child interaction styles and children's temperament have been related to children's stress during a medical experience as well as to their memory for the procedure (Goodman et al. 1994; Merritt et al. 1994). In a study of children's memory for the VCUG procedure, Goodman and her colleagues investigated the effects of parent–child communication and interaction on children's later memory (Goodman et al. 1994; Goodman & Quas 1996). The researchers observed children undergoing the VCUG procedure and rated children's stress levels. Between 1 and 3 weeks later, children were interviewed about what happened. The researchers obtained judgments from parents concerning their relationship styles and how mothers had comforted and talked with their children since the procedure's occurrence. The results indicated that mothers who were emotionally supportive (e.g. who comforted their children following the medical test) had children who were less upset during the VCUG and who evidenced better memory. On the other hand, mothers who ignored their children and did not provide emotional support had children who tended to make increased errors during the memory test. In Merritt et al.'s (1994) study of children's memory for the VCUG procedure, temperament measures were associated with children's distress during the medical test and their memory performance later. Specifically, children who scored higher on adaptability and approach-withdrawal tendencies were rated by technicians as being less upset during the VCUG and evidenced better recall than children who scored lower on these two temperament indices (lower scores on approach-withdrawal indicate tendencies to avoid new social circumstances).

Although these studies tapped only a subset of potential individual differences, they provide considerable insight into possible explanations for the "now-you-see-it, now-you-don't" results in the literature concerning the relation between stress and memory. As studies of individual difference variables imply, the relation between stress and memory is probably dependent upon other mediating factors that lead some children to evidence better recall for stressful events and other children to evidence worse recall for stressful events. Because this is a new area of research, there is still much to learn about the ways in which individual differences affect children's stress levels, and how these mediating factors interact with one another to influence children's stress and memory. It is likely, however, that individual difference variables determine or reflect variability in children's interpretations of events, which in turn affects memory.

Context and demand effects

Ideally, witnesses answer questions honestly based on accurate memory. However, the context of the interview situation can, at times, influence the accuracy of witnesses' reports and their suggestibility during an interview, regardless of accurate memory. These contextual influences or "demand characteristics" serve as cues that indicate, directly or indirectly, what the appropriate response should be in a particular situation. These cues can affect what a child (or even an adult) believes are the correct answers and how important it is to answer questions in accordance with the implied correct responses. Repeated questioning, as discussed previously, can create one type of demand characteristic in that children may interpret the repeated question as an indication that their first response was incorrect. Other demand characteristics include the authority status of an interviewer, the presentation style of the interviewer, and the accusatory context of a forensic interview.

Children and adults tend to be more suggestible when a person with authority provides misinformation (e.g. Loftus 1979). For children, having an adult rather than a child provide misinformation can increase suggestibility. In Ceci et al.'s (1987) study, children falsely acquiesced more frequently after exposure to an adult interviewer's misleading questions than they did after a child interviewer's misleading questions. There are many reasons why children may acquiesce to adult interviewers' suggestions. First, from early in their lives, children are taught that adults are authority figures. Children may try to please an adult interviewer by answering questions in manners consistent with how the questions were phrased (Walker 1994). Second, children learn basic conversation rules early. They know that, when an adult asks them a question, they should provide an answer. As such, children may try to provide answers to questions they are asked, even if they do not understand the questions or if they do not or could not know the answers (e.g. Saywitz 1995; Winer & McGlone 1993).

The presentation style of the interviewer can also affect the accuracy of children's memory reports. Some legal scholars fear that children's suggestibility increases when interviewers are too supportive because children will then try to please the interviewers. However, empirical research is less clear as to the effect of interviewer support on suggestibility. In fact, in some studies, the opposite appears true: Children's suggestibility decreases when they are interviewed by a warm interviewer (Carter et al. 1996; Goodman et al. 1991a; Moston 1990). For example, Goodman et al. examined children's memory for an inoculation and varied whether the children were questioned by a cold interviewer (e.g. one who did not maintain eye contact, smile, or encourage children and who kept a closed-body posture) or a warm interviewer (one who maintained open-body posture, eye contact, and a pleasant face and gave children positive feedback during the interviewer). Goodman (1991a) et al. found that the children who were questioned by the cold interviewer made more memory errors and were more suggestible than children who were interviewed by the warm interviewer. In a study by Goodman et al. (1995b), mother interviewers solicited more accurate free recall from their children than did stranger interviewers when both groups of interviewers were misled about the actual event. Presumably, the children felt more comfortable with their mothers than with the strangers, which helped the children maintain accuracy.

Finally, the accusatory context of a forensic investigation can affect children's perceptions of their experiences as well as their responses to questions. The forensic setting can include being questioned by police officers or social workers, understanding that there is an investigation because something bad may have happened, and knowing who may have done the bad things or what those things may have been. These contextual factors can influence children's perceptions of their earlier experiences, how they talk about their experiences, and the accuracy of their statements (Tobey & Goodman 1992). To examine the effects of forensic context on children's memory, Tobey and Goodman examined 4-year-old children's memory for a play session they experienced with an adult male. Prior to the memory interview, a police officer told some children that something bad may have happened when they played with the man (the forensic context condition). During the interview, children who were told that something bad may have happened made more errors than children who were not provided with this information. Interestingly, although the police officer implied that something bad happened, most children did not report that anything bad actually happened or indicate the man with whom they played did something bad. In fact, when individual children's reports were examined, only two children out of thirteen who were assigned to the forensic context condition made decidedly false reports about specific bad things happening, and only one of these two children implicated the man as doing something bad. Morever, to abuse-related questions, only one child

317

made an error: He agreed that the man kissed him when in fact the man had not done so. Aside from this one error, the children were highly accurate in answering the abuse-related questions despite the police officer's suggestion that something bad had happened.

In summary, many aspects of an interview can influence children's accuracy and suggestibility. Being asked questions by an adult stranger can increase children's suggestibility or lead children to try to answer questions they do not know or understand. On the other hand, contrary to some popular beliefs, a warm and supportive interviewer does not generally appear to increase children's suggestibility during an interview. Rather, children may actually be more suggestible when an interviewer is cold and unsupportive. The accusatory context of a forensic interview may also affect the accuracy of children's reports.

Given that many types of demand characteristics are often unavoidable, it is crucial to determine if interviewers can find ways to combat these social influences. Although researchers have begun to examine the effects of different types of instructions to children prior to the interview, such as ensuring children know that it is all right to say "I don't know" or giving children practice interviews (e.g. Geiselman et al. 1993; Saywitz & Snyder 1993), more research is clearly needed, especially research with preschool-aged children.

Facilitating children's performance

Numerous techniques have been developed to help children recall information of value to the legal system. Some of these innovations alter the ways in which children are questioned, with the goal of avoiding highly leading questioning and reducing the number of times children are interviewed.

Interview procedures

Guidelines and procedures have been developed to enhance accurate memory reports while at the same time decrease inaccurate reports. For example, one set of guidelines appeared in the late 1980s that dealt with ways to utilize anatomically detailed dolls in interviews to obtain information from children without unduly influencing their reports (Boat & Everson 1988). Other techniques deal specifically with the types of verbal prompts used to elicit information. Recently, two procedures have received considerable attention in the child witness arena. One is called the step-wise interview and the other is the cognitive interview.

The step-wise interview consists of guidelines to help minimize inaccurate reports from children (Yuille et al. 1993). The interview begins by asking a child free-recall questions (e.g. "Tell me what happened when. . .") about a particular experience. Next, the child is asked a series of directive questions which are designed to clarify and elaborate on her or his free-recall responses. According to the step-wise procedure, the directive questions should be as open-ended as possible and probe for increasingly specific information based on the child's earlier responses. Thus, if a child mentioned that he or she was playing during free recall, an appropriate follow-up directive question might be: "Tell me more about what you played?" An inappropriate follow-up directive question would be: "What games did you and the man play?" if during free recall the child had not mentioned playing games with any man. This procedure has been adopted by the UK as the formal method of interviewing young children for investigative purposes (see also Bull 1995). There have been few rigorous evaluations of the step-wise interview, however.

The other method of enhancing witnesses' reports that has received considerable attention is the cognitive interview (CI). The CI was originally developed to enhance adults' eyewitness testimony (Geiselman et al. 1984) and, since the mid-1980s, it has been adapted for use with children (e.g. McCauley & Fisher 1995; Saywitz et al. 1992). Briefly, the CI consists of four retrieval methods, each of which is designed to increase the amount of information recalled: (a) mentally reconstructing the situational and personal context of the original event; (b) reporting everything, even partial information that seems trivial; (c) recounting the event in a variety of orders (e.g. What happened next? or What happened right before that?); and (d) reporting the event from other prominent people's perspectives (e.g. Put yourself in the body of _____ and tell me what you would have seen or heard if you had been that person). In addition, the CI provides guidelines to help witnesses recall specific information about appearance, speech characteristics, conversations, names, and numbers.

Some studies indicate that the CI can be effective in eliciting information from children about their experiences (Geiselman et al. 1993; McCauley & Fisher 1995; Saywitz et al. 1992). For example, in one study, 7- to 11-year-old children experienced a staged, private event with an adult male confederate (Saywitz et al. 1992). Two days later children were interviewed by off-duty detectives who employed either a standard interview or the CI procedure. Both interviews began with free narrative questions about "what happened," which were followed by direct questions. For the CI condition, CI questions were interspersed within the direct questions (e.g. after children responded to a particular question, the CI interviewer would prompt for more information by saying "What happened right before that?"). When children appeared to have exhausted their memory of some aspect of the event, the CI interviewers instructed children to take the perspective of another prominent person (e.g. the adult male confederate) and asked children to answer the questions according to that person's viewpoint. The CI significantly increased the number of correct facts children reported compared to the standard interview condition, and there were no differences between the standard interview and CI in the number of incorrect facts children reported. Furthermore, no significant differences emerged between the conditions in how many direct questions children were asked. Thus, the increase in the amount of correct information children provided with the CI compared to the standard interview cannot be attributed to a greater number of questions in the CI.

Although the CI appears promising in increasing older children's and adults' reports, there may be age limits on its utility (Bekerian & Dennett 1995; Saywitz et al. 1992). Specifically, given young children's limited cognitive capabilities, they may not understand some of the CI retrieval methods. For example, it is not until children are beyond the preschool years (i.e., 5 or 6 years old) that they can consistently take another person's perspective in a variety of situations. Piaget was one of the first researchers to document children's lack of perspective-taking capabilities, and this inability is one of the hallmarks of the preoperational stage of development (Piaget & Inhelder 1956). Although recent researchers have shown that young children can perform some perspective taking tasks, young children are typically only successful when the task is familiar, simple, and in the present tense (Flavell 1995; Flavell et al. 1981). Thus, asking children to explain what happened during a particular event according to someone else's point of view may be too difficult for young children to understand and perform. In support of the view that developmental limitations exist in the utility of the CI, Memon et al. (1993) interviewed 6- and 7-year-olds with or without the CI. The researchers found that the CI was only partially effective in enhancing children's reports because not all children understood the CI procedures.

Anatomically detailed dolls (AD dolls)

The use of anatomically detailed dolls (dolls with genitalia), has been an especially controversial issue in forensic interviews with suspected child sexual abuse victims (Koocher et al. 1995). Proponents of using AD dolls believe that the dolls help children demonstrate sexual experiences that they either cannot or are not willing to describe verbally (Boat & Everson 1988, Landers 1988). Opponents of the use of the dolls believe that exposing dolls' genitals leads nonabused children to make false reports about abuse, especially when leading questions are also asked (Bruck et al. 1995; Ceci & Bruck 1995).

At present, research indicates that whether or not AD dolls are useful or harmful to children's eyewitness memory reports depends on a number of factors. Some of the factors that contribute to the effectiveness or harmfulness of AD dolls include children's cognitive capabilities (e.g. DeLoache & Marzolf 1995) and the type of information to be recalled (Goodman et al. 1995a; Saywitz et al. 1991).

DeLoache and her colleagues have conducted a number of studies that indicate very young children, particularly those below 3.5 years, have difficulties using dolls as symbols of themselves during a memory task (DeLoache 1995; DeLoache & Marzolf 1995). Specifically, children can demonstrate a previous experience successfully on themselves, but fail to do so successfully when asked to demonstrate the experience on dolls. For example, in one study, young preschoolers were touched on various parts of their bodies and then asked to demonstrate what happened on themselves or on dolls. Children were better at demonstrating where they were touched on their bodies than they were at demonstrating on the dolls (DeLoache & Marzolf 1995). DeLoache explains young children's inability in terms of task complexity in relation to their cognitive capabilities. When asked to perform tasks separately, young preschoolers can remember earlier experiences and can play with dolls in symbolic manners. However, when asked to remember an experience and use the dolls as symbols simultaneously, the task exceeds the children's cognitive capabilities. Congruent with this perspective, Bruck et al. (1995) examined 2.5 to young 3-year-olds' memory for a medical check-up and found that children responded at chance levels when they were asked to show what happened using AD dolls. It is likely that these young children failed to understand that the dolls were supposed to represent themselves.

The type of to-be-remembered information can further influence the utility of AD dolls (Goodman et al. 1995a; Saywitz et al. 1991). A study by Goodman et al. (1995a) provides a clear example of this point. In the study, 3- to 10-year-old children experienced a painful medical procedure that involved genital contact. (Doctors required the children to undergo the procedure, the researchers did not!) Children were interviewed a few weeks later about what happened during the procedure and asked to show what happened with AD dolls. In regard to the amount of correct information provided, 3- to 4-year-olds did not benefit from use of the AD dolls, but older children did. In fact, the 3- to 4-year-olds provided as much incorrect information with the dolls as correct information. However, the dolls were not useless. All children, regardless of age, benefited from the dolls in regard to a specific type of information. Specifically, children were significantly more likely to indicate that their genitals were contacted when recounting what happened using AD dolls than in free recall. Thus, although the AD dolls were effective in eliciting more correct information overall from only the older children, the dolls were effective for all children in obtaining information about genital contact specifically.

In summary, numerous formal and informal techniques have been employed to help children recount accurate information in forensic investigations. Both the step-wise interview and CI procedures provide interviewing guidelines. The step-wise procedure offers guidelines in the hope of increasing the accuracy of the information children report. The CI outlines specific procedures to increase how much information is reported, but the CI may only be effective in eliciting information from older children and adults who understand CI instructions. AD dolls are also employed at times to help children report sexual experiences that they may not want to talk about or may not have the vocabulary to discuss. However, the usefulness of AD dolls in interviews depends on children's cognitive development and the type of information being requested in the interview.

The techniques described in this section are only a sample of many that exist. The effectiveness of any particular technique depends on multiple factors, and it is often difficult to draw general conclusions when evaluating each one's utility in experimental situations. Clearly it is important to find the best and least intimidating ways to interview children about their experiences, and the aforementioned techniques represent important steps in the direction of reaching such goals.

Special populations

Despite the growing scientific literature on children's eyewitness memory, important groups of children have been overlooked in research studies. These groups include children with special needs, such as disabled or mentally challenged children. Statistics indicate that children (and adults) in special populations may be especially at risk for physical abuse, sexual abuse, and neglect (Sobsey & Doe 1991; Sullivan et al. 1987). Because of these children's status, the abuse often goes unnoticed or unreported, and once reported, not believed (Horton & Kochurka 1995). Here we discuss eyewitness memory in two groups of children with special needs: deaf children and mentally retarded children. It is possible that the problems associated with abuse, disclosure, and testimony in these children generalize to children in several other special populations as well.

A case in Canada exemplifies the problems associated with allegations of sexual abuse in deaf children. The case began in the mid-1980s when a worker at a residential home for deaf children was accused of sexually molesting dozens of deaf children enrolled at the school (Jericho Hill 1993). When the allegations first arose, even some of the social workers and education professionals viewed the children as incompetent to recount sexual experiences accurately, and the children's allegations were subsequently dismissed for several years.

Although previous researchers have demonstrated that deaf children's cognitive capabilities are equivalent to hearing children's capabilities, much less is known about deaf children's eyewitness memory. Porter et al. (1995) compared 8- to 10-year-old hearing versus deaf children's memory reports of a witnessed event. All children were rated by their teachers as being of average intelligence. Children viewed a film about a woman's wallet being stolen. Then they were interviewed about what happened. The interview structure followed the step-wise procedure, developed by Yuille (see pp. 318–19 in this chapter); that is, first children were asked free-recall questions and then a series of more directive questions based on information they provided in free recall. An American Sign Language (ASL) interpreter posed the interviewer's questions to the deaf children. There were no differences in the overall amount of information recalled by hearing and deaf children. However, the accuracy of information provided in response to the directive questions significantly differed for deaf children compared to hearing children. Specifically, deleterious effects of direct questions were more evident for deaf than hearing children. Porter et al. (1995) propose that because deaf children may be more reliant than hearing children on adults for assistance, deaf children may be more susceptible to adults' suggestions. Additionally, the format of ASL may have been more suggestive than the format of the verbal questions. For example, when asking a question about whether or not someone was wearing jewelry, the ASL interviewer pointed to the ear, neck, and fingers to convey the question, thus providing information about the specific type of jewelry. Thus, the increased errors by deaf children may have been because there were higher levels of suggestion inherent in the questions rather than because of deaf children's greater suggestibility *per se.*

Mentally retarded children are at a particular disadvantage when it comes to reporting abuse and maltreatment. In fact, mentally retarded individuals are often presumed incompetent as witnesses unless their competency can be demonstrated (Quinn 1986). Although research suggests that compared to normal children and adults, mentally retarded children and adults make more memory errors (Dent 1986; Sigelman et al. 1981), their increased errors tend to be evident mainly when specific questions are asked. For example, Gordon et al. (1994) compared mentally retarded and normal children's ability to remember real and imagined events. The researchers found that both groups of children were equivalent in their performance when asked open-ended questions, but the mentally retarded children performed worse when asked specific questions. Dent (1986) examined the effects of different types of questions on the accuracy of mentally retarded children's memory for a witnessed social interaction and found that their responses were less accurate when asked specific versus general questions about what happened.

In summary, studies indicate that children in special populations are at increased risk for various types of abuse and neglect. Although traditionally these children's reports were met with considerable skepticism, it appears that such children can provide accurate information about their experiences. However, when children with special needs are interviewed, increased consideration of the power of the question format must be taken into account. To the extent that children in special populations feel increased reliance on adults, leading questions may have a particularly strong effect on these children's responses. When translating into any language, including ASL, attention needs to be paid to ensure translations do not unintentionally increase the suggestive or leading nature of particular questions.

Currently there is a dearth of research concerning the eyewitness testimony capabilities of children from special populations, and there is a need for increased efforts to understand the conditions that enhance or deter these children's memory accuracy. One important group of children not yet included in studies of eyewitness memory consists of children diagnosed with Attention Deficit Hyperactivity Disorder (ADHD). Because of the behavioral and attentional problems these children display, they may be at particular risk for physical abuse or neglect. Also, because of their attentional problems, they can be quite difficult to interview. Finding ways to question them to determine what happened in their past may be an especially challenging yet necessary task for future researchers.

Children in the courtroom

Although children may be called as witnesses in any type of legal case, in many countries (e.g. UK, USA) children are by far most likely to take the stand in cases involving charges of child sexual assault (e.g. incest, sexual exploitation). Changes in laws and legal standards implemented mainly in the 1980s opened the courtroom doors to greater participation of children as witnesses in prosecutions of child sexual assault.

Still, compared to testimony by adult witnesses, children's testimony at trial is relatively infrequent. In the USA, for example, most child abuse cases never reach trial in criminal court, and thus most children involved in such cases, though interviewed in pretrial investigations, do not testify in criminal court. Instead, the case may be handled by child protective services, and the family referred for counseling, the child temporarily or permanently removed from the home, or the like; such interventions are particularly probable when intra-familial abuse is alleged. However, if the case is deemed of a sufficiently serious nature, whether or not it involves intra- or extra-familial abuse, it will be referred by the police for prosecution. In most such cases, the accused and the prosecutors typically end up agreeing to a plea bargain, which means the accused pleads guilty, often to a less severe charge, and subsequently receives a lighter sentence. A trial is thus avoided. Even so, a number of pretrial hearings may be held in which the child may be asked to testify. And in some cases, the child victim/witness will indeed testify at trial (see Goodman et al. 1992; Gray 1993).

The link between children's memory capabilities and their performance in the courtroom has been under heavy scrutiny in recent years. With a relative influx of children into courtrooms in child abuse cases, numerous controversial issues have arisen, such as the competency of children to testify, the stress associated with testifying, and special techniques to reduce children's stress. This segment of the chapter addresses these issues, in addition to reviewing children's overall experience in the courtroom and child witnesses' treatment in other countries.

Witness competency

As recently as the mid-1980s children under a certain age (e.g. 10–14 years in the USA, with the exact age dependant on State law) were presumed to be incompetent witnesses unless they could correctly answer a series of questions establishing their competence to testify. In other words, they were considered incompetent until proven competent. In the mid-1980s most courts supported the notion that children, even as young as 3 years of age, have the cognitive and moral ability to serve as witnesses (Myers 1994). Indeed, the Federal Rules of Evidence states that "every person is competent to be a witness except as otherwise provided in these rules" (Burton & Myers 1992: 449–50).

Whether a child is deemed competent or not is left to the discretion of the judge. In 1992, only four States required children to demonstrate competency before testifying in child sexual abuse cases. Traditionally, the cognitive and moral abilities a child witness must possess to be considered competent are: (a) the capacity to observe; (b) sufficient memory; (c) the capacity to communicate; (d) the ability to differentiate the truth from a lie (or fantasy from reality); and (e) an understanding of the obligation to tell the truth (Myers 1993). The following section focuses on the fourth criterion, namely, the ability to differentiate between the truth and a lie and between fantasy and reality. This criterion is typically considered of particular importance by the courts and has been the focus of several research studies. We also consider whether the traditional legal criteria serve as valid predictors of children's eyewitness memory accuracy.

Generally, even 3- and 4-year-old children are able to distinguish between the truth and a lie sufficiently to meet testimonial-competence standards (Haugaard et al. 1991; Melton 1981). Nevertheless, research has shown that concepts of truth and lie develop and change with increasing age. For example, preschoolers tend to consider something to be true if it can be matched factually. In contrast, older children and adults are more likely than preschoolers to consider the intent and the belief system of the speaker, in addition to factuality, when deciding if something is true or not (Strichartz & Burton 1990). In a study examining the effects of cues and secrets on 6- and 10-year-old children's memory reports, Pipe and Wilson (1994) examined children's understanding of truth and lies. When children were asked "Do you know the difference between the truth and a lie?", 10-year-olds were significantly more likely to provide an adequate definition (31 per cent) or description (41 per cent) than were the 6-year-olds (8 per cent and 9 per cent respectively). However, when asked a more concrete question, "If I said that you are 12 years old, would that be a truth or a lie?", the two age groups were not significantly different from each other. More importantly, Pipe and Wilson (1994) found that answers to the truth-lie questions were not associated with errors in free recall or in reporting a secret. In other words, children's understanding of truth and lie concepts did not predict accuracy of children's memory reports. Goodman et al. (1991b), in the first study to examine the relation between competence questions and accuracy on memory tasks, asked two groups of children (3- and 4-year-olds, and 5- and 6-year-olds) five competence questions to measure understanding of truth and lie concepts. Accuracy on only one question, "What happens if you tell a lie?" was predictive of children's accuracy on memory measures, and only for the 5- and 6-year-olds. Goodman et al. (1991b) concluded that the court's reliance on typical truth-lie questions to assess children's competency could potentially misclassify many children, at least in regard to the accuracy of their eyewitness memory.

Furthermore, it is unclear that children are any more likely than adults to lie (Spencer & Flin 1990). As Melton (1981) notes, there are no clear developmental trends in terms of honesty. Of course, both adults and children do lie, but there is little reason to suspect that a child would be more likely to lie. Indeed, children, particularly under the age of 7 years, have been found to have difficulty maintaining lies (Leekam 1992; but see Quas et al. 1996). In any case, young children's understanding of truth and lie is often considered satisfactory for courtroom testimony, at least by the time children reach 5 or 6 years of age, despite probable developmental differences in: defining truth-lie concepts; the relation between such knowledge and memory; and children's ability to maintain a lie.

Related to the dimension of distinguishing the truth from a lie is the ability to separate fantasy and reality. In general, research has shown that children understand the basic differences between fantasy and reality (Johnson & Foley 1984; Saywitz et al. 1993). There are few studies, however, examining children's ability to distinguish between fantasy and reality linked specifically to the types of events about which children testify in court. Rather, the majority of the research conducted in this area (e.g. Lindsay et al. 1991; Woolley 1995) relates to children's theory of mind and developmental differences in source monitoring on laboratory tasks. Although some developmental theories suggest that young children make a less clear distinction than older children between reality and fantasy (Piaget 1926), recent studies show that children as young as 4 years of age readily distinguish between certain types of reality and fantasy. In a study by Harris et al. (1991), 4- and 6-year-olds reliably described ghosts, monsters, and witches as not real. However, young children's distinction between reality and fantasy is still fragile, as evidenced by the fact that as many as 25 per cent of the children in Harris et al.'s sample thought that the pretend creature in the experiment could become real. Furthermore, developmental differences in source monitoring may in some cases affect children's ability to distinguish suggested misinformation from reality.

Saywitz et al. warned against interpreting children's occasional use of fantasy-based vocabulary to measure overall competence and memory accuracy. They note that younger children's tendency to engage at times in magical thinking and illogical thought "does not render the rest of the testimony inaccurate or irrelevant" (Saywitz et al. 1993: 68). In addition, Annon states on the topic of reality–fantasy confusion, "Children do not seem more likely than adults to make such confusions of fact and fantasy, as long as the material is encoded well and not a complex event that the child does not understand" (Annon 1987: 19). In general, as with the truth–lie distinction, even young children typically possess adequate ability to discriminate between reality and make-believe, at least as far as most courts are concerned.

In sum, up until the mid-1980s children were considered to be incompetent witnesses. However, the need to prosecute abuse cases involving young children coupled with research establishing children's ability to discriminate between the truth and a lie and between fantasy and reality has helped to change this view. In the mid-1990s, most courts consider children to be competent witnesses unless proven otherwise.

Children's experiences in the courtroom

In many ways, child witnesses are treated like adult witnesses once they qualify to testify. Although prosecutors are often nervous about having a child serve as the star witness in a trial, as a general rule, prosecutors prefer to put child witnesses on the stand than to use alternative types of testimony because prosecutors believe that live witnesses are more memorable and have more of an emotional impact on juries than do videotaped interviews or other innovative techniques such as testifying via closed-circuit TV (Davies & Noon 1991; Myers 1994; Quas et al. 1996b; Tobey et al. 1995). In addition, if an innovative technique is used in lieu of the child testifying, the case has a higher likelihood of being overturned in an appeal because of the controversies surrounding innovative techniques. As more children testify in court, certain accommodations to make children feel more at ease have been suggested, for example, child-friendly courtrooms, court schools for child witnesses to prepare them to testify, and allowing a support person to sit nearby during testimony, although even these accommodations are controversial in US courts (Myers 1994).

Language, communication, and testimony

Saywitz and her colleagues accurately note that "Child witnesses' communicative competence is affected by the interaction between memory processing and communication skills" (Saywitz et al. 1993: 70–1). Children's competence to communicate their memories in court can be profoundly affected by children's abilities to understand attorneys' questions. Research indicates that an important accommodation for children in the courtroom would be the reduction of "legalese" used in the questioning of child witnesses. Although most young children have the language skills necessary to answer simple questions, their ability to communicate may be impeded by stress (Hill & Hill 1987) and inappropriate questioning (e.g. Perry 1995). Child witnesses are frequently asked questions that are difficult even for adults to understand. For example, a 4-year-old witness was asked "On the evening of January 3rd, you did, didn't you, visit your grandmother's sister's house and did you not see the defendant leave the house at 7:30, after which you stayed the night?" (Saywitz et al. 1993: 60). Unfortunately, questions such as these are not rarities in the courtroom. Studies examining comprehension of simple versus complex legal questions reveal increased accuracy with simple questions in comparison to complex legal questions (e.g. Brennan & Brennan 1988; Perry et al. 1995; Carter et al. 1996). For example, Perry et al. (1995) found that for kindergartners, fourth-graders, ninth-graders, and undergraduates, mean accuracy was significantly higher for simplified versions of five types of legalese questions (e.g. double negatives and multifaceted questions). To obtain the most reliable accounts from children in court, Lamb and his colleagues suggest: (a) that children should be encouraged to explain what they witnessed in their own words; (b) that attorneys and other interviewers use direct, nonsuggestive questions to structure children's accounts when necessary; and (c) that interrogaters avoid asking children questions that they are incapable of answering (Lamb et al. 1994).

To summarize, efforts to improve children's experience in the courtroom are slowly being made, but not without controversy. Although prosecutors sometimes feel obligated to put children on the stand, attempts to make the courtroom less menacing are being implemented. In addition, recent studies are beginning to alert legal professionals to the difficulties children have in answering complex, legalese questions. In a survey of 227 state trial court judges, all but two believed that "specific attention should be paid to posing questions at a level the child can understand" (Hafemeister 1994: 12, as cited in Perry et al. 1995). To avoid the problems associated with developmentally inappropriate questioning of child witnesses, researchers are recommending "language advocates" in the courtroom and child development training classes for judges and lawyers (Carter et al. 1996).

Stress and testifying

Some mental health professionals worry that testifying live in court may be too traumatic for many children, whereas others propose that as long as children are adequately prepared for the experience and emotionally supported, most children can face the process with considerable resilience (Berliner & Barberi 1984; Runyan et al. 1988). Goodman et al. (1992) found that for a subset of children involved with the criminal courts, testifying live was associated with prolongment of behavioral disturbance (e.g. depression, somatic symptoms), with the act of facing the defendant particularly distressing for frightened child witnesses. Across studies, researchers have found that the emotional effects of testifying depend on numerous factors, such as the number of times the child must take the stand, the use of hostile cross-examination by attorneys, the child testifying against a family member, the social support the child receives, and the overall resiliency of the child (Goodman et al. 1992; Whitcomb 1992).

The stress of testifying live in court can also affect children's memory performance. In a number of laboratory and mock trial studies, children made more errors of omission (e.g. saying "I don't know," leaving information out, refusing to identify the defendant) when having to face the accused or testify in a court-like setting (e.g. Dent 1977; Hill & Hill 1987; Saywitz & Nathanson 1993). In actual legal proceedings, children who expressed pre-trial fear of the defendant and were then observed testifying live in court had a particularly difficult time answering the prosecutors' questions (Goodman et al. 1992).

In a US Supreme Court decision (*Maryland v. Craig* 1990), the effects of testifying live in court on children's abilities to communicate their memories fully was addressed. By a marginal vote, it was decided that if a child's stress of testifying live in court was so high as to deter a child's ability to communicate reasonably, the judge could decide to have the child testify from a separate room via closed-circuit TV. However, according to this ruling, a child's stress due to the courtroom setting in general is insufficient to deny defendants their right to face-to-face confrontation. Rather, the child's stress must be shown to be due to the defendant specifically, and the child must demonstrate an emotional distress "more than de minimus" (Whitcomb 1992).

The controversy surrounding stress and testifying has led to a variety of proposed reforms (often called "innovative techniques") that seek to reduce the number of children testifying live in court. Such reforms include testimony through hearsay witnesses, closed-circuit TV (called "live link" in the UK), and videotaped forensic interviews. In general, there is a paucity of research concerning the efficacy of these reforms, even though they are being used in the USA and other countries.

One of the most controversial of these reforms is the substitution of children's live appearances with that of hearsay testimony. Hearsay evidence is defined as "a statement, other than one made by the declarant while testifying at the trial or hearing, offered into evidence to prove the truth asserted" (Burton & Myers 1992: 449). As a general rule, hearsay evidence is inadmissible in court because the legal system considers it impossible to determine the trustworthiness of statements made out of the courtroom. However, in child sexual abuse cases, for example, the most compelling evidence is often hearsay (Whitcomb 1992). For instance, when the child's initial, vivid disclosure of abuse to a parent or the police is repeated by the parent or police officer in court, such hearsay testimony can be quite compelling. Although courts have been very reluctant to admit hearsay testimony for fear that defendants will be convicted solely on someone testifying in place of a witness who is unavailable to testify and be cross-examined, in practice the courts have been more liberal in admitting hearsay in child sexual abuse cases.

To date, little is known from scientific research about the effects of hearsay testimony on jurors' judgments. However, legal scholars and research psychologists are starting to study issues surrounding hearsay evidence. In general thus far the studies concerning hearsay testimony have found that, first, jurors do not use hearsay evidence to corroborate children's statements of the identity of abusers (i.e., in one mock trial study, the medical evidence, which was considered as hearsay, influenced perceptions of the child's credibility regarding the abuse but not the identity of the abuser: Pathak & Thompson 1993); second, eyewitnesses are rated as more reliable and accurate than hearsay witnesses (Bull-Kovera et al. 1992; Meine et al. 1992); and third, defendants are more likely to be convicted in the presence of eyewitness accounts than hearsay accounts (Meine et al. 1992).

Other alternatives to having children testify live in court include videotaped testimony and closed-circuit TV. Videotaped testimony often consists of presenting a videotaped forensic interview between an investigator and a child to the court. Videotaped testimony significantly reduces the number of times the child has to retell the story, and allows the judge and jury to see the manner in which the child was interviewed, the exact words that were said, and the spontaneity and expressions of the child (McFarlane & Krebs 1986). In a field study of actual jurors in real trials in the UK in which jurors either heard children's evidence via videotape or live testimony, Davies and his colleagues (1995) reported no statistical difference in the number of guilty verdicts across the different presentations of testimony. The authors concluded that videotaped testimony had no more or less of an impact than live testimony.

Testimony via closed-circuit TV is when the child sits in another room (e.g. the judge's chambers) during the trial and testifies while the judge, jury, defendant, and so on watch the testimony on a television in the courtroom. Tobey et al. (1995) investigated the effects of receiving testimony via closed-circuit TV on mock jurors' perceptions of child witnesses. In the study, the authors had children interact with a male confederate and later testify about this experience. Mock jurors who saw children testify via closed-circuit TV (i.e., the "closed-circuit" condition) perceived the child witnesses (6- and 8-year-olds) as less believable, less accurate, less attractive, less intelligent, and less confident than did mock jurors who saw the child testify live (i.e., the "regular trial" condition). Despite these significant pre-deliberation differences in modality of testimony on mock jurors' perceptions of the child, post-deliberation analyses revealed no effect of modality of testimony on guilt judgments: The defendant was no more likely to be viewed as guilty or innocent in either condition (see also Davies & Noon 1991 for similar results from a field study of actual jurors).

In summary, findings concerning the effects of stress on children's emotional well-being and memory performance in the courtroom indicate that for some, but not all, children confrontational stress can have an adverse effect. In addition, studies comparing different modalities of testimony have found that mock jurors are not significantly more likely to convict the defendant when the child witness is physically available versus when the child witness testifies via videotape or closed-circuit TV, although children who testify live are viewed more favourably than those who do not testify live.

Child witnesses outside the USA

In some countries, some of the above-listed techniques proposed to spare children from testifying live are being implemented and are less controversial than in the USA. Although legal professionals in other countries are also interested in protecting the rights of the accused, the right to face-to-face confrontation is not constitutionally guaranteed. For example, Denmark, Sweden, and the UK commonly use videotaped, instead of live, testimony in cases involving children (Higgins 1988). Preliminary studies in the UK found that trained court observers rated children who testified via videotaped interview as less anxious than those who testified live at trial. It was also found that interviewers were more accommodating and more supportive towards child witnesses in comparison to attorneys who questioned children at trial (Davies et al. 1995). The UK has also implemented closed-circuit TV as a method to decrease the number of children testifying live in court. This practice is quite common in the UK and has been in successful operation since 1988 (Myers 1994). In a report on the efficacy of closed-circuit testimony in the UK, Davies and Noon (1991) noted that while there was less stress on and more complete testimony from the children who testified via closed-circuit TV, there remained the risk of loss of influence of the children's testimony on the jury.

Finally, in Israel most child victims, witnesses, or even suspects under the age of 14 years do not testify live in court. In approximately 86 per cent of the cases a specially trained investigator interviews the child before the trial and then testifies in lieu of the child (Higgins 1988). Overall, the experience of child witnesses in other countries is quite different from that in the United States. It is to be hoped that legal systems in all countries will learn optimal practices based on the diverse approaches taken internationally toward children's eyewitness testimony (Bottoms & Goodman 1996).

Conclusion

In this chapter, we have attempted to provide readers with an overview of current issues and research regarding children's eyewitness memory. In general, children are capable of providing accurate eyewitness memory about personally significant events in their lives. However, like the memory of many adults, but at times more so, children's memory can be adversely affected by false suggestions. Researchers still search to uncover the optimal ways to elicit accurate eyewitness memory from children, whether children are interviewed in forensic investigations or in courts of law. The study of children's eyewitness memory has led to theoretical advances in our understanding of many important and heretofore largely overlooked issues in the scientific study of memory development, such as the effects of trauma on children's memory, children's memory malleability and suggestibility, children's source-monitoring confusions, and the power of social forces on memory reports. The study of children's eyewitness memory also holds important practical potential, especially the potential to help protect children from victimization and to further the cause of justice for all involved when allegations "from the mouth of babes" arise.

References

Ackil, J. K. & M. S. Zaragoza 1995. Developmental differences in eyewitness suggestibility and memory for source. *Journal of Experimental Child Psychology* **60**, 57–83.

Annon, J. S. 1987. The four-year-old child as competent witness. *American Journal of Forensic Psychology* **5**, 17–21.

Baker-Ward, L., B. N. Gordon, P. A. Ornstein, D. Larus, & P. A. Clubb 1993. Young children's long-term retention of a pediatric examination. *Child Development* **64**, 1519–33.

Bartlett, F. C. 1932. *Remembering*. Cambridge: Cambridge University Press.

Bauer, P. J. 1996. What do infants recall of their lives? Memory for specific events by 1- to 2-year-olds. *American Psychologist* **51**, 29–41.

Bauer, P. J. & G. A. Dow 1994. Episodic memory in 16- and 20-month-old children: Specifics are generalized not forgotten. *Developmental Psychology* **30**, 403–17.

Bauer, P. J. & J. M. Mandler 1989. One thing follows another: Effects of temporal structure on 1- to 2-year-olds' recall of events. *Developmental Psychology* **25**, 197–206.

Bauer, P. J. & J. M. Mandler 1992. Putting the horse before the cart: The use of temporal order in recall of events by one-year-old children. *Developmental Psychology* **28**, 441–52.

Bekerian, D. A. & J. L. Dennett 1995. An introduction to the cognitive interview technique. In *True and false allegations of child sexual abuse: Assessment and case management*, T. Ney (ed.), 192–206. New York: Brunner/Mazel.

Belli, R. F. 1989. Influences of misleading postevent information: Misinformation interference and acceptance. *Journal of Experimental Psychology: General* **118**, 72–85.

Belli, R. F., D. S. Lindsay, M. S. Gales, & T. T. McCarthy 1994. Memory impairment and source misattribution in postevent misinformation experiments with short retention intervals. *Memory and Cognition* **22**, 40–54.

Belli, R. F., P. D. Windschitl, T. T. McCarthy, & S. E. Winfrey 1992. Detecting memory impairment with a modified test procedure: Manipulating retention interval with centrally presented event items. *Memory and Cognition* **18**, 356–67.

Berliner, L. & M. K. Barberi 1984. The testimony of the child victim of sexual assault. *Journal of Social Issues*, **40**, 125–37.

Boat, B. W. & M. D. Everson 1988. Interviewing young children with anatomical dolls. *Child Welfare* **67**, 337–52.

Boat, B. W. & M. D. Everson 1994. Exploration of anatomical dolls by nonreferred preschool-aged children: Comparisons by age, gender, race, and socioeconomic status. *Child Abuse and Neglect* **18**, 139–53.

Bohannon, J. N. 1988. Flashbulb memories for the space shuttle disaster: A tale of two stories. *Cognition* **29**, 179–96.

Bohannon, J. N. & V. L. Symons 1993. Flashbulb memories: Confidence, consistency, and quantity. In *Affect and accuracy in recall: Studies of "flashbulb" memories*, E. Winograd & U. Neisser (eds.), 65–91. New York: Cambridge University Press.

Bottoms, B. L. & G. S. Goodman (eds.) 1996. *International perspectives on child abuse and children's testimony*. Newbury Park, CA: Sage.

Bottoms, B. L., P. R. Shaver, & G. S. Goodman 1996. An anlaysis of ritualistic and religion-related child abuse allegations. *Law and Human Behavior* **20**, 1–34.

Bowers, J. M. & D. A. Bekerian 1984. When will postevent information distort eyewitness testimony? *Journal of Applied Psychology* **69**, 466–72.

Brainerd, C. J. & P. A. Ornstein 1991. Children's memory for witnessed events: The developmental backdrop. In *The suggestibility of children's recollections*, J. Doris (ed.), 10–20. Washington, DC: American Psychological Association.

Brainerd, D. J. & V. F. Reyna 1988. Memory loci of suggestibility development: Comment on Ceci, Ross, and Toglia. *Journal of Experimental Psychology: General* **118**, 197–200.

Brainerd, C. J., V. F. Reyna, M. L. Howe, & J. Kingma 1990. The development of forgetting and reminiscence. *Monographs of the Society for Research in Child Development* **55**.

Brennan, M. & R. E. Brennan 1988. *Strange language: Child victims under cross examination*. Wagga Wagga, Australia: Riverina Literacy Center.

Briere, J. & J. Conte 1993. Self-reported amnesia for abuse in adults molested as children. *Journal of Traumatic Stress* **6**, 21–31.

Brown, R. & J. Kulik 1977. Flashbulb memories. *Cognition* **5**, 73–99.

Bruck, M. & S. J. Ceci 1995. Amicus brief for the case of state of New Jersey v. Michaels presented by committee of concerned social scientists. *Psychology, Public Policy, and Law* **1**, 272–322.

Bruck, M., S. J. Ceci, E. Francoeur, & A. Renick 1995. Anatomically detailed dolls do not facilitate preschoolers' reports of a pediatric examination involving genital touching. *Journal of Experimental Psychology: Applied* **1**, 95–109.

Bugental, D. B., J. Blue, V. Cortez, K. Fleck, & A. Rodriguez 1992. The influence of witnessed affect on information processing in children. *Child Development* **63**, 774–86.

Bull, R. 1995. Innovative techniques for the questioning of child witnesses, especially those who are young and those with learning disability. In *Memory and testimony in the child witness*, M. S. Zaragoza, J. R. Graham, G. C. N. Hall, R. Hirschman, & Y. S. Ben-Porath (eds.), 179–94. Thousand Oaks, CA: Sage.

Bull-Kovera, M., R. C. Park, & S. D. Penrod 1992. Jurors' perceptions of eyewitness and hearsay evidence. *Minnesota Law Review*, **76:703**, 703–22.

Burton, K. & W. C. Myers 1992. Child sexual abuse and forensic psychiatry: Evolving and controversial issues. *Bulletin of the American Academy of Psychiatry and Law* **20**, 439–53.

Carter, C. A., B. L. Bottoms, & M. Levine 1996. Linguistic and socio-emotional influences on the accuracy of children's reports. *Law and Human Behavior* **20**, 335–58.

Case, R. 1991. *The mind's staircase: Exploring the conceptual underpinnings of children's though and knowledge*. Hillsdale, NJ: Erlbaum.

Cassel, W. S. & D. F. Bjorklund 1995. Developmental patterns of eyewitness memory and suggestibility: An ecologically based short-term longitudinal study. *Law and Human Behavior* **19**, 507–32.

Ceci, S. J. & M. Bruck 1993. Suggestibility of the child witness: A historical review and synthesis. *Psychological Bulletin* **113**, 403–39.

Ceci, S. J. & M. Bruck 1995. *Jeopardy in the courtroom: A scientific analysis of children's testimony*. Washington, DC: American Psychology Association.

Ceci, S. J., D. F. Ross, & M. P. Toglia 1987. Age differences in suggestibility: Psycholegal implications. *Journal of Experimental Psychology: General* **116**, 38–49.

Christianson, S. A. 1992. Emotional stress and eyewitness memory: A critical review. *Psychological Bulletin* **112**, 284–309.

Davies, G. & E. Noon 1991. *An evaluation of the live link for child witnesses*. London: Home Office.

Davies, G., C. Wilson, R. Mitchell, & J. Milsom 1995. *Videotaping children's evidence: An evaluation*. London: Home Office.

DeLoache, J. S. 1995. The use of dolls in interviewing young children. In *Memory and testimony in the child witness*, M. S. Zaragoza, J. R. Graham, G. C. N. Hall, R. Hirschman, & Y. S. Ben-Porath (eds.), 160–78. Thousand Oaks, CA: Sage.

DeLoache, S. J. & D. Marzolf 1995. The use of dolls to interview young children: Issues of symbolic representation. *Journal of Experimental Child Psychology* **60**, 155–73.

Dent, H. R. 1977. Stress as a factor influencing person recognition in identification parades. *Bulletin of the British Psychological Society* **30**, 339–40.

Dent, H. R. 1986. An experimental study of the effectiveness of different techniques of questioning mentally handicapped child witnesses. *British Journal of Clinical Psychology* **25**, 13–17.

Dent, H. R. & G. M. Stevenson 1979. An experimental study of the effectiveness of different techniques of questioning child witnesses. *British Journal of Social and Clinical Psychology* **18**, 41–51.

Duncan, E. M., P. Whitney, & S. Kunen 1982. Integration of visual and verbal information in children's memories. *Child Development* **53**, 1215–23.

Easterbrook, J. A. 1959. The effect of emotion on cue utilization and the organization of behavior. *Psychological Review* **66**, 183–201.

Eisen, M. L., G. S. Goodman, & J. J. Qin 1995. *Eyewitness testimony in victims of child maltreatment: Stress, memory, and suggestibility*. Paper presented at the Society for Applied Research on Memory and Cognition invited symposium, Vancouver, Canada.

Farrar, M. J. & G. S. Goodman 1990. Developmental differences in the relation between scripts and episodic memory: Do they exist? In *Knowing and remembering in young children*, R. Fivush & J. A. Hudson (eds.), 30–64. New York: Cambridge University Press.

Farrar, M. J. & G. S. Goodman 1992. Developmental changes in event memory. *Child Development* **63**, 173–87.

Fischer, K. W. 1980. A theory of cognitive development: The control and construction of hierarchies of skills. *Psychological Review* **87**, 477–531.

Fivush, R. 1984. Learning about school: The development of kindergartners' school scripts. *Child Development* **55**, 1697–709.

Fivush, R. & N. R. Hamond 1989. Time and again: Effects of repetition and retention interval on 2-year-olds' event recall. *Journal of Experimental Child Psychology* **47**, 259–73.

Fivush, R., & N. R. Hamond 1990. Autobiographical memory across the preschool years: Toward reconceptualizing childhood amnesia. In *Knowing and remembering in young children*, R. Fivush & J. A. Hudson (eds.), 223–48. New York: Cambridge University Press.

Fivush, R. & J. R. Shukat 1995. Content, consistency, and coherence of early autobiographical recall. In *Memory and testimony in the child witness*, M. S. Zaragoza, J. R. Graham, G. C. N. Hall, R. Hirschman, & Y. S. Ben-Porath (eds.), 5–23. London: Sage.

Flavell, J. H., B. A. Everett, K. Croft, & E. R. Flavell 1981. Young children's knowledge about visual perception: Further evidence for the Level 1–Level 2 distinction. *Developmental Psychology* **17**, 99–103.

Flavell, J. H., A. G. Friedrich, & J. D. Hoyt 1970. Developmental changes in memorization processes. *Cognitive Psychology* **1**, 324–40.

Flavell, J. H., F. L. Green, & E. R. Flavell 1995. Young children's knowledge about thinking. *Monographs for Research in Child Development* **60** (no. 243).

Flavell, J. H., P. H. Miller, & S. A. Miller 1993. *Cognitive development*. Englewood Cliffs, NJ: Prentice-Hall.

Flin, R., J. Boon, A. Knox, & R. Bull 1992. Children's memories following a five-month delay. *British Journal of Psychology* **83**, 323–36.

Foley, M. A., F. T. Durso, A. Wilder, & R. Friedman 1991. Developmental comparisons of explicit versus implicit imagery and reality monitoring. *Journal of Experimental Child Psychology* **51**, 1–13.

Foley, M. A. & M. K. Johnson 1985. Confusion between memories for performed and imagined actions: A developmental comparison. *Child Development* **56**, 1145–55.

Freud, S. 1915/1957. Repression. In *The standard edition of the complete psychological works of Sigmund Freud, Vol. XIV*, J. Strachey (ed). London: Hogarth.

Freud, S. 1938. Psychopathology of everyday life. In *The writings of Sigmund Freud*, A. A. Brill (ed.). New York: Modern Library.

Geiselman, R. E., R. P. Fisher, I. Firstenberg, L. A. Hutton, S. Sullivan, I. Avetissian, & A. Prosk 1984. Enhancement of eyewitness memory: An empirical evaluation of the Cognitive Interview. *Journal of Police Science and Administration* **12**, 74–80.

Geiselman, R. E., K. J. Saywitz, & G. K. Bornstein 1993. Effects of cognitive questioning techniques on children's recall performance. In *Child victims, child witnesses: Understanding and improving testimony*, G. S. Goodman & B. L. Bottoms (eds.), 71–93. New York: Guilford.

Goodman, G. S. & C. Aman 1990. Children's use of anatomically detailed dolls to recount an event. *Child Development* **61**, 1859–71.

Goodman, G. S., C. Aman, & J. E. Hirschman 1987. Child sexual and physical abuse: Children's testimony. In *Children's eyewitness memory*, S. Ceci, M. Toglia, & D. Ross (eds.), 1–23. New York: Springer Verlag.

Goodman, G. S., B. Bottoms, B. Schwartz-Kenney, & L. Rudy 1991a. Children's testimony about a stressful event: Improving children's reports. *Journal of Narrative and Life History* **7**, 69–99.

Goodman, G. S., J. Dunn, & J. A. Quas 1995a. Children's memory for a stressful event: Developmental, individual difference, and interviewing considerations. In *Children's memory for emotional and traumatic experiences*, G. S. Goodman & L. E. Baker-Ward (chairs), symposium presented at the biennial meeting of the Society for Research in Child Development, Indianapolis, IN.

Goodman, G. S., J. E. Hirschman, D. Hepps, & L. Rudy 1991b. Children's memory for stressful events. *Merrill-Palmer Quarterly* **37**, 109–58.

Goodman, G. S. & J. A. Quas 1996. Trauma and memory: Individual differences in children's recounting of a stressful experience. In *Memory for everyday and emotional events*, N. L. Stein, C. Brainerd, P. A. Ornstein, & B. Tversky (eds.), 267–94. Hillsdale NJ: Erlbaum.

Goodman, G. S., J. A. Quas, J. M. Batterman-Faunce, M. Riddlesberger, & J. Kuhn

1994. Predictors of accurate and inaccurate memories of traumatic events experienced in childhood. *Consciousness and Cognition* **3**, 269–94.

Goodman, G. S. & R. S. Reed 1986. Age differences in eyewitness testimony. *Law and Human Behavior* **15**, 13–30.

Goodman, G. S., L. Rudy, B. L. Bottoms, & C. Aman 1990. Children's concerns and memory: Issues of ecological validity in children's testimony. In *Knowing and remembering in young children*, R. Fivush & J. Hudson (eds.), 249–84. New York: Cambridge University Press.

Goodman, G. S., A. Sharma, S. F. Thomas, & M. G. Considine 1995b. Mother knows best: Effects of relationship status and interviewer bias on children's memory. *Journal of Experimental Child Psychology* **60**, 195–228.

Goodman, G. S., E. Taub, D. P. H. Jones, P. England, L. P. Port, L. Rudy, & L. Prado 1992. Emotional effects of criminal court testimony on child sexual assault victims. *Monographs of the Society for Research in Child Development* **57** (no. 229).

Gordon, B. N., K. G. Jens, R. Hollings, & T. E. Watson 1994. Remembering activities performed versus those imagined: Implications for testimony of children with mental retardation. *Journal of Clinical Child Psychology* **23**, 239–48.

Gordon, B. N., C. S. Schroeder, & J. M. Abrams 1990. Children's knowledge of sexuality: A comparison of sexually abused and nonabused children. *American Journal of Orthopsychiatry* **60**, 250–57.

Gray, E. 1993. *Unequal justice: The prosecution of child sexual abuse*. New York: Free Press.

Hafemeister, T. L. 1994. Efforts to minimize trauma to child witnesses: A judicial appraisal of the best means to bring related information to their attention. In *Disseminating information to the judiciary*, M. J. Saks (chair) presented to the biennial meeting of the American Psychology-Law Society, Santa Fe, NM.

Hamond, N. R. & R. Fivush 1991. Memories of Mickey Mouse: Young children recount their trip to DisneyWorld. *Cognitive Development* **6**, 433–48.

Harris, P., E. Brown, C. Marriott, S. Whittall, & S. Harmer 1991. Monsters, ghosts and witches: Testing the limits of the fantasy reality distinction in young children. *British Journal of Developmental Psychology* **9**, 105–23.

Haugaard, J. J., N. D. Repucci, J. Laird, & T. Nauful 1991. Children's definitions of the truth and their competency as witnesses in legal proceedings. *Law and Human Behavior* **15**, 253–71.

Hembrook, H. & S. J. Ceci 1995. Traumatic memories: Do we need to invoke special mechanisms? *Consciousness and Cognition* **4**, 75–82.

Herman, J. L. & E. Schatzow 1987. Recovery and verification of memories of childhood sexual trauma. *Psychoanalytic Psychology* **4**, 1–14.

Higgins, R. B. 1988. Child victims as witnesses. *Law and Psychology Review* **12**, 159–66.

Hill, P. E. & S. M. Hill 1987. Videotaping children's testimony: An empirical review. *Michigan Law Review* **85**, 809–33.

Horton, C. B. & K. A. Kochurka 1995. The assessment of children with disabilities who report sexual abuse: A special look at those most vulnerable. In *True and false allegations of child sexual abuse: Assessment and case management*, T. Ney (ed.), 275–89. New York: Brunner/Mazel.

Howe, M. L. 1991. Misleading children's story tell: Forgetting and reminiscence of the facts. *Developmental Psychology* **27**, 746–62.

Howe, M. L., M. L. Courage, & C. Peterson 1995. Intrusions in preschoolers' recall of traumatic childhood events. *Psychonomic Bulletin and Review* **2**, 130–4.

Hyman, I. E., T. H. Husband, & F. J. Billings 1995. False memories of childhood experiences. *Applied Cognitive Psychology* **9**, 181–97.

Jericho Hill 1993. Jericho Hill School abuse: Government urged to pay compensation. *Vancouver Sun* B1.

Johnson, M. K. & M. A. Foley 1984. Differentiating fact from fantasy: The reliability of children's memory. *Journal of Social Issues* **40**, 33–50.

Johnson, M. K., S. Hastroudi, & D. S. Lindsay 1993. Source monitoring. *Psychological Bulletin* **114**, 3–28.

Johnson, M. K. & C. L. Raye 1981. Reality monitoring. *Psychological Review* **88**, 67–85.

Jones, D. P. H. & R. Krugman 1986. Can a three-year-old child bear witness to her sexual assault and attempted murder? *Child Abuse and Neglect* **10**, 253–8.

Kail, R. 1990. The development of memory in children, 3rd edn. New York: Freeman.

Koocher, G. P., G. S. Goodman, S. White, W. N. Friedrich, A. B. Sivan, & C. C. R. Reynolds 1995. Psychological science and the use of anatomically detailed dolls in child sexual-abuse assessments. *Psychological Bulletin* **118**, 199–222.

Lamb, M. E., K. J. Sternberg, & P. W. Esplin 1994. Factors influencing the reliability and validity of statements made by young victims of sexual maltreatment. *Journal of Applied Developmental Psychology* **15**, 255–80.

Landers, S. 1988. Use of "detailed dolls" questioned. *APA Monitor* **19**, 24–5.

Leekam, S. 1992. Believing and deceiving: Steps to becoming a good liar. In *Cognitive and social factors in early deception*, S. J. Ceci, M. D. Leichtman, & M. Putnick (eds.), 47–62. Hillsdale, NJ: Erlbaum.

Leichtman, M. D. & S. J. Ceci 1995. The effects of stereotypes and suggestions on preschoolers' reports. *Developmental Psychology* **31**, 568–78.

Lewis, C., R. Wilkins, L. Baker, & A. Woobey 1995. "Is this man your daddy?" Suggestibility in children's eyewitness identification of a family member. *Child Abuse and Neglect* **19**, 739–44.

Lindsay, D. S., M. K. Johnson, & P. Kwon 1991. Developmental changes in memory source monitoring. *Journal of Experimental Child Psychology* **52**, 297–318.

Loftus, E. F. 1977. Shifting human color memory. *Memory and Cognition* **5**, 696–9.

Loftus, E. F. 1979. The malleability of memory. *American Scientist* **67**, 312–20.

Loftus, E. F. 1993. The reality of repressed memories. *American Psychologist* **48**, 518–37.

Loftus, E. F. 1994. The repressed memory controversy. *American Psychologist* **49**, 443–5.

Loftus, E. F., D. G. Miller, & H. J. Burns 1978. Semantic integration of verbal information into a visual memory. *Journal of Experimental Psychology: Human Learning and Memory* **4**, 19–31.

Loftus, E. F. & J. E. Pickerell 1995. The formation of false memories. *Psychiatric Annals* **25**, 720–25

Mandler, J. M. 1990. Recall of events by pre-verbal children. In *The development and neural bases of higher cognitive functions*, A. Diamond (ed.), 485–516. New York: New York Academy of Science.

Maryland v. Craig, 47 CrL 2258 US SupCt 1990.

McCauley, M. R. & R. P. Fisher 1995. Facilitating children's eyewitness recall with

337

the revised Cognitive Interview. *Journal of Applied Psychology* **80**, 510–16.

McCloskey, M. 1993. Special versus ordinary memory mechanisms in the genesis of flashbulb memories. In *Affect and accuracy in recall: Studies of "flashbulb" memories*, E. Winograd & U. Neisser (eds.), 227–35. New York: Cambridge University Press.

McCloskey, M. & M. S. Zaragoza 1985. Misleading postevent information and memory for events: Arguments and evidence against memory impairment hypotheses. *Journal of Experimental Psychology: General* **114**, 1–16.

McFarlane, K. & S. Krebs 1986. Videotaping of interviews and court testimony. In *Sexual abuse of young children*, F. McFarlane & J. Waterman (eds.), 164–93. New York: Guilford.

Meine, P., R. C. Park, & E. Borgida 1992. Juror decision making and the evaluation of hearsay evidence. *Minnesota Law Review* **76**, 683–701.

Melton, G. B. 1981. Children's competency to testify. *Law and Human Behavior* **5**, 73–85.

Meltzoff, A. N. 1988. Infant imitation and memory: Nine-month-olds in immediate and deferred tests. *Child Development* **59**, 217–25.

Memon, A., O. Cronin, R. Eaves, & R. Bull 1993. The Cognitive Interview and child witnesses. In *Children, evidence and procedure: Issues in criminological and legal psychology, Vol. XX*, N. K. Clark & G. M. Stephenson (eds.), 3–9. Leicester, UK: British Psychological Society.

Merritt, K. A., P. A. Ornstein, & B. Spicker 1994. Children's memory for a salient medical procedure: Implications for testimony. *Pediatrics* **94**, 17–23.

Moston, S. 1990. How children interpret and respond to questions: Situational sources of suggestibility in eyewitness interviews. *Social Behavior* **5**, 155–67.

Myers, J. E. B. 1992. *Evidence in child abuse and neglect*, 2nd edn. New York: Wiley.

Myers, J. E. B. 1993. The competence of young children to testify in legal proceedings. *Behavioral Sciences and the Law* **11**, 121–33.

Myers, J. E. B. 1994. Adjudication of child sexual abuse cases. In *The future of children: Sexual abuse of children, Vol. IV*, R. E. Behrman (ed.), 84–118. David & Lucile Packard Foundation.

Nelson, K. 1986. *Event knowledge: Structure and function in development*. Hillsdale, NJ: Erlbaum.

Nelson, K. 1991. Emergence of autobiographical memory at age 4. *Human Development* **34**, 172–77.

Nelson, K. 1992. Remembering and telling: A developmental story. *Journal of Narrative and Life History* **1**, 109–27.

Oates, K. & S. Shrimpton 1991. Children's memories for stressful and nonstressful events. *Journal of Science, Medicine and the Law* **31**, 4–10.

O'Sullivan, J. T., M. L. Howe, & T. A. Marche (in press). Children's beliefs about long-term retention. *Child Development*.

Parker, J. F. 1995. Age differences in source monitoring of performed and imagined actions on immediate and delayed tests. *Journal of Experimental Child Psychology* **60**, 84–101.

Pathak, M. K. & W. C. Thompson 1993. *Do people correctly evaluate evidence partially corroborating hearsay in molestation cases?* Paper presented at 101st annual conference of American Psychological Association, Toronto.

Perry, N. W., B. D. McAuliff, P. Tam, L. Claycomb, C. Dostal, & C. Flanagan 1995. When lawyers question children: Is justice served? *Law and Human Behavior* **19**,

609–29.

Peters, D. P. 1987. The impact of naturally occurring stress on children's memory. In *Children's eyewitness memory*, S. J. Ceci, M. P. Toglia & D. F. Ross (eds.), 122–41. New York: Springer-Verlag.

Peters, D. P. 1991. The influence of stress and arousal on the child witness. In *The suggestibility of children's recollections: Implications for eyewitness testimony*, J. Doris (ed.), 60–76. Washington, DC: American Psychological Association.

Pezdek, K. & R. Chantal 1994. Memory for childhood events: How suggestible is it? *Consciousness and Cognition: An International Journal* **3** 373–87.

Piaget, J. 1926. *Language and thought of the child*. London: Routledge.

Piaget, J. 1983. Piaget's theory. In *Handbook of developmental psychology*, P. Mussen (ed.), 103–28. New York: Wiley.

Piaget, J. & B. Inhelder 1956. *The child's conception of space*. London: Routledge & Kegan Paul.

Pipe, M-E. & J. C. Wilson 1994. Cues and secrets: Influences on children's event reports. *Developmental Psychology* **30**, 515–25.

Poole, D. A. & D. S. Lindsay 1995. Interviewing preschoolers: Effects of nonsuggestive techniques, parental coaching and leading questions of reports of nonexperienced events. *Journal of Experimental Child Psychology* **60**, 129–54.

Poole, D. A. & L. T. White 1991. Effects of question repetition on the eyewitness testimony of children and adults. *Developmental Psychology* **27**, 975–86.

Poole, D. A. & L. T. White 1995. Tell me again and again: Stability and change in the repeated testimonies of children and adults. In *Memory and testimony in the child witness*, M. S. Zaragoza, J. R. Graham, G. C. N. Hall, R. Hirschman, Y. S. Ben-Porath (eds.), 24–43. Thousand Oaks, CA: Sage.

Porter, S., J. C. Yuille, & A. Bent 1995. A comparison of the eyewitness accounts of deaf and hearing children. *Child Abuse and Neglect* **19**, 51–61.

Putnam, F. 1989. Pierre Janet and modern views of dissociation. *Journal of Traumatic Stress* **2**, 413–29.

Putnam, F., K. Helmers, & P. Trickett 1993. Development, reliability, and validity of a child dissociation scale. *Child Abuse and Neglect* **17**, 731–41.

Qin, J. J., G. S. Goodman, B. L. Bottoms, & P. R. Shaver 1996. Repressed memory: An inquiry into allegations of ritual abuse. In *Truth in memory*, S. Lynn (ed.). New York: Guilford.

Quas, J. A., V. DeCicco, J. Bulkley, & G. S. Goodman 1996b. *District Attorneys' views of legal innovations for child witnesses*. American Psychology-Law News **16**(2), 5-8.

Quas, J. A., M. Denton, G. S. Goodman, & J. Myers 1996a. *Consistency and accuracy of children's true versus untrue reports of body touch*. Biennial Conference of the American Psychology-Law Society, Hilton Head, SC.

Quinn, K. M. 1986. Competency to be a witness: A major child forensic issue. *Bulletin of the American Academy of Psychiatry and the Law* **14**, 311–21.

Rapaport, D. 1942. *Emotions and memory*. Menninger Clinic Monograph Series, no. 2. New York: Wiley.

Rosenthal, R. 1995. State of New Jersey v. Margaret Kelly Michaels: An overview. *Psychology, Public, and Law* **1**, 246–71.

Rudy, L. & G. S. Goodman 1991. Effects of participation on children's reports: Implications for children's testimony. *Developmental Psychology* **27**, 527–38.

Runyan, D., M. Everson, G. Edelsohn et al. 1988. Impact of legal intervention on sexually abused children. *Journal of Pediatrics* **113**, 647–53.

Saywitz, K. 1995. Improving children's testimony: The question, the answer, and the environment. In *Memory and testimony in the child witness*, M. S. Zaragoza, J. R. Graham, G. C. N. Hall, R. Hirschman, & Y. Ben-Porath (eds.), 113–40. Thousand Oaks, CA: Sage.

Saywitz, K., R. E. Geiselman, & G. K. Bornstein 1992. Effects of cognitive interviewing and practice on children's recall performance. *Journal of Applied Psychology* **77**, 744–56.

Saywitz, K. & G. S. Goodman 1996. Interviewing children in and out of court: Current research and practice implications. In *The APSAC handbook of child maltreatment*, J. Briere, L. Berliner, J. A. Bulkley, C. Jenny, & T. Reid (eds.), 297–318. Thousand Oaks, CA: Sage.

Saywitz, K., Goodman, G. S., Nicholas, E. & Moan, S. 1991. Children's memories of physical examinations involving genital touch: Implications for reports of child sexual abuse. *Journal of Consulting and Clinical Psychology* **59**, 682–91.

Saywitz, K. & R. Nathanson 1993. Children's testimony and their perceptions of stress in and out of the courtroom. *Child Abuse and Neglect* **17**, 613–622.

Saywitz, K. J., R. Nathanson, & L. S. Synder 1993. Credibility of child witnesses: The role of communicative competence. *Topics in Language Disorders* **13**, 59–78.

Saywitz, K. J. & L. Snyder 1993. Improving children's testimony with preparation. In *Child victims, child witnesses: Understanding and improving testimony*, G. S. Goodman & B. L. Bottoms (eds.), 117–46. New York: Guilford.

Sigelman, C. K., E. C. Budd, C. L. Spanhel, & C. J. Schoenrock 1981. When in doubt, say yes: Acquiescence in interviews with mentally retarded persons. *Mental Retardation* **19**, 53–8.

Sobsey, D. & T. Doe 1991. Patterns of sexual abuse and assault. *Sexuality and Disability* **9**, 243–59.

Spencer, J. & R. Flin 1990. *The evidence of children: The law and the psychology.* London: Blackstone.

Stein, N. & T. Boyce 1995. The role of physiological reactivity in attending to, remembering, and responding to an emotional event. In *Children's memory for emotional and traumatic events*, G. Goodman & L. Baker-Ward (Chairs), symposium presented at the Society for Research in Child Development Meetings, Indianapolis, IN.

Steward, M. S. 1993. Understanding children's memories of medical procedures: "He didn't touch me and it didn't hurt!" In *Memory and affect in development: Minnesota Symposium on Child Psychology, Vol. XXXVI*, C. A. Nelson (ed.), 171–225. Hillsdale, NJ: Erlbaum.

Strichartz, A. F. & R. V. Burton 1990. Lies and truth: A study of the development of the concept. *Child Development* **61**, 211–20.

Sullivan, P. M., M. Vernon, & J. M. Scanlan 1987. Sexual abuse of the deaf youth. *American Annals of the Deaf* **132**, 256–62.

Terr, L. C. 1991. Childhood traumas: An outline and overview. *American Journal of Psychiatry* **148**, 10–20.

Tobey, A. E. & G. S. Goodman 1992. Children's eyewitness memory: Effects of participation and forensic context. *Child Abuse and Neglect* **16**, 779–96.

Tobey, A. E., G. S. Goodman, J. Batterman-Faunce, H. Orcutt, & T. Sachsenmaier 1995. Effects of closed-circuit testimony on children's accuracy and fact finders' perceptions of child witnesses. In *Children's and adults' eyewitness testimony* M. S. Zaragoza, J. R. Graham, G. C. N. Hall, R. Hirschman, Y. S. Ben-Porath (eds.), 214–39. Thousand Oaks, CA: Sage.

Usher, J. A. & U. Neisser 1993. Childhood amnesia and beginnings of memory for four early life events. *Journal of Experimental Psychology: General* **122**, 155–65.

Vandermaas, M. O., T. M. Hess, & L. Baker-Ward 1993. Does anxiety affect children's reports of memory for a stressful event? *Journal of Applied Psychology* **7**, 109–28.

Walker, A. G. 1994. *Handbook on questioning children: A linguistic approach.* Washington DC: American Bar Association.

Warren, A. R. & P. Lane 1995. Effects of timing and type of questioning on eyewitness accuracy and suggestibility. In *Memory and testimony in the child witness*, M. S. Zaragoza, J. R. Graham, G. C. N. Hall, R. Hirschman, & Y. S. Ben-Porath (eds.), 44–60. Thousand Oaks, CA: Sage.

Warren, A., K. Hulse-Trotter, & E. C. Tubbs 1991. Inducing resistance to suggestibility in children. *Law and Human Behavior* **15**, 273–85.

Whitcomb, D. 1992. *When the victim is a child*, 2nd edn. Washington DC: US Department of Justices, Abt Associates Inc.

Williams, L. M. 1994. Recall of childhood trauma: A prospective study of women's memories of child sexual abuse. *Journal of Consulting and Clinical Psychology* **62**, 1167–76.

Williams, L. M. 1995. Recovered memories of abuse in woman with documented child sexual abuse histories. *Journal of Traumatic Stress* **8**, 649–74.

Winer, G. A. & C. McGlone 1993. On the uncertainty of conservation: Responses to misleading conservation questions. *Developmental Psychology* **29**, 760–69.

Woolley, J. D. 1995. The fictional mind: Young children's understanding of imagination, pretense, and dreams. *Developmental Review* **15**, 172–211.

Yerkes, R. M. & J. D. Dodson 1908. The relation of strength of stimulus to rapidity of habit-formation. *Journal of Comparative Neurology of Psychology* **18**, 459–82.

Yuille, J. C., R. Hunter, R. Joffe, & J. Zaparniuk 1993. Interviewing children in sexual abuse cases. In *Child victims, child witnesses: Understanding and improving children's testimony* G. S. Goodman & B. L. Bottoms (eds.), 95–115. New York: Guilford.

Zaragoza, M. S. & J. W. Koshmider 1989. Misled subjects may know more than their performance implies. *Journal of Experimental Psychology: Learning, memory and cognition* **15**, 246–55.

Zaragoza, M. S. & S. M. Lane 1994. Source misattributions and the suggestibility of eyewitness memory. *Journal of Experimental Psychology: Learning, Memory and Cognition* **20**, 934–45.

Zaragoza, M. S., M. McCloskey, & M. Jamis 1987. Misleading postevent information and recall of the original event: Further evidence against the memory impairment hypothesis. *Journal of Experimental Psychology: Learning, Memory and Cognition* **13**, 36–44.

Acknowledgement

We thank Victoria Symons for her assistance.

CHAPTER 12

The development of remembering in cultural context

Jayanthi Mistry

Contextual approaches to the study of development have become particularly significant in current theoretical and scholarly discussions on the development of cognition. This, however, was not the case prior to the 1970s when contextual factors and their influence on performance were ignored in much of the research on cognitive development (Butterworth 1993) and memory (Schneider & Pressley 1989). Cognitive skills were typically conceptualized as context-free competencies located within the individual. Thus, experimental paradigms using laboratory tasks were commonly used in order to study cognitive processes such as memory as "pure" processes. For example, the influence of contextual factors such as an individual's prior knowledge was removed by studying memory for nonsense words.

In the early 1930s Bartlett had described memory as a social phenomenon, emphasizing that "both the manner and the matter of recall are often predominantly determined by social influences" (Bartlett 1932: 244). He documented the prodigious retentive capacity of Swazi herdsmen to recall the individual characteristics of their cattle and argued that this was not surprising since Swazi culture revolved around the possession and care of cattle. Bartlett also demonstrated that when the purpose for remembering did not have such social or economic importance then Swazi herdsmen's recall was not so impressive. He related the case of a Swazi herdsman who was able to remember details of all the cattle his owner had bought a year ago, yet the same youth when asked to recall a message of 25 words was not able to recall any more than did typical European youth.

Interest in the social context of cognition began to gather steam in the 1980s with a shift away from delineating context-free skills towards an understanding of the social and contextual factors that lead to situational differences in performance. Cross-cultural research on cognitive development conducted in the 1970s and 1980s and the writings of Soviet sociocultural scholars have typically been credited for influencing this shift. Emphasizing the important lessons to be drawn from research on culture and cognition, Rogoff and Chavajay (1995) trace how the critical transition from viewing culture as an independent variable affecting cognition to regarding cognitive processes as inherently cultural has significant potential for guiding research in cognitive development in general.

343

I begin this chapter with a brief discussion of some important lessons learned from cross-cultural research that have implications for the study of memory in general, leading to an overview of a sociocultural perspective on the development of children's remembering. From this perspective, developing remembering skills are assumed to be structured, constrained, and supported through features of the activity, its purpose, and the social and cultural contexts in which remembering occurs. Cross-cultural research in the study of memory is thus presented to demonstrate how individual remembering is supported or constrained by features of the activity in which remembering takes place.

Lessons from cross-cultural research on memory

Much of the cross-cultural research on memory, like cross-cultural research in general, has been motivated by interest in testing Western theories for their universality or variability across cultures. Many cross-cultural psychologists have emphasized this goal, claiming the importance of testing the cross-cultural generality of psychological principles before considering them to be established (Segall et al. 1990). Typically such studies, especially those in the area of memory, used procedures derived from laboratory studies in the USA to examine whether people in other cultures perform in a similar manner to their North American counterparts on the memory tasks.

In much of this cross-cultural research, the relation of culture and memory has been examined using a model in which culture serves as an independent variable and memory serves as the dependent variable or outcome of variation in cultural variables (Rogoff & Mistry 1985). Culture and memory are conceived as separate variables, and the influence of culture on the individual is frequently studied by comparing the memory performance of individuals from two (or sometimes more) different cultures. For example, in the typical "free-recall" task individuals are presented lists of words and then asked to recall these. Often the lists contain items from several categories (e.g. food, clothing, utensils). Individuals from the USA or other Western countries typically group items into categories (categorization) to help in remembering or use other mnemonic strategies such as verbal rehearsal (repeating words to memorize). Evidence from cross-cultural research in the 1960s and 1970s indicated that individuals from non-Western cultures did not use such mnemonic strategies and their recall of items was lower than that of Western individuals. Though initial explanations focused on the individual's ability, evidence from descriptions of non-Western people's memory in their everyday life suggested that though they did poorly on free-recall tasks, they could remember very well in other situations (as in the example from Bartlett 1932 presented earlier). The pioneering cross-cultural studies conducted by Cole and his colleagues in the 1970s (Cole et al. 1971; Cole & Scribner 1977; Sharp et al. 1979) were particularly notable for their insightful use of ethnographic methods combined with experimental procedures to elaborate features of the memory tasks and materials that mediated cultural differences in memory performance. Thus, the tendency to use laboratory tasks of memory to examine the universality of memory processes was seriously challenged by this work.

Within the broad field of cross-cultural psychology, another goal is also often emphasized: To explore other cultures to discover and examine psychological variations that are not present in one's own cultural settings (Berry & Dasen 1974). Studies addressing this goal have highlighted another important lesson for research on memory in general. Cross-cultural research enabled researchers to separate variables which can vary simultaneously in the USA but are separable in other cultures. For example cross-cultural comparisons of memory performance by individuals varying in schooling experience allowed consideration of whether the changes in memory performance observed across childhood in the USA might be due to experience with school rather than maturation (Rogoff 1981; Sharp et al. 1979). Western children enter school at about age 5, and there is high correlation between age and grade in school thereafter until adulthood. Hence, there is a danger that "cognitive-developmental research has been measuring years of schooling, using age as its proxy variable" (Laboratory of Comparative Human Cognition 1979: 830). In many non-technological societies, formal schooling is not yet universal, so the relative independence of age and amount of schooling provides investigators with a natural laboratory for investigating the effects of age and schooling separately. Cross-cultural research demonstrated that performance on free-recall tasks and related tasks was closely related to the extent of schooling that individuals had received (Rogoff 1981; Rogoff & Mistry 1985). Thus, when non-Western individuals did not perform as well as their Western counterparts, "culture" in terms of a specific aspect of background experience (e.g. formal schooling) was used to explain the difference.

These two lessons from cross-cultural research, questioning the tendency to generalize the universality of memory processes based on laboratory studies and the recognition that developmental differences may in fact be a function of schooling, have also been important for research on the development of memory in general. Previews of research on memory conducted in the USA suggest an increasing recognition of similar issues (Paris et al. 1985; Schneider & Pressley 1989; Weinert & Perlmutter 1988). These reviews have attempted to synthesize what has been learned so far about the development of memory from research influenced by an information-processing perspective. Several of these reviews document how early attempts to explain memory development as the development of increasingly flexible and more general memory strategies that develop between the ages of 5 and 11 have proved to be premature (Schneider & Pressley 1989). Research demonstrating that even young preschool children used intentional memory strategies when they were dealing with familiar tasks or contexts (Wellman 1988), and that knowledge and familiarity play an important role in developmental improvements in memory performance (Chi 1978) have been credited with highlighting importance of context and the problems with decontextualized generalizations about memory development.

Several authors of these reviews acknowledge that while most researchers in the USA accept a model of memory in which contextual and motivational variables are presumed to be important determinants of memory, they continue to study memory without regard to naturalistic situational or motivational states (Paris et al. 1985; Perlmutter 1988; Schneider & Pressley 1989). However, there are now encouraging and emerging trends towards examining memory in naturalistic situations and contexts, such as in the study of eyewitness memory (Neisser 1982; Rubin 1995; see also Chap. 11 in this volume).

While cross-cultural research has drawn attention to the importance of social and cultural context in remembering, Cole claims that "despite its surface attractiveness and important lessons that can be learned from it, there are difficulties inherent in the cross-cultural enterprise that limit its usefulness for explicating culture-cognition relationships" (1995a: 26). While such research typically focuses on cross-cultural variations in the products of developmental history, Cole states that it does not adequately elucidate "the cultural mechanisms of developmental change" (1995a: 30). In a related vein, Rogoff and Chavajay (1995) argue that a critical transformation has taken place in scholarly thinking about culture and cognition. They note the drop-off of research on cross-cultural comparisons of cognitive development and a transition towards understanding and explaining the processes of development.

Arguing that sociocultural theory has provided promising frameworks and constructs for conceptualizing and understanding the processes of change and the integral relation between culture and individual development, I now elaborate a sociocultural perspective on remembering.

A sociocultural perspective of remembering

There has been increasing interest in the contributions of sociocultural theory to the fields of psychology and education. The work of Vygotsky (1962, 1978), Leont'ev (1981), and their colleagues laid the groundwork for what is now widely known as a sociohistorical or sociocultural theory of human development and learning. Recent writings on sociocultural theory clearly emphasize its deep distinction from theories of human development which focus on the individual and attempt to derive decontextualized, universalistic representations of development in cognitive, language, and socioemotional domains. Sociocultural theorists have emphasized that the integration of individual development in social and cultural context requires a fundamental reconceptualization of mind and its development in social practice (Cole 1990; Minick et

346

al. 1993; Rogoff 1990; Valsiner 1989; Werstch 1991). The essence of this conceptualization is elaborated below.

From a sociocultural perspective, individual development is conceptualized as the acquisition and appropriation of culturally defined modes of speaking, thinking, and acting (Laboratory of Comparative Human Cognition 1983; Vygotsky 1978). In the course of our socialization, we have each learned the particular ways of using language, telling stories, remembering information, and making inferences that are valued and practised in our homes and cultural communities. Development is assumed to take place through an individual's participation with others in the activities that constitute daily life within the cultural community. Thus, human development, conceptualized as particular modes of thinking, speaking, and behaving, is assumed to *arise from* and remain *integrally tied* to concrete forms of social practice (Cole 1990; Vygotsky 1978; Wertsch 1985).

Three central and related assumptions of sociocultural theory are first discussed to lay the framework within which cross-cultural research on the development of remembering is then reviewed. These assumptions are: (a) the inseparability of individual and cultural context; (b) the notion that human development arises from and is constituted in social and cultural practice; and (c) the focus on activity as the unit of analysis in the study of human development.

Inseparability of individual and cultural context

The sociocultural emphasis on the inseparability of individual and cultural context is most clearly distinguished from perspectives on development in which culture is viewed as an independent variable that influences developmental outcomes. The latter view assumes that cultural factors are separable from the processes of individual development. For example, within traditional theories of memory, the role of prior knowledge is viewed simply as an amplifier of a pure process of memory which operates separately from experience and cultural patterns. Usually, the goal is first to document the decon-textualized skills characterizing a particular stage of individual development and then to consider how social experiences or cultural influences modify or affect these skills. For example, one generally accepted view within the information-processing approach to memory is that individuals are hypothesized to have a basic capacity to remember 7+2 bits of unrelated information, and that the use of deliberate memory strategies helps us to remember more than the amount this basic capacity enables us to hold in memory. Repeating to-be-remembered words (verbal rehearsal), clustering together items that have similar features (e.g. grouping all food items), or making a story out of them, are some mnemonic strategies that have been demonstrated to improve an individual's memory. The ability to use these strategies is often viewed as a decontextualized skill. Within the informational-processing perspective, cultural or background experiences such as schooling are viewed as an independent influence on an individual's propensity to use mnemonic strategies.

In contrast, in the sociocultural approach, the central claim is that human action or psychological functioning (e.g. thinking, remembering) is mediated by tools and signs (such as literacy systems and mnemonic aids) which are socio-culturally situated and derived (Cole 1990; Rogoff 1990; Vygotsky 1978; Wertsch 1985, 1991). To elaborate, the focus is on the action of remembering, and remembering is assumed to be mediated by tools and signs. Mnemonic strategies such as verbal rehearsal and clustering are examples of such mediational tools, and the assumption is that the use of these tools is integrally tied to situational context. In other words, the use of particular strategies is not viewed as a decontextualized ability that an individual can apply in a variety of situations.

The fundamental difference between sociocultural approaches and traditions in which individualistic assumptions are built into the very basic conceptualization of psychological phenomena is clearly manifest in how terms are used (Wertsch & Tulviste 1992). Terms such as cognition and memory are automatically assumed to apply exclusively to the individual. This assumption is so ingrained that theorists describing the social nature of mental functioning tend to use modifiers to reflect "socially shared," as in socially distributed cognition (Resnick et al. 1991) and collective memory (Middleton & Edwards 1990). Wertsch and Tulviste suggest that such modifiers continue to reflect the "derivative, or nonbasic, status that mental functioning carried out on the social plane is assumed to have in contemporary paradigms" (1992: 549). In contrast, in sociocultural approaches mental functioning is viewed as a kind of action that may be carried out by individuals, dyads, or larger groups. "Mind, cognition, memory, and so forth are understood not as attributes or properties of the individual, but as functions that may be carried out intermentally or intramentally" (Wertsch & Tulviste 1992: 549). This means that instead of conceptualizing individuals as "having abilities and skills," the focus is on the "person-acting-with-mediational-means" as the appropriate unit of analysis (Wertsch 1991: 119). Thus, rather than viewing school-age children as having the ability to use mnemonic strategies, from a sociocultural perspective the focus is on the "child using mnemonic strategies in school-like tasks." In other words, the "ability" or "tendency" is not separated from the contexts in which they are used. When the focus is on human "actions," we are immediately forced to account for the context of the actions and therefore cannot separate context from human functioning.

Culture as the context for development

Early interpretations of Vygotsky's theory (from 1970 to the mid-1980s) emphasized the social origins of cognitive skills and led researchers to focus on the social interactional processes through which children acquired valued cognitive skills (Rogoff & Gardner 1984; Wertsch 1978; Wood & Middleton

1975). Vygotsky's construct of the zone of proximal development became central to understanding the mechanisms or processes of developmental change. The construct was widely interpreted as providing assistance at a level slightly above which the child is functioning. Such interpretations have been criticized as being narrow and of robbing the concept of its potential for understanding how individual actions and functioning are situated within specific social systems of interaction (Griffin & Cole 1984; Minick 1987).

Fortunately, recent developments in sociocultural theory have focused specifically on providing theoretical concepts and discussions to understand and study the sociocultural context of development. Concepts such as context, activity (Leont'ev 1981; Wertsch 1985), cultural practices (Miller & Goodnow 1995), and situated practice (Lave 1990) have been discussed as various means of operationalizing cultural context. Cole (1995b) offers a particularly comprehensive discussion of these concepts as attempts to define a "supraindividual sociocultural entity" that is the cultural medium within which individual growth and development takes place. If we are to be able to examine how individual functioning is situated within a social and cultural context, we need to have a specific definition of this "supraindividual" (or outside the individual) entity in which the individual is enveloped. Cole draws on both the sociohistorical school of thought (represented in the writings of Vygotsky, Luria, and Leont'ev) and on anthropological theory to offer a conceptualization of such an entity, defining "culture as a medium constituted of artifacts" (Cole 1995b: 31). Artifacts refers to the tools and objects used in a cultural community that are developed by prior generations. Calculaters, books, and computers are common examples of physical artifacts or tools of our present-day technological society that mediate how we interact with our social and physical world (and thus are examples of mediational means). Written language, the alphabet, numeral systems, the decimal system (as a way of organizing numbers), and the calendar (organizing time into years, months, days) are examples of conceptual artifacts (or mediational tools) that also regulate human functioning and behavior. Culture is seen as uniquely human in that human beings are distinct from other creatures because they live in an environment transformed by the artifacts (mediational means), created by prior generations, which regulate and mediate their interaction with the social and physical world. Taking examples more relevant to memory, children in formal school settings remember in an environment (cultural medium) in which artifacts such as verbal rehearsal, note-taking, list-making, and categorization are valued and effective means. Children in living in peasant communities may live in an environment in which mediational means such as songs, chants, poems, oral stories, and legends may be the valued and effective means for remembering.

This notion of culture as a medium constituted of historically developed artifacts which are organized to accomplish human growth highlights the study of culture as central to understanding the processes or mechanisms of human development (Cole 1995a). But this begs the next question: What is the appropriate unit of analysis that will enable us to focus on both individual functioning and the supraindividual context within which this is situated? From a sociocultural perspective the appropriate mode of research is to analyze the way in which human thinking occurs within culturally organized forms of activity.

Activity as the unit of analysis

Based on the assumption that human functioning cannot be separated from the contexts of activities through which development takes place, it follows that rather than focusing on individuals as entities, the aim should be to examine individuals as participants in culturally valued activities. In fact, sociocultural theory posits that the integration of individual, social, and cultural/sociohistorical levels takes place within the analytic unit of activity (Cole 1985, 1995a; Leont'ev 1981; Tharp & Gallimore 1988; Wertsch 1985, 1991). In other words, the assumption is that activities mediate the impact of the broader sociocultural system on the lives of individuals and groups (Gallimore & Goldenburg 1993).

Using activity as the unit of analysis contrasts with the independent/dependent variable approach which separates individual responses from environmental stimuli as the units of analysis. On the other hand, activity as the unit of analysis consists of individuals engaged in goal-directed behavior, carrying out actions, using culturally valued tools and mediational means, within a framework of shared cultural assumptions and expectations (Cole 1985; Leont'ev 1981; Tharp & Gallimore 1988; Wertsch 1985). If we think of memory as the "action of remembering in a particular activity," rather than as a context-free capacity, then it becomes easier to understand how culture is integrally a part of every aspect of remembering. An activity involves goals, materials, and procedures for how the activity is to be carried out, which we have learned to value and use through prior practice and interaction with more experienced people in our cultural environments.

From this perspective, even in the laboratory experiment paradigm used in much memory research, the unit of analysis would not just be the "individual" but the "individual-using-mediational-means-within-an-activity." Thus, in order to keep a focus on the individual and the supraindividual context integrally related, the analytic unit would be "the child using verbal rehearsal in a laboratory free recall task." In the following sections, I synthesize and discuss cross-cultural research on remembering using a sociocultural framework to organize this work.

Cross-cultural research on remembering

Though much of the cross-cultural research in the study of memory has not been conducted within a sociocultural perspective, this body of research is reviewed to examine how it elucidates a cultural theory of memory development. If the notion of culture as elaborated within a Vygotskian framework is to be widely useful, it must take into account contemporary ideas and findings in the field (Wertsch & Tulviste 1992). In the following sections, I begin by summarizing major findings regarding cross-cultural differences in remembering, but focus primarily on research that elaborates aspects of the supraindividual sociocultural environment (Cole 1995b) in which individual remembering occurs.

On tasks resembling those used in Western research, non-Western subjects are widely observed to perform more poorly than subjects from the culture where the tests originated (see influential reviews by Cole & Scribner 1977 and Wagner 1981). Some of the most commonly used tasks derived from US research have been serial recall of lists of words or series of pictures, and free recall of lists of words or pictures. The usual finding has been that non-Western people do not perform as well as Western individuals (Rogoff & Mistry 1985). Following the prevalent approach in cross-cultural research, researchers have typically examined characteristics which commonly vary between cultures (such as the amount of formal schooling, degree of modernization, and urban versus rural residence) as an explanation for these differences in remembering. However, research that simply documents differences in remembering as a function of such variables does not really elaborate the cultural context of remembering unless it "unpackages" (Whiting 1976) specific aspects of the environmental or experiential context which differentiate the groups being compared (rural vs. urban, schooled vs. nonschooled, Western vs. non-Western, and so on). It is towards this goal that sociocultural theory's perspective on culture may be most useful, because it provides a useful framework to elaborate and unpackage the cultural context of remembering.

A central assumption of the sociocultural perspective discussed earlier is that human thinking is constituted from and remains integrally tied to practices and activities contexts within which it develops. For the study of memory, this means that the development of memory is considered to be situated in the social contexts, cultural practices, and activities in which children remember and use remembered information. Thus, their developing remembering skills are structured, constrained, and supported through features of the activity, its purpose, and the social and cultural contexts in which remembering occurs (Mistry & Rogoff 1994; Rogoff & Mistry 1985). In other words, what processes and skills of remembering are used will be a function of the features of the activity in which they are being used. In the following sections, I use the various components of the activity construct (defined from a sociocultural perspective) as an organizing framework within which to discuss existing cross-cultural research to demonstrate how individual remembering is supported or constrained by features of the activity in which remembering takes place.

In an activity individuals engage in goal-directed behavior, carrying out actions and using culturally valued tools and mediational means within a framework of shared cultural assumptions and expectations (Cole 1985; Leont'ev 1981; Tharp & Gallimore 1988; Wertsch 1985). Using this framework, I discuss cross-cultural research demonstrating differences in remembering as a function of (a) variations in goals or purposes of remembering, (b) variations in medi-ational means and materials used, and (c) variations in cultural assumptions regarding appropriate social roles and social-interactional behavior. An important underlying assumption highlighted throughout the chapter is that differences between cultures are interpreted as a function of differences in the demands of particular task settings and activities, rather than in terms of the general level of subjects' mental functioning or of a groups' mental functioning.

Remembering as a function of goals and purposes

While Western, schooled people generally perform better than non-Western, non-schooled people on typical laboratory memory tasks, there have been many accounts of outstanding memory performance by non-Western people in the anthropological and cross-cultural literature. For example, Micronesian navigators demonstrate extraordinary skills in memory, inference, and calculation in navigating between islands (Gladwin 1970). Similarly, the exceptional memory of Arabian shaykhs in remembering information about battles and raids has been documented (Mack 1976), as well as that of oral historians who remember detailed information about the genealogy and history of families and clans in Africa (D'Azevedo 1982). In most of these cases, the memory feat is usually accomplished in the service of a culturally important non-mnemonic goal. Thus, meaningful purposes integrate the memory task in an appropriate cultural activity.

One explanation offered for such accounts of outstanding memory among people in societies with oral traditions is that lack of a written language or means of record-keeping has necessitated a reliance on remembering large amounts of information, thus enhancing the memory skills of individuals in these societies. Some cross-cultural studies of the early 1970s attempted to test these notions. For example, Ross and Millsom (1970) hypothesized that since African societies are generally characterized as relying on oral traditions, Ghanaian university students would remember more details in orally presented stories than would a comparable group of American students. The Ghanaian students did, in fact, perform better than did the American students in remembering stories that were read aloud to them. However, the extensive experiments conducted by Cole and his colleagues among the Kpelle of Liberia did not reveal any generalized superior memory skills among them compared to American adults (Cole & Scribner 1977).

Rather than searching for explanations of superior generalized or inherent memory skills among Western or non-Western people, sociocultural theory focuses on examining aspects of the situation in which remembering takes place to understand why particular groups of people may perform better than others. Thus, one of the explanations offered for the superior performance of Western people on laboratory memory tasks, contrasted with the outstanding memory of non-Western people in certain situations of their daily life, may lie in the role of meaningful goals for remembering. While most laboratory-based memory research has utilized situations in which memory is a goal in itself, remembering in everyday life is usually in the service of accomplishing some other goal rather than being itself the end for the activity (Rogoff & Mistry 1985). Young or non-schooled children who are unfamiliar with performing solely for evaluation are likely not to understand the purpose of remembering items in a memory test, thus giving Western children a performance advantage. Though tests may not be a comfortable situation for schooled children, they at least understand what is expected of them and have had practice in exercising memories for no other practical purpose than to comply with the request of the researcher. Children who do not share such expectations or purposes are likely to approach the memory task differently.

The importance of understanding how meaningful goals and purposes guide efforts to remember became the focus of many investigations of children's memory, even those that focused on single cultural contexts (Rogoff & Mistry 1990). For example in the USA, efforts to investigate young children's remembering in ecologically valid and naturalistic settings led to research documenting that even preschoolers exhibited deliberate effort and use of strategies to remember when the purpose for remembering was made more realistic and familiar (Paris et al. 1985; Wellman 1988). Research suggested that children as young as 3 years of age made deliberate efforts to remember aspects of events, locations, and names of "lost" objects when the purpose for remembering was embedded in a meaningful activity (Nelson & Ross 1980; Wellman & Somerville 1980). Brewer and Dupree (1983) found that memory was enhanced when the goal of an action was known.

Istomina's (1977) landmark study investigating the development of voluntary memory also sparked interest in understanding the importance of meaningful goals for children's recall. Her study reported that preschoolers' performance on a free-recall task was better when they were asked to remember items for the purpose of buying them from a store (in the "game" condition) than when they were asked to remember for the sole purpose of demonstrating memory (in a "lesson"). While replications of her study in the USA and Germany have produced contradictory results (Mistry & Rogoff 1987; Mistry et al. 1995; Schneider & Brun 1987; Weissberg & Paris 1986), one of the explanations offered has focused on broad contextual differences between the Soviet children of the 1930s in Istomina's study and the test-wise children in American preschools in the 1980s. In explaining their finding of better performance in the lesson than in the game condition, Weissberg and Paris (1986) argue that middle-class children are now used to requests from adults to remember through the influence of television and preschools. Children who are frequently tested in activities that adults label as "games" may in fact treat being tested for adult evaluation as having a meaningful purpose.

Remembering as a function of mediational means and materials

In the USA the dominant trend in research on the development of children's memory has been to search for changes in underlying competencies that characterize universal development (Perlmutter 1988). Based on over two decades of experimental studies of children's deliberate remembering in controlled situations, there is general consensus on a model that explains memory development in terms of changes in functional memory capacity, use of verbal memory strategies, nonstrategic knowledge, and metamemory (Perlmutter 1988; Schneider & Pressley 1989). Age-related increases in operative knowledge (i.e. knowing how to use mnemonic strategies), epistemic (content) knowledge, and metacognitive knowledge are assumed to contribute to age-related improvements in memory performance (Perlmutter 1988). In relation to this body of research, cross-cultural research on the effects of school experience on memory have been particularly useful in evaluating whether the changes in memory performance observed across childhood in the USA might be due to experience with school rather than maturation (Rogoff 1981; Sharp et al. 1979).

Reviews of cross-cultural research on cognitive development (Rogoff 1981) and memory (Rogoff & Mistry 1985) conclude that, taken together, results document a powerful effect of schooling on performance on the memory tasks that have been used. Non-schooled subjects generally have less success than do schooled subjects on tasks such as paired-associate learning (J. W. Hall 1972), free recall (Cole et al. 1971; Sharp et al. 1979), and serial recall (Fahrmeier 1975; Stevenson et al. 1978). However (as mentioned earlier), merely documenting differences in remembering as a function of schooling does not explain how and why these differences occur. We need to understand what processes mediate the better performance of schooled people.

Variations in remembering as a function of mediational processes Along with emphasizing the importance of understanding how goals and purposes of activities are integrally related to people's performance on a memory task, sociocultural theory also posits that remembering is a function of culturally valued tools and mediational means used in the activities in which remembering takes place. The insightful series of memory experiments conducted by Cole and his colleagues with schooled and unschooled Kpelle in Liberia (Cole et al. 1971; Cole & Scribner 1977) shed much light on how a key explanation for the difference in performance between the two groups lay in the use of organization strategies (an example of mediational means). Non-schooled subjects were unlikely to engage spontaneously in strategies that provide greater organization to help remember the unrelated items that were presented in such tasks. But if an appropriate organizational strategy was made explicit, non-schooled subjects were able to make use of it, suggesting that the difference lay in preference for particular strategies, not ability to use these strategies. For example, in paired-associate learning, if there was an explicit relationship between the items in the pairs (such as bull-sheep, from the same semantic category), the effect of schooling was attenuated compared to when there was little relationship between items (e.g. bull-root; Sharp et al. 1979).

Similarly, in free-recall tasks, recall and clustering by nonliterate subjects increased when the category organization of the items was made clear. The category structure of lists of items was used more by nonliterate subjects when the categories were marked simply by sorting items and holding the items randomly over different chairs (Cole et al. 1971). Free recall and clustering also improved when nonliterate subjects were told the category names at the time of presentation of the list and recall was cued through category names. Interestingly, when such cuing was discontinued, recall and clustering remained high (Cole et al. 1971). Further, if personally meaningful organization of free-recall items was made available by having subjects sort items into piles until a stable organization was reached, nonliterate subjects made use of their personal organization in structuring later free recall (Scribner 1974).

To summarize from these studies, it is apparent that the difference in memory performance between schooled and non-schooled people appeared to be mediated by the use of organization strategies. People with schooling tended to use organizational strategies which enhanced their recall, while people not exposed to Western schooling tended not to use such mnemonic strategies. Further, since differences between schooled and non-schooled groups do not generally appear until the schooled sample has received several years of schooling (Cole et al. 1971), cross-cultural research suggests that some experience at school influences learning of organizational strategies (Rogoff & Mistry 1985). Actively constructing connections between unrelated items may seldom be necessary for subjects who do not have to learn to remember lists of initially unrelated items (as in school). School is one of the few situations in which a person has to remember information deliberately, as a goal in itself, and make initially meaningless, unrelated pieces of information fit together sensibly. Many of the strategies used in laboratory memory tasks (which share these same characteristics) may be taught and encouraged by schooling. As evidence that the correlation between schooling and test performance may be a tautology, Cole et al. (1979) point out that versions of many of the memory tests used in cross-cultural research can be found in Binet's early work searching for behavior that predicted performance in school. It should not be surprising that greater schooling predicts performance on tests designed to discriminate children's school performance (Rogoff & Mistry 1985).

Another relevant line of cross-cultural research conducted by Wagner (1978, 1981) has suggested that the explanation for cultural differences may lie in the particular processes of memory being used. The general hypothesis is that on memory tasks requiring the deliberate use of mnemonic strategies, cultural differences would be heightened, whereas in tests that rely less on such strategies the cultural differences would be less. However, studies that compare performance on recognition tasks (which are assumed to require less use of strategies than recall tests) in different cultures show an inconsistent pattern that does not support the idea that cultural differences are minimized on such tests (Rogoff & Mistry 1985). Reviews of cross-cultural studies of recognition memory each point to the inconclusiveness of data on cultural differences in recognition: Cole and Scribner state that "under some conditions, for some response measures, recognition of unacculturated peoples can exceed that of their educated counterparts" (1977: 254). Rogoff (1981) suggests that familiarity with the response demands of recognition tests may underlie the occasionally better performance of schooled than non-schooled subjects. Thus research on recognition memory is not sufficiently consistent to test the idea that cultural differences are less on these tasks presumed to required less deliberate use of mnemonic strategies.

However, several studies using the probed serial recall task support the idea that cultural differences reside more in the use of strategies than in structural aspects of memory (Rogoff & Mistry 1985). Such tasks involve showing the subject a series of cards with pictures and then turning them face down in linear order. The subject is then shown a "probe card" with a picture corresponding to one of the face-down cards and asked to point to the location of its mate. With American subjects, heightened recall for the first items shown ("primacy effect") has been explained in terms of the use of rehearsal as a recall strategy. Heightened performance on the last item(s) shown ("recency effect") has been attributed to use of the sensory memory store, considered a structural feature of memory.

Wagner (1974) found greater recall and a greater primacy effect for Yucatan subjects with more schooling than for those with less schooling. Schooling differences in the recency effect, while significant, were not as striking as differences in the primacy effect. In a later study with Moroccan males, Wagner (1978) found that schooled subjects at older ages (over 13 years) showed greater recall, much greater primacy, and only slightly greater recency than non-schooled subjects. He concluded that control processes (e.g. rehearsal) are much more subject to environmental influences than are structural features of memory.

Variations in remembering as a function of modality While the bulk of memory studies have involved verbal materials (usually lists of words), there is some interest in whether the usual pattern of poorer performance by non-Western compared to Western subjects occurs with spatial materials. Intriguing anecdotes credit some non-Western people with impressive skills in finding their way in large-scale space: Eskimos and Australian aborigines are reputed to be very skilled in remembering their way through local terrain; Polynesian sailors similarly impress Western observers with their skill in remembering the lay of the ocean in complex navigation from island to island (Gladwin 1970; Levy-Bruhl 1926; Lewis 1976).

Empirical work on cultural differences in spatial memory is rather sparse, but there are several findings of superior or equivalent spatial memory performance by non-Western populations compared to Western groups. Kleinfeld (1971) found better recall for drawn designs among Eskimo children than urban Caucasian children. Kearins (1981) found better recall for spatial arrangement of objects by aborigines dwelling in the Western Desert of Australia than by suburban white Australian youth. The suburban adolescents' performance was especially poor for arrays of objects that were not easily labeled (sets of different rocks or different bottles). Drinkwater (1976) showed that non-tribal Aborigine youth equated in schooling with a white suburban sample performed the same on a spatial array as the white suburban subjects. These findings of Eskimo and Aborigine superiority on spatial tests have been interpreted in terms of the needs of Eskimo and desert Aborigine people to develop good spatial memory to find their way in environments which appear to the Western eye to be bleak and short of landmarks, changing with the wind and storms.

However, studies with non-Western populations in less extreme environments also show enhanced memory for location and spatial arrangement contrasting with the more usual performance decrement of non-Western subjects (Rogoff & Mistry 1985). Rural Guatemalan ladino children demonstrated better recall for location of objects than for the identity of objects, while children in Buffalo showed equal recall for a memory task requiring recall of spatial arrangement of digits in a grid. Rogoff and Waddell (1982) found slightly (nonsignificantly) better performance by Guatemalan Indian children compared to US children on reconstruction of the placement of objects in a model panorama. Together, these results suggest that non-Western people perform equally or better on spatial material than Western people.

What aspect of spatial memory tasks encourages good performance by non-Western people? One interpretation is that spatial information requires little deliberate effort to be encoded, and thus people who have difficulty implementing deliberate strategies do not have difficulties with spatial tasks. However, this explanation may be too simplistic and does not take into account that there are other features of the remembering task that may also influence the actions of the individual faced with it. For example, contextual support is present in some spatial tasks and contrasts with the absence of organizing links in the usual lists of verbal materials. The presence of organizing context may account for some of the findings of excellent performance by non-Western people in spatial tasks.

Similarly, differences in mediational means used by Western and non-Western individuals in spatial memory tasks have also been used to explain the findings. Some of the studies discussed earlier (Kearins 1986; Rogoff & Waddell 1982) suggest that the relatively poor performance of Western individuals on spatial memory tasks may be due to their use of verbal rehearsal strategies which are not necessarily effective for remembering spatial information. For example, Kearins (1986) noted the different methods of memorizing used by the aboriginal and white children in her series of studies. The aboriginal children sat still and silent, as if visually memorizing the location of objects in the array, while the white children were fidgety, restless, and seemed to be muttering to themselves as if using verbal rehearsal, a strategy that is effective for recall of lists, but not necessarily for spatial arrays. Similarly, in Rogoff and Waddell's (1982) study, about a third of the 30 American children, but only 1 of the 30 Mayan children, rehearsed the names of the objects in the panorama as they studied the items to be recalled.

To summarize, studies of spatial memory tasks suggest that non-Western people perform equally or better than Western people on these tasks. Further, explanations that seek to specify what particular aspects of context facilitate recall of spatial materials appear to be more promising than assumptions of general superior spatial ability or lack of ability to use deliberate strategies.

Variations in remembering due to familiarity with materials Cross-cultural researchers who supplement their "experimental" measures of performance with ethnographic observations of everyday activities are struck by the difficulty that people have with particular skills in the laboratory while spontaneously using the skills of interest in their everyday activities (Cole et al. 1978; Laboratory of Comparative Human Cognition 1979; Rogoff 1981). As a first attempt to make laboratory tasks more culturally appropriate to the population tested, researchers attempted to use familiar materials to enhance the ecological validity of the work. A few studies directly compared performance on memory tests when familiar materials versus unfamiliar materials were used. For example, a comparison of the dialect used for testing with American children revealed that recall of stories was equal for white children tested in Standard English and black children tested in Black English dialect, though white children recalled more than black children when they were tested in Standard English and black children did better than white when they were tested in Black English dialect (W. S. Hall et al. 1975). Similarly, Hawaiian dialect speakers recalled more information from stories presented in dialect than in standard English, while Standard English speakers from Hawaii recalled more from stories presented in Standard English than in Hawaiian dialect (Ciborowski & Choy 1974).

Studies conducted within a single cultural context have also demonstrated the significance of familiarity of materials, thus raising questions about the notion that developmental or age differences in memory are primarily due to the acquisition of underlying generalized competencies. Chi's (1978) study that 10-year-old chess experts could learn meaningful chess positions better than adult chess novices was particularly influential in this regard. In a related vein, studies on memory and aging have demonstrated that memory differences between younger and older adults may not be due to aging, but because of lack of familiarity with the to-be-remembered material. When the generational familiarity of words was manipulated, Barrett (1978; cited in Gorfein

& Spata 1989) found that recall of the older and younger adults varied. When a word list consisting of words more familiar to older adults (such as "fedora", "poultice") was used, older adults recalled more than did younger adults, and the opposite was true when a list of words more familiar to younger adults was used (e.g. "disco," "afro"). Similarly, historical shifts in frequency of word usage have been cited to account for differences in the free recall of young and elderly American adults: Elderly adults recalled words that were commonly used in their youth better than those that were frequent in contemporary usage (Worden & Sherman-Brown 1983).

In addition to familiarity of the to-be-remembered materials, familiarity with particular categorizing systems also appears to benefit recall. Black adolescents recalled more words and clustered to a greater extent than white adolescents in a task using categories elicited from the Black subjects (Franklin 1978). While the white subjects were familiar with the words on the list, their lack of familiarity with the categorization scheme put them at a disadvantage. Similarly, Super and Harkness (1981) noted that on free-recall lists designed to reflect taxonomic categories, American adults clustered more than did Kenyan adults, while on comparable lists designed for clustering more on the basis of function, Kenyan adults clustered more. In another study demonstrating different methods of categorizing, Lancy and Strathern (1981) compared clustering in free recall by children from two societies in Papua New Guinea, that varied in the complexity of the folk taxonomies employed in their language. Ponam folk classification used taxonomic categories similar to those common in Western societies. In contrast, Melpa folk classification has a paucity of suprageneric terms. Melpa people use a strategy for classification which they call "making twos" or grouping by pairs. For example, plant, animal, and color terms are ordered in pairs of polar opposites (e.g. planted vs. wild, light vs dark). On free-recall tasks, Ponam children exhibited greater recall as well as more clustering of items than did Melpa children.

The importance of familiarity with materials has also been documented in studies that examine the interaction between knowledge and use of strategies in free-recall tasks. Tarkin (1981; cited in Ornstein et al. 1988) demonstrated that repetition strategies used by third-graders varied as a function of the meaningfulness of the learning material. When third-grade children learned especially meaningful materials their rehearsal set sizes were as large as those typically produced by sixth-grade children, but were much smaller when they processed relatively unfamiliar materials.

Bartlett (1932) argued that memory is essentially a social phenomenon. First stimulated by Bartlett's work, there has now been much research demonstrating that familiarity of schemas seems to aid recall of stories. In culturally foreign stories, recall shows importations or distortions from familiar schemas. For example, North Americans distort stories in recall to avoid ending a story on a negative note or with unresolved problems (Rice 1980). US college students recall more from stories whose schemas are familiar than from stories taken from other cultural groups (Kintsch & Greene 1978). Harris et al. (1992) also document the powerful effect of culturally based knowledge on memory for stories about people performing common activities. College students in the USA and Mexico heard three stories of everyday activities. There were two versions of each story, consistent with either an American or a Mexican cultural script. In a delayed recognition test for information in the stories, both groups of students mistakenly recalled the stories from the other cultures as being more like their own culture than they actually were. Similarly, Stefensen and Colker (1982) asked American women and Australian aboriginal women to recall two stories about a child getting sick. In one case the sick child was treated by Western medicine and in the other by aboriginal native medicine. Results documented that each group recalled the story consistent with their own knowledge better than they did the other story.

Thus, there is now little doubt that memory performance is related to the familiarity that subjects have with the materials to be remembered. Familiarity involves both experience with the specific materials and experience with how they are used. Even urban–rural differences in memory performance have been explained on the basis of familiarity of materials and tasks. Wagner (1981) explained the better performance of the rural subjects on a recognition task with pictures of rugs and rug patterns by suggesting this was due to their greater familiarity with the materials.

Organization of remembering in social and cultural practice

Research discussed so far has dealt with specific aspects of the activity context within which remembering occurs. In these studies, particular aspects such as the purpose for remembering, familiarity with materials, and mediational means (e.g. organizational strategies) have either been experimentally manipulated or compared cross-culturally to examine the effect of these variables on memory performance. While the results of these studies are all interpretable as highlighting the importance of specific aspects of the sociocultural context of activity, they do not illustrate how the various aspects of goal, task, materials, mediational means are integrated in a particular situation.

In recent years, there has been an emerging trend in mainstream memory literature on examining "environmental context" factors in early memory development (Perlmutter 1988: 369). There is increasing recognition that to understand memory performance, or to compare performances of individuals from different cultures, it is essential to place memory performance in the context of each group's interpretation of the task to be accomplished, the goal in performing the activity, and the broader social context of such activities in their experience (Rogoff & Mistry 1985). We now recognize that in investigations of memory performance, even if the materials and the memory processes used are familiar, if these are not integrated into an activity which resembles some familiar activity, the task is likely to be perceived as foreign (Rogoff & Mistry 1985). For example, the performance advantage that schooled Western children have compared to non-schooled children may be due to the fact that the former have experience and practice in the social script for participating in a test situation, which the latter lack.

The role of institutional and cultural practices To examine the notion that cultural practices organize the ways that individuals remember, Scribner and Cole (1981) designed a memory task resembling the incremental method of learning the Quran practised by literate Arabs (i.e., adding a new word to a series at each attempt). They compared the performance of Vai people who varied in the use of several types of literacy: Arabic literacy gained in study of religious script in traditional Quranic schools, literacy in the indigenous Vai script learned through informal means for practical correspondence in trade, and literacy in English learned in Western-style schools. The Arabic literates had a great advantage over the other groups on recall of words when the preservation of word order was required, consistent with memory practices used in learning the Quran. However, on recall tests of words irrespective of order or on recall of stories, the Arab literates did not perform better than the other groups. Scribner and Cole (1981) concluded that learning to be literate in the Quran influences recall only when the format and sequencing of the to-be-remembered material models previous learning habits.

Cultural tools for mathematical operations also hold a specific functional role for remembering information related to their use. Japanese abacus experts use internalized representations of the abacus which allow them to calculate mentally without an abacus as accurately as with one (Hatano 1982). Their mental abacus is of extended size and can represent a number of many digits. While abacus experts can recall a series of 15 digits either forward or backward, their memory span for the Roman alphabet and for fruit names is not different from the usual 7+2 units found for most adults in memory span tasks. The special processes involved in their impressive mental abacus operations are tailored to the activities in which they were practised. Similarly, Ho et al. (1991) found that a 19-year-old male Chinese calendar savant's exceptional proficiency in calendar calculation was not based on skills in eidetic imagery, rote memorization, or high-speed calculation. Rather the savant's calculation ability appeared to be brought about by specific familiarity with 14 calender templates and the knowledge of matching the templates to every year, based on culture-specific practice in converting the Gregorian calendar to the Chinese calendar.

Cross-cultural findings on the effect of schooling on memory can also be interpreted and understood as an instance of how a cultural institution (schooling) provides practice in performing on memory tasks. Western schooling provides children with culturally based definitions of cleverness and acceptable means for solving problems (Rogoff & Mistry 1985). It provides an emphasis on fast performance as in timed tests, which are unusual outside of school in many cultures. It may provide practice in specific approaches to memory problems, such as the imposition of organization on arbitrary items.

Aside from specific practice, the cultural tools and techniques generally used in school also involve conventions and formats which are useful in typically memory studies, such as organizing a list by taxonomy rather than function, or using multiple-choice formats.

The role of social interactional contexts of remembering Along with the institutional and cultural practices which organize memory development, the immediate social interactional context also influences an individual's use of memory skills. Research that elaborates how social interactions and people's interpretations of the task support or constrain their remembering is summarized from Rogoff and Mistry (1985). Social aspects of experimental situations are unfamiliar to some groups. The relationship between experimenter and subject may be rapidly understood by children familiar with testing in school, but may be highly discrepant from familiar adult–child interactions for non-Western children and adults. Children who have had school experience are familiar with an interview or testing situation in which adults ask questions to which they already know the answer. Schooled children have typically had practice in figuring out what an adult is asking when the adult does not structure the problem or reveal what aspects of performance will be evaluated (Rogoff et al. 1984). This often gives them an advantage over children who have not had experience with formal schooling. On the other hand, non-schooled children may be concerned with showing respectful behavior to the tester rather than figuring out the problem. In Weisner's (1976) study, rural children in Kenya outperformed urban children in digit recall, which Weisner suggested was due to their greater compliance, attentiveness, and deference to the experimenter, which probably influences performance on digit recall and other rote memory tasks.

Another example of how conventions for social interaction can influence memory performance is provided by a study on story recall by Rogoff and Waddell (1982; cited and summarized from Rogoff & Mistry 1985). In the Rogoff and Waddell study, 9-year-old Guatemalan Mayan and American children were asked to recall stories that were adapted from the Mayan oral literature. Extensive efforts were made to make the task culturally appropriate for the Mayan children. The stories were told to the children by a familiar teenager speaking the local Mayan dialect, in a room that the children had become familiar with through several play sessions and parties. In the effort to make story recall more like telling the story rather than being tested by the same person who had just told it to them, the children told the stories to another familiar local adult who had not been present when the teenager told the stories to the children. In-spite of all these efforts, the Mayan children remembered far less of the stories than did the American children. They averaged 54.3 information units from two stories while their American counterparts remembered an average of 79.0 information units.

In addition to remembering less information, the Mayan children appeared to be excessively bashful in the story recall situation. Some could barely be induced to speak at all; many spoke in whispers, fidgeting and looking at their knees. Their utterances were punctuated with the word "cha." Apparently, there were important social features of the test situation that made the Mayan children very uncomfortable. It is culturally inappropriate for Mayan children to speak freely to an adult. When carrying messages to adults, they must politely add the word "cha" (which means "so I have been told") in order to avoid conveying a lack of respect by impertinently claiming greater knowledge than the adult. Though the Mayan children heard stories told by their elders, it was a strange and uncomfortable experience for them to attempt to tell a story to an adult, no matter how comfortable they were with the adult. On the other hand, retelling a story to an adult is a very familiar situation for children in the USA. In fact, it is one of the tasks of the early school years to teach children to produce and retell narratives to an audience that includes adults (Snow 1989). Children typically get practice in such story retelling through their participation in activities such as "show-and-tell" and "sharing-time," which are specifically designed for this purpose.

The inseparability of memory performances from the social circumstances of the task is also illustrated in Tannen's (1980) study of American and Greek college students who were asked to recall a cinematically presented story. The two groups of students varied in their approach to the task. The American students treated it as a recall task, worrying about temporal sequence and inclusion of details, including technical detail pertinent to the cinematic presentation. The Greek students treated it as a story-telling task, interpreting events and actor's motives, frequently omitting details that did not contribute to the story theme. They focused on the events without commenting on the cinematic technique. Most importantly, Tannen (1980) provided evidence that these differences related to cultural values. Published reviews by prominent American and Greek film critics reviewing the same films showed similar differences in approach, with the American critics focusing on the film director's technical accomplishments, while the Greek critics focused on the film's message and artistic vision rather than its technique.

Thus, recall is clearly embedded in the immediate and broader social context of the activity in which it occurs. Hence, the performance of an individual in an experiment cannot be considered a window on some pure aspect of memory functioning. It is inherently grounded in the social situation of the current performance and the situations in which the individual is used to remembering things (Rogoff & Mistry 1985).

Summary

This chapter argues that in order to understand the process of remembering in cultural context we need to examine the practices of children and those around them in their usual activities. Memory skills develop for the purpose of solving practical problems, which vary according to the specific situation and the cultural context. Memory performance must be examined in the context of the familiarity of the material to be remembered, the individual's interpretation of the tasks to be accomplished, the relation of the task goals to culturally important activities, and the relation with the social interactional and the broader sociocultural contexts of people's practice in remembering (Rogoff & Mistry 1985).

References

Barrett, T. R. 1978. *Aging and memory: Declines or differences*. Paper presented at the Psychonomic Society meeting, San Antonio, TX.

Bartlett, F. C. 1932. *Remembering*. Cambridge: Cambridge University Press.

Berry, J. W. & P. Dasen, P. (eds.) 1974. *Culture and cognition*. London: Methuen.

Brewer, W. F. & D. A. Dupree 1983. Use of plan schemata in the recall and recognition of goal-directed actions. *Journal of Experimental Psychology* 9, 117–29.

Butterworth, G. 1993. Context and cognition in models of cognitive growth. In *Context and cognition: Ways of learning and knowing*, P. Light & G. Butterworth (eds.). Hillsdale, NJ: Erlbaum.

Chi, M. 1978. Knowledge structure and memory development. In *Children's thinking: What develops?*, R. S. Siegler (ed.), 73–96. Hillsdale, NJ: Erlbaum.

Ciborowski, T. & S. Choy 1974. Nonstandard English and free recall. *Journal of Cross-Cultural Psychology* 5, 271–81.

Cole, M. 1985. The zone of proximal development: Where culture and cognition create each other. In *Culture, communication, and cognition: Vygotskian perspectives*, J. V. Wertsch (ed.). Cambridge: Cambridge University Press.

Cole, M. 1990. Cognitive development and formal schooling. In *Vygotksy and education*, L. Moll (ed.). New York: Cambridge University Press.

Cole, M. 1995a. Culture and cognitive development: From cross-cultural research to creating systems of cultural mediation. *Culture and Psychology* 1, 25–54.

Cole, M. 1995b. The supra-individual envelope of development: Activity and practice, situation and context. In *Cultural practices as contexts for development*, J. J. Goodnow, P. J. Miller, & F. Kessel (eds.). Los Angeles, CA: Sage.

Cole, M., J. Gay, J. A. Glick, & D. W. Sharp 1971. *The cultural context of learning and thinking*. New York: Basic Books.

Cole, M., L. Hood, & R. P. McDermott 1978. Concepts of ecological validity: Their differing implications for comparative cognitive research. *Quarterly Newsletter of the Institute for Comparative Human Development* 2, 34–7.

Cole, M. & S. Scribner 1974. *Culture and thought*. New York: Wiley.

Cole, M. & S. Scribner 1977. Cross-cultural studies of memory and cognition. In *Perspectives on the development of memory and cognition*, R. V. Kail & J. W. Hagen (eds.). Hillsdale, NJ: Erlbaum.

D'Azevedo, W. A. 1982. Tribal history in Liberia. In *Memory observed: Remembering in natural contexts*, U. Neisser (ed.), 274–92. San Francisco, CA: Freeman.

Drinkwater, B. A. 1976. Visual memory skills of medium contact Aboriginal children. *Australian Journal of Psychology* 28, 37–43.

Fahrmeier, E. D. 1975. The effect of school attendance on intellectual development in Northern Nigeria. *Child Development* **46**, 281–5.

Franklin, A. F. 1978. Sociolinguistic structure of word lists and ethnic group differences in categorized recall. *Quarterly Newsletter of the Institute for Comparative Human Development* **2**, 30–4.

Gallimore, R. & C. Goldenburg 1993. Activity settings of early literacy: Home and school factors in children's emergent literacy. In *Contexts for learning: Sociocultural dynamics in children's development*, E. A. Forman, N. Minick, & C. A. Stone (eds.). New York: Oxford University Press.

Gladwin, T. 1970. *East is a big bird*. Cambridge, MA: Belknap.

Gorfein, D. S. & A. V. Spata 1989. When can we say memory differs from age to age and/or culture to culture? In *Cross-cultural research in human development: Lifespan perspectives*, L. L. Adler (ed.). New York: Praeger.

Griffin, P. & M. Cole 1984. Current activity for the future: The ZoPed. In *Children's learning in the "Zone of Proximal Development,"* B. Rogoff & J. V. Wertsch (eds.). San Francisco, CA: Jossey-Bass.

Hall, J. W. 1972. Verbal behavior as a function of amount of schooling. *American Journal of Psychology* **85**, 277–89.

Hall, W. S., S. Reder, & M. Cole 1975. Story recall in young black and white children: Effects of racial group membership, race of experimenter, and dialect. *Developmental Psychology* **11**, 628–34.

Harris, R. J., L. M. Schoen, & D. L. Hensley 1992. A cross-cultural study of story memory. *Journal of Cross-Cultural Psychology* **23**, 138–47.

Hatano, G. 1982. Cognitive consequences of practice in culture specific procedural skills. *Quarterly Newsletter of the Institute for Comparative Human Development* **4**, 15–17.

Ho, E. D., A. K. Tsang, & D. Y. Ho 1991. An investigation of the calendar calculation ability of a Chinese calendar savant. *Journal of Autism and Developmental Disorders* **21**, 315–27.

Istomina, Z. M. 1977. The development of voluntary memory in children of preschool age. In *Soviet developmental psychology*, M. Cole (ed.), 349–65. While Plains, NY: Sharpe.

Kearins, J. M. 1981. Visual spatial memory in Australian aboriginal children of desert regions. *Cognitive Psychology* **13**, 434–60.

Kearins, J. M. 1986. Visual spatial memory in Aboriginal and White Australian children. *Australian Journal of Psychology* **38**, 203–14.

Kintsch, W. & E. Greene 1978. The role of culture-specific schemata in the comprehension and recall of stories. *Discourse Processes* **1**, 1–13.

Kleinfeld, J. 1971. Visual memory in village Eskimo and urban Caucasian children. *Arctic*, **24**, 132–7.

Laboratory of Comparative Human Cognition 1979. Cross-cultural psychology's challenges to our ideas of children and development. *American Psychologist* **34**, 827–33.

Laboratory of Comparative Human Cognition 1983. Culture and cognitive development. In *Handbook of child psychology*, P. H. Mussen (ed.), *Vol. I* of *History, theory, and methods*, W. Kessen (ed.). New York: Wiley.

Lancy, D. F. & A. J. Strathern 1981. Making twos: Pairing as an alternative to the taxonomic mode of representation. *American Anthropologist* **83**, 773–95.

Lave, J. 1990. The culture of acquisition and the practice of understanding. In *Cultural psychology*, J. W. Stigler, R. A. Shweder, G. Herdt (eds.). New York: Cambridge

University Press.

Leont'ev, A. N. 1981. The problem of activity in psychology. In *The concept of activity in Soviet psychology*, J. V. Wertsch (ed.), 37–71. Armonk, NY: Sharpe.

Levy-Bruhl, L. 1926. *How natives think*. London: Allen & Unwin.

Lewis, D. 1976. Observations on route finding and spatial orientation among the Aboriginal peoples of the Western Desert region of Central Australia. *Oceania* **46**, 249–82.

Lonner, W. 1980. The search for psychological universals. In *Handbook of cross-cultural psychology: Perspectives, Vol. 1*, H. C. Triandis & W. W. Lambert (eds.), 143–204. Boston, MA: Allyn & Bacon.

Lord, A. B. 1965. *Singer of tales*. New York: Atheneum.

Mack, J. E. 1976. *A prince of our disorder: The life of T. E. Lawrence*. Boston, MA: Little, Brown.

Middleton, & D. Edwards (eds.) 1990. *Collective remembering*. London: Sage.

Miller, P. J. & J. J. Goodnow 1995. Cultural practices: Toward an integration of culture and development. In *Cultural practices as contexts for development*, J. J. Goodnow, P. J. Miller, & F. Kessel (eds.). Los Angeles, CA: Sage.

Minick, N. 1987. Introduction. In *Thinking and speech*, L. S. Vygotsky. New York: Plenum.

Minick, N., C. A. Stone, & E. Forman 1993. Integration of individual, social and institutional processes in accounts of children's learning and development. In *Contexts for learning: Sociocultural dynamics in children's development*. E. Forman, N. Minick, & C. A. Stone, (eds.). New York: Oxford University Press.

Mistry, J. & B. Rogoff 1987. *Influence of purpose and strategic assistance on preschool children's remembering*. Poster presented at the meetings of the Society for Research in Child Development, Baltimore, MD.

Mistry, J. & B. Rogoff 1994. Remembering in cultural context. In *Psychology and culture*, W. Lonner & R. Malpass (eds.). Needham Heights, MA: Allyn & Bacon.

Mistry, J., B. Rogoff, & H. Herman 1995. *Contexts for children's remembering: Meaningful purpose and parental assistance*. Unpublished paper, Medford MA: Tufts University.

Moll, L. 1990. Introduction. In *Vygotksy & education*, L. Moll (ed.). New York: Cambridge University Press.

Neisser, U. 1982. *Memory observered: Remembering in natural contexts*. San Francisco, CA: Freeman.

Nelson, K. & G. Ross 1980. The generalities and specifics of long-term memory in infants and young children. In *New directions for child development, Vol. X, Children's memory*, M. Perlmutter (ed.). San Francisco, CA: Jossey-Bass.

Ornstein, P. A., L. Baker-Ward, & M. J. Naus 1988. The development of mnemonic skill. In *Memory development: Universal changes and individual differences*, F. E. Weinert & M. Perlmutter (eds.), 31–50. Hillsdale, NJ: Erlbaum.

Paris, S. G., D. R. Newman, & J. E. Jacobs 1985. Social contexts and functions of children's remembering. In *Cognitive learning and memory in children*, C. J. Brainerd & M. Pressley (eds.). New York: Springer-Verlag.

Perlmutter, M. 1988. Research on memory and its development: Past, present, and future. In *Memory development: Universal changes and individual differences*, F. E. Weinert & M. Perlmutter (eds.), 353–80. Hillsdale, NJ: Erlbaum.

Resnick, L. B., J. M. Levine, & T. D. Teasley 1991. *Perspectives on socially shared cognition*. Washington, DC: American Psychological Association.

Rice, G. E. 1980. On cultural schemata. *American Ethnologist* **7**, 152–71.

Rogoff, B. 1981. Schooling and the development of cognitive skills. In *Handbook of cross-cultural psychology, Vol. 4*, H. C. Triandis & A. Heron (eds.), 233–94. Boston, MA: Allyn & Bacon.

Rogoff, B. 1990. *Apprenticeship in thinking*. New York: Oxford University Press.

Rogoff, B. & P. Chavajay 1995. What's become of research on the cultural basis of cognitive development? *American Psychologist* **50**, 859–77.

Rogoff, B., S. Ellis, & M. Gauvain 1984. Development viewed in its cultural context. In *Developmental psychology*, M. H. Bornstein & M. E. Lamb (eds.). Hillsdale, NJ: Erlbaum.

Rogoff, B. & W. P. Gardner 1984. Adult guidance of cognitive development. In *Everyday cognition: Its development in social context*, B. Rogoff & J. Lave (eds.). Cambridge, MA: Harvard University Press.

Rogoff, B. & J. Mistry 1985. Memory development in cultural context. In *Cognitive learning and memory in children*, M. Pressley & C. Brainerd (eds.), 117–42. New York: Springer-Verlag.

Rogoff, B. & J. Mistry 1990. The social and functional context of children's memory skills. In *Knowing and remembering in young children*, R. Fivush, J. Hudson, & U. Neisser (eds.). New York: Cambridge University Press.

Rogoff, B. & K. J. Waddell 1982. Memory for information organized in scene by children from two cultures. *Child Development* **53**, 1224–8.

Ross, B. M. & C. Millsom 1970. Repeated memory of oral prose in Ghana and New York. *International Journal of Psychology* **5**, 173–81.

Rubin, D. 1995. *Memory in oral traditions: The cognitive psychology of epic, ballads, and counting-out rhymes*. New York: Oxford University Press.

Schneider, W. & H. Brun 1987. The role of context in young children's memory performance: Istomina revisited. *British Journal of Developmental Psychology* **5**, 333–41.

Schneider, W. & M. Pressley 1989. *Memory development between 2 and 20*. New York: Springer-Verlag.

Scribner, S. 1974. Developmental aspects of categorized recall in a West African society. *Cognitive Psychology* **6**, 475–94.

Scribner, S. & M. Cole 1981. *The psychology of literacy*. Cambridge, MA: Harvard University Press.

Segall, M. H., P. R. Dasen, J. W. Berry, & Y. H. Poortinga 1990. *Human behavior in global perspective: An introduction to cross-cultural psychology*. New York: Pergamon.

Sharp, D., M. Cole, & C. Lave 1979. Education and cognitive development: The evidence from experimental research. *Monographs of the Society for Research in Child Development* **44**, 1–2, no. 178.

Snow, C. E. 1989. Understanding social interaction and language acquisition; sentences are not enough. In *Interaction in human development*, M. H. Bornstein & J. S. Bruner (eds.). Hillsdale NJ: Erlbaum.

Stefensen, M. S. & L. Colker 1982. Intercultural misunderstandings about health care: Recall of descriptions of illness and treatments. *Social Science and Medicine* **16**, 1949–59.

Stevenson, H. W., T. Parker, A. Wilkinson, B. Bonnevaux, & M. Gonzalez 1978. Schooling, environment, and cognitive development: A cross-cultural study. *Monographs of the Society for Research in Child Development* **43**, 3, no. 175.

Super, C. M. & S. Harkness 1981. Looking across at growing up. In *Developmental plasticity: Social context and human development*, E. S. Gollin (ed.). New York: Academic.

Tannen, D. 1980. A comparative analysis of oral narrative strategies: Athenian Greek and American English. In *The pear stories: Cognitive, cultural and linguistic aspects of narrative production*, W. L. Chafe (ed.), 51–87. Norwood, NJ: Ablex.

Tarkin, B. 1981. *The effects of stimulus meaningfulness on children's spontaneous rehearsal strategies*. Senior honors thesis, University of Massachusetts.

Tharp, R. G. & R. Gallimore 1988. *Rousing minds to life: Teaching, learning and schooling in social context*. Cambridge: Cambridge University Press.

Valsiner, J. 1989. *Human development and culture: The social nature of personality and its study*. Lexington, MA: Lexington.

Vygotsky, L. S. 1962. *Thought and language*. Cambridge, MA: MIT Press.

Vygotsky, L. S. 1978. *Mind in society: The development of higher psychological processes*. Cambridge, MA: Harvard University Press.

Wagner, D. A. 1974. The development of short-term and incidental memory: A cross-cultural study. *Child Development* **45**, 389–96.

Wagner, D. A. 1978. Memories of Morocco: The influence of age, schooling, and environment on memory. *Cognitive Psychology* **10**, 1–28.

Wagner, D. A. 1981. Culture and memory development. In *Handbook of cross-cultural psychology, Vol . 4*, H. C. Triandis & A. Heron (eds.), 187–232. Boston, MA: Allyn & Bacon.

Weinert, F. E. & M. Perlmutter (eds.) 1988. *Memory development: Universal changes and individual differences*. Hillsdale, NJ: Erlbaum.

Weisner, T. S. 1976. Urban–rural differences in African children's performance on cognitive and memory tasks. *Ethos* **4**, 223–50.

Weissberg, J. A. & S. G. Paris 1986. Young children's remembering in different contexts: A replication and reinterpretation of Istomina's study. *Child Development* **57**, 1123–9.

Wellman, H. M. 1988. The early development of memory strategies. In *Memory development: Universal changes and individual differences*, F. E. Weinert & M. Perlmutter (eds.), 3–30. Hillsdale, NJ: Erlbaum.

Wellman, H. M. & S. C. Somerville 1980. Quasi-naturalistic tasks in the study of cognition: The memory related skills of toddlers. In *Children's memory*, M. Perlmutter (ed.), *Vol. X*, of *New Directions for Child Develoment*. San Francisco, CA: Jossey-Bass.

Wertsch, J. V. 1978. Adult–child interaction and the roots of metacognition. *Quarterly Newsletter of the Institute for Comparative Human Development* **2**, 15–8.

Wertsch, J. V. 1985. *Vygotsky and the social formation of the mind*. Cambridge: Harvard University Press.

Wertsch, J. V. 1991. *Voices of the mind*. Cambridge, MA: Harvard University Press.

Wertsch, J. V. & P. Tulviste 1992. L. S. Vygotsky and contemporary developmental psychology. *Developmental Psychology,* **28**, 548–57.

Whiting, B. B. 1976. The problem of the packaged variable. In *The developing individual in a changing world*, K. F. Riegel & J. A. Meacham (eds.). Chicago, IL: Aldine.

Wood, D. J. & D. Middleton 1975. A study of assisted problem-solving. *British Journal of Psychology* **66**, 181–91.

Worden, P. E. & S. Sherman-Brown 1983. A word-frequency cohort effect in young versus elderly adults' memory for words. *Developmental Psychology* **19**, 521–30.

About the contributors

Chapter 1. Introduction
See Chapter 7.

Chapter 2. The development of infant memory

Carolyn Rovee-Collier received her PhD from Brown University in 1966 and is Professor II of Psychology at Rutgers University. She is editor of *Infant Behavior and Development*, co-editor (with Lewis P. Lipsitt) of *Advances in Infancy Research*, and past president of the International Society for Infancy Research. She studies the development of learning and long-term memory in infancy.

Peter Gerhardstein received his PhD from the University of Minnesota with Irving Biederman in 1993 and is a Research Associate at Rutgers University studying the interface between selective attention, visual perception, and memory retrieval in infants.

Chapter 3. The neurobiological basis of early memory development

Charles A. Nelson is Professor of Child Psychology, Neuroscience, and Pediatrics and Director of Graduate Studies at the Institute of Child Development, University of Minnesota. He received his PhD from the University of Kansas in 1981. Dr Nelson's research interests are in cognitive neuroscience, with a particular interest in the relation between brain and memory development. He is currently an associate editor of *Child Development*, and until 1995 served as editor of the *Minnesota Symposium on Child Psychology*.

Chapter 4. Development of memory in early childhood

Patricia Bauer is an Associate Professor at the Institute of Child Development, University of Minnesota. She received her PhD from Miami University in 1985 and then was a post-doctoral fellow at the University of California, San Diego. Dr Bauer's research is on cognitive development, with particular emphasis on developments in memory during the period of transition from infancy to early childhood. She is associate editor of *Developmental Psychology* and co-edited *Developmental spans in event comprehension and representation: Bridging fictional and actual events* (1997).

Chapter 5. The development of procedural and declarative memory

Alan Parkin is Professor of Experimental Psychology at the University of Sussex, Brighton UK. He originally trained as a zoologist but obtained a DPhil in Psychology from the University of Sussex in 1979. His research interests are primarily concerned with human memory and its various pathologies. He is the author of four books including *Memory: Phenomena, experiment and theory* (1993) and *Explorations in cognitive neuropsychology* (1996).

Chapter 6. Event memory in early childhood

Robyn Fivush is Professor of Psychology and the Director of the Institute for Women's Studies at Emory University. She received her PhD from the City University of New York in 1983 and was an NSF post-doctoral Research Fellow at the University of California, San Diego. Her research focuses on the content and organization of children's developing memories for both routine and novel events. Dr Fivush recently edited *Knowing and remembering in young children* with Judith Hudson (1990), and *The remembering self* with Ulric Neisser (1990); she has co-authored *Gender development* with Susan Golombok (1990).

Chapter 7. The development of working memory

Nelson Cowan is Middlebush Professor of the Social Sciences in the Psychology Department at the University of Missouri, Columbia. He received his PhD from the University of Wisconsin, Madison, in 1980. Dr. Cowan's research is on aspects of short-term memory storage, its relation to selective attention, and its change with development in childhood. He is associate editor of the *Journal of Experimental Psychology: Learning, Memory, and Cognition*, and author of *Attention and memory: An integrated framework* (1995).

Chapter 8. The development of memory strategies

David Bjorklund is a Professor of Psychology at Florida Atlantic University. He received his PhD from the University of North Carolina, Chapel Hill, in 1976. Dr Bjorklund's research has focused on factors related to developmental and individual differences in strategic memory. He is a member of the editorial boards of *Cognitive Development, Developmental Psychology*, and the *Journal of Experimental Child Psychology* and the author of *Children's thinking: Developmental function and individual differences* (1995, 2nd edition).

Rhonda Douglas is a doctoral student in psychology at Florida Atlantic University. She is currently conducting research on children's eyewitness memory.

Chapter 9. Memory development and processing resources

Robert Guttentag is a Professor of Psychology at the University of North Carolina, Greensboro. He received his PhD from the University of Denver in 1980. His research has focused on the effects of resource limitations on children's acquisition and use of remembering strategies and on children's developing understanding of what it means to be remembering. Dr Guttentag has served on the editorial boards of *Developmental Psychology* and *Monographs of the Society for Research in Child Development*.

Chapter 10. Metamemory development

Mary Holland Joyner recently completed her graduate studies at the University of North Carolina, Chapel Hill, receiving her PhD in May 1996. Her research interests include family influences on children's school achievement and investigating predictors of school truancy and dropout.

Beth Kurtz-Costes is Associate Professor of Psychology at the University of North Carolina, Chapel Hill. She received her PhD from the University of Notre Dame in 1984. Dr Kurtz-Costes' research examines family and cultural influences on children's self-perceptions and school achievement.

Chapter 11. Children's eyewitness testimony:
Memory development in the legal context

Jianjian Qin received his Master's degree in experimental psychology from East China Normal University and is currently an advanced doctoral student in cognitive psychology at the University of California, Davis. His research interests include children's memory and suggestibility and adults' true and false memory of childhood events.

Jodi Quas, MA, is an advanced doctoral student in developmental psychology at the University of California, Davis. Her research interests include the effects of trauma on children's memory, attachment theory, and individual differences in children's memory and suggestibility. She has co-authored several articles and chapters that address these issues.

Allison D. Redlich is a doctoral student in psychology at the University of California, Davis. Her research interests include children's allegations of sexual abuse, perpetrators' motivations and modus operandi in committing abuse, and jurors' reactions to child witnesses. Ms Redlich received her undergraduate degree from Pennsylvania State University and worked as a researcher with Dr Michael Lamb and Dr Kathleen Sternberg at the National Institute of Child Health and Human Development.

Gail S. Goodman is Professor of Psychology at the University of California, Davis. Her research on children's eyewitness memory has been supported by numerous federal grants and cited in US Supreme Court decisions. She has served as President of Division 37 (Child, Youth and Family Services) and Division 41 (Psychology and Law) of the American Psychological Association.

Chapter 12. The development of remembering in cultural context

Jayanthi Mistry is an assistant professor in the Eliot-Pearson Department of Child Study at Tufts University. She received her PhD from Purdue University in 1983. She has conducted research on the social contexts of remembering, and her current research interests include investigations of the sociocultural contexts of children's learning. Dr Mistry has served as a consulting editor for the *Journal of Cross-Cultural Psychology*.

Author index

373

381

Subject index